Border Security

What kind of a world is one in which border security is understood as necessary? How is this transforming the shores of politics? And why does this seem to preclude a horizon of political justice for those affected? *Border Security* responds to these questions through an interdisciplinary exploration of border security, politics and justice. Drawing empirically on the now notorious case of Australia, the book pursues a range of theoretical perspectives – including Foucault's work on power, the systems theory of Niklas Luhmann and the cybernetic ethics of Heinz Von Foerster – in order to formulate an account of the thoroughly constructed and political nature of border security. Through this detailed and critical engagement, the book's analysis elicits a political alternative to border security from within its own logic: thus signaling at least the beginnings of a way out of the cost, cruelty and devaluation of life that characterises the enforced reality of the world of border security.

Peter Chambers lectures in criminology at Deakin University, Melbourne.

Space, Materiality and the Normative

Series Editors: Andreas Philippopoulos-Mihalopoulos and Christian Borch

www.routledge.com/Space-Materiality-and-the-Normative/book-series/SMNORM

Space, Materiality and the Normative presents new ways of thinking about the connections between space and materiality from a normative perspective. At the interface of law, social theory, politics, architecture, geography and urban studies, the series is concerned with addressing the use, regulation and experience of space and materiality, broadly understood, and in particular with exploring their links and the challenges they raise for law, politics and normativity.

Books in this series:

A Jurisprudence of Movement
Common Law, Walking, Unsettling Place
Olivia Barr

Animals, Biopolitics, Law
Lively Legalities
Irus Braverman

Spatial Justice
Body, Lawscape, Atmosphere
Andreas Philippopoulos-Mihalopoulos

Urban Commons
Rethinking the City
Christian Borch and Martin Kornberger

Border Security
Shores of Politics, Horizons of Justice
Peter Chambers

Forthcoming:

Placing International Law
Authority, Jurisdiction, Technique
Fleur Johns, Shaun McVeigh, Sundhya Pahuja, Thomas Skouteris, and Robert Wai

Border Security

Shores of Politics, Horizons of Justice

Peter Chambers

Routledge
Taylor & Francis Group
LONDON AND NEW YORK

First published 2018 by Routledge

2 Park Square, Milton Park, Abingdon, Oxfordshire OX14 4RN
52 Vanderbilt Avenue, New York, NY 10017

Routledge is an imprint of the Taylor & Francis Group, an informa business

First issued in paperback 2019

British Library Cataloguing-in-Publication Data
A catalogue record for this book is available from the British Library

Library of Congress Cataloging-in-Publication Data
A catalog record for this book has been requested

ISBN: 978-1-138-94313-1 (hbk)
ISBN: 978-0-367-23233-7 (pbk)

Typeset in Galliard
by Apex CoVantage, LLC

Brief contents

Detailed contents

Preface

Mad systems, global complexity, political justice

The impetus for this book struck me in 2012, while I was on my way to a roundtable on borders in Berlin. On a layover between Tokyo and Frankfurt, sitting on the second floor of an actual superjumbo at Narita. I was wondering about 3/11, the destructive power and the tenacity of the Tepco Old Boys Network. The tsunami wiped entire regions from the east cost of *honshu*, blew in and sucked out and blew it in again as teddy bears and children face down in piles of plywood, trawler and Toyota. There were photographs of ships atop three storey school buildings. There was no one left alive. There were ghost boats appearing on the Pacific Coast of the US, seething with living rats, living by eating one another. More than a year after the initial devastation wrought by the surging Pacific, Tepco remained afloat, employed, unflushable to a man, even as the Fukushima Diachi Plant continued to leak radioactive water into the surrounding sea. The old men of Tepco confronted their mess with the same flatness of face they'd used their whole lives for everything: faces that would make death blink and just blink back. How was it that the entire coastal region of Fukushima had been exposed as so fragile, yet Tepco clung tenaciously together? On the plane I wondered, staring at the men moving the baggage containers onto the rollers, bringing line to plane and fuel to wing: why doesn't everything just fall apart?

The phrase – 'mad systems!' – suddenly gripped me, the irresistible enmeshment of complete human psychosis and meticulous technical excellence, connecting madness to madness at all scales in a delicate, precisely timed and user friendly way, everything brought into its coupling or boiling point where and when it could be dumped into something else without spilling a mL or losing a suitcase. Yet on the other hand a whole society seemingly incapable of thinking critically or in public or directly confronting those who'd presided over the near miss catastrophe, the most recent one – and the last and the next. Yet 3/11 isn't a Japanese issue, after all: the GFC happened, and the middle classes of the OECD paid for it; then growing numbers got angry at immigrants but still wanted cheap stuff and overseas holidays. Mad systems: more than a million Australians visit Bali each year now, in a way that is regarded as uncontroversial; alongside this, 69,605 or so people sought asylum by boat in Australia between 1976–2014, a much smaller number of people – a months' supply of 2015 Australians to

Bali – yet over nearly four decades. It's these numbers of boat arrivals that have sustained the passions and divisions that powered the emergence of border security I explore in the pages that follow.

I've grown to love the pressurised cabins on planes, being flung through the air by jets under wings, awaiting the next meal service, paying as much attention to the George Clooney film as he and it deserves, or leafing through the inflight magazines, slightly worse every year. I linger over the gilt pens and ugly watches on offer, stay awhile in the duty-free perfume section and wonder how prices stay so high in the presence *such supply*. There is so, so much perfume in airports. There's so much that they even have it on the plane, in case you didn't get a chance to buy it at the airport (but if you buy too much, they'll confiscate it, because 'terrorists'). Who buys it, especially on the plane, and why is it still so expensive if there's absolutely heaps everywhere? In the cabin of the airborne aircraft, once we level out and the seatbelt tone pings, I can finally release myself into the fate of modernity, feel what Sloterdijk, following Heidegger, would call *galassenheit*, wonder about these scents and the smell of avgas without being able to disavow in any way that 'we are embarked', and that there's room on the plane for me and everyone else and all the perfume and ugly gold-plated stationery and jewellery – but not the occupants of the boats.

'Mad systems' has been ghosting my thinking for four years since that silvered sunny morning at Narita, the way that, just as the technical realm's complexity fades into the animated control magic of intuitive end-user experiences, so the human factor entering data into its enchanting interfaces becomes evermore psychotic and surreal. The thinner the phones get, the woollier the thinking, the madder and stupider the Internet, the more cause and effect gets stretched. All of it, stretched thin, credulity and civility and tenderness. All you satirists are out of a job. This book traces the emergence of 'the ring of steel', a thing that was once 'not worth the candle'. How, as Foucault might ask, did something once unnecessary become possible, then necessary? How did my mobility come to be girded by the mad systems of the ring of steel? *Border Security* traces key lines of this political emergence.

Mad systems led me along the border and into theories of complexity and systems, and complexity in security returned to me not 'agency' but its absence: a sharpened sense of where and why we lack and desire it. An inkling of complexity gives us some respect for the dynamics in play, plate tectonics and the weather, the slow grind of continents *and* the Wednesday afternoon inability of supercomputers to tell their humans if it will rain on Thursday morning, the limits of our knowledge, our abyssal ignorance in the face of death on the fate of the universe, and the co-knowledge that causality is real, the caterwaul of a cat amongst the aeons. Things are happening and interacting, we don't know and we don't control, the effects and relations come at one another then some of them rush at us, confronting us with polyrhythmic effects we perceive through whatever tiny traces our perceptual apparatuses can use to glean. What does a sudden sneeze mean when thunderstorms killed eight people with asthma in November 2016;

what of Donne's 1624 wondering about a promontory washed into the sea, is Europe the less?

As for systems, in *Border Security* I seek a more precise sense of the ways in which things sit upon other things, which is a story of the subtleties of domination and the operativity of complexity. A more attuned appreciation of how and why some things couple and entwine while others side by side do not mix or know of one another, yet how all of this pulsates in Luhmann's punctuated spasms of mis/understanding. Being released back into the environment of communication was a huge relief for me, like a zoo animal tagged and released back into the wild, out of the human zoo, still hobbling but recovered from the impact of the car. Because it was a reprieve from the guilting conceit that, as some kind of sovereign subject or individual I'd been taught to be as a consumer, I had responsibility for all these choices I made 'authoritatively', as if climate change were in any way like Christmas shopping, as if Brunswick K Mart or the refugee scanning fast fashion at the counter were the same as humanity being doomed to piped carols and mandatory Santa hats for all eternity.

So: so much escapes, yet in what follows I find in this is a greater possibility for knowing our actual agency and accepting our *almost* inconsequential moving place in the cosmos and on this earth now. I take an older commitment from the humility of this wisdom of critical theory, so as to try to keep responding to the political present by asking why and how things came to be how they are, yet to do so without succumbing either to the conceit of knowing or the paralysis of an individual or subject who wants to make a difference and thinks they can't and so does nothing and then feels depressed – but still commutes and applies for a promotion, and gets to work and gets a raise, and feels depressed staying in the Hotel Grand Abyss, yet still claims the stay as a business expense, then tweets about their new book. On the very day of Trump's election, an on-the -rise scholar with a book out on populism tweeted: 'I'm thinking my book might have just got even more relevant'. I winced at what careerism has done: all the ladder-climbing adders, all the impact factor and churn. I don't wish to think of my work as important or consequential, but neither is it without its effects. I don't know what those might be: early 70s Zhou on 1789 – 'it's too early to say'. I know that everything I do makes *almost* no difference at all, so let's put this book falling dead born in that pile. But we also do not know which among our actions might make a positive difference that we might wish into the world. A brilliant career of many decades might not turn up much; a spur-of-the-moment choice can make waves and trigger a cataclysmic cascade; groups of people seeking protection might be cast as existential threats to the nation; a 'we' might have to live and move within a ring of steel in order to remain secured citizens. Some of us are capable of careers, some of us will trigger cataclysms. We are mostly ineffectual, but causality is real. This book seeks to side with causality, and focuses on political effects engendered by deep, diffuse desires and socially constructed systems, among whose contributors are some notable careerists.

The normative concerns of *Border Security* are driven by the conviction that the only way to be as humans to one another is to be together somehow, even with all the idiots and assholes in our midst: “we must love one another or die”/ “we must love one another and die”. No wonder W.H. Auden found his poem and its fame over him – a fame found once more in 2016 – sticking in his craw. We know and control very little, but must live together somehow and can only do so well when we share futures we can hope our way toward together, however much that means limping, muddling through, mucking it up and needing to tear it up and start again. The young mistake in political thinking is that we can reach utopia; the old mistake is to abandon utopia and still think we're thinking politically, and not just policing in the interests of management. This work is oriented by these horizons.

Only justice as fairness can transform the seeing spite of knowing someone wrongly got other than they deserved, the resentment of never having what was rightly theirs. The politics we've had so much of in the recent West, strongest of all in the neoliberalised Anglosphere, the politics that avoids justice, that avoids the attempt to transform vengeance into justice with fairness. The past few decades have seen a mean economistic atomism dominate other visions and peoples, when times are good, and it has made large numbers of people hot for punitive hardening – and this is especially so when the easy victims outweigh the opportunities for short-term gain. The mine of the bull and the thine of the bear in the *gemeinshaft*. A cacophony of aggrieved animal spirits in the human zoo, I can hear it from the forest I'm released into, more utterance than information in it.

Only justice as responsibility can restore the links between actions and systems, between people's un/intentions and their un/intended consequences: lines to make right, to attribute actants to their actions, to hold people to their promises and to bind back the unbound to their unbounded ambitions. Any politics that cuts these lines between the did and the ‘done over’ risks the little of the world we still have now via more avoidance and evasion, the restless search for havens away from the lines of action, islands apart from the causal chains and the chains of command, a slice of the actions we actually engaged in and knowingly ran and hid from, the things we did not know but should have, shouldn't we, the avarice and cowardice, all the hiding and avoidance that goes on almost without restraint these days, and sometimes even passes as freedom.

Only justice as the good can involve us in trying to live our way together toward a better imagined future; the best that we can hope for but most likely will not achieve, all the horizons of the world. A politics incapable of imagining and enacting its way toward its own utopia is bereft of direction and a future, and fundamentally this is where I see us at this moment. For Weber, his 1905 spirit of capitalism and its nullity imagined that it had attained a level of civilisation never before achieved. In 2016, our nullity failed to imagine its nullity.

The heart of my concern in *Border Security* says: ‘look to the good, consider our vision, what do we want, where do we want to get to?’

The dreamers of modernity gave us ways to think ourselves into better futures, and now I see instead so much self absorption and identity cartwheeling atop the mad systems, the surface play fronting the manic cyclone of circulation, pulling us into its maddening currents but also tethering us into the microworlds of little habits and patterns, not just microaggressions but the everyday hate of toiling after an email. Office life is a succession of timestamped microaggressions; email is its nest. Until recently the alternatives to office life and its comforts – for us, for now– seemed impossible to imagine, and they are nearly so now. But everything else – we know it, don't we? yet?– is just obeying the stupidity, aligning with management's promotion of itself, rolling over on the expedient lies, resigning ourselves to the repetition of violence and repetition, "The habit-forming pain, Mismanagement and grief: We must suffer them all again". Worlds of bystanders not so innocently watching the careerists and the vandals wrecking everything, undoing the *demos*: that common wealth so hard won, so fragile and so precious that in spite of everything still surrounds us.

Acknowledgements

Any book stands atop a lifetime's worth of accrued thanks and debts. First and foremost, I must thank my parents and sister for my extraordinary upbringing and the incredible good fortune to have been born who I was, as I was, when I was, in Sydney. I grew up living high on a hill overlooking Pittwater, staring at Scotland Island, some sunny afternoons playing with crabs on the mudflats at Salt Pan Cove. As I complete the book, it's become obvious to me how much that estuarine country possesses my imagination: in one sense the entirety of this work and its preoccupations was, if you will, determined by the contingency of my fortunate upbringing – standing on the sand, staring at the blue sea.

I returned to scholarly work trying to reassemble the mess and horror of post-911 counter-terrorism and the Invasion of Iraq, after living for three years in Tokyo: this double alienation – from the West, in the East – shaped the inception of my theoretical interest, and it's always reminded me that the world is already on fire. Through my intellectual apprenticeship in the first decade of the twenty-first century, was extremely grateful to catch the tail end of a pedagogy oriented around excellence and critical acuity. More than anything it was the exceptional people studying social and critical theory at the now defunct Ashworth Centre for Social Theory at Melbourne Uni, especially my excellent good friends who I developed the TAP reading group with, who deserve greatest thanks for helping me develop a theoretical understanding of the political present battle tested in weekly dialectical encounters. I also want to thank Chris Hobson for his friendship, and for keeping the ssg bbq going all these years; alongside all the ssgs. Thank you, my friends.

In the final years of my PhD I relied heavily on the good guidance in supervision I received, and especial thanks to Peter Rush for carefully reading my work, and to Alison Young for being an advocate and mentor who saw something in me and gave me some wonderful opportunities to lecture and teach with creative control: an amazing privilege. In the years between PhD and my settled field in criminology, I want to note the efforts of the members of the Research Unit in Public Cultures and the Institute for International Law and Humanities: Nikos and Scott, and Alison once more, but again and especially the amazing group of RUPC and IILAH colleagues whose collegiality and friendship has meant so much. In my settled field lecturing in criminology, special thanks to the amazing team at Deakin, a wonderful group of people to work with and a great support to me during these past two years.

In my current life, I would never have finished this work without the unstinting support of both families: thank you Chambers and Summers clans for all your love, help and support.

Finally, to my love, Arwen, and to my two wonderful boys, Magnus and Albie: if you foolishly choose to read this one day, I hope what you find here is history and not politics.

Introducing border security's world

1.1 The emergence of border security's world in Australia

This book explores border security by focusing on a nation-state where its emergence can be seen starkly: the Commonwealth of Australia. In less than four decades, Australia went from a nation-state in which the phrase 'border security' and its practices and norms had no meaning or currency to a global vanguard policy model that, as we shall explore, is now being selectively taken up by European nation-states in the face of the 'European' 'Migration' 'Crisis'.

And yet, *Border Security* is not a book *about* Australia. Although its emergence emanates from Australia, in what follows, I read Australia as a global political laboratory and international export policy model. Australia is a site of imagining and enaction, a worksite where border security's tensions and contentions emerged, unfolded and solidified more clearly than nearly anywhere else. To tell its story is to try to understand how something highly improbable emerged, then became politically urgent, electorally necessary, then became muted critical infrastructure, in ways that now constrain how people live together and what they can hope for in the future.

This work is an attempt to understand how border security came to be what it is in the political present;[1] a global space of contention in which a common concern is being played out with the enforcement arms of states, the sovereignty of nations and the electoral attention of large minorities of citizens, and the bodies of vulnerable noncitizens seeking asylum. *Border security is a unilateral projection of national sovereignty in global space*, one whose spread and adoption by nation-states as an urgent and necessary response to 'crises' of human mobility raise the common question of global justice in order to negate its possibility.

As a study addressing its topic by focusing on one of its clearest global locations, *Border Security: Shores of Politics, Horizons of Justice* is about the implied social relations and political effects of the choices and commitments involved in a

1 See: Foucault, Michel, 'Kant on Enlightenment and Revolution', *Economy and Society*, 15: 1, 1986, pp. 88–96.

social transformation that took border security from something improbable to a fully integrated infrastructure as nationally vital and studiously ignored as plumbing. Border security's integration process has been *fundamentally* political: not only because it expresses basic values as its severances produce spaces, materialities and norms, but because in doing so it has reoriented the shores of politics and the horizons of justice.

Above all, as of this writing, the Australian story of border security's becoming infrastructural offers a message in a bottle[2] for the European project and North America. The fundamental danger of border security is that its normal operation negates the very possibility of asylum, and with it, a society in which the possibility of justice has been replaced by the indefinite angst and urgent emptying out of security – an evacuated polis whose siege conditions apply differentially to noncitizens *and* citizens alike.[3]

I.2 'Complex continuum', global space: first observations of border security's world

In this section, I lay out a set of claims that stake out the assumptions underpinning the systems theoretical approach taken throughout *Border Security*. I've attempted to express these assumptions in as bare and direct a way as possible, and so to prepare the reader, as a consequence this section may require sitting slowly with some of the sentences. Alternatively, readers more interested in empirical detail might wish to skip this section – either until a greater familiarity with the concepts has been achieved in the course of spending time with the examples that follow (sections i.7–i.11), or until such time as later points that build cumulatively prompt curiosity or require retrospective clarification. In any case, the following points laid out in this section are fundamental.

Border security is a creative, constructive social process; border security is a way of making the world inhabitable by dividing it. The inaugural theoretical assumption underpinning my approach is that: "a universe comes into being when a space is severed or taken apart".[4] Or, put positively: "draw a distinction and a universe comes into being".[5]

Following the systems theory of Niklas Luhmann and its epistemological foundations in second-order cybernetics,[6] I observe distinction making – thus the

2 in Jeffries, Stuart, *Hotel Grand Abyss: The Lives of the Frankfurt School*, Verso, London, 2016, pp. 10–11.

3 Dreyfus, Hubert and Rabinow, Paul, *Michel Foucault: Beyond Structuralism and Hermeneutics*, University of Chicago Press, Chicago, 1982, p. 232.

4 Spencer-Brown, George, *Laws of Form*, The Julian Press, New York, 1969, p. V.

5 Von Foerster in Poerkson, Bernhard, *The Certainty of Uncertainty: Dialogues Introducing Constructivism*, Imprint Academic, Exeter, 2004, p. 15.

6 Clarke, Bruce, 'Heinz von Foerster's Demons: The Emergence of Second-Order Systems Theory', in Clarke, Bruce and Hansen, Mark B. (eds.), *Emergence and Embodiment: New Essays on Second-Order Systems Theory*, Duke University Press, 2009, pp. 34–61.

recursive enaction of boundaries – as constitutive of the genesis and construction of social systems. On this epistemological basis, I explore border security as a social system that exists in communication and "reproduces itself in its imaginary space of reference"[7] through operations. Based on these assumptions, this book traces the way Australian agents of border security represent its severances. To do this, I begin from the key distinctions of border security's world and understand its agents' work as world making:[8] for in communication, severance is also suture.[9] We can see this by looking at Australian Border Force's (Border Force's) diagrammatic explanation of the continuum concept of the border (Figure I.1).

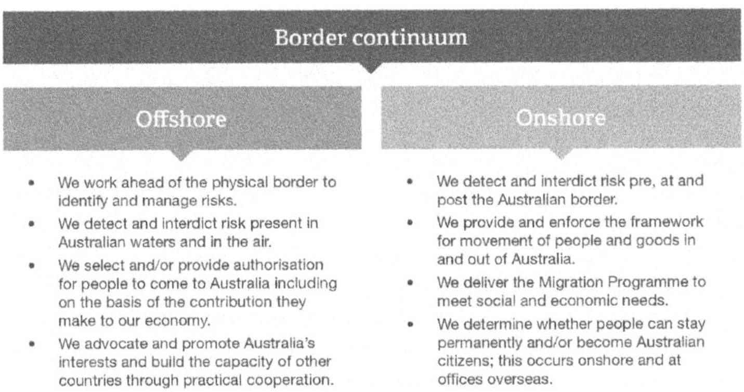

Figure I.1 Border continuum

Source: Australian Government, Department of Immigration and Border Protection, Creative Commons[10]

Border Force observes the border as "a complex continuum that stretches", *then* makes a subordinate distinction between onshore and offshore. Within the 'continuum', *the* border is not divided into *two* 'sides' of a 'line'.[11] Rather, as different points along the same continuum – different observations of 'the same difference' – offshore and onshore are two of a number of continuous ways in which 'the same border' can be observed by Border Force as its space of operations.

7 Luhmann, Niklas, *Theory of Society, Volume 1*, Stanford University Press, Stanford, 2012, p. 53.
8 Salter, Mark, 'Theory of the/: The Suture and Critical Border Studies', *Geopolitics*, 17: 4, 734–755, 2012, pp. 734–736.
9 Op.Cit.
10 'Where Do We Work', *Department of Immigration and Border Protection*. www.border.gov.au/AustralianBorderForce/PublishingImages/australian-border-force-abf/protecting/where-do-we-work/Border%20continuum.png
11 Balibar, Étienne, 'At the Borders of Europe', in *We, the People of Europe? Reflections on Transnational Citizenship*, Princeton University Press, Princeton, 2004, p. 1 and Salter, Mark, 'Theory of the/: The Suture and Critical Border Studies', *Geopolitics*, 17: 4, 734–755, 2012, p. 737.

In the severances represented and re-described here, both shores, onshore *and* offshore, are proper to Australia: not as a relation to country, nor a monopoly over territory, nor a willingness to die for the homeland, nor a public realm in which rights and justice can be rationally contended. For Border Force, 'Australia' is a space of interest that must be secured[12] (see section I.11). In the language of Luhmann's systems theory, the Australian border is predicated on the observed unity of the difference of the two 'shores' that differentiate the boundaries of Australia.[13]

As border security, operation by operation, this process of differentiation reproduces Australia as a boundary that is meaningful for anyone who exists in relation to it[14] (section 6.6); for some people these meanings are matters of life and death. *Border security's world comes into being wherever 'Australia' is observed as a threatened space of interest severed or taken apart by Border Force in order to be secured as a border.*

The distinction between shores will become essential in the chapters to come, especially in Chapter 3. But what I want to draw attention to first – as we set up what is, after all, Border Force's theory of itself and border security – is the clear and repeated articulation of the 'we' in the continuum diagram. In Border Force's conception of the border continuum, each dot implicates the co-ordinated action of a group agent,[15] working as an observing system, as its enabling constraint. For each 'point' of the stretching continuum to be kept 'taut' a 'we' must keep working, and this gives Border Force a number of definite tasks that span a space and time of interest that 'stretches across' Australia's shores in order to make border security's world – and keep it made. As Border Force's current CEO, Mike Pezzullo, asserts: the border is part of a global order, and can only be sustained through "human agency and practice".[16]

Within its space of interest, Border Force describes how its agents work ahead, and what the work on each point of the continuum is about:

- identifying
- detecting
- interdicting
- providing

12 See: Border Force, 'Our Operating Environment'. www.border.gov.au/australian-border-force-abf/protecting#Our%20operating%20environment

13 Luhmann, Niklas, *Theory of Society, Volume 1*, Stanford University Press, Stanford, 2012, pp. 26–27 and Nevins, Joseph, 'Remote Places at the Heart of Empire', *Political Geography*, 30, 2011, pp. 351–354.

14 Luhmann, Niklas, *Theory of Society, Volume 1*, Stanford University Press, Stanford 2012, pp. 30–31 and p. 113.

15 Pettit, Philip, 'Responsibility Incorporated', *Ethics*, 117: 2, 2007, pp. 171–201.

16 Border Force News Room, 'New Thinking About Borders: ACBPS CEO Michael Pezzullo'. http://newsroom.border.gov.au/channels/Speeches/releases/ceo-speech-to-university-of-canberra-national-security-lecture-series

- advocating
- promoting
- enforcing
- delivering
- determining.

Border Force's own observations of its world of operations, as one 'autodescriptive' window onto border security's world, already tell us important things about how *this* work of border security understands itself in and through its relations to its operating environment. Each one of the dot points denotes the tensioning of attentive work, but the putative unity of the continuum – and by extension 'Australia' as a secured, bordered, sovereign space '*in* which' the nation is secured – cannot function unless all points are *in communication* with each and every other one. This is also one precise reason why I develop a theoretical understanding that explores how and why border security's world is constructed and evolves *in society*, in Luhmann's sense (sections 2.2–2.3).

The metaphoric threads and literal threats that keep the points connecting to one another show how Border Force's severances *suture*, stitching together "the domestic, the international, and the global, rendering those lines both a visible sign of state legitimacy in the face of the international and invisible as a sign of the artificiality of the state and the international".[17] The stretching continuum orders Border Force's group agents to engage in the co-ordinated work of securing Australia's interests. These points of suture are specific to Australia, but they're also unthinkable without the historically complex and constraining international division of the world into shores *and* a contemporary understanding of global space as a realm of 'threatened interest' that can, should and must – rightly – provide security work with a definite set of tasks. This doesn't mean that 'Australia's interests' reside 'inside Australia' as a territorial form, Giddens' "bordered power container",[18] but it does mean that a growing number of entities that seek to approach Australia are recognised as threats 'entering the space of interest' – including, of course, 'the boats' and asylum seekers aboard them, until they're bodies in the water (sections 1.11–1.12). The spatially challenging and theoretically interesting implication that emerges from this is that anyone can enter the space of interest from anywhere in the world. Border Force's continuum indicates the sense in which Australia's space of interest is global, because its threats emerge in global space. This alone obviates any analysis that remonstrates that 'Australian border security is merely a domestic or regional matter'. On the contrary, it grows, moves and secures national sovereignty in

17 Salter, Mark, 'Theory of the/: The Suture and Critical Border Studies', *Geopolitics*, 17: 4, 2012, pp. 748, 734–755.

18 Giddens, Anthony, *The Nation-State and Violence: Volume Two of a Contemporary Critique of Historical Materialism*, Polity Press, Cambridge, 1985, p. 120.

global society,[19] and for these reasons its differentiation of the world into 'threat environment' and 'secured sovereign space' via the border implicates all of us differentially in our relation to systems of global mobility, such as civil aviation (sections i.7 – i.8).

With all this in mind, I offer a preliminary theoretical description of 'global space', a phrase that I will return to and build on in the chapters to come. In *Border Security*, global space names three things:

1. the lived experience of severe exposure and the routine threat of domination and death faced by groups of people such as asylum seekers (which we can only delineate by observing it as political spaces beyond protection and care, but not beyond authority and domination[20])
2. the operating environment of security work, based (in circular fashion) on an understanding of global space as an urgent co-existent field in which challenges, threats, and opportunities *just keep emerging* and *must be responded to* decisively
3. a set of instances disclosing what globalisation actually means *in* the mobility differential maintained as a boundary between border security's operating environment and the lived experience of asylum seekers

As enacted, Border Force's theory of the border, security and Australia enjoins its agents to attend to 'the borders of Australia' on the understanding that the continuum and their work within global space is variously 'about' risk, authorisation, the framework of movement, the Migration Program and whether people can stay. This work is no longer about two-dimensional lines, a simple and clear division between inside/outside, or the aligned relation between territory, law and population, nor has it been conducted as if it were for some time. Rather, in Border Force's theorisation,

> We consider the border not to be a purely physical barrier separating nation states, but a complex continuum stretching offshore and onshore, including the overseas, maritime, physical border and domestic dimensions of the border. To protect the safety, security and commercial interests of Australia, we are working with our partner agencies to develop intelligence-based profiles of risk across each dimension of the border continuum.[21]

To sum up, then, *in Border Force's terms, 'the' border does not exist*: not as a line, nor a territorial limit, barrier or fixed location. Rather, Border Force's phrasing

19 Luhmann, Niklas, 'Globalization or World Society: How to Conceive of Modern Society?' *International Review of Sociology*, 7: 1, 1997, pp. 67–79.

20 See section I.10.

21 'Protecting Our Borders', Australian Border Force. www.border.gov.au/australian-border-force-Border Force/protecting

and the elaborated understanding and implications of the border continuum evinces a nuanced understanding that shows a reflexive application of the polysemy, vacillation and dispersion of borders *in* contemporary state work.[22] To paraphrase Marx's eleventh thesis on Feuerbach, with all due irony, this is not just a way of interpreting the border as a complex continuum,[23] it's about the active work of changing it into one, then relocating 'Australia' as that which prospers 'within' it.

I.3 The shores of politics in border security's world: sovereignty, security, offshore

Border Force's complex continuum, at all its points, resides 'within' the nation's sovereignty in ways we will explore. The maritime jurisdictions that comprise vast zones of Australia's space of interest are fields of work in which Border Force's front line workers labour to secure *national* sovereignty by interdicting noncitizens far beyond the territorial limit of *state* sovereignty. In other words: one thing border security's agents require to secure Australia is the ability to deploy 'human agency and practice' (to paraphrase a phrase from Pezzullo's speech quoted above) to enact *national* sovereignty – in maritime jurisdictions where *state* sovereignty does not exist (sections 1.10–1.12). Does this mean that national sovereignty in Australia is now no longer grounded in or limited by the territorial limit of law, thanks to border security's emergence? Or does it mean that the Commonwealth's agents of border security "create(s) the meaning for the border *in* its transgression"?[24] Is the difference between the national and the state indicative of a disjuncture few have noticed, a contradiction most have failed to reckon with, or a paradox that these operations of sovereignty rely upon? In *Border Security*, I encourage us to observe the latter as the most critically revealing theoretical possibility (sections 1.10, 3.2). As with its emergence in communication and the constitutive use of onshore/offshore, the centrality of paradox offers another precise reason why Luhmann's systems theory is an excellent guide to understanding border security (sections 2.11–2.12 and 3.1–3.4).

In what follows, I argue that Border Force's ordinary operation in Australia's area of maritime interest enacts a theory of sovereignty bolder and more influential than most recent academic theorists have managed. This makes it rich, interesting, of general social theoretical interest. As a matter of methodology, I urge, the way border security's world and its enacted theory of borders and sovereignty has run ahead of conventional conceptual resources means we have to 'catch up'

22 Vaughan-Williams, Nick, *Border Politics: The Limits of Sovereign Power*, Edinburgh University Press, Edinburgh, 2009, pp. 5–7.

23 Bigo, Didier, 'Internal and External Security(ies): The Möbius Ribbon', in Albert, Matthias, Jacobson, David and Lapid, Yosef (eds.), *Identities, Borders, Orders*, University of Minnesota Press, Minneapolis, 2001, pp. 91–116.

24 Salter, p. 736, italics mine.

to the continuum concept and what it implies. Like border security, sovereignty is a practice, 'it takes making'[25] (to paraphrase both Saskia Sassen ***and*** Mike Pezzullo), and has already been practiced for some time. For fifteen years to the time of writing the enforcers of national sovereignty have gone out as agents of border security and interdicted the threatening entities whose entry-seeking existence ensure Border Force's future as defender of Australia – nation, sovereign and border – far beyond the territorial limit where sovereignty supposedly 'lives'.

Within border security's world, Border Force's tasks are parsed out as professional and technical work whose existence is necessary where Australia's border is a space severed by the distinctions of risk analysis and sutured through enforcement operations. That is: all the identifying, detecting, interdicting, providing, advocating, promoting, enforcing, delivering and determining that work along the continuum actually involves, day after day. Within border security's world this is avowedly and totally security work, and observing Border Force's tasks in these ways, in turn, transforms the complex continuum into a space of security for Border Force *while* enabling security work to be conducted in a nebulous field now stably describable, in any case, as a 'complex continuum'.[26]

Border Force's boundary-making distinctions are not observable by its enactor-agents as partial, passionate or political. This is for two reasons that bring us to one of *Border Security's* key political points while helping us locate the shores of politics in border security's world. First, they are not political because the distinctions of politics – that can ask of a contention or critically enquire of a decision 'is it good, is it fair, is it right, is it just?' –[27] are not operative for Border Force's agents. In systems theoretical terms, we could say that "politics and justice are not distinctions that reproduce border security operations; their appearance in the operating environment is perturbing to the system".[28] Put more plainly, in border security's world, politics and justice are irritants – not just a nuisance, but things that border security's agents try to expel, contain and control as much as possible. A humanistic perspective on this might judge this as 'bad' or a 'lack' or 'absence' of elements that should rightly exist: this has been the basis for many powerful human rights and radical Christian campaigns critical of the human costs of border security (section 6.6). But it's also why many detention-critical campaigns – especially liberal and human rights-based campaigns for asylum seekers' rights – fail to fully see the normative implications of the following crucial point.

25 Sassen, Saskia, *Territory, Authority Rights: From Medieval to Global Assemblages*, Princeton University Press, Princeton, 2006.

26 Von Foerster, Heinz, 'Objects: Tokens for (Eigen-)Behaviors', in *Understanding: Essays on Cybernetics and Cognition*, Springer, Berlin, 2003, pp. 261–273 and Luhmann, Niklas, *Theory of Society, Volume 1*, Stanford University Press, Stanford, 2012, p. 130.

27 See: Judt, Tony, 'Ill Fares the Land', *New York Review of Books*, April 29, 2010. www.nybooks.com/articles/2010/04/29/ill-fares-the-land/

28 Luhmann, Niklas, *Theory of Society, Volume 1*, Stanford University Press, Stanford, 2012, pp. 66–67.

As agents of security working along the border continuum, Border Force's agents do not require the distinctions of politics and justice to operate. In this sense, which I pursue through many recombinations and codas in the chapters that follow, ***border security's world operates beyond the shores of politics, beyond horizons of justice.***

The expulsion of politics from border security operations, secondly, is a creative process. As I explore, enacting and integrating border security's world in society has recursively generated durable structures with significant societal momentum and their own heavy materiality and durable normativity. Much of it is observed by Border Force as logistical and infrastructural (see Chapter 4), thus as reflexive as Mike Pezzullo and other leading agents of border security are, the politics of security operations remains stubbornly implicit, and the iteration of border security's necessity by Border Force and others has proven very resistant to ethical or reflexive consideration of the human and living environmental effects of border security operations.

In a number of senses whose precise texture and normative implications I explicate, over time border security is a social learning process conducted through the border continuum that continually places unobservable effects 'back out' into the unmarked sides of its own boundaries. Through operations, day after day, and in the course of responding to inchoate perturbations and expelling clearly identified irritants, border security's agents have learned to avoid repeat irritations, they seek to teach others ways of avoiding and expelling them, and they have learned how to studiously turn the border continuum away from its own 'back side' (sections 3.3, 4.9). Over time, in space, in society, these 'lessons of operations', on-water and off (sections 2.11–2.12, 3.11–3.12), have been integrated into border security's institutional and cultural memory, and because this web of intrasystemic semantic reference is, Luhmann argues, what steers "structural developments in certain directions",[29] the work of irritation and expulsion can direct us toward salient points of political transformation. This is one sense in which border security is about power in transformation.

Relatedly, Border Force's distinctions *cannot* be observed as partial, passionate or political – within the system. In the language of systems theory, this is described as the cause and effect of operational closure. In the public language of the then Minister, maritime interdictions are 'on-water operational matters' (section 2.11): they *cannot* be discussed in public, and journalists who open border security agents to basic questions of politicisation are routinely attacked and denounced.[30] This shows us another sense in which politics and justice are constitutive blindspots (sections 1.12, 6.1–6.6) of border security's world as Border

29 Luhmann, Niklas, *Theory of Society, Volume 1*, Stanford University Press, Stanford, 2012, p. 67.

30 Begley, Patrick, 'Gillian Triggs Refuses to Resign in Face of "Personal Attacks" From Abbott Government', *Sydney Morning Herald*, June 12, 2015. www.smh.com.au/federal-politics/political-news/gillian-triggs-refuses-to-resign-in-face-of-personal-attacks-from-abbott-government-20150611-ghm56b.htm

Force's agents practice it, because enacting sovereignty cannot occur *as border security* unless politics and justice are kept on the unmarked side of the boundary (sections 1.11–1.12). For this reason, border security's routine operation raises the following operational paradox that we will circle again and again.

Border security is an observing system whose agents are engaged in political action[31] placed beyond the shores of politics. Where Clausewitzean war was "the continuation of politics by other means",[32] border security can be cast through this phrasing as "the political negation of politics for reasons of security".[33] Even as Border Force enforces national sovereignty offshore, its agents, as agents of security, *cannot* see border security's passionate, partial, political aspects of the line carved by the wake of a ship's hull gliding across the ocean's surface to interdict people seeking asylum.

Border security is not political where it is most political, then. One clear example of where the lived contradictions raised by this paradox plays out is offered by a recent protest action involving Border Force's own staff. Border Force workers, who have been involved in a two-year pay dispute, organised a rally, during which employees wore 'fake uniforms'. A senior immigration official remonstrated that the fakes, which simulated Border Force's designed choice of a paramilitary uniform, undermined the community's perception of the department:

> Some of our employees chose to participate in a rally, which actively promoted voting against a political party. . . . These employees chose to wear clothing that simulated the Australian Border Force uniform, which included the words 'Border Protection Officer' on the back and 'Protecting our Community' on the front. . . . This type of action has the potential to associate the official activities of the department with the rally in the eyes of the public and undermine the community's perception of the department. . . . The Australian Public Service is apolitical. . . . As employees of the APS we have a responsibility to maintain the confidence of the community by being professional and impartial.[34]

The thicket of contradictions here is dense with political significations and their disavowal. Applying general liberal-democratic assumptions, whether offshore or onshore, border security is public service work conducted by authorised persons on behalf of a nation-state for whose citizens such actions are representative

31 Foucault, Michel, 'The Subject and Power', *Critical Inquiry*, 8: 4, 1982, p. 790.

32 Foucault, Michel, *Society Must Be Defended: Lectures at the Collège de France*, 1975–1976, Picador, London, 2003, pp. 15–16.

33 Agamben, Giorgio, 'On Security and Terror', *www.libcom.org*, September 24, 2006. https://libcom.org/library/on-security-and-terror-giorgio-agamben

34 Towell, Noel, 'Border Force Accused of Wearing Fake Uniforms to Campaign Against Turnbull', *Canberra Times*, May 17, 2016. www.canberratimes.com.au/national/public-service/border-force-accused-of-wearing-fake-uniforms-to-campaign-against-turnbull-20160516-gow3aq.html

expressions of a degree of contested popular will, and border security policy emerged in a parliamentary liberal democracy where its adoption was and is a durably popular though contested and divisive political choice. After the election in 2013, cabinet ministers in the Abbott government even spoke repeatedly of having 'received a mandate' to carry out *Operation Sovereign Borders* (sections 3.5, 2.11–2.12). As a specific measure proper to the politics of that conjuncture, the introduction of the very dark navy paramilitary uniform was a source of controversy when it was introduced with the Border Force Act, in force from July 1, 2015.[35] The paramilitary uniform and all that it implied generated fierce opposition, especially on the Immigration 'side' of the forced unity of the arranged marriage between Immigration and Customs forced by the Act.

The appearance of the 'black shirts', finally, happened in the months following a TV advertisement whose starring actor was one of the most senior members of the Australian Defence Force (ADF), General Angus Campbell, who appeared as the Commander of *Operation Sovereign Borders* in a video shot for YouTube to publicly send the message: 'No Way: You Will Not Make Australia Home' (section 2.2). The uniform, like General Campbell's acting foray, has been observed as a quintessential symbol of the politicisation of the public service through border security during the Operation Sovereign Borders 'era', a process that has not only militarised Customs but also politicised the military.[36]

Since the 'victory' of *Operation Sovereign Borders* – from early 2014 to the time of writing – *border security itself* has also become a tacit cultural situation in Australia, a muted social fact that 'mainstream' political parties and most news media outlets avoid politicising in any way. To be clear, this absence of critical attention to border security has transpired alongside sustained, fierce and meaningful ethical and political opposition to conditions faced by asylum seekers, and offshore detention (sections 5.8, 5.9, 6.1–6.6). All the same, political discussions of border security itself, in its immanence, are extremely rare in Australia. More importantly, its existence, now fully integrated in society, is no longer regarded by most as politically up for grabs: it is presumed as secured in perpetuity – perhaps awful, but nonetheless necessary.

Simultaneously, border security lives in Australian political rhetoric as an important electoral cudgel for the Coalition. The latter's situational definitions became so culturally hegemonic after their 2013 victory that the Labor party didn't dare contend with them *at all* during the following 2016 federal election.[37] By 2016,

35 'Australian Border Force Act, 2015'. www.austlii.edu.au/au/legis/cth/consol_act/abfa2015225/

36 Grattan, Michelle, 'Morrison Reacts to Heat Over Politicising the Military', *The Conversation*, November 13, 2013. http://theconversation.com/morrison-reacts-to-heat-over-politicising-the-military-20325

37 Laughland, Oliver, 'Angus Campbell Warns Asylum Seekers Not to Travel to Australia by Boat', *The Guardian*, April 11, 2014. www.theguardian.com/world/2014/apr/11/angus-campbell-stars-in-videos-warning-asylum-seekers-not-to-travel-by-boat

border security had become a studiously constructed nontopic for Labor. The watchword in the 2016 election among the Labor faithful expressed a simple and complete ceding of this ground: 'don't get wedged on national security'.

Finally, as rhetoric and topic, border security is an electoral weapon of the resurgent populist right: and we see this repeated all over the world at present, especially in post-Brexit Northern and Western Europe and 'build a wall' Trump era United States. Yet returning to prosaic micropolitics of the 'fake uniforms' and the email warning employees protesting Border Force for just one final moment, somehow 'all of the above' – with its conspicuously and intentionally public, political and (arguably) slightly farcical cast – is intrasystemically legible as apolitical. Or, at least, it is bald-facedly upheld as such. That is to say, within border security's world by 2015, only a protest action *critiquing* Border Force had 'the potential to associate the official activities of the department with politics' and undermine 'the community's perception of the department'. Only opposition to border security is regarded by border security as political; it *demands* support from its citizens, like former Prime Minister Tony Abbott's demand that Australia's national broadcaster show 'affection for the home team' in its reporting of the government, in order that it be part of 'Team Australia'.[38] Beyond its Australian-national cultural peculiarities, in whose dramas Mr Abbott played notable and surreal part –[39] yet with a style that's also a piece with the current global wave of (on the) offensive populists – a key task of *Border Security* is to trace out and think through the following question: how has such an intensely (a)political situation become so quietly integral to the way a polity studiously fails to recognise the politics of its own political practices?

I.4 The shores and horizons of a society of border security

Exploring Australia as a space secured by these severances and sutures, 'border continuum' begins to tell us about the shores and horizons of a society of border security, marked by evacuations of politics and justice from border security's world, such as those just discussed. But what might these recurring evacuations of the *polis* might mean if we think about a *society* of border security, if we follow Aristotle and Arendt by saying – approvingly – that any communal life of the *polis* distinct from that of the barbarians needs to be founded on a shared sense of justice?[40]

38 Ireland, Judith, 'Tony Abbott Blasts National Broadcaster: ABC Takes "Everyone's Side But Australia's"', *Sydney Morning Herald*, January 29, 2014. www.smh.com.au/federal-politics/political-news/tony-abbott-blasts-national-broadcaster-abc-takes-everyones-side-but-australias-20140129-31lt8.html

39 See: Williams, Evan, *Australian Leader Eats Raw Onion Whole: Headlines From the Government That Broke Satire*, Black Inc, 2015.

40 Salter, Mark, Theory of the/: 'The Suture and Critical Border Studies', *Geopolitics*, 17: 4, 2012, pp. 744, 734–755. See also: Philippopoulos-Mihalopoulos, Andreas, 'On Absence: Society's Return to Barbarians', *Soziale Systeme*, 14, 2008, Heft 1, S. pp. 142–156.

If border security only concerned itself with a highly specific modern state function, like espionage or diplomacy, we might remonstrate that, within a complex and functionally differentiated society, politics and justice just take place 'elsewhere': the *polis* is still vibrantly and contentiously there, it's just several kilometres (or, we might say, '12+ nautical miles') 'in that direction'. Justice is onshore; justice is for citizens. But in a society of border security where securing takes place at many different points in a continuum – in space, over time, in communication – the diffuse entrenchment of border security makes it infrastructure which is not only tacit, but also vital. The enaction of border security's world supports and secures the living conditions of a whole lifestyle through which a culture's reward structure is channelled.

Through its long-term integration, and the conflicts this expels, negates and precludes, who or what can thrive, or even live, outside the border continuum? As citizens, residents and campaigning politicians have come to depend upon border security for their social and civil mobility and paycheck, who can live and move in and out of the geopolitical orbits of Australia *except* through the border continuum's secured circuits, and with Border Force's authorisation? These questions prompt further considerations of shared spaces and futures, such as the following. As a trajectory enacted as a social system, what are the political spaces, materialities and norms of a society solidified with the tightening strengthening of Border Force's border continuum? I pose response to this key sociological question through border security's emergence; *in lieu* of the chapters to come, I offer the following introductory description.

The waxing of a world that waits for threat objects to appear on the horizon is the waning of a world made good through the possibility of justice among a *people* who share one another's *lives*. We may be talking, in other words, of communities where fairness and responsibility, as a right, as an obligation, a utopian horizon and shared imaginary, fades into a future in which residents must circulate within the space of interest in order to live and prosper, but can only do so without impedance to the extent that their work is recognised as unthreatening and of value to the system as a whole[41] (section I.11). The continuum concept and its repeated 'we' calls its group agents to their national task of bringing border security's world more strongly into being, but can this call a people into being: we, the onshore and offshore people of Australian Border Force?[42] Let's consider offshore detention more closely as one important societal effect of border security's emergence, because it gives a concrete way in to thinking about what has happened as border security's a(nti)political operations have become routinely conducted beyond horizons of justice.

41 Garland, David, 'The Limits of the Sovereign State: Strategies of Crime Control in Contemporary Society', *The British Journal of Criminology*, 36: 4, 1996, p. 466.

42 Balibar, Étienne, *We, the People of Europe? Reflections on Transnational Citizenship*, Princeton University Press, Princeton, 2004, p. ix.

Conducting operations offshore generates a highly selective dialectic of visibility and invisibility, spectacle and silencing – as it's meant to (section 3.1–3.4). That is, the political effects of offshoring are as well known as the aesthetic choice of a paramilitary uniform, the introduction of regulations necessitating that 'apolitical' APS officers wear it and salute senior officers, and the sending of an email reminding employees of the consequences for the 'choice' of attending a political rally critiquing Border Force. Offshore detention was carefully considered and chosen in a precisely calibrated pattern as part of an overall policy design *for its known benefits* (section 3.11–3.12). The design benefits of offshore operations I explore in detail in Chapter 3 speak to why offshore comprises a major part of the border continuum, which makes understanding how and why offshore works – and for whom – a key critical focus of this book.

In the fifteen years since its implementation, operating offshore has done what it was designed to do, and it works by its own measures: it effectuates deterrence and control by keeping asylum seekers beyond courts and critical scrutiny (section 3.10); it mutes their suffering; it ensures that maritime interdiction is a security matter; and it means indefinite detention can be conducted logistically, so that people can be warehoused without moral scrutiny, beyond care (Chapter 4). Detention is offshore so that anything that happens in detention can be defended as a matter of moral indifference – even where allegations of a five-year-old boy being raped are concerned. Moral lecturing on such matters, said Border Force's head in a public response to these rape allegations, is unhelpful:

> No amount of moral lecturing by those who seem not to comprehend the negative consequences of an open-borders policy will bring forth solutions. . . . Yielding to emotional gestures in this area of public administration simply reduces the margin for discretionary action.[43]

Mike Pezzullo's response shows a point of sovereign suture made using the severances of border security's world; it begs us to ask about the kind of society that 'rightly' secures its sovereignty through the indefinite offshore detention of children, and considers concerns about their possible rape in its care 'moral lecturing'[44] that reduces the space of discretionary action. This brings us to why this work retains a stubborn focus on 'border security' and not borders, security, seeking asylum, immigration detention and human rights.

43 Anderson, Stephanie, 'Immigration Department Secretary Michael Pezzullo Denies 5yo Asylum Seeker Raped on Nauru', *abc.net.au*, February 26, 2016. www.abc.net.au/news/2016-02-08/5yo-asylum-seekers-not-raped-on-nauru-immigration-official-says/7147492

44 McKenzie-Murray, Martin, 'Nauru Rapes: "There Is a War on Women"', *The Saturday Paper*, August 22, 2015. www.thesaturdaypaper.com.au/news/immigration/2015/08/22/nauru-rapes-there-war-women/14401656002263, and Hall, Bianca, 'Federal Court Finds Australia Owes Nauru Rape Victim a Duty of Care', *The Sydney Morning Herald*, May 6, 2016. www.smh.com.au/national/federal-court-finds-australia-owes-nauru-rape-victim-a-duty-of-care-20160506-goohbm.html

I.5 The focus of this work: why 'border security' and not borders, security, seeking asylum, immigration detention or human rights?

This work is emphatically about border security: this means quite stubbornly following border security's severances and the worlds its agents build through the recursive effects of applying its distinctions through operations (sections i.1–i.2). It is only by grappling with how border security's agents enact border security's world that we can understand its power and appeal as something that might migrate and be adopted and adapted by other authorities and polities. By understanding the implications and effects of enacting these distinctions, we can understand how warehousing people takes place in a logistical space where the proper task of those who govern it involves maintaining the margin for discretionary action while *never* yielding to emotional gestures where the possible rape of children is concerned. In the space of security cognised as the border continuum, the ability to respond urgently as security is what counts, in order to 'protect the border', in order to effectuate deterrence and control, in order to project sovereignty (sections 3.10, 3.12) – and this means discounting people as such, as well as discounting their systemically produced suffering.

The focus of this work remains on border security, second, because its operation negates asylum. This is my own normative concern, prompted by what I see as a very dangerous societal effect of border security's emergence,[45] based on what we can learn from the Australian experience *and* its lineages in the deeper history of US-Haitian interdictions (Chapter 3).

This asylum negating aspect of *Border Security's* focus is also intended as what I described earlier as a 'message in a bottle' – *especially* for Europe, but also for the global futures that confront border security's world, wherever it emerges as an authoritative response to the threats that emerge from global space (section I.2). To the extent that the negation of asylum occurs, the selective adoption of border security policies by nation-states in the coming decades will affect the lives of tens of millions of vulnerable people by denying them protection as refugees, abandoning them to the spreading wastelands of our global warzones and destroyed cities. If current trajectories continue and intensify, large and growing populations may find their lives aligned with border security's circuits, detained in its centres, destroyed with indifference as an effect of its norms: warehoused, traumatised, abandoned.

But the globalising negation of asylum that would be carried along with the spread of border security's world returns to this section's basic point: if we don't *first* try to understand that the enaction of border security's world negates asylum and is indifferent to justice *because* its agents are pursuing other strategic aims via their own distinctions – not because of a lack or an absence, but precisely

45 Dreyfus, Hubert and Rabinow, Paul, *Michel Foucault: Beyond Structuralism and Hermeneutics*, University of Chicago Press, Chicago, 1982, p. 232.

through the fullness and political creativity of border security's world – we will never understand what 'we' may be supporting, condemning, implicated in. I intend this as a vital point for critics of border security writing from a social justice perspective, because it helps get at why so many political, legal and ethical demands for protection, fairness and responsibility seem to keep going unheard, why well-evidenced claims that indefinite offshore detention centres are 'factories of mental illness' are ignored,[46] why senior officials who bear evidence of the destroyed lives of children are personally attacked for delivering it,[47] why the systemic nature of all of this is minimised or excused in the face of overwhelming and undeniable evidence,[48] and why border security continues to resonate as a sensible 'hopeful model' for Europe.[49]

I maintain an analytic focus on border security, third, to engage critically with the societally diffused idea that global mobility is 'about' people, or that economic globalisation and the expansion of trade and GDP growth procures prosperity, rights and justice for them as a beneficent effect of its spread. And that, by extension, globalisation pursued as the expansion of global logistics and trade will 'deliver' a world of shared prosperity (see Chapter 4). For nearly four decades, the ideology of global trade has insisted that 'a rising tide lifts all boats'; what I explore instead is how the rising tide of border security in Australia sought to 'stop the boats', and how this discloses the myth of global mobility as the spreading rise of freedom and prosperity by showing what's actually happened at this one complex, evolving worksite of globalisation.

A critical examination of the normativity implicit in border security's world is also a way in to salient questions of global inequality. This is because it gives us a way to observe *global* class relations being worked out, as some seek protection and others who would care are secured *from* protecting them, or silenced in the name of security for speaking openly out about what they have seen done in the name of national sovereignty. This is also intended to encourage those of us working in and across critical studies of borders, security, the international

46 'Detention Centres Are Factories for Mental Illness', *ABC The Drum*. www.abc.net.au/news/2011-11-18/tatz-ryan-detention-centres/3677942

47 Begley, Patrick, 'Gillian Triggs Refuses to Resign in Face of "Personal Attacks" from Abbott Government', *Sydney Morning Herald*, June 12, 2015. www.smh.com.au/federal-politics/political-news/gillian-triggs-refuses-to-resign-in-face-of-personal-attacks-from-abbott-government-20150611-ghm56b.html and Kelly, Joe, 'Gillian Triggs Debases Her Position: Peter Dutton', *The Australian*, June 7, 2015. www.theaustralian.com.au/in-depth/terror/australian-born-jihadis-to-lose-citizenship-says-peter-dutton/news-story/0474b153fead5fd3ba82b1678659c3b3

48 Evershed, Nick, Liu, Ri, Farrell, Paul and Davidson, Helen, 'The Nauru Files: The Lives of Asylum Seekers in Detention Detailed in a Unique Database', *The Guardian*, August 10, 2016. www.theguardian.com/australia-news/ng-interactive/2016/aug/10/the-nauru-files-the-lives-of-asylum-seekers-in-detention-detailed-in-a-unique-database-interactive

49 Frum, David, 'Closing Europe's Harbors: The Urgent Case for Stopping the Flow of Illegal Migrants Across the Mediterranean', *The Atlantic*, July/August 2015. www.theatlantic.com/magazine/archive/2015/07/closing-european-harbors/395321/

and human rights to bring the constitutive background of operations into the foreground (section 4.2), not just by locating and explicitly voicing the tacit predicates and silent commitments attached to the nebulous global spaces securing our citizenship, but through a more directly avowed encounter with the ways capitalism draws us through its screened circuits,[50] where we are sorted according to our value and integrated according to our alignment with the norms of global logistics (sections 4.6–4.9, 5.6–5.7). If we are privileged enough, much of this savage sorting[51] escapes our attention; if we were Hazaras fleeing war and seeking protection in Australia by boat, we would experience the boundary of the same system as total domination.

1.6 Border security and the normative: horizons of justice

In the normative thrust that emerges from this book to become its increasing focus by the final chapters, I argue that asylum seeking raises a basic question about a possible global meaning and location of political justice, and that border security negates this possibility *because* it could exist. Considering this by way of historical analogues, we can think of the spaces, materialities and norms underpinning other modern 'dividing practices'[52] such as South African apartheid, the Berlin Wall and state security in East Germany, and racial segregation in the United States. I explicitly consider the emergence of border security along such 'lines'. I develop this as an explicitly normative set of considerations not because border security is an evil entity or conspiracy, a nebulous 'it' whose human masterminds must be identified and denounced. I do so because the operative distinctions of border security's world are but one among a number of sets of political possibilities we share, some less improbable than others, that constitute ways of doing politics in the face of global complexity and its *recognised* challenges. Border security means we're already implicated in this politics: all of us. To the extent that the suffering it produces is conspicuous and unnecessary, it also means we're responding very badly.

The fact that border security has been so popular, and urgent calls for its adoption, defence and expansion have become loud and clear in these first two decades of the twenty-first century shows us its seductive power, its creativity, it follies and perils. But I hope this might take us beyond critique to the serious task of imagining and developing better futures together. That border security's world operates

50 Balibar, Étienne, '*Homo nationalis*: An Anthropological Sketch of the Nation-Form', in *We, the People of Europe? Reflections on Transnational Citizenship*, Princeton University Press, Princeton, 2004, p. 18, italics in original, and Mezzadra, Sandro and Neilson, Brett, *Border as Method, or, The Multiplication of Labor*, Duke University Press, Durham, 2013.

51 Sassen, Saskia, *Expulsions: Brutality and Complexity in the Global Economy*, Belknap Press, Cambridge, 2014.

52 Foucault, Michel, 'The Subject and Power', *Critical Inquiry*, 8: 4, 1982, pp. 777–778.

with no intrasystemic relation to justice, rights, people or life – except insofar as these elements appear within the border continuum as risks approaching the other side of the boundary – is not just my critical assessment of a key societal effect of operating using its distinctions. It's also a warm invitation do otherwise. Other responses are possible; my wager is that the problems and contradictions of these other ways may well be better, in the way that, for all their faults, Berlin, Johannesburg and Belfast are less violent places since the end of the Cold War, apartheid and the Troubles. A world without border security would not be some paradise on earth; but nor would 'the world end' or sovereignty wither and die if Australians stopped destroying the mental health of noncitizen children in order to stop the boats. A world without border security would offer neither emancipation nor damnation. As with the cities and conflicts just mentioned, an Australia not divided by border security's world would not be 'less divided', it would be 'divided differently'. The differences might be profound, subtle and slightly disappointing all at once.

Apart from anything else, a key critical observation that emerges in this book is that enacting border security's world commits society to a waste of life, space and time that also involves the infliction of extreme violence and cruelty to children as key systemic features. Indeed, the use of cruelty to procure deterrence is recognised as a benefit that not secures sovereignty while keeping open a 'space of discretion' for public administration in the border continuum, as Mr Pezzullo indicates (section I.4). When viewed against other historically viable ways of achieving it, destroying the lives of children is but one catastrophe in what has become a grotesquely costly way to enact sovereignty. As I contend border security demoralises and disfigures the society involved in its expansion, then refuses to speak of this, then threatens jail time for those who would.[53]

I.7 *Palapa*'s crossing into global space and its capture by border security

The ships, islands and reefs that confront the asylum seekers in this work – with the shores of politics and horizons of justice they carry aboard, as their 'baggage' – are figures of global political alternatives we might imagine and enact together. The following particular group of passengers and their fateful crossing into global space (section I.2) also inaugurate the story of border security's emergence in Australia. In this section I shift focus a little, gathering the epistemological foundations and normative concerns of the book to zoom in and focus on an empirical example highly significant in the Australian emergence of border security, the story of the *Palapa* (sections 1.1, 2.8) and the fate of its asylum-seeking passengers.

53 Whyte, Sarah, 'Doctors and Teachers Gagged Under New Immigration Laws', *Sydney Morning Herald*, June 4, 2015. www.smh.com.au/federal-politics/political-news/doctors-and-teachers-gagged-under-new-immigration-laws-20150603-ghft05.html

At around 2am on Thursday August 23, 2001, several busloads of people arrived at a wharf in Pantau, near Pelabuhan Ratu, on the south coast of west Java. The people, mostly Afghanis,[54] had arrived by bus from hotels near Jakarta, four hours north. Among them: 350 unaccompanied males (40 of them boys),[55] 21 families, 43 children and 6 Sri Lankans – a total of 438 people.[56]

Pelabuhan Ratu is popular with Australian surfers, but none of those who made this four-hour bus trip from the outskirts of Jakarta had come to the south coast of Java for its reef breaks. They had come to get on a boat they'd been promised would to take them to Australia. All of them were departing Indonesia to arrive in Australia, where they were told they could claim asylum, with the hope of being found to be refugees. Then as now, Indonesia is not a signatory to the Convention on refugees, and with high levels of urban overcrowding, corruption, poverty and inequality is not an easy country for the majority of its citizens, let alone a place of peace and stability where most asylum seekers can easily rebuild meaningful futures. As Assadullah Naziri, one of those aboard *Palapa*, reminds us, "[we were fleeing repression and persecution in Afghanistan". Attempting to arrive in Australia by boat was a "pathway for people like us who wanted to escape the country".[57] The people getting aboard *Palapa* were fleeing extreme violence, risking their lives to seek protection and a viable future for themselves and their families.

This leg of their promised passage to safety, shelter and care involved taking a re-purposed 20 metre wooden fishing vessel, *KM Palapa 1*, across the Indian Ocean to Christmas Island, approximately 400km south.[58] To the extent it is remembered at all, *Palapa* is best remembered globally as the fishing boat rescued by *MV Tampa*, triggering the 'Tampa Affair'.[59] For those aboard it, like Hussain Ewazi, the *Palapa* was etched in memory as a voyage of fear, panic and the stench of vomit.[60]

54 Marr, David and Wilkinson, Marian, *Dark Victory*, Allen and Unwin, Melbourne, 2004, p. 8 and Toohey, Paul, 'That Sinking Feeling', *Quarterly Essay*, 53, March 2014. www.quarterlyessay.com.au/essay/2014/03/that-sinking-feeling

55 Dusevic, Tom, 'Tampa Refugees Resurface as Kiwis', *The Australian*, August 20, 2011. www.theaustralian.com.au/national-affairs/tampa-refugees-resurface-as-kiwis/story-fn59niix-1226117936857

56 See: Marr, David and Wilkinson, Marian, *Dark Victory*, Allen and Unwin, Melbourne, 2004, p. 1–8.

57 Dusevic, Tom, 'Tampa Refugees Resurface as Kiwis', *The Australian*, August 20, 2011. www.theaustralian.com.au/national-affairs/tampa-refugees-resurface-as-kiwis/story-fn59niix-1226117936857

58 Approximately 400 km or 248 miles, which is 215 nautical miles. This is also the rough distance between the port of Mariel, in Cuba, and Miami, Florida (see chapter three, sections 3.6–3.10).

59 Crock, Mary, 'In the Wake of Tampa: Conflicting Visions of International Refugee Law in the Management of Refugee Flows', *Pacific Rim Law and Policy Journal*, 12: 1, 2003, pp. 49–95.

60 Op.Cit.

Palapa and the Tampa Affair jump scales in the public imagination, being seen as part of a whole constellation of post 9/11 border security responses. Yet none of the August 23, 2001 *Palapa* embarkees could have suspected the strange way in which the trajectories of their lives would be affected by the causal chain that would attach them to *MV Tampa*, the question of Australia's sovereignty and national security posed by the Tampa Affair, and in turn to a pair of 767s that would smash through the sky-raised steel and glass of the Twin Towers, less than three weeks later. Both the proximity and antecedence of *Palapa*'s voyage are important. This tangle of larger, later events and their long and complex lineages envelop the afterlife of the *Palapa*, and as many of them are crucial to understanding the Australian emergence of border security via the Tampa Affair, I dwell on them in detail in Chapter 2 (sections 2.8–2.9). Yet the Tampa Affair, 9/11 and the Global War on Terror that (we know in retrospect) ensued from September 2001 render the *Palapa* a somewhat forgotten minor detail of these big stories; a tiny boat among large ships, angry men of violent conviction and important matters of global security. Its passengers' moment of embarkation – sheltering in the lee of *Tampa*, and the storm unleashed by 9/11 – is worth pausing to remember. It was a life-defining moment for those aboard, but it's also the precise moment where boat-borne, Australia-bound asylum seeking's fateful crossing into global space began (section I.2).

I.8 From the difference between system and environment to seafaring, via operational closure and navigation

Unlike so many similar boat trips undertaken across the Mediterranean as of writing, *Palapa* and its occupants escaped oblivion: much of this is due to the norms of seafaring that ensured their rescue (section 1.11). Given the importance of 'the boats' and ships throughout *Border Security*, it would be remiss to think about *Palapa*'s miraculous survival of its crossing into global space without considering seafaring as that which buoys it up, because like the occupants of the *Palapa* and their actual human fates, the importance of seafaring, of boats and ships and navigations and their place in the normative order of global logistics, tends to disappear. It is as if 'the boats' are blank matters of fact that just began appearing one threatening day on an otherwise featureless surface,[61] rather than a group of living humans contending with actual vessels enmeshed in a murky smuggling economy and floating atop the dangerous immense complexity of the ocean. Alongside an attempt to think directly about what it means for a maritime-emergent theory and practice of border security, thinking directly about seafaring is also a second way in to my interpretation of Luhmann's systems theory. Thus

61 Steinberg, Philip E., *The Social Construction of the Ocean*, Cambridge University Press, Cambridge, 2001, pp. 159–211.

the following points append the epistemological assumptions laid out earlier (section I.2): as there, the reader may dwell on or skip them as they wish; as there, they fundamentally shape my basic understanding.

The design of a hull that floats in all conditions is a seaworthy observation of the difference between system and environment.[62] This difference exists on a number of levels: physical differences of mass and density that exist between wood and water, such that wood floats; the chemical differences that contribute to the paradoxical resistance and attraction of water and wood such that wood repels water, for a time; the transformative differences of states created by a human apprehension of a biological material that in its living state is structured to sustain the life of a tree by conducting water, yet in its dead state can be sawn, hammered, assembled and caulked until it becomes a seaworthy hull, such that wood can become a boat capable of sustaining human lives for many years, even through a violent storm on the open ocean. In this sense, all boatbuilding and seafaring is a practiced understanding of systems theory. To broaden this point, throughout *Border Security* I observe many instances of intuitive systems thinking, which is why I work on the assumption that, for this work's purposes, Luhmann's systems theory is less about fidelity to Luhmann's insights and syntax, and more a way of thinking about world making. Both border security and seafaring are viable ways of making worlds that proceed by constructing viable boundaries and enacting socio-spatial processes using their own operative distinctions. A seaworthy hull understood and used for seafaring already presents us with a practiced understanding of systems theory, a *phronesis* of operational closure and structural coupling upheld as communication, circulating in society. This *phronesis* is simultaneously theoretical, practical and causal-effective; as I unfold a little now, it also nurtured, sheltered and carried with it cultures of seafaring that made and change *and are changing* the worlds in which we live.

Once we have a seaworthy hull, we have a structure that is operationally closed from an environment that it becomes for those aboard the moment they undertake seafaring – which, in circular form, they become capable of doing after observing the hull's purpose as the underpinning of a boat. Seafaring aboard a boat transforms the ocean into a differentiated environment that the hull 'upholds' for those who sail across its surface. As sailing happens, those aboard simultaneously become structurally coupled to an ocean they must remain distinct from, for as long as seafaring continues: this is what swimming and drowning are, human relations to a sinking boat and the ocean's surface.

A seaworthy hull used for seafaring cannot just float; it must enable navigation. As a hull moves, its shape has to slide over or carve into the water it glides on and pushes into, *while* the water pushes back and buoys the hull up. For a hull to move in such a purposive way, it must obey constraints that enable it *to be* while

62 Luhmann, Niklas, *Theory of Society, Volume 1*, Stanford University Press, Stanford 2012, pp. 28–40.

shaping *how it can be*. This gives us a clear way of seeing the selective pressures involved in all evolved forms, and from a human point of view, it gives us a way of understanding design effects and constraints through observation, purpose, what we might call 'enabling constraints', or what Alicia Juarrero, following Chuck Dyke, calls "structured structuring structures".[63] In respect of these constraints, when the purpose of seafaring is navigation, a hull is typically longer than it is wide, with a low centre of gravity, with a shape and (usually) keel and/or a rudder that take into consideration the method of propulsion (pulled through the water by the translation of wind into propulsion through sails, or pushed through the water by an oar, propeller or jet), the speed at which the boat will travel, and the sea conditions it will have to withstand. The collier *Earl of Pembroke* was chosen to become the *Endeavour* because its hull was designed so it could carry heavy loads through rough seas and sail safely through shallow water: the cost of this design compromise was speed and manoeuvrability (section 4.3–4.5). *MV Tampa*'s hull was designed to safely carry enormous volumes of roll-on, roll-off and containerised cargo across the high seas, all year round – this is what made it a capable part of global logistics (section 4.2, 4.5). The enormous hull this design commitment produced for global logistical seafaring made *MV Tampa* capable of carrying all 438 rescuees, and even meant they could be housed from the sun and rain in spare shipping containers on deck. But the Commonwealth's agents, most conspicuously Phillip Ruddock, cited this co-produced design effect – size, hull, lack of port – as the factor that made it impossible for *Tampa* to dock at CI's Flying Fish Cove and disembark the asylum seekers 'in Australia' (section 1.8–1.9).

Even with an understanding capable of observing an operations-enabling difference *then* constructing a hull and a seaworthy boat, we still require the conditions of seafaring, which are social. 'Seafaring' could only emerge once communication about it became possible (section 2.2–2.3). In the first place, this is because seafaring necessitates a world imagined-and-experienced as out there, open, capable of being traversed, worth risking exploring. For the time in which the world was 'known to be known'[64] as flat, traversing the world's oceans was precluded on the grounds of prudence and safety, concerns about angering the Gods and persistent rumours of dragons and monsters. The cultural availability – and bold use (section 4.3–4.5) – of seaworthy boats and crews is another part enabler of the world of seafaring, but without information about such navigation-prompting elements as nearby islands of plunder, stories of new worlds and rumours of the existence of undiscovered continents, there would have been nowhere capable of inspiring the risk of such a journey.[65] And without an understanding of celestial and cartographic navigation and its mathematical predicates and instrumentation, there

63 Juarrero, Alicia, *Dynamics in Action: Intentional Behaviour as a Complex System*, MIT Press, Cambridge, 2002, p. 129.

64 Luhmann, Niklas, *The Reality of the Mass Media*, Stanford University Press, Stanford, 2000, p. 13.

65 See: Sloterdijk, Peter, *In the World Interior of Capital*, Polity Press, Cambridge, 2013.

would be no way of getting 'there' and 'returning home' (section 4.3–4.5). All of these points around seafaring, diffusely, are also important to this book as grounding my understanding of globalisation, following Peter Sloterdijk. It tells us nothing of the stories of those climbing aboard *Palapa* who would become rescuees aboard *Tampa*, but without this regress of world making modern predicates, they are less likely to have been where they were, in motion as they were.

1.9 The fate of asylum seeking in the age of civil aviation: the emergence of a 'global' jet *civis* and 'the boats' as a co-produced jet age meaning

We should think likewise of civil aviation and its place in our political present. Throughout what follows, civil aviation follows seaborne navigation as the culturally prevalent way in which 'we' move: from seafaring to aeromobility. Co-observing 'the planes' also means that 'the boats' of border security are an offshore negation of seafaring made from an onshore, airborne culture in which civil aviation commands a normative value that, like the value of shipping and global logistics, is as pervasive and essential as it is generally unrecognised. 'We' expect to fly and do so without thinking; we consider even less how this has meant stopping 'them' from using other modes of transport, once we have denied them seats beside us in the skies we take for granted. For most Australian citizens, the Indian and Pacific oceans and the Asian continental landmass are 'flyover states'. With the people boarding *Palapa* still in the background, this means we should spend a moment thinking about the co-emergence of civil aviation and the arrival of asylum seekers as a profound political problem *in the West* which did not exist until the early 70s, and only coalesced around 1977 (chapters 2 and 3).

As the ex-military engineering innovations of the Boeing 707 (1958) were transferred into the 737 (1968), 747 (1969) and 767 (1981), civil aviation became a mass phenomenon, and business and tourist travel were set on the trajectory where they quickly became the atmospheric condition and banal social fact of global middle-class existence they remain to this day. This 'global' jet *civis* only emerged when civil aviation supplanted coal and diesel-powered shipping as the primary means of international mass transit it had been for most of the twentieth century (section 3.6, section 5.3–5.4). As a mass phenomenon, this tipping point came in the early 70s. This correlates with the rise of asylum seeking by boat as a mass phenomenon involving groups of people fleeing conflict who 'just arrive' at the territorial borders of other nation-states,[66] in ways that have increasingly come to be observed by state-related agencies as crises: of immigration,

66 Harding, Jeremy, 'The Uninvited', *London Review of Books*, 22: 30, 2000. www.lrb.co.uk/v22/n03/jeremy-harding/the-uninvited, Hugo, Graeme, 'From Compassion to Compliance? Trends in Refugee and Humanitarian Migration in Australia', *GeoJournal*, 55, 2001, pp. 27–37. The refugee/asylum seeker distinction is also explored by Mountz, Alison,

then of sovereignty and borders (section 2.5–2.10, 3.8–3.12). The first group of asylum seekers seeking protection in Australia arrived by boat in Darwin in 1975; 'boat people' was first politicised in Australia in the 1977 election, and throughout the rich West from 1975 with the Indochinese Exodus. It is also this point that comprises a tipping point in the shift to neoliberalism, financialisation and the intentional construction of global cities (Chapter 5).

The last ship to carry assisted migrants, the *Australis*, arrived in Melbourne in 1977. From around about this time, 'refugees' – seen from onshore Australia – became people whose asylum claims had been pre-processed in offshore camps as part of the offshore resettlement program, people brought onshore by plane.[67] Neither causally nor coincidentally, 'boat people' first became a matter of onshore political concern in the Anglophone West at this conjuncture. In a broader sense, 'boat people' are simultaneously 'those incapable of flight' and (*pace* Sloterdijk) 'people viewed from a plane at a comfortable distance': an existential situation co-generated by *their* aerial bombardment and *our* civil aviation, the way we have come to expect we can live, the way we have come to accept they must be exposed to death.

From roughly 1977, 'refugees' are people 'cleared to fly' because they have been documented through the international mechanisms of the UNHCR and IOM. In contrast, asylum seekers 'just turn up uninvited' and demand protection. Annual quotas of 'refugees', such as Australia's annual intake of roughly 12,000, don't trouble national sovereignty as the right to decide who can enter and how (Chapter 1), because these populations have already by been rendered controllable – locatable, identifiable and *therefore* jet mobile – via their compliance with the norms and processes of international human rights bureaucracies. Asylum seekers' requests for protection, made so directly, without clarifying conditions of hospitality beforehand, upset a whole global order of national sovereigns and international governance – completely dependent on the unexplicated background of civil aviation and global logistics – by short circuiting its norms in a way that throws nation-state identity, potency and existence into question. Such 'crises' are increasingly demanding decisive and punitive responses – which, in turn, resonate with the desires and anxieties of a growing percentage of the citizens of the rich West.

The 1970s-onward emergence of asylum seekers is the first sense in which boat people are *global* arrivals: harbingers of the global who, when they step outside the nationally sovereign and the international by embarking on these extraordinarily fraught and hazardous journeys, become entities from global space whose movement reveals the existence of smuggler networks and informal transport systems as the global shadow of our formal, secured networks and systems – that 'we' bar them from using. A counterworld of chaos, disorder and life-and-death demand *just* out there, just beyond the limit of sovereign enforcement; the fragility of

Specters at the Port of Entry: 'Understanding State Mobilities Through an Ontology of Exclusion', *Mobilities*, 6: 3, pp. 319, 317–334.

67 Op.cit.

a world of orderly life and secured privilege trembling with our screens in our hands right here in our safe suburban now – this is the dialectic of the political present that boat arrivals present us with as a social fact about global space. To understand 'the boat' as a figure of global space, something that people survive somehow, and 'that which must be stopped', I focus on how cultural norms driving calls for border security – norms that developed as civil aviation supplanted seaborne mass transport – placed shipping outside the purview of secured circulation *while* aerial bombardment continued its expansion as the rich world's military response of choice. In *Border Security*, I consider what it therefore means that there is a life and death demand for boat travel in the jet age.

1.10 The negated politics of the logistics of *Palapa*, and the operationally necessary co-presence of the threat environment in border security's world

With what I've just introduced about ships, boats, seafaring and civil aviation in mind, let us now return to the wharf at Pantau that fateful morning of August 23, 2001 to consider the logistics of boat-borne people smuggling in the jet age. Most of those who fatefully climbed aboard *Palapa* paid more than 10,000 Australian dollars for their passage to Australia.[68] *Palapa*'s passengers were offered a potentially deadly passage with no basic human comforts, for the same cost as a first-class airfare from London to Sydney or the same journey economy for a family of five. Consider this as you imagine the passengers taking their flimsy lifejacket (none provided to the children) and their spot among what the waves would soon make into a soup of vomit, shit, diesel and bilge water, sloshing around a slippery, leaking hull, screaming in fear for their lives. This description sounds histrionic; yet such conditions are a routine experience, and the fear, the smell and the screams are what many survivors report back as the traumatic signatures of these voyages.

In 2001, the year *Palapa* sailed for Christmas Island, there were 8,449,152 inbound international passenger movements to Australia; by 2015 this number more than doubled to 17,517,506[69] (section 2.8, section 4.9). In 2015, Melbourne Airport handled 33.1 million domestic and international passengers, and Sydney Airport handled 39.6 million. In 2015, more than 1 million Australians flew to Bali,[70] a figure that remains roughly consistent as of this writing; an aver-

68 Marr and Wilkinson note 11,500 AUD for one family, but each passage would have been subject to negotiation.

69 'Airport traffic data', Bureau of Infrastructure, Transport and Regional Economics (BITRE), June 2017. https://bitre.gov.au/publications/ongoing/airport_traffic_data.aspx

70 Duff, Eamonn, 'Indonesia Prepares to Welcome Millionth Aussie Tourist for the Year', *Sydney Morning Herald*, November 9, 2014. www.smh.com.au/national/indonesia-prepares-to-welcome-millionth-aussie-tourist-for-the-year-20141108-11iuv4.html

age return airfare to Bali from most Australian cities costs just a few hundred Australian dollars.

Keeping in mind what was introduced about seafaring in the previous section, consider the pitiful capacity of *Palapa* relative to its passenger numbers and route, and the completely inappropriate choice of design, crew and equipment as a vessel capable of conveying those aboard safely to their destination. 438 people, the number crammed aboard *Palapa* by the time it set off, is a 747-400 flying near capacity in most configurations. A 747-400 fits over four hundred people in a body 71 metres long. Local state authorities assisted the smugglers to forcibly cram 438 people aboard a vessel that was 20 metres long: chartered yachts of the same length carry no more than 12 wealthy tourists through the Indonesian archipelago. As detailed in *Dark Victory*, "[t]he cheap Chinese life jackets the adults were wearing had no whistles, no lights, and would not keep an unconscious person's head out of the water. There were none for the children. There was no galley, just a few scraps of food in plastic bags". Apart from a box compass "there was no navigational equipment at all. 'No sextant, no log, no charts, no nautical publications, no electronic communication devices, no GPS. They didn't have communication equipment, no radio, no nothing' ".[71] All aircraft that are part of global civil aviation are powered by engines engineered to withstand the stresses that routine operating conditions expose them to. They're regularly serviced by dedicated engineers, and flown by trained pilots with proper navigational equipment that is checked before each flight. *Palapa* had an incompetent crew and one dodgy engine, which broke down during a storm that arose between Java and Christmas Island, nearly drowning everyone aboard.

There's no shortage of blame for such situations: one of the lines of enquiry I undertake in *Border Security* seeks to locate the discursive absence of border security among those agents responsible for the co-production of such hazards as routine. Onshore in Australia, most of the blame for mass drownings is laid squarely at the feet of 'evil people smugglers' who profit from such conditions (section 2.1). Like border security, such approbation has bipartisan support in Canberra. Closer scrutiny (2.6–2.10) reveals a murkier picture, implicating many of those who condemn the smugglers, without absolving anyone of all responsibility. Rather than offering a moral lesson about blameworthy individuals, the following less noted condensation point, already indicated clearly by the above descriptions, is worth emphasising.

There is no technical impediment to the safe movement of 438 people from Afghanistan to Australia by plane, at a fraction of the inconvenience, cost and danger that smuggler networks routinely expose already vulnerable people to. The people bussed to the wharf at Pantau had arrived in Indonesia months earlier by plane. Between 2002 and 2014, Australia deployed 26,000 people to Afghanistan, the country that many of those aboard *Palapa* had fled. Over the duration

71 Wilkinson, Marian, *Dark Victory*, Allen and Unwin, Melbourne, 2004, p. 23.

of Operation Slipper, Australia's longest overseas military commitment – a war effort that lasted thirteen years – 41 people were killed, and 261 were wounded. In roughly the same period, 52,086 people attempted to seek asylum by boat in Australia, and as far as records indicate, 900 or so drowned.[72] Fleeing Afghanistan's wars for protection in Australia as a civilian was twenty-one times deadlier than fighting in Afghanistan as an Australian soldier. This begs a question as obvious as it is unasked: why didn't those arriving at the Pantau wharf in Pelabuhan Ratu avoid the grave danger of an extortionately priced sea journey aboard a hazardously overloaded, unseaworthy coastal fishing boat – and just fly to Australia from Bali, for a couple of hundred dollars?

Australia has a universal visa system. This means that all noncitizens seeking to arrive in Australia must have a visa authorising them to do so. Australia's universal visa system is codified in the *Migration Act*, whose purpose is 'to regulate the entry and presence of noncitizens'.

As the piece of legislation that replaced the White Australia policy's *Migration Restriction Act* (section 1.6, 5.3), that has been amended many times, such as in the wake of *Tampa*, the *Migration Act* can and has been changed in the context affecting those who were boarding *Palapa* from 2am on August 23, 2001. The universal visa system is a political choice that, like the choice of a paramilitary uniform or offshore processing, has consequences for all those subject to it, many of which escape the control of its intentional architects.

Among its other purposes, the universal visa system functions as a way of responding to global space by screening entry through an administrative process that is lawful and regulated. Physical geography aside, what's stark about Australia among contemporary nation-states contending with the complexity of global mobility via migration is that the universal visa system forms a key plank of what the border continuum refers to as the 'framework of movement', as we've explored (section I.2). Through the framework of movement, the Commonwealth claims to know *every one* of the people who has entered or is present in Australia, *omnes et singulatum*.[73] The universal visa system is therefore a key means toward the Commonwealth's normative goal of *total* control of human mobility as a way of governing population. The contingent choice of a universal visa system is a political technology, one co-produced by physical geography and the cultural norm – simultaneously a matter of technical capacity, personal convenience *and* enforced fact – of flying for overseas travel and inbound migration. 'Stop the boats', which emerged as the key slogan of 2013's *Operation Sovereign Borders* federal election, is just the terminus of an earlier-developed co-produced

72 Davies, Sara and Reilly, Alex, 'FactCheck: Have More Than 1000 Asylum Seekers Died at Sea Under Labor?' *The Conversation*, July 23, 2013. http://theconversation.com/factcheck-have-more-than-1000-asylum-seekers-died-at-sea-under-labor-16221

73 Foucault, Michel, 'Omnes et Singulatim: Towards a Criticism of "Political Reason"', *The Tanner Lectures on Human Values*, Stanford University Press, Stanford University, Stanford University Press, Stanford, October 10 and 16, 1979.

set of elements that comprise a framework of movement that seeks to *totally* screen out boat arrivals (section 2.7–2.8, 2.11). In this system of total control which necessitates that no extrasystemic arrivals transpire, the arrival of a boat – even *one* – prevents the goal from being achieved.

This already defines global space *per negationem* as 'that which must be screened out', and effectively precludes arrival by boat because, but for the socially invisible populations of seafarers involved in global logistics, or the handful of contrastingly conspicuous arrivals of round-the-world yachtspeople, *everyone* – post 1977 – arrives in Australia by plane. Seen this way, the political choice of a universal visa system is *the* key condition that makes 'the boats' necessary. If asylum seekers could get on a plane to Australia without a visa, they could arrive cheaply and safely in Australia without paying smugglers and taking boats. Their inability to do so is precisely what generates the demand for smuggler services using the mode of transport available between the Indonesian archipelago and the 'island continent' facing it across the Timor Sea. The political choice of a universal visa system is, for all these reasons, the deeply contradictory lynchpin of Boat Arrivals in Australia Since 1976,[74] though one seldom identified as such. Arguably, it's the most salient contingent condition shaping the lives people of people seeking asylum in Australia by boat, yet it's presented as the most necessary onshore in Australia, and to the best of my knowledge it has never been politicised in the context of border security.

Even a very persuasive rhetorical performance of the above points is unlikely to win over the majority of Australians – or Western Europeans, North Americans and the Japanese – to the ideal and reality of a borderless world. An immediate remonstration, following Pezzullo and others (section 2.6–2.9), is that *without* a framework of movement screening out irregular migration, national sovereignty is forever lost: *Après nous, le deluge*.

The Australian intensification of this increasingly common argument among the world's wealthiest polities, following the points just raised, is that sovereignty is lost without *total* deterrence of *all* unauthorised arrivals. In strengthening voices of populist, nationalist and xenophobic imagination, filled with passionate intensity by a seeming spiral of news media events of third-world rapists and terrorist atrocities,[75] a world of free movement, where the national 'we' would fully share 'our world' with the free mingling, unscreened co-presence of global mobility – is precisely *the* nightmare scenario, a dystopian future in which 'we' are

74 Phillips, Janet and Spinks, Harriet, 'Boat Arrivals in Australia Since 1976', *Parliament of Australia*. www.aph.gov.au/About_Parliament/Parliamentary_Departments/Parliamentary_Library/pubs/rp/rp1314/BoatArrivals

75 Coulter, Ann, *Adios, America: The Left's Plan to Turn Our Country into a Third World Hellhole*, Regnery Publishing, Washington DC, 2015 and Boyle, T.C., *The Tortilla Curtain*, Viking, New York, 1995 and Akerman, Piers, 'Rudd's Red Carpet to Asylum Seekers', *The Daily Telegraph*, November 14, 2009. http://blogs.news.com.au/dailytelegraph/piersakerman/index.php/dailytelegraph/comments/rudds_red_carpet_to_asylum_seekers/

swamped and overrun, lose 'our' sovereignty, our working and living conditions, our agency as individuals, our consent to be entered or refuse entry, our whole way of life.

The threat of losing a way of life to an unstoppable, inundating, devastating entry gives us a second sense of what global space *is recognised as meaning* within the observing systems we will spend time with in *Border Security*. Global space is not just the space of exposure, vulnerability and grave danger that those departing aboard the *Palapa* were entering, it's an imminent space of fear and a dark future spreading *in* here. It is an admixture of this imagination of 'threatening arrival' that growing numbers of the globally privileged are recoiling from and revolting against, in ways both politically symptomatic and electorally destabilising. Strangely, both populations peopling this tightening boundary, the fleeing and those secured from the fleeing who draw up the clamour of border security, are in their own ways seeking havens, places of asylum. The island paradise is the negated utopian horizon of global space, the non-existent place we are all seeking through our own biographical passages.

The politically disquieting fact produced by border security's negation of asylum is that 'our haven' is procured by 'abandoning them' to the conditions we fear for ourselves:[76] the observation of global space as a threat environment generates a zero sum game in which their lives are the price of our feeling secure.[77] The 'necessary existence' of an *enforced* framework for regulating the movement of noncitizens has provided an enormous impetus toward the emergence of border security in Australia, as elsewhere. In one related set of senses, border security is 'just' the militarisation of the norms co-produced by civil aviation, the universal visa system, the failure of international systems of governance to provide meaningful protection to civilian populations fleeing war and the proclivity of state actors for displacing the precarious, exposed and mortally vulnerable through earlier commitments, to return to a point already raised, the strategic choice of aerial bombardment as a way of dealing with the hostilities of the third world.

Recent works around this *topos* – walling, imperilled sovereignty, national and identity crises – have focused on 'our' fear, anxiety and especially sovereignty. Many such accounts tend toward psychoanalysing 'the nation' and the wishes its sovereignty might fulfil *for 'us'*[78] (*our* sovereignty, *our* nation, *our* invasion

76 Bauman, Zygmunt, *Wasted Lives: Modernity and Its Outcasts*, Polity Press, Berlin, 2004 and Agamben, Giorgio, *Homo Sacer: Sovereign Power and Bare Life*, Stanford University Press, Stanford, 1998.

77 Burke, Anthony, *Fear of Security: Australia's Invasion Anxiety*, Cambridge University Press, 1998 and *Beyond Security, Ethics and Violence: War Against the Other*, Routledge, Abingdon, 2005.

78 Brown, Wendy, *Walled States, Waning Sovereignty*, Zone Books, New York, 2010, p. 133 and Brown, Wendy, 'Desiring Walls', *LSE Public Lecture*, November 12, 2008. www.lse.ac.uk/publicEvents/events/2008/20080821t1104z001.aspx

See also: Hage, Ghassan, *White Nation: Fantasies of White Supremacy in a Multicultural Society*, Pluto Press, London, 1998, Hage, Ghassan, 'Multiculturalism and White Paranoia

anxieties). Less noted is that the 'framework of movement', such as it appears in Border Force's border continuum (section I.2) has become enforceable and societally resonant to the extent that a conception of 'global space' as a complex threat environment has co-emerged. It is this socio-spatial observation, and its normative implications, that I follow throughout *Border Security*, as a rejoinder, alternative and complement to psycho-social accounts whose semantic load is located in variants of the national subject.

As a unilateral projection of sovereignty, border security only makes compelling sense to a society with an apprehension of global space. By focusing only on sovereignty or anxiety, we miss the co-productivity of system and environment. To specify this, where screening is involved, the projection of sovereignty must have a 'somewhere' in which to see its agents' actions taking decisive effect. This is true not only because border security is a response to what is recognised as problematic and threatening within the complexity of global mobility. It's also because, in order to respond to this complexity, agents along the border continuum recursively posit the border continuum as their field of security, a space of rightful operations where urgent, decisive responses to 'threats and opportunities' are good, proper and necessary. To each battle its field: border security's battles for orderly mobility are contested in global space. Sovereignty is a produced effect of this work, at least as much as it is the quest and longing that inheres in the desire for its projection.

At the same time, anxiety and fear has a political agency in the way observing systems apprehend their operating environment. 'In' an operating environment characterised by the presence of a dynamic mix of 'increasingly fluid, complex, continuously emerging' threats, the 'nebulous malevolents' of global space rush at the nationally-threatened 'us', threatening order with breakdown and necessitating 'our' decisive re-ordering – so this is also an involvement by which 'we' are captivated by security. As the screening boundary between what co-appears as the anomic chaos of global space and the threatened interior of national interest, unwelcoming yet exposed to a feared, unstoppable and ruinous penetration, *the* border – and the border as a thing rightly protected – has been interposed by Border Force as a way of securing that 'says' that *without* securing, 'we' would be overwhelmed by that which just keeps coming. By observing the threat objects that *then* keep appearing within its environment of operations, this apprehension of the environment of security operations expresses something like the following: 'left unsecured, this unknown, approaching future will overwhelm us. We must act decisively, and do what is necessary, urgently'.

This sense of a distinct common fate imperilled by 'today's globalised world' as a vague yet total, hostile and overwhelming environmental situation is something

in Australia', *Journal of International Migration and Integration*, 3: 3, pp. 417–437, Burke, Anthony, *Fear of Security: Australia's Invasion Anxiety*, Cambridge University Press, Cambridge, 1998 and Papastergiadis, Nikos, 'The Invasion Complex: The Abject Other and Spaces of Violence', *Geografiska Annaler*, 88: 4, 2006, pp. 429–442.

that was named in Australia much earlier, coeval with similar culturally specific speech acts of the post globalisation right. In her Maiden Speech to the House of Representatives on September 1996, xenophobic nativist chauvinist Pauline Hanson famously said: "I believe we are in danger of being swamped by Asians" (section 2.6, 5.5). Another of her comments passed less noted, but over time I believe it co-named the foreground anxiety and the background conditions of the age in which 'we' recognise ourselves *and* the world we believe is imperilled: seafaring, system and environment, taken together as a common fate.[79] She said: "[a]ll we need is a nail hole in the bottom of the boat and we're sunk".[80]

Border security's world, and its strange predicates in Australia's peculiar onshore obsessions with its identity and security, would be difficult to explain to the children aboard every leaky boat before and after the *Palapa*, *Tampa* and 9/11, not least of all the fact that despite their tiny bodies, no lifejackets, lack of swimming ability and huddled presence on a catastrophically overloaded unseaworthy boat – they became the threats.

To return to the overarching point of this section, as a negation of civil aviation, as a figure of human existence, as a metaphor for the state and as a deadly mode of transport characterising the routine crossings of global space in the contexts encountered throughout this book, the existence of 'the boat' is not a technical matter. But in *Border Security*, almost nothing is merely technical, and this is especially important because the most technical aspects of operations work hardest to occlude border security's most political aspects and greatest injustices. One way of apprehending the ends of all this is by examining border security's strategic vision for global space – secured circulation.

1.11 Border security's strategic vision: a society of secured circulation

In his classic paper 'The Limits of the Sovereign State', David Garland concludes by contending that

> Unlike the penal-welfare strategy, which was linked into a broader politics of social change and a certain vision of social justice – however flawed in conception and execution – the new penal policies have no broader agenda, no strategy for progressive social change and no concern for the overcoming of social divisions. They are, instead, policies for managing the danger and policing the divisions created by a certain kind of social organization, and for

79 Foucault, Michel, 'Governmentality', Burchell, Graham, Gordon, Colin and Miller, Peter (eds.), *The Foucault Effect: Studies in Governmentality*, University of Chicago Press, Chicago, 1991, pp. 87–104.

80 Hanson, Pauline, 'Pauline Hanson's Maiden Speech in the House of Representatives', September 10, 1996. http://australianpolitics.com/1996/09/10/pauline-hanson-maiden-speech.html

> shifting the burden of social control on to individuals and organizations that are often poorly equipped to carry out this task.[81]

As potent as Garland's critique is – and two decades on, a close reading reveals durable insights – when we turn our attention to the emergence of border security's world at and beyond the limits of the sovereign state, the contemporary Australian Commonwealth and its border security world is conspicuous for its audacious imagination of its future and our human place in its circuits.

Border security's world carries as its strategic vision a society integrated through secured circulation. Let's add this to the following two key assertions raised earlier:

1 border security is a unilateral projection of national sovereignty in global space (section I.2), and;
2 border security's world comes into being for Border Force where 'Australia' is observed as a threatened space of interest, via the threat environment, in order to be secured *from* global space *as* a border, through operations.

With these two points in mind, I conceptualise securing circulation[82] in the following ways:

- securing circulation is a way of 'locking down' global mobility as a location, using techniques grounded in control[83]
- securing circulation shapes mobility with a view toward successful securing: its goal is normative, the norm is circular (section 1.10)
- A secured location – control applied, securing achieved – serves as a conduit for authorised passages, which integrates mobility within profitable circuits: securing circulation is aligned toward accumulation for capital (section I.5–I.6, chapter 4).

81 Garland, David, 'The Limits of the Sovereign State: Strategies of Crime Control in Contemporary Society', *The British Journal of Criminology*, 36: 4, 1996, p. 466.
82 Foucault, Michel, *Security, Territory, Population*, Palgrave Macmillan, Basingstoke, 2007, O'Grady, Nathaniel, 'Securing Circulation Through Mobility: Milieu and Emergency Response in the British Fire and Rescue Service', *Mobilities*, 9: 2014, pp. 512–527 and Elbe, Stefan, Roemer-Mahler, Anne and Long, Christopher, 'Securing Circulation Pharmaceutically: Antiviral Stockpiling and Pandemic Preparedness in the European Union', *Security Dialogue*, 45: 5, 2014, pp. 440–457.
83 "The conception of a control mechanism, giving the position of any element within an open environment at any given instant". Deleuze, Gilles, 'Postscript on the Societies of Control', *October*: 59, Winter 1992, p. 7, Chambers, Peter, 'Smartphone', in Salter, Mark B. (ed.), *Making Things International 2: Catalysts and Reactions*, University of Minnesota Press, Minneapolis, 2016, pp. 195–216 and Kanngeiser, Anja, 'Tracking and Tracing: Geographies of Logistical Governance and Labouring Bodies', *Environment and Planning: D*, 31: 4, 2013, p. 598.

Let's begin in the place whose complications best clarify what this threefold theorisation of secured circulation means in the context of Australian border security: an island and territory not only specific to the Commonwealth of Australia, and the place where *Palapa*'s passengers were attempting to reach. A physically unique place possessing a remarkable and peculiar ecology whose political aspects will preoccupy us throughout *Border Security*: Christmas Island.

Christmas Island (CI) is the tip of an oceanic volcano that arose from the trench that surrounds it around sixty million years ago. As far as records indicate, CI was uninhabited by *homo sapiens* when it was spotted by Captain William Mynors, a master of the East India Company, from aboard the *Royal Mary*, on Christmas Day in 1643. This moment of observation and naming already places Christmas Island in a political space of modernity between Queen Elizabeth I's granting of the Charter to the East India Company, on December 31st, 1600, and Thomas Hobbes' publication of *Leviathan* in 1651.[84] Its inhabitants could not have known this, but on that day Captain Mynors placed CI in Britain's sovereign sights. The Island was annexed to the British Crown 244 and a half years after Mynors' 'discovery', on June 6th, 1888, based on the discovery of industry-enabling quantities of high quality phosphate of lime, right on the Island's surface.

From the 1880s until the 1970s, Christmas Island was one of the world's three significant phosphate mining islands, but it's also biologically notable for its endemic species, which led David Attenborough and others to label it the Galapagos of the Indian Ocean. Of all these species, one is world famous, because of its significant and spectacular annual migration. The Red Crab is an animal whose species identity is a story about the desire lines of an irrepressible and improbable migration, severed and sutured by secured circulation.

In the conclusion to her *Deadly Life of Logistics*, Deborah Cowen notes UPS' evaluation of the significance of the red crab migration on Christmas Island:

> Every fall, the red crabs of Christmas Island undertake a Great Migration made possible by great logistics. They have limited time to ensure the survival of their species. Departures are synchronized, contingency planning overcomes obstacles, and just in time, they deliver their eggs. In their world just like ours, on time arrivals depend on logistics.[85]

In both Cowen's chapter and UPS' copy, the crabs serve as a concept-metaphor for logistics. But their migration into global logistics as exemplary is loaded with

84 Galli, Carlo, 'Political Geometries', *Political Spaces and Global War*, University of Minnesota Press, 2010 and Elden, Stuart, 'Chapter 9', *The Birth of Territory*, University of Chicago Press, Chicago, 2013.

85 UPS' Great Migrations TV advertisement, quoted in Cowen, Deborah, *The Deadly Life of Logistics: Mapping Violence in Global Trade*, University of Minnesota Press, Minneapolis, 2014, p. 210.

a poetic irony and theoretical resonance that neither authors seemingly intended nor fully grasped – what both Cowen and UPS merely indicate is actually profoundly the case.

For most of the year, the majority of the Island's red crabs live in the rainforests at the island's centre, most of which are within Christmas Island National Park.[86] Then, just before the beginning of the wet season in late October and early November (not 'fall'), before the heavy rains set in, the crabs emerge from their burrows in the forest and begin moving toward the beach. The Island's crab population, something like 50 million, all make the annual journey from the forests to the beach and back. Most of the crabs move northwest from the island's centre toward the beaches along its north shore. Each year, the crabs – on an individual and population level – follow a route remarkably similar to the one from the year before. Unlike comparable species, like the red land crabs of Cuba, both female and male crabs migrate to the beach and back annually: the former to spawn, the latter to fertilise the millions of eggs released. The female red crabs time their spawning so that it takes place just as the high tide of the last quarter of the moon turns. We do not know how the red crabs know to do this.[87]

The majority of Christmas Island's 'permanent' human residents, roughly two thousand people, live in three areas to the northeast, skirting the coastal edge, in a strange micocosmic parody of mainland Australia's residents, clinging to the airconditioned jobs and coastal climate of the south-east's cities and suburbs, dreaming of its beaches, recoiling from the bush. In the two decades since CI became a place where interdicted asylum seekers are brought, a transient and fluctuating population of human arrivals keep arriving on the Island. Not just detainees, in the Island's detention centre, but the full spectrum of Australian politicians, administrators and federal police, as well as international contractors, missionaries and human rights observers who make up the shifting groups of people drawing a wage by governing the political economy of detention on the island in different ways.

Construction of the Christmas Island Immigration Detention Centre (IDC) began in 2002, and it opened in 2008. It was built to the west of the crab's main forest habitats, on an old mining lease in a part of the National Park to the north west of the island. Construction of the Centre was allowed in the sensitive and globally significant ecology of this part of the island after the proposed site was exempted from environmental Acts, on the grounds of national interest. Nonetheless, the choice of site means that the detention centre's construction (2002–8) and routine operation (2008-present) continues to depend on the daily, heavy use of a road that cuts across the red crab's migratory path. The

86 'National Parks', *australia.gov.au*. www.australia.gov.au/about-australia/australian-story/national-parks

87 Section I.2 and Von Foerster, Heinz, *The Beginning of Heaven and Earth Has No Name: Seven Days With Second-Order Cybernetics*, Fordham University Press, New York, 2013, pp. 25–27.

ongoing, year-round, all weather operation of the centre – the logistics of the IDC in its entirety – has to somehow reckon with the migration of the red crabs, year after year.

As a measure ensuring Australia's national sovereignty is constructed to be compliant with all Commonwealth regulations, reckoning with the red crab migration must produce an outcome that's 'humane and secure' for all parties, human and nonhuman alike. The politics of border security bisects the annual migration of the red crab as a now-enmeshed matter of detention logistics and species survival.

Figure I.2 Crab Bridge, Murray Road, Christmas Island

Source: Parks Australia[88]

Figure I.2 is the Crab Bridge. To me, it offers a living picture of what securing circulation means, how its circumscription of movement into shaped canals make it different to mere 'global mobility'. In the foreground, running from east (the Island's population centres, the wharf and airport) to west (just the detention centre) is the lime white of the crabless road, cutting through the forest

88 'Crab Bridge', Murray Road, Christmas Island

in the background. On either side of the road, light green barriers, which exist right along the road, funnel crabs moving from the forest toward the road, then up the Crab Bridge. The bridge is five metres high, ample clearance height for a 30-seater bus like a Toyota Coaster (2.6 m) or a medium rigid vehicle (4.5m). Elsewhere along the route, the roadside barriers funnel crabs into crab grids, tunnels just below the road covered by grates, like cattle grids. There are thirty-four across the island, including all along the road to the detention centre. In anticipation of the crab's migration and the wet season, each year rangers have to rake the crab grids clean, one by one.[89] This gives us a way of thinking about secured circulation as a designed effect. As a successful and compliant design, the crab bridge 'knows' the crab's migratory habits and patterns, and was implemented accordingly. The crabs move across their own immigration detention 'channel', secured by their inability to jump the light green barriers, their willingness to climb the bridge, and their irrepressible desire to return to the exact spot on the beach they went to last year.

As a piece of public infrastructure developed in the era of neolilberal governance to ensure the unimpeded operation of an immigration detention centre,[90] the crab bridge was not constructed *for the crabs* – not out of love, not as an act of worship, nor to protect them from predation from invasive species. It's there because routine mass death events of crabs, run over by the logistics of offshore detention, could be read onshore as an unjustifiable cost of operations.

Seeing the bridge's designed function as part of 'securing circulation' means seeing the bridge as designed for the difference it makes to a system whose purpose is to continue detention as smoothly as possible. If the buses had to stop for the month in which the crabs were migrating, this would cause a bottleneck, spilling border security's operations, including detainees, into Christmas Island's resident communities, generating an unacceptable threat to national security.

The detention centre was also designed with an electrified fence running around its perimeter. This electric fence, intended to deter escaping human detainees, presents a deadly threat to the robber crabs, a much, much larger and less numerous species who roam freely across the island. Although there is a metal perimeter fence put in place to prevent the robber crabs making it to the electric fence, some get through from time to time, and some who reach the electrified boundary of the immigration detention centre are electrocuted. But as the robber crabs have no species-set migratory path, their individual death poses no design challenge for detention, and no routine threat to the smooth secured circulation required by detention logistics. I take the fate of the robber crab as also indicating our lives in the face of such circuits; on an individual level, the circuits of secured circulation are indifferent to the fate of the living. On a systemic level, the crab

89 Sloterdijk, Peter, *Terror From the Air*, MIT Press, Cambridge, MA, 2009, p. 9.

90 Chambers, Peter, 'The Passage of Authority: Imagining the Political Transformation of Australia's Christmas Island, from Sovereignty to Governance', *Shima: The International Journal of Research into Island Cultures*, 6: 2, 2012, pp. 124–131.

bridge is a passage for the medium of authority, and whenever 'we' approach the border continuum, whether at this bridge or the aerobridge, we are as red crabs.

Securing circulation, then, describes the transformation of 'global flows' into profitable circuits whose intrasystemic side is differentiated from the complexity of the world in which it co-exists, drawing energy, drawing boundaries, reducing complexity, producing structures, reproducing 'itself'.

To break frame by way of concluding, I return to second order cybernetics and the normative implications of its epistemological insights, with the fate of the crabs and ourselves in our circuits in mind. In the earliest Macy Conferences, the pioneers of cybernetics pinpointed 'circularity' as the operating principle common to biological, electrical and social systems that also functioned for them as the common ground for their interdisciplinary explorations.[91] While emphasising the extraordinary productivity of circularity and circuits (and let us note that it was one group of cyberneticists who morphed into Silicon Valley's fathers, but not the other), Heinz Von Foerster recalls us to a key difference between observing systems and what he called 'trivial machines'. As an exemplary trivial machine, a vending machine relies upon the reliable application of a number of circuits: that connect it to the electrical grid, that ensure its thermostat triggers the fan that passes over the refrigerant and keeps the drink cold. Triviality means we get our cold drink when we insert the correct change and press the right button, each and every time we do so. As Sloterdijk might add: *while* the broader regress of logistical circuits that keep the machine stocked, the machines producing drinks, the materials for the drink containers in production and the sugar growing in the field under the sun, remain in the un-explicated background, outside the purview of our rapt attention, let alone critical concern, as soft drink consumers enjoying the prompt return of correct change, then a cool drink.

Following Von Foerster's insight, observing systems such as the border continuum, Border Force, securing circulation – indeed such as you and I as writer and reader here – are not trivial machines, because we always interpose our own state into operations. We already do this the moment we engage with questions such as: *what is securing circulation? What is border security? How did such an improbable state of affairs come to be accepted and integrated into society?* A consequence of nontriviality that Luhmann draws from von Foerster, is that both border security – and 'us' as its observers – must be considered incalculable and unpredictable. Surely we should 'know' this after two great 'oopses' of the past decade: when the world's best economists missed systemic risk in 2008; when political 'science' predicted a Clinton victory until the very moment when Trump was elected. If the vending machine is a paradigmatic trivial machine for Von

91 Pias, Claus (ed.), *The Macy Conferences 1946–1953: The Complete Transactions*, University of Chicago Press, Chicago, 2016 and Clarke, Bruce, 'Heinz von Foerster's Demons: The Emergence of Second-Order Systems Theory', in Clarke, Bruce and Hansen, Mark B. (eds.), *Emergence and Embodiment: New Essays on Second-Order Systems Theory*, Duke University Press, Durham, 2009, pp. 34–62.

Foerster, the crab bridge, for me, is a striking example of a very politically contemporary human attempt to trivialise crab mobility; yet neither the crabs, nor their mobility, are trivial machines. Connecting this back to the strategic vision of secured circulation that is the obsessive focus of border security's world, we can see the many senses in which border security attempts to trivialise the complexity of global mobility. Like those who 'knew' that subprime was not a risk and that Hillary would win, the world's confident careerists fail to reckon both with our abyssal ignorance[92] and with what I observe as the emergent, swerving, devastating, world making realities – unknowable, open, yet deadly – of causality.[93]

Placing this thought amidst border security's world and the political present in which it thrives, I ultimately intend *Border Security* as a way toward open thinking *about* border security that points *beyond* the distinctions of border security's world. Border security represents its severences and circularity as necessary and urgent; in what follows, I seek to show how this too came to be, explore how it has resonated and became integrated in society, consider the shores it sets out from and the horizons it seeks to navigate us toward, and finally, try to imagine how we might pursue other, probably much better worlds and other possible ways of living together.

92 Von Foerster, Heinz, *The Beginning of Heaven and Earth Has No Name: Seven Days with Second-Order Cybernetics*, Fordham University Press, New York, 2013, p. 26.

93 Connolly, Willliam, *The Fragility of Things: Self-Organizing Processes, Neoliberal Fantasies, and Democratic Activism*, Duke University Press, Durham, NC, 2013.

Part I

The emergence of border security in Australia

Chapter 1

Girt by sea

Transformations of sovereignty and border security

1.1 Introduction: for an analytic of *statifications* and a systems theoretical understanding of power from 'moments in the elements of sovereignty'

Sovereignty in all its forms remains central to any practiced understanding of power. The practices of sovereignty that predominate in society tell us important things about that historical conjuncture and the politics of how it was gathered in a specific place. Yet the form sovereignty takes and the medium it generates through its formation not only differs in each case,[1] it differentiates each case. Thus when in 2013 the Coalition formulated *Operation Sovereign Borders* – a pamphlet, a catchphrase, an electoral cudgel and eventually a policy affecting the lives of thousands of asylum seekers – it did so as an intensification of an earlier Australian iteration of national sovereignty that was, at one stage I will explore later in this chapter, literally and stridently voiced by megaphone at people seeking protection, on the open ocean.

With projections of national sovereignty such as these in mind, the purpose of this chapter is to trace moments from Australian sovereignty's morphogenesis that can render the complex emergence of border security intelligible.[2] I consider the emergence of border security as a societally dominant way to practice sovereignty by enacting it as a projection, such that a decade or so later, in 2013, *Operation Sovereign Borders* could become societally possible, plausible, necessary, urgent.[3] To do so, I closely follow practices of sovereignty across time and space:

1 in Australia's past and present (section 1.2–1.7),
2 as it evolved on Christmas Island (CI) (section 1.8–1.9), and
3 'out there' in Australia's maritime jurisdictions (section1.10–1.12),

for what they reveal about the shifting morphology of political spaces.

1 Luhmann, Niklas, *Theory of Society, Volume 1*, Stanford University Press, Stanford, 2012, pp. 113–123.
2 Op.cit., p. 252.
3 Op.cit., p. 43.

As I explore, sovereignty appears through material expressions of evolving relations of subjection and resistance that take place and make space politically: the shores of politics ebb and flow in tides of contestation, in waves of domination, from the nation to the ocean, between populations in their sometimes violent and never settled co-habitation of spaces a people names and takes as sovereignly its own.

I want to urge us to think about sovereignty as a political relation unfolding between people in their contentious sharing of space. Sovereignty is not just a settled matter, a 'thing' that can be possessed, transferred, contained within 'the state'; a threatened legitimacy that must be responded to urgently. Sovereignty is a complex, active, transitive, dynamic political relation we remain subject to; sovereignty remains a relation of subjection, then, but of a certain kind. In the contexts of *state-led* sovereignty processes, integral for the emergence of border security in all its global worksites, I follow Foucault's description in *The Birth of Politics* around *statifications*, where this refers to:

> incessant transactions which modify, or move, or drastically change, or insidiously shift sources of finance, modes of investment, decision-making centers, forms and types of control, relationships between local powers, the central authority, and so on.[4]

In the interpretation of Foucault I pursue here, *statifications* denotes processes of recombinant assembly, state-related, state-mobilising formations that are never finished, always ongoing, in the present, and take shape as political projects shared by a number of interested, benefiting agents. In the transformations of sovereignty at issue in this chapter, I therefore pursue how conduits for the passage of sovereign authority proper to each historical conjuncture were made and re-made.

The implication of understanding sovereignty as a political relation of subjection enacted through *statifications* – active, transitive processes – is the following. Worlds of sovereignty come into being and are worked into political spaces each time the distinctions of that shifting assembly are made and remade (section I.2). Each sovereign political formation is an actualisation of a constrained set of possible others sitting within its horizon of imaginability, drawing utopian energy from the vision of justice that sits just over that world's horizon.[5] Australia gives a stark example of how this unfolds because it was a political laboratory from its

4 Foucault, Michel, *The Birth of Biopolitics: Lectures at the Collège de France*, Palgrave Macmillan, Basingstoke, 2008, p. 77. Foucault's coinage of *statifications* was made in the context of thinking about political formations as shifting assemblies of power relations without recourse to '*the* state'.

5 More, Thomas, *Utopia*, Penguin, 2012, Plato, *The Republic*, Penguin, London, 2007, Swift, Jonathan, *Gulliver's Travels*, Penguin, London, 2003, Adorno, Theodor, *Critical Models: Interventions and Catchwords*, University of Chicago Press, Chicago, 2005.

inception, and remains 'a society of the state'[6] representable to itself and others through the seeming congruity of the 'island continent' (section 1.7). Yet Australia is also a live political experiment containing utopias and dystopias, an unseceding succession of political spaces whose basic legitimating elements remain passionately contested, and whose most significant political projects large numbers of its peoples remain deeply ambivalent about and opposed to. Australia's national sovereignty recurs as the demand of an unsettled society, enacted by its state agents as border security.

The following account of sovereignty's Australia-emanating statifications also explores how the tight congruence of land, law and people in *state* sovereignty (section 1.4) is never as neat or snug as the identities most invested in it desire it to be, especially wherever identity is celebrated (section 1.3). All *national* sovereignty – and some key distinctions between state sovereignty and national sovereignty will be offered in what follows – relies on highly selective acts of historical incoherence in order that a nation might set and celebrate its identity. A crucial point appending this is that incongruence and incoherence are no barrier to decisive action where vital distinctions and the boundaries of identity are concerned. As presented in the introductory chapter, every set of distinctions that continue to be drawn in communication perpetuate, entrench and integrate the construction of that world (section I.2): national sovereignty, and border security as one way of practicing national sovereignty, are worldmaking and world destroying, because they mark and defend the boundaries of the nation as a matter of who can live 'here', in language, in steel, in concrete. This transforms what the risk of death by drowning means, and generates defensible contexts in which the mental health of children is rightly destroyed in offshore detention, if it procures deterrence (section 2.10, 3.10). By implicating a national 'us' in all of this, both via sovereignty and through the systems that secure circulation so that 'we' can move and 'they' must not arrive (section I.7–I.9), the making of social relations through sovereignty involves *us* in creative, world-making processes. The normative swerve, which will come into increasing focus as *Border Security's* chapters proceed, is this: as citizens subject to sovereignty, or as noncitizens who move freely into and through the border continuum, these are world-making relations that we are all a part of, never apart from – though ours is the choice to accept or reject this communicated account.[7]

As we examine these important aspects of subjection and their reifications as codifications of the violent land appropriation processes that colonial and imperial

6 Kapferer, Bruce and Morris, Barry, 'The Australian Society of the State: Egalitarian Ideologies and New Directions in Exclusionary Practice', *Social Analysis: The International Journal of Social and Cultural Practice*, 47: 3, 2003, pp. 80–107.

7 Borch, Christian, 'Social Systems', *Niklas Luhmann*, Routledge, Abingdon, 2011, pp. 31–37.

colonisations name,[8] I am urging an analytic orientation that keeps returning attention to sovereignty's always shifting, always relational forms. Just as Marx wrote that 'moments are the elements of profit',[9] the *statifications* that follow throughout this chapter can be thought of as 'moments in the elements of sovereignty', which I offer as observations of power in transformation.

As per the tripartite division of this chapter numbered above, I begin tracing these moments in the elements of sovereignty by contouring the emergence of national sovereignty in Australia, helping us to focus on the morphogenesis of national sovereignty over an extended period of time. Second, I move to a fine-grained examination of land appropriation, territory and population on Australia's Christmas Island. This will enable us to pinpoint the implications of these general contours, show the replication of general dynamics in microcosm, and key in on their inconsistencies and lacunae as the particularities of these sovereign pasts were grafted on to Australian sovereignty's contemporary form. This also 'shows the shifting' in the tensions that produce the violent demand for sovereignty, between state, nation and population, over space and time. Third, I look that the intrasystemic distinctions that enable maritime border security to be enacted as a unilateral practice of national sovereignty 'in' Australia. This third section looks at an extensive space, Australia's maritime distinctions, and its application to the highly time-sensitive matters of two groups of people seeking to approach Australia before and after the emergence of border security. In this third section, I pay close attention to the selective and inconsistent importation of international norms and definitions by the agents of border security in their production of a navigable discursive topography, and the application of these ways of observing and operating to bodies *on the water* and bodies *in the water*. By way of foreshadowing the terminus of this chapter, marked by a boat's sinking into the Indian Ocean, the relation of bodies to water returns us to a fundamental aporia that exists whenever the agents of states claim jurisdiction over spaces and peoples: how can one claim *authority over* something or someone without also somehow taking *responsibility for* it?

1.2 National sovereignty 'in' Australia: an untimely (boat) arrival

The arrival of national sovereignty 'in' Australia continues to be untimely. In October 2001 – during an election campaign, post–Tampa Affair, post 9/11 – John

8 Schmitt, Carl, *The Nomos of the Earth in the International Law of the Jus Publicum Europaeum*, Telos Press, New York, 2006 and Kapferer, Bruce and Morris, Barry, 'The Australian Society of the State: Egalitarian Ideologies and New Directions in Exclusionary Practice', *Social Analysis: The International Journal of Social and Cultural Practice*, 47: 3, 2003, p. 86.

9 Marx, Karl, 'The Production of Surplus Value', *Capital, Volume 1: A Critique of Political Economy*, Penguin, London, 1992 and in Harvey, David, *A Companion to Marx's Capital, Volume 1*, Verso, London, 2010, p. 142.

Howard expressed the matter of Australia's national sovereignty as a decisionist prerogative, a sovereign decision on who could arrive, voiced by the Prime Minister in the name of the people:

> we will decide who comes to this country and the circumstances in which they come.

Yet many of the 19.4 million who then comprised 'the we who willed' came to Australia at a time when national sovereignty was not; and the ancestors of a few million among their number came under maritime circumstances not of their choosing, as part of a British policy of penal transportation. In the ensuing twenty-one decades between the First Fleet's 'arrival' in 1788 and what became 'this country' by the 2001 of the above assertion, the land that today's deciders now live on – as private property – had first to be taken from the peoples whose country it was.

In a 2016 essay, six months after losing the Prime Ministership he had made by standing atop Howard's decisionist prerogative and yelling 'stop the boats' in order to wreck the electoral prospects of his political opponents, ex Prime Minister Tony Abbott offered the following remark:

> unlike France or Britain, we lack a colonial past to complicate the present.[10]

On any level we may wish to interpret it, Mr Abbott's assertion should give us pause. To the extent that it sovereignly 'is', Australia is the nation-al net effect of still complicated land appropriation processes: colonising, colonial and imperial. These land appropriation processes are the continuation 'as Australia' of a period of contested British conquest that lasted more than a century, before the colonies became a federation of states in 1901. From early colonisation as penal settlements[11] (1788–1868) to federation (1901) *via* the period of explicit, intentional imperial conquest (1835–1901), what later became the Australian nation emerged through British processes of land appropriation. Colonisation, colonialism and imperialism spread the jurisdictions and settlements that framed and

10 Abbott, Tony, 'Abbott: I Was Right on National Security', *Quadrant Online*, March 26, 2016. https://quadrant.org.au/opinion/qed/2016/03/abbott-right-national-security/

11 Penal transportation came to be widely opposed in Britain from the 1830s. New South Wales was removed from the list of places to which convicts could be sent in 1840; Victoria became a state in 1851, and never admitted convicts as Victoria; Van Diemen's Land became Tasmania on August 10, 1853, which coincided with the end of transportation. Transportation continued to Western Australia until 1868. 'Convicts and the British Colonies in Australia', *australia.gov.au*. www.australia.gov.au/about-australia/australian-story/convicts-and-the-british-colonies

housed society across 'the island continent'. As Dorsett and McVeigh put it (and this assertion may be read back over those of Howard and Abbott):

> As the settlers pushed out from Sydney Cove, towards the Blue Mountains and beyond, sovereignty followed in their wake.[12]

The colonisation and land appropriation that comprised conquest *were* the primary processes whose major contingent effect was the production of Australia: to say that 'we lack a colonial past to complicate the present' is to avow the national we by asserting that it lacks itself.

This strange picture of the nation is further complicated by the interposition of border security. In the name of a threatened national sovereignty Australians would now interdict and detain a hypothetical First Fleet. Contemporary sovereign practice would preclude the national origin it also celebrates, *if* then was now. It is through the dialectical frame of this fundamental contradiction that I explore the emergence of Australia's national sovereignty: how the historical, political interaction of *earlier* non-sovereign, non-Australian colonial and imperial predicates *later* became the sovereign nation-state of Australia.

1.3 Australia Day: celebration of the nation

'Australia Day' celebrates the arrival of the First Fleet as part of the British policy of penal transportation, whose exclusive focus on Britain's American colonies from 1718–1776 was put to an end with the success of the American Revolution in 1783. That which would later become Australia was born as an unintended consequence of another nation's political revolution, a key part of which involved seeking to end Britain's use of the American colonies as 'dumping grounds'. Australia Day emerged to prominence since 1988 (the bicentenary of the First Fleet's arrival) and has thrived since 1996 in the absence of a unifying cultural memory outside imperial and European wars,[13] through an era where, when presented with the opportunity in 1999, 54% of Australians voted against becoming a republic. At the time of writing, Australia Day is popularly represented by its proponents as the 'celebration of the nation',[14] a day when those who get

12 Dorsett, Shaunagh and McVeigh, Shaun, 'Just So: The Law which Governs Australia is Australian Law', *Law and Critique*, 13, 2002, p. 295.

13 ANZAC Day is a day of remembrance that, since 1996 or so, has been about the glorification of Australia's role in armed conflict, including wars of aggression such as the invasion and occupation of Afghanistan and Iraq.

14 'About our National Day', *Australia Day*, www.australiaday.org.au/australia-day/about-our-national-day/

For an excellent critical account, see: Sparrow, Jeff, 'The Real Problem Is Not the Lamb ad But the Militarisation of Australian Nationalism', *theguardian.com/au*. www.theguardian.com/commentisfree/2016/jan/12/the-real-problem-is-not-the-lamb-ad-but-the-militarisation-of-australian-nationalism

involved revel in their identity, often by barbecuing and eating red meat together in the summer outdoors, displaying the flag, and binge drinking.[15] Like celebrations of nation the postwar world over, Australia Day can only function as a 'celebration of *the* nation' in attentive ignorance: an active forgetting of some of its peoples and the nation's murky, complex, contradictory, ambivalent historical depths; and of Australia's common political relations to the spaces taken to make it – colonial, imperial, colonising.

'*Australia* Day' is interestingly named. There was no such thing as Australia[16] on January 26, 1788 when the First Fleet arrived at Botany Bay; there was no *express* intention of establishing New South Wales as anything more than a place of punishment for convicts.[17] Of the 13–1500 people who arrived aboard the First Fleet, most were British subjects, most were English, some were Irish, most, but not all, were Anglo-Celtic and white, and none expressed 'nationalities' or 'indigeneity' self-conscious or distinct from Britain and Ireland that might, retrospectively, be described as 'Australian'. The arrivals' commonality was that they faced an unknown and possibly hostile, inhospitable environment together, almost unimaginably far from home –[18] either as punishment, or to administer and govern a colony whose purpose was its infliction. They did so with inappropriate equipment, very poor knowledge of the local environment and soil, and inadequate support from a colonial centre eight months away. For all these reasons, contemporary Australia Day celebrates the eighteenth-century arrival of a group of non-Australians to a place that was not Australia, where most did not want to be, where most had been sent. Yet strangely for our purposes, and for anyone observing January 26 as a day of national origins, it does concede that 'Australia' was a boat arrival.

Eleven ships and 13–1500 people arrived on the First Fleet; the continental aboriginal population in 1788 was somewhere between 315,000 and over one million.[19] Given this spectrum of estimates, the colonists were outnumbered anywhere between 200 and 700 to one. From 1788, what many people now call Australia *had* a permanent population who *did* to enter into relations with the

15 Feldman, Allen, 'Strange Fruit: The South African Truth Commission and the Demonic Economies of Violence', *Social Analysis*, 46: 3, 2002, pp. 242–246.

16 The term 'Australia' in 1814 by Matthew Flinders after his circumnavigation confirmed the existence of the world's only 'island continent', completing the British European 'discovery' of *terra Australis incognita*, the great (unknown) southern land (section 4.3–5). 'Australia' was in social circulation by the mid-1820s in New South Wales and Van Diemens Land, though 'New Holland' was still the common way to refer to the continental land mass at that time.

17 Clendinnen, Inga, *Dancing with Strangers: Europeans and Australians at First Contact*, Cambridge University Press, Cambridge, 2005.

18 The First Fleet set sail from Plymouth on May 13, 1787, sailed for Rio De Janeiro, then to Cape Town, before arriving in what we call Sydney Harbour on January 26, 1788.

19 'Aboriginal and Torres Strait Islander Population, Year Book Australia, 2008', Australian Bureau of Statistics. www.abs.gov.au/ausstats/abs@.nsf/0/68AE74ED632E17A6CA2573D200110075?opendocument

representatives of an internationally recognised political formation, the British officers who began administering what they had been instructed to observe as their colony to govern.

Late eighteenth-century 'New South Wales' was a way of governing a settled colony from first arrival, 'for the purposes of its acquisition and the application of English law'.[20] Doing so involved disavowing the taking and violence of the land appropriation processes that colonisation necessarily involves. At the time, a key method of disavowal was seeing the land as uninhabited by (what its agents were prepared to recognise as) meaningful human communities,[21] who had of course to be "led by a sovereign and with recognisable institutions and laws".[22] In the boat-brought mirror of late eighteenth-century Britain, the colonists looked at what surrounded them and saw no monarch, no buildings, no crops, no People, no sovereignty;[23] so they began erecting their own in the King's name, expropriating the people who were and were not there for the purposes of the process.

Fast forwarding to remain with our line of national sovereignty's Australian emergence, on November 1, 1828 Governor Arthur declared martial law in Van Diemen's Land:[24] contemporary Tasmania, a second British penal settlement and colony, 630 nautical miles (1170km) to the south of Sydney.[25] Arthur's declaration of martial law gave military personnel the authority to arrest Aboriginals without a warrant, shoot them on sight wherever they came within settled areas and hang them for violent actions against settlers, such as spearings. In 1830, the use of deadly force against indigenous groups impinging on 'settled areas' was expanded across the entire island as rightful government action. The Black Line enacted this by enlisting every able-bodied colonist in Van Diemen's Land to form a human chain that moved south and east across the island; an act of island-continental expulsion – that was apiece with British colonial practices of the time.[26] For the first time – perhaps – we might see a population united, not

20 'Aboriginal Customary Laws and Anglo-Australian Law After 1788 Australian Law as Applied to Aborigines', *Australian Law Reform Commission*. www.alrc.gov.au/publications/4.%20Aboriginal%20Customary%20Laws%20and%20Anglo-Australian%20Law%20After%201788/australian-law-applied

21 Manne, Robert, 'The History Wars', *The Monthly*, November 2009. www.themonthly.com.au/issue/2009/november/1270703045/robert-manne/comment

22 'Aboriginal Customary Laws and Anglo-Australian Law After 1788 Australian Law as Applied to Aborigines', Australian Law Reform Commission. www.alrc.gov.au/publications/4.%20Aboriginal%20Customary%20Laws%20and%20Anglo-Australian%20Law%20After%201788/australian-law-applied

23 Echoing Hobbes, Thomas, *Leviathan*, Penguin, London, 1982, p. 186.

24 Boyce, James, *Van Diemen's Land*, Black Inc, Melbourne, 2008.

25 80 hours of sailing at 8 knots, the rough speed in favourable conditions.

26 Ryan, Lyndall, 'The Black Line in Van Diemen's Land: Success or Failure?' *Journal of Australian Studies*, 37: 1, 2013, pp. 3–18, Paton, Diana, 'An Injurious Population: Caribbean-Australian Penal Transportation and Imperial Racial Politics', *Cultural and Social History: The Journal of the Social History Society*, 5: 4, 2008, pp.449-464 and Ford, Lisa, 'Indigenous Policy and Its Historical Occlusions: The North American and Global Contexts of Australian Settlement', *Australian Indigenous Law Review*, 12: 1, 2008, pp. 69–80.

by deciding who can arrive and how (sections 1.2, 2.6–2.10), but by drawing a boundary whose purpose was the destruction of another population, in order that another might live peacefully and profitably on its newly fenced properties.

Are these frontier relations *Australia's* national struggles? Are the Black Wars a formative part of Australia, or are they apart from Australia, events rightly left in Van Diemen's Land when some among its population fled across Bass Strait in 1834 to establish the colony of free settlers around Port Phillip Bay that would later become Melbourne; or when Van Diemen's Land exorcised penal transportation upon becoming Tasmania in 1856?[27] The extent to which Australians evaluate these matters places us on the 'side' of a culture 'war' whose rhetorical contours indicate that this remains political for some Australians, intensely so for indigenous people disenfranchised through expropriation, and assertively so for ideologically driven conservatives invested in disavowing the violence that colonisation involves in the course of asserting the lack of the colonial past.

Then as now, such events were also part of broader conflicts within British colonisation processes based on incommensurable patterns of land use triggered by the need for an order of land as property to guarantee exclusive possession; eventually co-generative of capitalism. It was this transformation, worked out on the ground in one of its colonial worksites – Van Diemen's Land in the 1820s – that enabled the conquest of the continent that later became Australia from 1835.[28] Tony Abbott's 2016 declaration that the national 'we' lacks 'a colonial past to complicate its presence' would seem to excise the Black Line from *Australia's* past altogether, sending responsibility for the Black Wars back to Governor Arthur, and to Britain, from where, like Arthur, Mr Abbott came to Australia, by boat. Yet Mr Abbott, as Prime Minister, does not disavow Australia's connection to Britain and its monarchy. As Prime Minister on Australia Day on January 26, 2015, Mr Abbott unilaterally granted Prince Phillip a Knighthood of the Order of Australia.

1.4 1835–1850s: trespass, void, *terra nullius*; intentional conquest, criminal jurisdiction and aboriginal imprisonment

The shift toward the intentional conquest of Australia, which took place around 1835, was predicated on nullifying the contestation of frontier relations between indigenous groups and settlers that had unfolded over the nearly half century between 1788 and 1835, including Batman's treaty with the Kulin Nation.[29]

27 In contemporary tourist projections Tasmania is represented as 'the apple isle' (fruit production, but also an Edenic and tempting island), while its 'devils' are cute if incredibly vicious marsupials.

28 Boyce, James, *Van Diemen's Land*, Black Inc, Melbourne, 2008, Boyce, James, *1835: The Founding of Melbourne and the Conquest of Australia*, Black Inc, 2012 and Hobsbawm, Eric, 'The Land', in *The Age of Capital: 1848–1975*, Abacus, London, 1975, pp. 205–228.

29 Turnbull, Malcolm, 'Beneath the Boulevards: Malcolm Turnbull on James Boyce's 1835: The Founding of Melbourne & the Conquest of Australia', *The Monthly*, July 2011.

A detailed example of the rationality attending this moment can be found in the precise wording of Governor Bourke's Proclamation of August 28th, 1835, in reference to relations that took place on Kulin nation lands most residents now call Melbourne (sections 5.3–5.4):

> Whereas, it has been represented to me, that divers of His Majesty's Subjects have taken possession of vacant Lands of the Crown, within the limits of this Colony, under the pretense of a treaty, bargain, or contract, for the purchase thereof, with the Aboriginal Natives; Now therefore, I, the Governor, in virtue and in exercise of the power and authority in me vested, do hereby proclaim and notify to all His Majesty's Subjects, and others whom it may concern, that every such treaty, bargain, and contract with the Aboriginal Natives, as aforesaid, for the possession, title, or claim to any Lands lying and being within the limits of the Government of the Colony of New South Wales . . . is void and of no effect against the rights of the Crown; and that all Persons who shall be found in possession of any such Lands as aforesaid, without the license or authority of His Majesty's Government, for such purpose, first had and obtained, will be considered as trespassers, and liable to be dealt with in like manner as other intruders upon the vacant Lands of the Crown within the said Colony.[30]

On October 10, 1835 Governor Bourke, governor of New South Wales, refigured the entire continent as 'terra nullius' in order to facilitate its British conquest on the semblance of legal grounds[31] (see also section 4.3). From this time onward, indigenous peoples in all the British colonies of Australia were forcibly expropriated from their country with the full force of law, formalising what, until that date, had transpired through informal contact, conflict over food and water resources, and squatting. From 1835 the indigenous inhabitants faced off against the colonists and the representatives of the Crown as trespassers and intruders – their contracts 'void', the country they had lived in for tens of thousands of years 'vacant' – while the spreading occupation of white squatters was carefully translated into lawful occupation as private property.

In 1836, the case of Murrell brought indigenous people within the criminal jurisdiction of the Colony of New South Wales for the first time,[32] resolving a

30 'Governor Bourke's Proclamation 1835 (UK)', Museum of Australian Democracy. www.foundingdocs.gov.au/resources/transcripts/nsw7_doc_1835.pdf and 'Governor Bourke's 1835 Proclamation of Terra Nullius', Migration Heritage Centre. www.migrationheritage.nsw.gov.au/exhibition/objectsthroughtime/bourketerra/

31 On August 22, 1770 Captain Cook had 'only' claimed the entirety of the East Coast at 'Possession Island' in the name of His Majesty King George III. An intention to colonise the west coast coagulated as the Swan River Colony in 1829, prompted by Napoleonic fears of French colonisation, and enabled by the broadening of Britain's post-Napoleonic attention and ambition.

32 Notably, just two years later, in 1838, the Swan River Colony began imprisoning aboriginal men on Rottnest Island, a practice that lasted nearly a century, until 1931.

question about whether aborigines were 'within' the law, whether it applied to them, whether they could be arrested and punished.[33] As Dorsett and McVeigh emphasise, this contributed toward the further "erasing of any legal memory of a time in which the common law's jurisdiction was anything other than complete and unified".[34] By the middle of the century the issue of criminal jurisdiction over aboriginal populations was treated as settled in New South Wales, transforming the once disparate matters of jurisdiction and sovereignty into a modern political equation,[35] and adding to it the component of land ownership as property.

Considering the emergence of sovereign Australia through land appropriation, then, it is only from 1850 or so that we can begin considering the emergence of *state* sovereignty and strict territoriality, considered as a congruence of law, territory, authority and population capable of producing itself – nationally – as a 'bordered power container' (section I.2). These weren't settled facts; the co-production of this knowledge as enforceable social and legal facts were integral to the work of settlement between 1788–1835. Governing toward settlement by expanding jurisdiction – by appropriating land, by expropriating indigenous populations, through deforestation, grazing, squatting and the transformation of country into territory and property, right across the continent – opened the field to what expanded into a century long process of land appropriation whose intent was conquest.

1.5 1851–1901: the Gold Rush, imperial Victoria, property boom and bust

When the Australian Gold Rush took off in the Antipodean winter of 1851, it did so just as Victoria became a separate colony,[36] after legislation was passed by the New South Wales Legislative Council on July 1, 1851, following the signing of a British Act of Parliament separating Port Phillip District from New South Wales by Queen Victoria on August 5, 1850. Victoria came into being via correspondence arriving from Sydney and London. But Victoria was not a place – nor was Melbourne a city – that was yet 'in' or 'from' Australia in any sovereign sense contemporary political formations might recognise.

From 1851, the lawful order of land as property that had emanated from Melbourne from 1835 catalysed with the discovery of world-significant deposits of alluvial gold, then property speculation and mass migration (sections 5.3–5.7). The interaction of these factors turned Victoria into what it is best described as

33 Ford, Lisa, 'Indigenous Policy and Its Historical Occlusions: The North American and Global Contexts of Australian Settlement', *Australian Indigenous Law Review*, 12: 1, 2008, pp. 69–80.

34 Dorsett, Shaunagh and McVeigh, Shaun, 'Just So: The Law Which Governs Australia Is Australian Law', *Law and Critique*, 13, 2002, p. 296.

35 Dorsett, Shaunagh and McVeigh, Shaun, *Jurisdiction*, Routledge, Abingdon, 2012.

36 From 1835 until 1851, the Port Phillip Settlement, named Melbourne in 1837 by Governor Arthur Phillip, was a part of New South Wales.

for the half century between 1851–1901: a major engine of British capital in its first phase of imperial expansion. By 1881 Melbourne was one of the fastest growing and most prosperous cities in the world; within a generation Melbourne had gone from being an illegal squatters camp on the banks of the Yarra to the British Empire's second city.[37] Ten years after its heady high point in the early 1880s, the Rush was subsiding, and the speculative urban real estate bubble it fuelled burst in 1889,[38] giving way to the lean conditions of the 1890s. In 1901, just as the effects of the Victorian gold and boom conditions ebbed almost fully away and protectionist white insularity ascended to cultural dominance, with 'the nation' becoming a central question among local white British subjects, Melbourne became the capital city of the new federation of colonies, the Commonwealth of Australia.

1.6 "Aborigines not to be counted in reckoning population"[39]: accounting for sovereignty through population from federation, January 1, 1901

At Federation in 1901, 'Australia' was a name for a set of British colonies, far-flung peripheries of imperial capital, still largely politically and economically independent from one another. By this time, it is certainly plausible to begin speaking of cultural distinctions: distinct*ness* which was more than just an accent, but still far less than a dialect. In a curious fallow historical potentiality, in the months leading up to federation, New Zealand was poised to join (sections i.7, 2.4), and a provision remains in the preamble, where it is described as one of its original states.

Unlike the sovereignty of 'Australia's indigenous peoples', sovereignty was not a question that could have provoked a *national* response in 1901. Like the congruence of territory, authority and population expressed in the ideal-typical strict territoriality of the sovereign nation-state, the equation of sovereignty with federation, the turn into the twentieth century and the wording, legal meaning and cultural value of Australia's constitution is not simple, neat or coherent. When the colonies federated as Australia on January 1, 1901, the sovereignty of them all unquestionably lay with the Empress of India.[40] In this sense, the birth of black letter 'Australian history' – something distinct from 'British colonial and imperial history', or 'the political economy of imperialist capitalism' – coincides precisely with

37 See: Davison, Graeme, *The Rise and Fall of Marvellous Melbourne*, Melbourne University Press, Melbourne, 2004.

38 See: 'Land Boom in 1880s Melbourne', *Museum Victoria*. http://collections.museumvictoria.com.au/articles/2676

39 'Commonwealth of Australia, Constitution Act, Section 127', www.austlii.edu.au/au/legis/cth/consol_act/coaca430/s126.html

40 Although Queen Victoria died only three weeks later, on January 21, 1901, four days before the first Australia Day of the twentieth century.

twentieth-century history, the end of the Victorian era and the beginning of what would be seven decades of racialist protectionism, parochial insularity and anxious, paranoid imperial deference. Yet nobody in Australia celebrates Federation Day.

At federation in 1901 the European population was 3,773,801 people:[41] 3.5 times what it had been in living memory in 1861, and between 3–10 times the estimated total number of indigenous inhabitants before conquest, in 1788.[42] By 1920, Australia's indigenous populations were held to be in terminal decline: 'a dying race'[43] whose tribal components required paternalist protection, and whose 'mixed race' populations needed to be assimilated gently into the dying of the tribal light. On a policy level, most states had legislated special laws and Protectors by the 1920s, and the forcible removal of children from their families, ostensibly for their own welfare, became systemic: what is now known as the Stolen Generations.[44] As this happened, post-dispossession spaces such as reserves, missions and stations spread across the island continent.

As the paternalist, assimilationist *statifications* of White Australia spread and strengthened their grip around indigenous lives, diverse tribal groups – peoples the Empire had spent more than a century in land-appropriating conflict with – were officially dis-counted from the nation's population in the constitution. Section 127:

> [I]n reckoning the numbers of people of the Commonwealth, or of a State or other part of the Commonwealth, aboriginal natives shall not be counted.[45]

Between the arrival of the First Fleet in 1788 and the celebration of a nation, ongoing and expanding rapidly since 1988, Australian history also involved the discursive negation Australia's indigenous populations. But as a way of integrating the counted population as known and governed, this was also politically creative.

41 'A snapshot of Australia, 1901', Australian Bureau of Statistics. www.abs.gov.au/websitedbs/D3110124.NSF/24e5997b9bf2ef35ca2567fb00299c59/c4abd1fac53e3df5ca256bd8001883ec!OpenDocument

42 Federation Australia's population was roughly the same as Ireland, 70% that of Canada, roughly one-tenth of the total population of Great Britain.

43 The figures at federation are 150,000 people; in 1920 the population is estimated here at 20,000. 'Indigenous Australia Timeline', Australian Museum. http://australianmuseum.net.au/indigenous-australia-timeline-1901-to-1969

44 "In 2008, 8% (26,900 people) of Aboriginal and Torres Strait Islander people aged 15 years and over had been removed from their natural family, consistent with the rate reported in 2002 (also 8%) . . . 12% of people aged 45 years and over experienc(ed) separation. Of those aged 15–44 years, 7% had personally experienced removal from their family". '4704.0 – The Health and Welfare of Australia's Aboriginal and Torres Strait Islander Peoples, Oct 2010', Australian Bureau of Statistics. www.abs.gov.au/AUSSTATS/abs@.nsf/lookup/4704.0Chapter470Oct+2010

45 'Commonwealth of Australia Constitution Act, Section 127', *austlii.edu.au*. www.austlii.edu.au/au/legis/cth/consol_act/coaca430/s126.html

In the language of Timothy Mitchell, ways of counting some populations were established through methods that discounted others.[46]

Section 127, which remained part of the constitution until 1967, needs to be understood in relation to the main planks of the White Australia policy, a set of measures that sought to regulate population in order to maintain Australia as a White British Imperial enclave. The turn of the century shift toward the 'benevolent protection' of a 'dying race' sat side by side with the need to restrict the arrival of non-European boatborne newcomers. The Immigration Restriction Act's[47] purpose was to limit Asian migration in order to ensure European predominance, based on anxieties that had arisen throughout the colonies between the 1870s and 1890s. For its first seven decades as a nation-state, White Australia expanded and integrated the hegemonic position of white Australians among the populations the Commonwealth and state governments governed: both by aligning Australia and Australian lives with the majesty and blood of the British Empire, far overseas; and, at home, through the discounting and paternalist shepherding of its 'dying' first nations and the regulation of immigrant populations on racial grounds, while its colonial-settler populations settled in as 'typical Australians'. With these Australian-imperial *statifications* in mind, this chapter now transitions from a schematic re-description of national sovereignty to a closer focus on islands, via the following intermezzo.

1.7 'Girt by sea': unity in the boundedness of the island continent

Australian border security is projected from a contemporary nation-state whose boundedness is not only sung to life each time Australians sing their recent official anthem.[48] 'Australia' appears naturally obvious on most typical twentieth-century European maps – in a way that few continental nation-states do – because of way the physical geography of the mainland is represented, as 'girt by sea'.[49] In considering the place of national sovereignty in the emergence of border security on an 'island continent', two things about Australia's seeming twentieth-century boundedness are striking, and they both append the racialist insularity secured through the exclusions of federation and pursued through White Australia.

46 Mitchell, Timothy, 'The Character of Calculability', *Rule of Experts: Egypt, Techno-Politics, Modernity*, University of California Press, Berkeley, 2002, pp. 114–119.

47 'Immigration Restriction Act (1901)', Museum of Australian Democracy. www.foundingdocs.gov.au/resources/transcripts/cth4ii_doc_1901a.pdf

48 In 1878, a Scot, Peter Dodds McCormick penned a song named *Advance Australia Fair*. It replaced 'God Save the Queen' as Australia's national anthem in 1984. It contains the lyrics, 'with golden soil, and wealth for toil, our home is girt by sea'.

49 See Butler, Judith and Spivak, Gayatri, *Who Sings the Nation-State? Language, Politics, Belonging*, University of Chicago Press, Chicago, 2007 and Perera, Suvendrini, *Australia and the Insular Imagination: Beaches, Borders, Boats, and Bodies*, New York: Palgrave Macmillan, 2009.

For the first nearly six decades of its existence as a nation-state, Australia's physical geography *was* observed as a strategic threat. Australia's continental landmass relative to population, its peripheral colonial status and travel distance from the imperial centre,[50] and its regional location, were all the subject of enormous governmental *and national* worrying. In this sense, 'the Australian nation' is something a 'we' worries will be invaded, and knows must be defended. By World War Two the stakes were considered nothing less than existential: as Arthur Calwell declared on July 13, 1945, the day he became Australia's first Minister for Immigration, Australia must 'populate or perish' (sections 5.3–5.6).

Australia's seeming boundedness – as a physical fact that might be capable of constituting the borders of Australia based on its *being* an 'island continent' – also belies the geography of Australia's many islands, the diversity of their climates and populations, and the historically incomparable connective power of the world's oceans.[51] Boundedness is not just a collective act of insular imagining that's about actively forgetting the politically creative role of seafaring, Van Diemens Land, British colonial and Imperial violence, and the Black Line 'in' Australian history; it's about leaving every other 'island'[52] out of national Australia's mainland picture of itself – while enacting a cultural memory of invasion whose events are as selective as its lacunae are large. This touches on a key point about islands we keep arriving at in *Border Security.*

Island transformations involve the complex interaction of materiality and ideality, the gravitational pull of dreams, the warp and woof of jurisdictional weaving *and* the walls and roofs of their specific concretion. Problems are conceived, plans are drawn up, red crabs are corralled so they can circulate and sometimes the robber crabs outside these mobility circuits get electrocuted by electrical circuits installed to deter humans attempting to escape into the crabs' natural habitat (section I.10). Islands are not only ways of seeing separation where there is also relation, they're also constructions of enacted imagination, and political representations of space[53] that only make sense within grander historical orderings and orientations of 'the world',[54] such as those I have just glossed (sections 1.2–1.6).

To herald the focus of Chapter 3, we can clarify this thinking of islands by touching upon their use as offshore. The application of the form of offshore to effectuate an offshoring process of any kind, involves specific mobilisations 'off,

50 The First Fleet was at sea for 109 days; Gold Rush passages were ninety days or so. A 1909 passenger liner trip was still fourty-five days. The voyage by ship reduced the journey to *just* under a month by the early 60s 'Passenger ships to Australia: a Comparison of Vessels and Journey Times to Australia between 1788 and 1900', Australian National Maritime Museum. www.anmm.gov.au/Learn/Library-and-Research/Research-Guides/Passenger-Ships-to-Australia-A-Comparison-of-Vessels-and-Journey-Time

51 Steinberg, Philip E., *The Social Construction of the Ocean*, Cambridge University Press, Cambridge, 2001, p. 10.

52 McWilliams, *Southern California: An Island on the Land*, Peregrine Smith, Utah, 1980, p. 14.

53 Galli, Carlo, *Political Spaces and Global War*, University of Minnesota Press, Minneapolis, 2010.

54 Schmitt, Carl, *The Nomos of the Earth in the International Law of Jus Publicum Europaeum*, Telos Press Publishing, New York, 2006.

in and on' particular sites with definite environs for a number of reasons (sections 3.1–3.4). As raised in the introduction, this produced island-specific design challenges on CI which were solved through intentional action by group agents (i.2, i.4) working with a brief, like the Crab Bridge (section I.10); but this, in turn produced effective hazards unforeseen by the designers' designs. In these instances, both the death of robber crabs and the possibility of sovereign shipwreck transpired through the offshore emergence of border security on Christmas Island. But here is the important complication. Some of the 'islands' produced as offshore may be geo-physical islands, "land surrounded by water on all sides".[55] But for offshoring to emerge as a process at all, on any island, it must be accompanied by a general imagination of the two-sided form of offshore and an enacted imagination of a specific island as an offshore site. To be able to establish a shore, one must be able to place it in relation to one's horizons – and to return us to our systems theoretical epistemology – this relies on the production of boundaries as authoritative distinctions and horizons as the possibility of their actualisation.

In the context of a dependent island like CI, dependency takes a number of forms, in which we can see shifting shapes of *statifications* working toward sovereignty in this chapter. Dependency might be reducible to communicative arrangements that ensure the seasonal return of supply ships, preparations made on the expectation of the reliable arrival of tourists, the punctual receipt of remittances or the light speed relay of data pulsing through an undersea cable running through abyssal oceanic darkness. At issue for understanding island-based *statifications* that work through colonisations of land, capital and labour toward the production of sovereignty is that dependency ensures ongoing fealty or loyalty to the dominant partners. This also indicates the irreducible yet inseparable relations between dependency, safety and perception in the production of security, including border security. This is important as we consider the way islands such as CI can be made to work toward to securing a number of political goals that 'we' desire, believe is achievable, but can never see or know definitively. CI makes Australia sovereign, within border security's world; yet for this to become possible, CI first had to become sovereignly Australia. The following sections now explore this in detail through the microcosmic example of CI's Australian-sovereign becoming.

I.8 CI 1888–1958: from annexation under British Imperial jurisdiction to valid transfer to the Commonwealth of Australia

As a territory of the Commonwealth, Christmas Island is one part of Australia that belies the unifying boundedness of 'the island continent'.[56] Recalling the

55 Mountz, Alison, 'Specters at the Port of Entry: Understanding State Mobilities Through an Ontology of Exclusion', *Mobilities*, 6: 3, 2011, p. 317.

56 This section reprises and develops points raised in Chambers, Peter, 'Society Has Been Defended: Following the Shifting Shape of State through Australia's Christmas Island', *International Political Sociology*, 5, 2011, pp. 18–34.

introductory chapter, CI is the tip of an oceanic volcano 320km to the south of Java and 2,630km northwest of Perth (section I.10). In becoming a part of Australian border security from September 2001, CI was not only the place 'in' Australia *Tampa* was interdicted on its way towards during the Tampa Affair, the month before; it was carefully chosen as the location for Australia's first and (thus far) only purpose-built immigration detention centre (constructed 2002–2008, opened 2008). Among other reasons, CI was chosen for this purpose because of the political tensioning generated by the combination of its isolation from the mainland and its physical proximity to Java, where the small smuggling trade is located, which is also what makes it attractive as the part of Australia nearest to Indonesia. Until *Tampa*, Reach CI and you reached Australia. This was the rationale behind the smugglers' sending the *Palapa*'s occupants towards this tiny island in late August 2001, just as it was the rationale behind excising CI from the Migration Zone in the September 2001 wake of Tampa (sections 3.11–3.12).

CI is the home to several endemic species: we've already encountered the crabs and the logistical problems their migratory patterns present for securing circulation. Yet when CI was 'discovered' by European explorers in 1888 (245 years after Captain Mynor of the British East India Company sighted and named it), it was 'uninhabited'. Certainly, as far as archives indicate, though it has teemed with life for millions of years, CI was never occupied or colonised by a human community – until the late nineteenth century.

In 1886, *H.M. Flying Fish*, captained by Captain Maclear, visited the island under instruction from the British Admiralty. Maclear left the crabs but, under instruction, took mineral samples back to Britain. The mineral samples were analysed in Edinburgh by John Murray, who didn't fail to notice a pebble of almost pure phosphate lime among the specimens. A second pebble-prompted visit returned more samples of equally high quality. Murray wrote to the Duke of Argyll, who wrote to Prime Minister Lord Salisbury, who instructed the admiralty to "bring Christmas Island under British jurisdiction".[57] The island was annexed to the British Crown on June 6, 1888.

From the turn of the century until the outbreak of the Second World War, CI was one of the world's most significant phosphate islands – in an era when organic phosphate was the world's most significant fertiliser. Along with Nauru and Ocean Island, CI 'donated' the phosphate-driven phase of the Green Revolution to Australia, New Zealand, Japan (the single biggest customer) and export markets throughout the world. As a 'phosphate island', early twentieth-century CI was a British Imperial extraction economy powered by 'coolie' labour sourced from China via labour agents in Singapore. The Island was strictly divided on race and class lines and overseen by a District Officer, who personated the sovereign

57 Williams, Maslyn and Macdonald, Barrie, *The Phosphateers: A History of the British Phosphate Commissioners and the Christmas Island Phosphate Commission*, Melbourne University Press, Melbourne, 1985, p. 45.

authority of the British monarch through his body and office[58] – indeed, he remained on the Island in order to do so.[59]

Crucially, although annexed by the British, under British jurisdiction and administered through the Straits Settlements of Singapore, CI was not a territory. Likewise, the communities who laboured and lived there were not citizens who could claim rights, nor were they recognised as indigenous groups who could self determine. At this conjuncture, sovereignty emanated from the British Crown and remained unified in the person of the District Officer; it was not located in the territory. In the political formation of this island world, the ***statification*** enabling the passage of authority was effectuated by the official representations made by the District Officer, whose body in uniform, attending to the matters of its office, became the conduit for sovereign authority on the Island. British imperial sovereignty on CI at this time was experienced by its labouring populations as a personal, imperial relation of subjection,[60] not a territorial, state-guaranteed form of citizenship (sections 5.5–5.7).

In the years immediately after its invasion and occupation by the forces of Imperial Japan in March 1942,[61] the strategic value of CI began to be recognised as far away as Canberra and Wellington. In the postwar period, under the aegis of postwar national reconstruction, the development of Keynesian mass economies, and the cultivation of export-oriented crops, and with an emergent understanding of the logistical value of supply chains,[62] superphosphate was recognised as being of strategic importance. Agricultural lobbies on both sides of the Tasman began a decade long process of lobbying in order to bring CI securely into their sphere of influence, or even transfer sovereignty from the British Empire to Australia.

In the early 50s, expressed fears of 'Asiatic penetration'[63] prompted a Canberra-led re-cognition of CI's strategic value as a military asset. At this time, in an age of iron curtains and domino effects, Australia was taking a defensive position on the 'arc of islands' surrounding the island continent, and CI was re-figured as a component part of a reinforced archipelago that would allow Australia to "exert a dominant political influence in the area with a view to maintaining Australian

58 Hobbes, Thomas, *Leviathan*, Penguin, London, 1982, pp. 217–222.

59 Chambers, Peter, 'The Passage of Authority: Imagining the Political Transformation of Australia's Christmas Island, From Sovereignty to Governance', *Shima: The International Journal of Research into Island Cultures*, 6: 2, 2012, pp. 123–124.

60 Op.Cit., p. 122.

61 CI was occupied one month after Singapore had fallen, Darwin had been bombarded and midget submarines had managed to attack as far south as Sydney, where a midget submarine sunk a Manly ferry. All this only three months after Pearl Harbor. Hunt, John, 'Revolt on Christmas Island', *Sydney Morning Herald*, March 14, 2012. www.smh.com.au/entertainment/revolt-on-christmas-island-20120313-1uy5q.html

62 Cowen, Deborah, *The Deadly Life of Logistics: Mapping Violence in Global Trade*, University of Minnesota Press, Minneapolis, 2014, p. 3.

63 Lowe, David, *Menzies and the Great World Struggle: Australia's Cold War 1948–1954*, UNSW Press, Sydney, p. 48.

security behind a peripheral screen of islands".[64] In this postwar, Cold War context, Australian sovereignty was visible as 'mainland territorial integrity' threatened by the aggressive penetration of an expansionist 'Asia' that loyal subjection to the British monarch had been unable to repulse when Singapore fell in 1942 (section 5.5). Simultaneously, trans-Tasman Antipodean national interests saw the phosphate deposited on the surface of CI as a resource that ought to be secured – thus steps were taken to monopolise access to what was, at this time, a prehistoric guano deposit of national strategic and regional economic importance.

The transfer of CI's sovereignty from Great Britain to Australia formally began on March 14, 1955, with formal meetings taking place in Singapore. CI's structural Cold War role as part of the peripheral screen faded into the background, both as the atmosphere thawed, and as CI came to be seen as a piece of transferrable property. Between 1955 and 1958, the transfer of CI's sovereignty was less about human communities focusing on violence, territory and monopolisation (*pace* Weber) than it was the recurrence of discussions about taxation and royalties taking place between legal persons entering into international relations on behalf of their populations' national interest, in order to possess something profitable. On October 22, 1956, the British informed the Australian and New Zealand governments of their intention to detach Christmas Island from Singapore, in order to administer it as a separate entity. On January 1, 1958, the island was detached from Singapore by Britain. On October 1, 1958, the detached colony became a territory of the Commonwealth of Australia under the *Christmas Island Act (1958)*.

Australia's October 1958-onward sovereignty over CI derives from the following factors, whose co-formation produced a medium enabling the island's authoritative passage from Britain to Australia, via the transfer:

- effective British occupation and administration of the Island
- a valid transfer to Australia by complementary legislation
- continual governmental and judicial activities by Australia
- the absence of any competing claims to sovereignty, especially from an indigenous population.[65]

As explored earlier in this section, agents of Great Britain annexed the island and placed it under British jurisdiction on June 6, 1888. We've also seen that sovereignty was enacted through the living person of the colonial district officer, whose presence and administration ensured effective occupation throughout the British Imperial decades of CI's twentieth century as a phosphate island. The validity of the transfer, in turn, was ensured by reciprocal legal norms and procedures

64 in Goldsworthy, David, *Losing the Blanket: Australia and the End of Britain's Empire*, Melbourne University Press, Melbourne, 2002, p. 51.

65 Report of the House of Representatives Standing Committee on Legal and Constitutional Affairs, *Islands in the Sun: The Legal Regimes of Australia's External Territories and the Jervis Bay Territory*, Canberra, Australia, 1991.

shared between representatives of states capable of entering into relations with one another on behalf of their governments. On the matter of CI's sovereignty *in 1958*, the transfer relied on general, international normative framings of sovereignty akin to those theorised in Montevideo a quarter of a century earlier.[66] But these, in turn, relied on earlier forms of sovereign subjection that were peculiarly British and Imperial, and that existed because agents of the Crown had taken the contingent action of annexing the Island 'in the first place'. In order to be given, CI had first to have been taken.[67]

From October 1, 1958 onwards, the validity of the transfer was to be maintained by the continuation of government by agents of the Australian Commonwealth. This indicates that only a continuous process of government was – and is – capable as maintaining sovereignty on the island from this time, and only in the 'presence of an absence': neither an indigenous population nor a self-determining nascent citizenry capable of claiming CI as theirs for themselves. On this account, 'Australia' was there (governing every day), and no one else was (living there ever, as a distinct people).

Let's summarise the *statifications* working toward sovereignty we can glimpse through the above descriptions. In its shifting re-cognition through CI, we can grasp how, under the British Empire, the formation of sovereignty went via *the monarch and the Crown*. In the immediate postwar and Cold War context, the formation of state sovereignty went via *territory and violence*. In the period of transfer, only *legal persons capable of entering in to relations with one another* could have enacted the passage of sovereign authority from Great Britain to the Commonwealth of Australia. Yet from the moment of transfer, the Australian Commonwealth inaugurated *the ceaseless routine work of 'governmental and judicial activities'* that it continues to the time of writing – including through the detention of noncitizens.

1.9 CI from 1958: producing a conduit for Australian sovereign authority through the government of the island territory's living population

From October 1, 1958, Australian sovereignty could only be retained by actually governing *all* of the Island and *all* of the *populations* residing there all of the time, establishing a relation between territorial and popular entirety and making the maintenance of sovereignty depend on it. As governmental activities would only remain unquestionably legitimate in the absence of competing claims from an indigenous population, from 1958 the Commonwealth produced a conduit

66 'Montevideo Convention on the Rights and Duties of States', Article 1, Council on Foreign Relations. www.cfr.org/sovereignty/montevideo-convention-rights-duties-states/p15897

67 Schmitt, Carl, *The Nomos of the Earth in the International Law of the Jus Publicum Europaeum*, Telos Press, New York, 2006, pp. 324–356.

for the passage of sovereign authority by attending to the matter of population – as follows.

Since 1888, who had come to CI; who had stayed, who had never left, who was born or had lived their entire life there? To 1975, the majority of the island's population was comprised of ethnic Chinese workers who had been brought to CI to extract phosphate. In 1975, a Commonwealth representative wrote the following:

> [A]lthough it is quite clear that Christmas Island is geographically separate from Australia, neither ethnic nor cultural distinctiveness apply permanently to the territory.[68]

This statement is consistent with the distinction Australia's nation-state agents had held since 1958, in order to prevent UN interference through the possible recognition of CI's being a non-self-governing territory:[69] CI was separate but not distinct from Australia; CI was apart from, yet a part of Australia. In the eighty-seven years between annexation and the above statement (more than a decade longer than Australia had been a nation-state), were there any among these – ethnically and culturally 'indistinct' – people who had never left the island, were born there or never knew another home? The answer is almost definitely yes.

CI's population was shaped first of all by the pragmatics and logistics of human movement raised by labour conditions and transport infrastructures: the materiality of a political space and its norms. When major mining operations began on CI at the turn of the century, the cost of passage made regular return prohibitively expensive. As a single industry island, CI had one employer. The fear among workers was that people who left the Island would never be allowed to return; workers could be dismissed without appeal and deported within twenty-four hours. For most who came, a more general combination of political instability back home, paltry wages on the Island and pervasive addiction to opium – administered by the colonial district officer at a discount – made going home so hard that CI *was* home, effectively, then eventually. Some of these people had children – born on the Island – some of whom, in turn, had children. *The Union of Christmas Island Workers* records that by the early 1970s, in the years leading up to the Commonwealth's position that 'neither ethnic nor cultural distinctiveness applied permanently to the territory':

> 'people born on the Island constituted at least ten percent of the total population. Some of these were almost 40 years old. This percentage, though

68 Australian Parliament Senate Standing Committee on Foreign Affairs, 'United Nations Involvement With Australia's Territories: Report From the Senate Standing Committee on Foreign Affairs and Defence', *Commonwealth of Australia*, 1975, pp. 110–111.

69 'The United Nations and Decolonization: Non-Self-Governing Territories', *www.un.org*. www.un.org/en/decolonization/nonselfgovterritories.shtml

> small, nevertheless did comprise what could be seen as a permanent, and even indigenous population.[70]

As the Annual Report of 1975 states that the population as of June 30, 1975 totaled 3,032, this suggests an intergenerational island-born population of perhaps a little over three hundred people.

As we will explore in some detail in Chapter 5, Australian citizenship emerged in the postwar period as a differential mechanism for deporting visitors and protecting permanent residents, just as Australia's first national migration program was developed (section 5.5). Notably, there were no Australian citizens until 1948, and even these postwar populations remained 'British subjects' on their passports until 1984, two years after Advance Australia Fair was made the official anthem, four years before the bicentennial triggered the 'celebration of the nation'[71] (section 1.3). The transfer of CI's sovereignty to Australia in 1958, only ten years after Australians had become capable of being citizens, rendered the civic status of the island's long-term residents contingent and complicated, rather than resolving it as unambiguously settled.

From the mid-1960s, steps were taken by the Commonwealth to preclude the emergence of a resident population capable of recognising itself as 'a people', and to minimise the possibility of their becoming Australian citizens. One way of effectuating this popular prophylaxis was to make no mention of actual historical conditions of residence in government reports. Throughout the sixties and in to the early 70s, the Commonwealth's Annual Report referred to the island's residents as 'persons recruited for employment'. In 1964, only six years after the transfer of sovereignty, the secretary to the Department of External Affairs wrote to the general manager of the British Phosphate Commission that "the Australian Government was anxious to limit the numbers of the Asian population which might, because of long residence, be considered by international agencies to have the rights of indigenous inhabitants".[72] As a result of this correspondence, the British Phosphate Commission instituted a policy that meant that workers were ***required*** to leave the island every three years and then reapply for work in China or Singapore: a governmental device with the explicit purpose of interdicting the emergence of permanent residents who could claim rights and citizenship, or self determine as a nation.

The transfer of sovereignty to Australia had transformed CI into a territory of the Commonwealth. At that conjuncture, sovereignty, territory and population catalysed to produce the ***possibility*** of CI's becoming an island peopled by a

70 Waters, Les, *The Union of Christmas Island Workers*, George Allen and Unwin, Melbourne, 1982, pp. 4–5.

71 The Department of Immigration advised that all travellers were required to carry a passport to enter Australia in 1980. See: 'A History of the Department of Immigration – Managing Migration to Australia', Commonwealth of Australia. p. 57. www.border.gov.au/CorporateInformation/Documents/immigration-history.pdf

72 Waters, Les, *The Union of Christmas Island Workers*, George Allen and Unwin, Melbourne, 1982, p. 14.

living, growing population of Australian citizens. Yet residents had to actualise this possibility through a declaration; citizenship had to be communicated as a desire filled out in institutionally legible forms of communication. Under the terms of the *Christmas Island Act 1958*, British subjects residing on the Island – *before* the transfer, who were *not* Australian citizens – could make a declaration that they wished to become Australian citizens within two years of that date. Residents who were under the age of twenty-one were required to make a declaration within two years of their twenty-first birthday. Notably, island-resident-subjects making such declarations did so as individuals in correspondence with the authorised representatives of the nation-state of Australia, not as a member of a people declaring itself to the United Nations.

Individual declarations were arriving in Canberra as further developments arrived on the Island from 1970s onshore Australia: the transformation from White Australia to multiculturalism (1966–1973), and the Union of Christmas Island Workers' fight for mainland pay and conditions (late 70s). Australia's policy-led cultural shift toward multiculturalism had several effects on CI, which was already substantively multicultural, far more than its newly aspirational mainland counterpart. The three most notable of these changes for the island's residents were:

1 the abandonment of policy-led segregated schooling and housing;
2 an end to the categorisation of island residents on the basis of race (in favour of 'ethnic group', from 1972);
3 and a winding down of the mainland resettlement plan that had complemented the 60s tactics of popular prophylaxis mentioned above.

An island-resident-citizen population was finally being allowed to finally emerge on the territory and inclusively merge with multicultural Australia. Not only that, but the residents' ethno-cultural difference was refigured as a positive feature to be celebrated, rather than a worrying problem to be addressed through enforced segregation and vigilant management.

The late 70s struggle of the Union of Christmas Island Workers, meanwhile, raised the question of 'the mainland' as one of justice, via wage parity and substantive equality: if CI's residents were Australians *like* everyone else, why shouldn't they be paid the same wages *as* everyone else? Christmas Islanders here glimpsed the meaning of sovereignty *as* living within the shores of a politics whose horizon was justice as fairness, and demanded 'the fair go'. Pay parity was achieved after a significant struggle, and by the early 1980s and into the early 1990s the explicit purpose guiding the government of CI by the Commonwealth was legal alignment with Australia[73] and the political integration of its multicultural citizenry. CI and its residents had finally and fully arrived in Australia, as Australians.

73 See: 'Islands in the Sun: The Legal Regimes of Australia's External Territories and the Jervis Bay Territory', Report of the House of Representatives Standing Committee on Legal and Constitutional Affairs, 1991.

Many of the Christmas Islanders who spotted *MV Tampa* when it appeared on the horizon in the final days of August 2001 were Australian citizens. Twenty-first-century Christmas Islanders who spotted *Tampa* lived in a sovereign territory of the Commonwealth of Australia, physically an offshore island, but politically onshore Australia (section 3.11). Such Australian lives are perhaps inconceivable to their diverse ancestors, a District Officer like Victor Purcell seventy years earlier, or 424 Afghan, three Pakistani and six Sri Lankan asylum seekers rescued from the *Palapa* from aboard the Norwegian freighter[74] named after the American city and bay, with its Scandinavian officers and Filipino crew. Yet were the Christmas Islander Australians in any meaningful way *like* the Special Air Services troopers from the mainland who boarded *Tampa* in their name at around 12:30pm Canberra time on Wednesday August 29, 2001? Did anyone living on CI during that week of declared 'sovereignty in crisis' live a relation to Australia's national sovereignty like that of the Prime Minister who insisted, from an island-continental electoral platform in 5,180km away in Canberra, that the *Tampa* must be stopped – as a decisive matter of national sovereignty?

John Howard's elevation of the interdiction of noncitizens into a matter of national sovereignty via the decisionist prerogative of 'we will decide' *made* CI central to the delineation of Australia from its others from that day to the time of writing. This is something improbable at the moment it became possible with the transfer of sovereignty on October 1, 1958, and it bears almost no relation to the rationality and techniques of the Island's 1888 annexation. This chapter has already examined transformations of sovereignty through Australia and CI that disclose how the island was:

- *annexed* and placed under British jurisdiction;
- *exploited* as a donor-resource for the Green Revolutions of Japan, Australia and New Zealand;
- *re-conceived* as part of a Cold War 'peripheral screen' capable of preventing 'Asiatic penetration';
- *transferred* like a piece of property from Great Britain to Australia, via talks in Singapore that facilitated a 'valid transfer';
- *governed* in a number of intricate, problem-responsive ways by the Australian Commonwealth: first to prevent the emergence of its residents as a people, then to ensure thee reproduction of its population as a diverse group of Australian citizens.

In line with the overarching contention I'm developing in this chapter, transferring an island and governing its population were both ways for the Commonwealth

74 Spinks, Harriet, 'Tampa: Ten Years On', *Parliament of Australia*. www.aph.gov.au/About_Parliament/Parliamentary_Departments/Parliamentary_Library/FlagPost/2011/August/Tampa_ten_years_on

of Australia to enact sovereignty that were observed as valid in their political conjunctures. Both meant attending to space and people in certain creative ways capable of transforming CI into a medium for the passage of sovereign authority at each time-sensitive moment. It would not have been possible to 'govern the Island's population' in 1888, nor did any of those involved in the question of its sovereignty in 1958 during the transfer suggest annexing it or preventing asylum seekers from seeking protection there. You never step into the same sovereignty twice.

1.10 From territorial to functional sovereignty, via maritime jurisdictions?

I now draw analytic attention away from population and territory and toward the ocean to focus a critical understanding of what's imagined and practiced in *maritime* border security, and what's therefore at stake in the shifting formations of sovereignty under examination. What does it mean when *Operation Sovereign Borders* seeks to use the ocean, parsed as maritime jurisdictions in Australia's area of maritime interest, in order to secure Australia's national sovereignty?

As a legacy of the Eurocentric, US-centric twentieth century and its powerful political imaginaries, the British colonial, Imperial and Australian Commonwealth *statifications* discussed so far were enacted by agents of states as if they emanated from the living bodies of monarchs, or territorial 'centres'. Yet as part of the transformations triggered from Tampa onward, Border Force's attempts to 'stop the boats' have taken place in maritime jurisdictions, vast oceanic spaces far from the limit of the territory with varying, attenuated, even tenuous relations to Australian land, law and history. Following one archive, we might examine such spaces of power as 'extraterritorial jurisdictions',[75] but in what follows, I hold to the way that border security's world carves out its space of operations by observing the ocean: in its immanence; in its relation to certain bodies of international law (but not others); and in its circular relation to the expedient needs of border security. Border security stretches practices of national sovereignty beyond the credulity of state sovereignty's grounding in strict territoriality: this is one precise sense in which it is a *projection* of *national* sovereignty,[76] an active, transitive *statification* that does not simply emanate from the territory, but makes its own space by 'taking the ocean' and people in relation to it, in a certain way. To broaden the implications here, examining how contemporary political relations to the ocean are parsed out in Australian border security's communications about

75 Colangelo, Anthony J., 'What Is Extraterritorial Jurisdiction?' *Cornell Law Review*, 99: 6, September 2014, pp. 1303–1352.

76 This section reprises and develops points made in: Chambers, Peter, 'The Embrace of Border Security: Maritime Jurisdiction, National Sovereignty, and the Geopolitics of Operation Sovereign Borders', *Geopolitics*, 20, 2015, pp. 1–34.

their purpose as jurisdictions, is also intended to explicate a shift from territorial to functional authority that we *may* be witnessing.[77]

The maritime zones Australian border security's agents use to project national sovereignty are jurisdictions. I interpret jurisdiction as an observed unity of 'authority over' and 'responsibility for': jurisdiction is a two-sided form that enables legally meaningful communication. Insofar as it is used to ask who 'is responsible for' or 'has authority over' something, someone or somewhere, jurisdiction contours a question about justice to which an authoritative response might give sharp focus.

The responsibilities of Maritime Border Command, the agents that the Commonwealth has authorised to conduct maritime interdiction, are delineated in the *Guide to Australian Maritime Security Arrangements* (GAMSA), a set of guidelines that function as a discursive topography of the agents and roles working as and for Australia's sovereignty, through border security, far out in the ocean. The document itself does not have the force of law, but it clearly says who does, where and why – and its agents do have the force of law. By way of presaging some key points to follow, it's important to note that GAMSA's reading of maritime jurisdictions is consistent with UNCLOS norms, but that its use of specific definitions is selective and expedient. In line with our epistemological commitment to following the intrasystemic severances of border security's world (section I.1), I read GAMSA as an indicative outline of border security's jurisdictions: 'Australia's area of maritime interest' is a significant field within the border continuum. The following paragraphs offer a close reading of these inaugural 'autodescriptions' of GAMSA's self, role and world. To prepare the reader, this is a rather 'dry' rendition of the ocean, but as with the introduction's sections on the border continuum (section I.2), the points raised are offered as an essential theoretical setup for the 'wet' example that concludes the chapter (section 1.12) by explicating how we might understand the fundamentally paradoxical nature of national sovereignty as enacted through border security in maritime space.

GAMSA's maritime security arrangements are aligned to Australia's 'national objective for maritime security'. The national objective seeks to "deter or prevent illegal activity from occurring in Australia's maritime jurisdiction and where necessary to interdict and enforce Australian laws".[78] Already we can see a number of co-operative factors:

- a mission imperative or task, aligned to a *national* security objective;
- an operational use of a jurisdictional understanding of the ocean, so made *for* (a threatened) national sovereignty.

77 Sassen, Saskia, *Territory, Authority, Rights: From Medieval to Global Assemblages*, Princeton University Press, Princeton, 2008 and Teubner, Gunther, *Constitutional Fragments: Societal Constitutionalism and Globalization*, Oxford University Press, Oxford, 2012.

78 Commonwealth of Australia, *'Introduction', in Guide to Australian Maritime Security Arrangements (GAMSA),* Commonwealth of Australia, 2013, p. 3. https://www.border.gov.au/AustralianBorderForce/Documents/GAMSA%202013.pdf

For Maritime Border Command to 'interdict and enforce Australian laws' and achieve its national objective, Australian law must be present – to some extent, for certain purposes, and with definite limits. Maritime Border Command cannot respond lawfully without a space *and time* of Australian law that is spatio-temporally already – and sovereignly – there.[79] We have seen how fraught this is (sections 1.2–1.7), as well the ontological and epistemological assumptions it makes about a nation's sovereign past, present and future: the political effects of routinely enacting these distinctions as border security, likewise, will come into increasingly sharp focus from this point on. In examining the emergence of population, territory and security on CI (sections 1.8–1.9), we've also seen how successive governments worked creatively with what was communicable as sovereignty *at each conjuncture* to reproduce a form of sovereignty capable of securing a workable passage of authority *for that conjuncture*. GAMSA is similarly creative with maritime jurisdictions, but its use of jurisdiction to achieve the sovereignty of the national objective begs the following question. If state sovereignty only *fully* exists to the territorial limit of twelve nautical miles from the territorial sea baseline, and Australian law only *fully* coincides with this, how is sovereignty possible where it is enacted as border security on the high seas?

As a set of jurisdictions capable of being transformed into a medium for the formation of national sovereignty as border security, GAMSA places its security arrangements in maritime zones that emerged in their current form in 1982 in the Convention on the Law of the Sea (UNCLOS).[80] In *GAMSA's description*, UNCLOS has three functions. It:

1 provides a comprehensive international legal regime for use of the sea and its resources . . .
2 establishes a legal order of the seas that seeks to balance the rights and responsibilities of coastal states against the rights and responsibilities of other sea users . . .
3 clearly establishes and delineates the various maritime zones over which states may exercise different degrees of jurisdiction.[81]

GAMSA relies on UNCLOS, for two reasons. First, GAMSA relies on UNCLOS as its recognised legal, international background. UNCLOS is a comprehensive international legal regime and order of the seas, a 'metacommunity' whose international legal existence and legitimacy grounds all GAMSA's

79 Dorsett, Shaunagh and McVeigh, Shaun, 'Just So: The Law Which Governs Australia is Australian Law', *Law and Critique*, 13, 2002.

80 'United Nations Convention on the Law of the Sea (UNCLOS)', *www.un.org*. www.un.org/depts/los/convention_agreements/texts/unclos/unclos_e.pdf

81 Commonwealth of Australia, 'Legal and Administrative Aspects to Australia's Maritime Jurisdiction', *Guide to Australian Maritime Security Arrangements* (GAMSA), 2013, p. 29.

claims:[82] the state and the international are co-produced in GAMSA's authoritative thinking around this maritime space. But notice the following scalar jumps that achieve this.

UNCLOS is an ordering of oceanic space that transcends *state* sovereignty – though only as an *international* convention agreed to by sovereign nation-states in order to stabilise the pacific unfolding of *globalising* commercial processes, and only where the world's oceans are understood in fundamental contradistinction to the full sovereignty of the territorial nation-state, but "with due regard for the sovereignty of all States".[83] UNCLOS crosses scales to which a number of different state-based agents can attach to, but it can only do *here* so because of the way it works as a *statification* enacted within border security's world, of which GAMSA is a discursive artefact and 'communicant'.

UNCLOS is recognised – here by the Commonwealth as GAMSA, but elsewhere by the agents of other states – as speaking authoritatively of the oceans in a way that is internationally grounded in its metacommunity and globally applicable as a common legal referent, to which all States Parties refer if contestation arises. However, once imported into GAMSA, UNCLOS is re-worked in line with the former's national objective, to offer a present-and-future place for international law within the orderly national space of the Commonwealth in its defence against the threatening global, through border security. GAMSA selectively takes UNCLOS and its distribution of 'responsibilities for' into itself to give itself a functional place to enact its 'authority over' *legitimately* – beyond the territorial limit of Australian law that exists for most persons and purposes.

GAMSA relies on UNCLOS, second and more particularly, as its means of delineating and exercising *its* jurisdiction – which border security's agents then enact as Australia's national sovereignty, including through interdiction. This is a unilateral taking of discursive elements from an authoritative telling of jurisdiction for the making and taking of a political space as sovereign. That is: GAMSA's use of UNCLOS' international norms is for explicitly national and unilateralist purposes. Notice how border security's distinctions scrambles the scales GAMSA's agents rely upon crossing – for their own operations. GAMSA lets UNCLOS' definitions speak of where Australia can be for the spatio-functional present and future.

In sum, through GAMSA's importation and re-description of UNCLOS' norms, agents embedded within institutions of state sovereignty are permitting a body of international law to tell Australia where and how the 'securers' of its borders can be nationally sovereign. As a further twist, the 'you may' of this letting and permitting evinces a highly selective and only partial respect for international law more generally: Australia's interdiction, transfer and indefinite offshore

82 Salter, Mark B., 'Theory of the/: The Suture and Critical Border Studies', *Geopolitics*, 17: 4, 2012, p. 742.

83 'United Nations Convention on the Law of the Sea (UNCLOS)', *www.un.org*. www.un.org/depts/los/convention_agreements/texts/unclos/unclos_e.pdf

detention of asylum seekers, all authorised by GAMSA's reading of its international responsibilities within this body of international law, has been conducted in open defiance of substantive, sustained criticisms made by agents of international humanitarian law[84] and maritime law (sections 6.3–6.6).

If a *nomos* is an 'observed unity' of order and orientation,[85] the *nomos* of Australian border security and national sovereignty is not optimally understood as an extraterritorial emanation from territorial sovereignty, the monopoly-securing violence of the territorial community (Weber) or a person of international law (Montevideo). Rather, the *nomos* of border security is read back for the future of the Commonwealth as a space of sovereign interest by the prior achievement of UNCLOS' functional international legal order of the seas.[86] In a document that contains no substantive discussion of territory,[87] GAMSA communicates an authoritative oceanic time, space and function set for national sovereignty.

Australia's maritime jurisdictions are then parsed out in GAMSA in alignment with the UNCLOS-agreed elements of the international legal order of the seas.[88] Consistent with these norms, the Australian Commonwealth only exercises *full* sovereignty over the territorial sea – to the limit of twelve nautical miles. In other maritime jurisdictions, Australia only exercises *partial* sovereignty, and only for certain purposes, such as fisheries and piracy – the latter of which will become highly significant in the following sections (sections 1.11–1.12). Yet: national sovereignty's effective formation through a border security capable of 'stopping the boats' relies on the decisionist prerogative, a *categorical assertion* of an absolute and supreme right of the authorised representatives of 'a people' to decide who can arrive and how. Only the authorised may enter and remain within the territory: Australian law recognises this by changing all 'nonlawful noncitizens' into unlawful noncitizens, which onshore rhetoric then re-codes as 'illegals' (section 2.6, 3.10). So when maritime interdiction takes place within or beyond a

84 Millar, Lisa, 'Australia's Asylum Seeker Policies Heavily Criticised at UN Human Rights Council Review', *abc.net.au*, November 10, 2015. www.abc.net.au/news/2015-11-10/australias-asylum-policies-heavily-criticised-at-united-nations/6926032

85 Schmitt, Carl, *The Nomos of the Earth in the International Law of the Jus Publicum Europaeum*, Telos Press, New York, 2006, pp. 42–50.

86 Derrida, Jacques, *The Beast and the Sovereign, Volume 2*, University of Chicago Press, Chicago, 2011, p. 51.

87 In GAMSA 'territory' only refers to the names of places under discussion (such as Northern Territory and Australian Antarctic Territory), and is referred to in delineating jurisdiction, such as through a description of a 'territorial sea baseline', or through the implied existence of coastal states and their entourage of claims and agents. There is as little focus on territory in GAMSA as there is discussion of the ocean and jurisdiction in Wendy Brown and Giorgio Agamben's theoretical discussions of sovereign walling and sovereign power: it is as if one world ends where the other begins, like the sky 'ending' at the horizon. Brown, Wendy, *Walled States, Waning Sovereignty*, Zone Books, New York, 2010 and Agamben, Giorgio, *Homo Sacer: Sovereign Power and Bare Life*, Stanford University Press, Stanford, 1998.

88 territorial sea baseline (TSB); internal waters; coastal waters; territorial sea; contiguous zone; exclusive economic zone (EEZ); continental shelf.

jurisdiction such as the Exclusive Economic Zone (EEZ), how does the partial sovereignty of Australia's international rights and responsibilities co-operate with the categorical sovereignty of Australia's threatened national border?

Beyond the EEZ there exist two further zones that GAMSA *unilaterally claims* Australian jurisdiction over. This last point is crucial: these are not international jurisdictions with normative heft arrived at through multilateral processes then imported into GAMSA from UNCLOS, like the EEZ and TSB. These are Australian distinctions made from within border security's world and projected offshore from onshore Australia. This gives us another precise sense in which border security is a unilateral projection of national sovereignty in global space (sections i.2–i.3).

The 'two' zones, the Australian Search and Rescue Region (SRR) and the Security Forces Authority Area (SFAA), are spatially co-extensive but functionally differentiated. GAMSA refers to the SRR as "that part of the world in which a nation has responsibility for the safety of life at sea . . . and for assistance to people in distress".[89] Like the TSB and EEZ, this is in line with Safety of Life at Sea (SOLAS) norms, relatively stable since the sinking of the Titanic in 1912, and codified in their current form between 1974–1980.[90]

GAMSA also emphasises that it "deals solely with *security* in Australia's maritime jurisdiction and does not address maritime *safety* issues, including the Safety of life at Sea (SOLAS) Convention".[91] Where maritime law is concerned, GAMSA creates its security field – the threat environment whose operationally necessary co-presence I am pinpointing throughout this book – by drawing a point of severance. In the absence of a national sovereignty observed as threatened by asylum seekers intending to cross the boundary and enter the territory, GAMSA's agents would have safety responsibilities. But security deals solely with security, not safety. How then can border security's agents deal safely with approaching security threats whose vessels are sinking, overloaded unseaworthy vessels carrying people who can't swim, and children without lifejackets (section I.7)? What happens when Maritime Border Command's threat objects start drowning? I return to consider this central dilemma raised by practicing sovereignty as border security in this chapter's conclusion. GAMSA's circular reasoning can only observe these points as fundamental contradictions. It does so only because they are essential for operations as security (authority over); it does so with no recognition that these political choices are existential for rescuees as safety (responsibility for). Who or what can suture this jurisdictional split by observing it sovereignly?

89 Commonwealth of Australia, 'Glossary', in *Guide to Australian Maritime Security Arrangements* (GAMSA), 2013, p. 163.

90 'International Convention for the Safety of Life at Sea (SOLAS), 1974, *www.imo.org*. www.imo.org/en/About/conventions/listofconventions/pages/international-convention-for-the-safety-of-life-at-sea-%28solas%29,-1974.aspx

91 'Legal and Administrative Aspects to Australia's Maritime Jurisdiction, Guide to Australian Maritime Security Arrangements' (GAMSA), 2013, Commonwealth of Australia, p. 4, italics in original. www.border.gov.au/AustralianBorderForce/Documents/GAMSA%202013.pdf

The concept of 'Security Forces Authority' Area (SFAA) was developed in International Maritime Organization (IMO) discussions in the early 2000s, and especially from 2005, informal talks and somewhat formal understandings organised and developed multilaterally to combat piracy, in the years when 'Somali pirates' became an object of international governmental worrying. One document where we can observe the concept of a Security Forces Area migrating into GAMSA is from IMO Circular 1073 of June 10th, 2003, which published directives for maritime rescue co-ordination centres dealing with 'acts of violence against ships', in a discursive context where these definitions were supposed to be applied to piracy. In this document, the IMO defines 'Security Forces Authority' and 'Security incident' as follows (and notice the direct importation of UNCLOS definitions):

> 'Security Forces Authority': For the purposes of this circular, and in accordance with the organization of and the decisions by the national Governments, the SFA (Security Forces Authority) is generally a national or regional command of a public agency such as the Navy, Coast Guard or Police in charge of providing the response to security incidents.
>
> 'Security incident'. SOLAS 1974. . . defines a security incident as 'any suspicious act or circumstance threatening the security of a ship, including a mobile offshore drilling unit and a high speed craft, or of a port facility or of any ship/port interface or any ship to ship activity'.[92]

The SFA concept appeared in Australian Commonwealth documents and PowerPoints by 2009.[93] The SFA*A* – the *area* of authority, the spatially extensive security field of this point on the border continuum – is a unilaterally projected functional security overlay nesting in the legitimacy of an internationally recognised area of safety and rescue responsibility. It is an oceanic Australian border security space generated by government-employed security experts taken from the context of combatting piracy. The key question, then turns on whether piracy is a threat *like* 'irregular maritime arrivals': the above IMO definition would observe them as distinct; GAMSA observes them as follows. GAMSA does not quote or reticulate UNCLOS 1974's definition of security incident: "any suspicious act or circumstance threatening the security of a ship . . . or of a port facility . . . or any ship to ship activity". GAMSA defines a security threat in the maritime domain as: "any action, device or event that has potential to cause consequences adverse to Australia's interests".[94]

92 International Maritime Organisation, 'Measures to Enhance Security Directives for Maritime Rescue Co-ordination Centres (MRCCS) on Acts of Violence against Ships (MSC/Circ.1073)', *www.imo.org*. www.un.org/en/sc/ctc/docs/bestpractices/1073.pdf, p. 2.

93 It appeared nowhere in the first 2006 edition of GAMSA, which was compiled when Joint Offshore Protection Command became Border Protection Command.

94 This definition will become central in chapter four (section 4.7–4.9). 'Introduction', in *Guide to Australian Maritime Security Arrangements (GAMSA)*, 2013, Commonwealth of Australia. www.border.gov.au/AustralianBorderForce/Documents/GAMSA%202013.pdf, p. 9.

In GAMSA, maritime boat arrivals appear as threat entities within the SFAA because piracy and boat arrivals are identified as threats – in GAMSA (note the circularity). The identification of piracy with boat arrivals generates a circuit of security reasoning that allows GAMSA to maintain maritime arrivals *as* matters for border security. The GAMSA-observed distinction of the SFAA maintains the border continuum as a space that can be imagined as sovereign within the nation and practiced as interdiction through security operations, beyond the territorial limit of law and responsibility for human life as population. But this, in turn, means that such security operations become necessary for the perpetuation of border security as a way of enacting national sovereignty.

For operational reasons, Australia's agents of interdiction are forced to assume GAMSA's (unilaterally expressed) position on national sovereignty in order to make border security's Australia-emanating distinctions authoritative, enabling the continuation of operations: otherwise interdictors would revert to being the frontline agents responsible for safely rescuing the very same people. For 'us', whether onshore in Australia or otherwise outside Australia's area of maritime interest, we can observe a disavowed politics in the decision to see vulnerable people seeking protection as threats like piracy, a threat that the IMO and UNCLOS would be unable to observe – because they use a different and more specific definition of threat.

In sum, then: the occluded politics of border security in GAMSA is predicated on disavowing the vulnerability of the entities it treats as threats, while the national sovereignty it defends is predicated on conflating pirates with asylum seekers. As the following concluding section pinpoints, this predication of national sovereignty continues to emerge at the very moment that operations switch from 'safety and rescue' to security.

I.11 Double visions of border security and their constitutive blindspot: bodies on and in the water, security and safety, and the life of the threat

In the final days of August 2001, *MV Tampa* (*Tampa*) hovered on the horizon of Australia, within the shores of its politics: its CI-visible hull buoying up what was still a floating, drifting question of politics, ethics and identity for all concerned.

Tampa's captain, Arne Rinnan, and his crew, were a node of global logistics conducting routine traffic between global locations (sections 4.2–4.3), en route to Singapore from Fremantle. They were interrupted when Surveillance Australia drew Captain Rinnan's attention to *Palapa* as a ship in distress (sections i.7–i.9). This interruption was unwelcome as very costly for Wilhelmsen Lines, but *Tampa* responded because of the absolute responsibility of the master to the safety of life at sea, the fundamental legal obligation of maritime law and a deeply held cultural norm of seafaring. If a ship is sinking, if people are in danger, you rescue them.

During the final days of August 2001, *Tampa*'s captain and crew were instructed by Wilhelmsen's lawyers to refer to those it rescued from *Palapa* and brought aboard *Tampa* as rescuees.[95] Within this situational definition, shared and upheld by the Norwegian government, those aboard were still:

- living people vulnerable to drowning;
- under a number of jurisdictions of international maritime law, and also;
- a group of asylum seekers who became rescuees when they were saved from drowning, a group to whom Captain Rinnan, and the governments of Norway, Indonesia and Australia, all owed a modicum of responsibility.

This was the situational definition that held between the rescue on Sunday August 26 until roughly 2pm on Tuesday August 28: 'rescuees' 'in limbo' generating a trilateral 'international relations situation' as the three nation-states involved attempted to shift or 'shirk responsibility' (section 2.9). None of the human agents involved – not even any of the key agents within the Howard government advocating a hardline stand – characterised the rescuees plucked from the foundering *Palapa* as security threats. By way of concluding this chapter's consideration of sovereignty, what I want to do by recalling this time-sensitive aspect of the Tampa Affair is show how the insertion of security into the matter of seeking asylum by boat transformed 'all of the above' into a matter of national security, generating the 'double vision' characteristic of national sovereignty enacted as border security, with authority over security threats as its focus, and responsibility for vulnerability as its 'blindness inherent'. With Luhmann and von Foerster as my theoretical and epistemological guides (section I.1), I regard this blindspot as constitutive: the negation of vulnerability is the 'invisible condition of seeing' threats. As Luhmann puts it, here following Michel Serres' phrasing,

> [T]he observer is the nonobservable. The distinction he uses to indicate the one side or the other serves as the invisible condition of seeing, as blind spot. And this can be said for all observation, whether the operation be psychic or social, whether it be carried out as actual process of consciousness or as communication.[96]

This constitutive blindspot of border security has upheld interdiction operations as sovereignly necessary from the precise moment this distinction was observed. Upholding it commits this practice of sovereignty to a conflation of vulnerable people with threats as a way of exercising 'sovereign authority over' without 'taking political and ethical responsibility for' that therefore exists for the

95 Marr, David and Wilkinson, Marian, *Dark Victory*, Allen and Unwin, Melbourne, 2004, pp. 76–77.

96 Luhmann, Niklas, *Theory of Society, Volume 1*, Stanford University Press, Stanford, 2012, p. 35.

time in which agents of border security's world rely on making this distinction. We can pin this down by continuing to follow the time-sensitive aspects of the Tampa Affair just introduced, then comparing them with the contrasting ways in which people were observed during the rescue of *SIEV 4* by *HMAS Adelaide*, in October 2001.

Before Captain Rinnan radioed his intention to sail *Tampa* toward CI at 11.39am on Wednesday 29 August, 2001, the situation was still ambiguous onshore among the responsible agents of three nation-states: Indonesia, Norway and Australia. Three days earlier, on the first day of the rescue, when Captain Rinnan transformed 'asylum seekers aboard *Palapa*' into 'rescuees aboard *Tampa*', hijacking was offered as a plausible explanation that moved around onshore Australia. Between 6pm and 7.30pm on Sunday August 26, "Canberra believed the *Tampa* might have been hijacked".[97] If the rescuees had wrested control of the ship, or if they had *forced* Rinnan to sail *Tampa* to CI, this would be an act akin to 'violence at sea', or even piracy, which would make *Tampa* a security matter to which the Commonwealth could respond with decisive force. This also fits with the following anecdote, which should be read closely against the above discussion of piracy and the IMO.

Two months before the Tampa Affair, in a discussion with the Indonesian Embassy's People Smuggling Group, Phillip Ruddock began quizzing Leigh Dixon of the Australian Federal Police about pirates. On Dixon's recollection, Ruddock asked all those in the room why it was that "boat loads of asylum seekers who often carried money and jewellery (were) not attacked by pirates active in waters around the archipelago".[98] In the same meeting, Ruddock also allegedly asked those in attendance to consider sabotaging vessels carrying asylum seekers: "could we interfere with the boats?" Ruddock allegedly asked.[99]

Perhaps Ruddock *was* joking; but this also indicates that, even jokingly, the spectre of 'violence' and 'manipulation' would have solved the problem of humanity posed by boat arrivals toward the responsible agents of nation-states, by enabling them to be re-cast as hostile villains and security threats, like pirates, or criminals (sections 3.9–3.10). Nonetheless, to presage the following chapter's focus, it was only the wake of the Tampa Affair, through the contingencies imposed as law by Prime Minister Howard's response – the way it resonated with the Australian electorate, *then* 9/11, *then* border security as instituted policy and culture – that *made* seeking asylum by boat the security matter that it was

97 Marr, David and Wilkinson, Marian, *Dark Victory*, Allen and Unwin, Melbourne, 2004, p. 28.

98 Marr, David and Wilkinson, Marian, *Dark Victory*, Allen and Unwin, Melbourne, 2004, p. 42. Following the clue left by Marr and Wilkinson, Mr Ruddock was making reference to the following article. 'Dangerous Waters: Regional Efforts to Combat Piracy Are Taking Shape', *The Economist*, July 19, 2001. www.economist.com/node/702508

99 Marr, David and Wilkinson, Marian, *Dark Victory*, Allen and Unwin, 2004, p. 43 and Wilkinson, Marian, 'Ruddock Discussed Piracy During Boat People Crisis', *Sydney Morning Herald*, March 8, 2003. www.smh.com.au/articles/2003/03/07/1046826532276.html

not beforehand, nor during the crisis itself. As we leave those aboard *Tampa* for a while, we need to be very clear: they were still vulnerable people who could drown and a group of rescuees, they were not security threats – and Tampa was not yet observed as a decisive matter of Australia's national sovereignty.

With the institution of *Operation Relex I*[100] on September 3, 2001, for the very first time, asylum seekers travelling toward CI from Java were explicitly approached on a security footing: because their ability to reach the territory without a visa would be in violation of the decisionist prerogative, and because of the universal visa system (section I.9). Noncitizens without visas are unlawful noncitizens; unlawful noncitizens seeking to approach the territory are security threats.

Suspected Unlawful Non Citizens (SUNCs) and Suspected Illegal Entry Vehicles (SIEVs) date from this time as the category of person and vessel co-produced by the prerogative and the universal visa system. Their typification through a sequenced set of like cases from that day forth – 'another operation, another SIEV, another boatload of SUNCs' – meant that asylum seekers' attempts to enter Australia's area of maritime interest generated a condensation point through which each SIEV became part of a sequence and set,[101] a horizon of operations in which those security threats, SUNCs, just kept floating in to Australia's area of maritime interest.

From September 1, 2001 with the arrival of SIEV 1, SUNCs approaching Australia aboard SIEVs were interdicted as threats to Australia's national sovereignty (GAMSA would emerge later, in 2008, with the definition of threat encountered above). For the first time, *Operation Relex I* used military assets to achieve deterrence, finally bringing to bear an on-water operational reality imagined aloud by then opposition leader Gough Whitlam in 1977 (section 2.5). Relex' strategic aim was 'to deter and to deny':[102] "to *prevent* . . . the incursion of unauthorised vessels into Australian waters such that, ultimately, people smugglers and asylum seekers would be *deterred* from attempting to use Australia as a destination".[103] As explored in Chapter 3 (sections 3.6–3.10), the 80s US Caribbean lineages of this maritime deterrence strategy are strong and clear, and were highly successful in preventing Cuban and especially Haitian people from seeking asylum by sea. The Commonwealth's 00s innovation was to use the Navy, not the Coast Guard, to cast this task as a militarised matter of national sovereignty, and to do so as

100 Wilkinson, Marian, 'Secret file: Operation Relex', *Sydney Morning Herald*, October 28, 2002. www.smh.com.au/articles/2002/10/27/1035683303429.html

101 Luhmann, Niklas, *Theory of Society, Volume 1*, Stanford University Press, Stanford, 2012, p. 38.

102 Whitmont, Debbie, 'To Deter and Deny: The Inside Story of Operation Relex – The Defence Forces' Mission to Stop Asylum-Seekers Reaching Australian Shores,' *4 Corners*, April 15, 2002. www.abc.net.au/4corners/archives/2002a_Monday15April2002.htm

103 'A Certain Maritime Incident', Commonwealth of Australia, October 23, 2002, pp. 13–14, italics in original. www.aph.gov.au/Parliamentary_Business/Committees/Senate/Former_Committees/maritimeincident/report/index

'*the* border' was made into a thing rightly protected through interdiction (sections 3.12. 4.6).

During the first days of *Operation Relex I*, deterrence began with a literal warning, read out on water using a megaphone. Here we can read another societally legible instance of national sovereignty speaking which can be read alongside the pull quotes that appeared earlier (sections 1.2–1.4):

> to the master and crew. The Australian government is determined to stop illegal migration to its territory. You should now consider immediately returning to Indonesia, and not enter Australia.[104]

On water, this 'megaphone diplomacy' generated confusion. "Between 6.13pm on 6 October and 4.32am on 7 October, five DIMA warning notices were issued, some several times, in both written and spoken form, and in English, Bahasa and Arabic".[105] This allows us to glance at how this unilateral projection of national sovereignty did not regard how it might be regarded, or that the Navy's interpretation of its task of voicing sovereign authority was initially given in too strident and too literal a way: a huge grey ship, a smaller, swift moving grey inflatable boat, a group of uniformed officers, one of them yelling things through a trumpet-like device.

When *HMAS Adelaide* (*Adelaide*) approached SIEV 4 on the evening of October 6, 2001 – a day before the bombardment of Afghanistan begun with Operation Enduring Freedom – matters proceeded according to the post-Tampa situational definition of 'deter and deny'. On the one hand, *Adelaide's* crew – in international waters at the time – were to deter those aboard SIEV 4 from entering Australian waters:

> If the vessel did gain entry to Australia's contiguous zone, a boarding party was to detain the SIEV, sail it to the outer edge of the zone and release *it if it were safe to do so.* If the vessel re-entered the contiguous zone, then a boarding party was to detain the SIEV, its passengers and crew, pending further direction from government. 'At no stage', however, 'were unauthorised arrivals to have access to the Australian migration zone.'[106]

104 'Inquest into the Death of Mohammed Hassan Ayubi, Muzafar Ali Sefarali, Mohammed Amen Zamen, Awar Nadar, Baquer Husani, (SIEV 36 Inquest)', *Darwin Coroner's Court*, 2010, p. 19. www.defence.gov.au/siev36/pdf/findings%20-%20SIEV%2036%20inquest.pdf

105 'A Certain Maritime Incident', Commonwealth of Australia, October 23, 2002, p. 32. www.aph.gov.au/Parliamentary_Business/Committees/Senate/Former_Committees/maritimeincident/report/index

106 'A Certain Maritime Incident', Commonwealth of Australia, October 23, 2002, p. 32, italics mine. www.aph.gov.au/Parliamentary_Business/Committees/Senate/Former_Committees/maritimeincident/report/index

However, in spite of repeated warnings, those aboard continued to sail toward CI. By 2.30am on October 7, 2001, SIEV 4 had entered the contiguous zone.

Throughout the morning of October 7, *Adelaide* upped the ante in their attempts to fulfill their mission objective: at 3.59am, Commander Banks ordered warning shots to be fired, and crew aboard *Adelaide* continued issuing verbal warnings via megaphone. At 4.30am, crew conducted an "assault type non-compliant boarding . . . whilst the vessel was still under way",[107] and by 4.45am, the boarding party had taken control and were steering the vessel back toward Indonesia.

Just after first light after 5am a number of man overboards were reported; a total of fourteen jumped into the water. After the Navy recovered these people from the water, Commander Banks ordered a second boarding party, which recovered control of the boat, steering it north towards Java once again. At 10.29am on October 7, *Adelaide*'s crew had re-placed everyone aboard, and "the boarding party were extracted . . . as the SIEV exited out of Australian jurisdiction 24 miles from Christmas Island".[108] By this time, the weather was deteriorating, and while the boarding party had been aboard, numerous attempts had been made to sabotage the boat.

Just after midday, at 12.19pm on October 7, 2001, SIEV 4 was observed dead in the water, with what appeared to be a white flag hoisted. Once on board again, the boarding party discovered evidence of deliberate sabotage: water in the fuel, a damaged starter motor. This meant that SIEV 4 was now a vessel in distress. After consulting with his superior onshore, *Adelaide*'s Commanding Officer decided to tow SIEV 4 – to CI.

After about a day's worth of towing, SIEV 4 began to sink. At 4.30pm on Monday October 8, 2001, the boarding party from "the *Adelaide* commenced serving the evening meal on the SIEV, but just before 5.00pm and 'largely without warning' it began to sink rapidly. . . . At 5.08pm, passengers from the SIEV began entering the water as its bow went under, and the first of the *Adelaide*'s life rafts was launched".[109]

This is where we grasp the difference that really makes a difference with the interposition of border security between asylum seekers and rescuers, and by extension the selective vision and inherent blindness of this practice of national sovereignty. Two and a half hours before the bow went under, Commander Banks had refused to disembark the women and children aboard SIEV 4, when requested by a boarding officer. On record, Commander Banks testified that "if I disembarked some to the *Adelaide* I would have failed in my mission aim and

107 'A Certain Maritime Incident', Commonwealth of Australia, October 23, 2002, p. 33. www.aph.gov.au/Parliamentary_Business/Committees/Senate/Former_Committees/maritimeincident/report/index

108 Op.cit., p. 35.

109 Op.cit., p. 36.

I might as well have embarked all of them. In my judgment we still had a boat that was still marginally seaworthy and I still had control of the situation".[110]

- On the one hand, Commander Banks had been given safety instructions proper to vulnerable people in a dangerous situation: 'no loss of life or injury'. As master, Banks had *responsibility for* safety of life at sea.
- On the other, his mission aim was to 'deter and deny' security threats their objective of crossing the border and reaching CI. As part of *Operation Relex I*, Banks had *authority over* asylum seekers as SUNCs.

For this combination of reasons, those aboard *Adelaide* were subjected to a *mise en scène* that, to any seafarer outside border security's world, such as Arne Rinnan and the crew of the *Tampa* weeks earlier, would have seemed a dangerous absurdity. *Adelaide*'s crew spent the afternoon observing the Commonwealth's security threat sink. And then, at 5.08pm, the precise moment that "passengers from the SIEV began entering the water as its bow went under . . . the first of the *Adelaide*'s life rafts was launched".[111]

1.12 Bodies on the water, bodies in the water: global space, vulnerable people, threat objects, national sovereignty, SUNCs aboard SIEVs

In the introductory chapter I presented Border Force's border continuum (section I.12) and descriptively analysed how border security emerged as a decisive response to a world understood as a complex, risky *threat* environment (sections i.2–3, i.9). Entities approaching from global space rush at the border, approaching it in a way that – without necessary and urgent responses that secure – would be overwhelming. To bring us full circle, this anxious apprehension of the threat environment sets in motion the urgent, decisive response framing tensioning the interposition of sovereignty as the voiced refusal of arrival: *we* will decide – no – *you* cannot arrive. As Howard hoarsely insisted the night of Wednesday, 29, at the end of the long day of his SAS-secured victory over the *Tampa* rescuees: "that boat will never land in our waters – never".[112] With this and this chapter's other sovereign voicings ringing in our ears, I further develop the co-implication of border security and global space, as follows.

Border security relies on a conception of global space as a threat environment with a store of threats who keep appearing and are capable of crossing and entering *the nation*: this produces the nation as that which must be secured,

110 Op.cit., p. 37.

111 Op.cit., p. 36.

112 Charlton, Peter, '*Tampa*: The Triumph of Politics', in Solomon, David (ed.), *Howard's Race: Winning the Unwinnable Election*, Harper Collins, Sydney, 2002, p. 95.

and practices of border security actualise this as a way of restoring sovereignty, 'protecting *the* border', and achieving the policy aims of deterrence and control. This requires some kind of 'threatened nation' as the side of the severance that can *and must* be secured because it is threatened, or which is threatened, *because* it was marked as a boundary,[113] *because* it can be crossed. Without the border as a boundary and a thing rightly protected, no one could 'cross', let alone would crossing be societally legible as a 'crossing and entering' the Commonwealth could determine as 'illegal migration to its territory' it had to stop – or cease being sovereign. A 'global citizen' would only see people moving around a world interior (*weltinnenraum*) (section 4.3), domestic transfers within the utopia of a hypothetical planetary Schengen.[114]

Where global space is the maritime context as unmarked background,[115] I've explored how only an intrasystemically observed threat is capable of transforming the Search and Rescue Zone into the urgent foreground as a border-as-threat-environment: only when Maritime Border Command observe threats do screen-able, interdict-able, movable objects emerge for its agents. Having been observed and interdicted, these threat objects have a number of onshore political functions. They can be removed as technical, operational matters – security – without having to be approached, engaged, listened to, welcomed or paid off.[116] They can be detained, and deterrence can be inflicted on them, both as punishment for them, and as a warning for those who would seek to come. GAMSA says to its agents: wherever there is a threat, our security work is necessary; wherever the border is threatened, border security is necessary.

Sovereignties emanating from earlier European society attached to the living persons of people occupying thrones or offices[117] (sections 1.4, 1.8). Border security attaches itself to living noncitizen persons to the extent that they *are* threats within its environment of operations, by being aboard boats approaching the territory of Australia. Border security relies upon a reified ontology of threats that are operationalised by observing entities moving through a space that, in turn, *is* a threat environment. This reified ontology only exists intrasystemically,[118] though it projects its distinctions out into the open ocean, in the above instance literally by megaphone. Entities that may or may not exist outside this environment do not exist to it as its concerns: flying fish may leap from the waves in the

113 Nevins, Joseph, "'Remote Places at the Heart of Empire', *Political Geography*, 30, 2011, p. 351.
114 Sloterdijk, Peter, *In the World Interior of Capital*, Polity Press, Cambridge, 2013 and Balibar, Étienne, 'World Borders, Political Borders', in *We, the People of Europe? Reflections on Transnational Citizenship*, Princeton University Press, Princeton, 2004, pp. 101–115.
115 Luhmann, Niklas, 'The Paradoxy of Observing Systems', *Cultural Critique*, 31, 1995, p. 39.
116 Gartrell, Adam, 'Tony Abbott Comes Close to Admitting People Smuggler Payments', *The Sydney Morning Herald*, June 20, 2015. www.smh.com.au/federal-politics/political-news/tony-abbott-comes-close-to-admitting-people-smuggler-payments-20150620-ght1kl.html
117 Dorsett, Shaunagh and McVeigh, Shaun, *Jurisdiction*, Routledge, Abingdon, 2012.
118 Luhmann, Niklas, *Theory of Society, Volume 1*, Stanford University Press, Stanford, 2012, p. 116.

area of maritime interest, but though they may provoke wonder among some of Maritime Border Command's officers on the high seas, their entry into Australian waters cannot prompt interdiction.

Maritime border security relies on the presence of *human* threats seeking protection from other countries to give itself the ability to exercise sovereign authority over vast maritime spaces that are otherwise not fully sovereign. At the heart of border security's maritime operations in Australia is a conception of threat broad enough to encompass both the ocean and what we might describe as 'human survival activities' now being undertaken by some of the planet's most disadvantaged and vulnerable people. Asylum seekers are people fleeing war, persecution, terror, poverty and the destruction of homes and supporting ecologies – yet operations cannot observe these distinctions. In the first decade of the twenty-first century, in a post 9/11 cultural moment, the Australian Commonwealth constructed a self-serving equivalence, observing these attempts at escape and asylum seeking as 'the same thing' as piracy and violence at sea. The threatened sovereign nation observed this alone; for the IMO, pirates are threats because they are 'violent *toward* ships', not because they are 'vulnerable *aboard* boats'.

Any security threat, any 'action, device or event that has potential to cause consequences adverse to Australia's interests' can trigger a border security response – *but only certain actions, devices and events do.* This point will become pivotal in our fourth chapter on global logistics (sections 4.8–4.9). For current purposes, the following final point is key. Asylum seekers themselves as bodies alone – whether as individuals or as whole populations –[119] are not 'actions, devices or events', except insofar as they are aboard vessels seeking to arrive, voyages whose grave hazards they are only risking because they are seeking protection.

'Threats aboard vessels' allows us to pinpoint the fundamental distinction between security and safety that animates sovereign Australia's maritime practice of border security: bodies *on* the water, bodies *in* the water. It's the water, the ocean upon whose surface this drama unfolds, that is the key element enabling and disabling border security's world. Insofar as there are bodies *on* the water, the ocean, for border security's agents, remains as Mark B Salter remarks: "emptiness, terra nullius, the desert, the sea, or outer-space".[120] But as soon as people are *in* the water, their potential to cause 'adverse consequences' is doused. Bodies in the water resume being humans in grave danger of drowning because of what the open ocean is for humans, transforming security threats into SOLAS matters that border security's agents must then attend to as a life-and-death responsibility to which they have a duty of care.

119 Vaughan-Williams, Nick, *Border Politics: The Limits of Sovereign Power*, Edinburgh University Press, Edinburgh, 2009, p. 7 and Lemke, Thomas, *Biopolitics: An Advanced Introduction*, NYU Press, New York, 2011.

120 Salter, Mark B., 'Theory of the/: The Suture and Critical Border Studies', *Geopolitics*, 17: 4, 2012, p. 742.

People can no more breathe water than chlorine gas: the disavowed materiality of the ocean, and its existential meaning for us as vulnerable humans who can so easily drown, provides the stage for the central paradox of national sovereignty when it is enacted through on-water operations. This is a paradox which remains implicit in the Commonwealth's onshore observations of offshore operations, but it is a paradox viscerally lived by asylum seekers in the water. This points us to a peculiarity of boat arrivals within border security's world: they are threat objects who under no circumstances must be eliminated.[121] Where vulnerable people seeking protection are threat objects who must be interdicted, security operations inflate around 'the life of the threat'. When life is threatened, the living are no longer a threat; the moment they resume their journey toward protection, they become threats once more.

121 Chambers, Peter, 'The Embrace of Border Security: Maritime Jurisdiction, National Sovereignty, and the Geopolitics of Operation Sovereign Borders', *Geopolitics*, 20, 2015, p. 22.

Chapter 2

"We will decide who comes here"

Sending the message of border security

2.1 Introduction: "Something that would resonate politically to the message of border security"

Border security is a unilateral projection of sovereignty publicly represented as a communicated message. One of the most senior enforcement agents involved in the Tampa Affair recalls his involvement in this key point of border security's Australian emergence as being *about* 'sending the message'.

> I can't help but feel that the Prime Minister, John Howard, viewed the SAS[1] as something that would resonate politically to the message of border security. You can't amp it up more in the public's mind than saying 'we're gonna send in the SAS, we'll show you how tough we are on border security'.[2]

By and large, news media have reticulated and disseminated this practiced understanding of 'the message of border security', our focus in this chapter.

Since the national problematisation of boat arrivals in Australia in 1999, state-led efforts – as policy, rhetoric and opinion – have continued to assert that 'we must send a message'. That is: the message of border security has remained broadly consistent since its Australian emergence, but its addresses and addressees in society[3] have shifted markedly. Around the turn of the century, the message was addressed to asylum seekers as 'people who come here illegally in defiance of the laws and queue jump on others who patiently wait their turn'.[4] Variants of this comment were made to talk back radio audiences comprised of Prime Minister Howard's 'rusted on' ideological and electoral base, and concretised an executive thematisation of 'queuejumpers' and 'illegals' that took place over the

1 Charlton, Peter, 'Tampa: The Triumph of Politics', in Solomon, David (ed.), *Howard's Race: Winning the Unwinnable Election*, Harper Collins, Sydney, 2002, p. 94.

2 Raschella, Adrian, 'Former SAS Commander Breaks Silence on Tampa', abc.net.au, updated July 8, 2013. www.abc.net.au/news/2011-07-07/former-sas-commander-breaks-silence-on-tampa/2785164

3 Luhmann, Niklas, 'What is Communication?' *Communication Theory*, 2: 3, 1992, pp. 215–259.

4 Prime Minister Howard, paraphrased in the documentary *Leaky Boat*. www.abc.net.au/tv/programs/leakyboat.htm

course of years, which I will give significant attention to (section 2.6). Notably however, the above comment makes no mention that people smuggling was *made* an offence in Australia by the Howard government in 1999,[5] not coincidentally three years or so after the Howard government began shifting to a deterrence-led response to asylum seeking by boat.

A decade after the Howard government's focus on sending a message to 'illegals', in a 2010 speech given to an Australian think tank, made less than two weeks after taking office as Prime Minister, Julia Gillard re-directed the message of border security to people smugglers, descrying smuggling as "an evil trade to be punished".[6] In 2013, while campaigning on a border security platform that excoriated the Gillard government's 'failure' to achieve border security by stopping the boats, the Coalition returned to border security's late 2001-era grounding in the nation's sovereignty, re-activating Howard's decisionist prerogative as "a statement of national sovereignty and the need for Australia to control our borders",[7] while using it alongside 'stop the boats' and the threat of moral responsibility for mass drownings – as a way of beating their electoral opponent.

On September 18, 2016, Prime Minister Malcolm Turnbull addressed Australian border security to the leaders of Europe and the United Nations, describing it as the world's best border security policy *and* the lynchpin of mutual respect and successful multiculturalism: "[u]ncontrolled migration flows start to destabilise countries and undermine support for migration, undermine support for multiculturalism, undermine the mutual respect which is the foundation of a successful multicultural society like ours".[8]

As we begin tracking the message of border security, we should note a political consistency among these shifting addresses: all of these speech acts speak to the necessity of border security, and all of them involve their audiences in this 'necessity'. In varying ways they are about sending the message of border security, which includes the idea that border security is *about* sending the message.

2.2 'Sending the message' of border security: a theory of communication *and* a theory of border security as communication

'Sending the message' of border security enacts a theory of communication; it also expresses the theory that border security is – or is about – communication.

5 Section 233A of the *Migration Act (1958)*. www.austlii.edu.au/au/legis/cth/consol_act/ma1958118/s233a.html

6 Gillard, Julia, 'Moving Australia Forward', *PM Transcripts, Commonwealth of Australia*, July 6, 2010. https://pmtranscripts.pmc.gov.au/release/transcript-17435

7 'The Coalition's Operation Sovereign Borders Policy', Liberal Party of Australia, 2013, p. 4. sievx.com/articles/OSB/201307xxTheCoalitionsOSBPolicy.pdf

8 Colgan, Paul, 'Malcolm Turnbull Talks Up Australia's Border Protection as "The Best in the World" Ahead of UN Talks', *Business Insider Australia*, September 18, 2016. www.businessinsider.com.au/malcolm-turnbull-talks-up-australias-border-protection-as-the-best-in-the-world-ahead-of-un-talks-2016–9

These societal aspects of border security form the observational basis of what follows, which I begin with a two-step enquiry into the 'sending a message' theory of communication. Readers not directly interested in these foregrounded theoretical concerns may wish to skip this and the next section and resume reading from section 2.4.

In border security's world, communication is conceptualised as the transmission of an object or package given to an addressee. With the help of one moment from Luhmann's theory of communication, we can see that this is "an understanding of communication in terms of action", and as such that it "views the process of communication as a successful or unsuccessful transmission of messages, information, or understanding expectations".[9] The action-based theory of communication has theoretical support from Habermas' influential critical theory,[10] and on the level of common sense it seems a simple, effective and necessary thing that the entities with whom 'we are communicating' 'get it' when we 'try to say something about something'. In the context of border security, this also speaks to how careful phrasing of the message at specific moments of address sought or achieved societal resonance, as on the public occasions mentioned above (section 2.1).

If communication is about 'sending a message', then sending the message of border security is about a process, a known delivery and a subsequent governing effect:

1 the transmission of messages,
2 the knowledge that they've reached their destination,
3 and a shift in the conduct of the addressee's conduct in accordance with the intentions or wishes of the transmitter.

This means that Australian border security *is* communication as transmission process, and the knowledge that – after transmission took place – a sovereignty-restoring power-effect was generated. 'Border security: we get it, it works, we are changing our behaviour in response'. We can accept this as sufficient if we wish, in line with the epistemological commitments described by Border Force in its description of the border continuum and the framework of movement (section I.2). That is to say, if 'sending the message' is how communication is understood by those observing systems practicing it as Australian border security, this is how we should understand border security as communication in Australia. But if we follow Luhmann and switch to a second level of observation where we

9 Luhmann, Niklas, 'What is Communication?' *Communication Theory*, 2: 3, 1992, p. 254.
10 Habermas, Jürgen, *Theory of Communicative Action Vol. 1: Reason and the Rationalization of Society*, and *The Theory of Communicative Action Vol. 2: Lifeworld and System: A Critique of Functional Reason*, Beacon Press, Boston, 1992.

take the immanent distinctions of the 'sending the message' theory and note the distinctions they indicate *in* their own web of reference, as we will shortly (section 2.3), matters are not so simple.

On closer examination, 'transmission and delivery' is something of a matryoshka doll. The process of transmission also contains the message of communication 'inside *the* communication', but only when it's sent in a way that 'we know' that it arrived. Where the package contains 'the message', sending it effectively conveys that the proper recipients 'get' border security when it's 'given to them'.[11] But this implies both that 'they' are capable of receiving it and that they reliably do so, because otherwise sending the message isn't routinely meaningful, like a message in a bottle thrown daily to the fish of the sea, or heartfelt prayers petitioning a non-existent God for divine intervention. *Somehow* – a big somehow to which we will give analytic attention – 'sending the message' means that, as communication, border security shifts shape in and through communication, instantiating itself as transmission, subject, object, package, message, receipt, process *and knowledge of this putative totality as effective*. No mean feat.

Glancing at the examples in the introductory section where border security was addressed to 'illegals' and 'evil people smugglers', 'sending the message' is expressed in a way that suggests that border security reaches its proper addressees on the outer side of the national boundary:

- 'people who come here illegally'
- 'evil people smugglers'

This border-crossing communication that 'makes it all the way there, overseas', in turn, expresses a belief that transnational audiences have an address or location they can be reached at, and that they can *and do* receive their 'border security' when it's sent their way. It also presumes that the putative interlocutors have heard tell of Australian legislation and moral value judgments – but what if asylum seekers haven't read the Migration Act, what if people smugglers are not really evil villains but rather amoral informal travel agents trying to make a buck in a market generated by the Commonwealth's unwillingness to let asylum seekers get on planes (sections i.8–i.9)? Recalling a key claim in the introduction, we have to think carefully about what it means that there's a demand for unsafe boat travel in the age of mass jet transit.

Australian border security's metaphorics are packaged up via a spectrum of modern technical practices common to the postal service, aerial bombardment

11 Feldman, Allen, 'Hardmen, Gunmen, Butchers, Doctors, Stiffs, and Ghosts', in *Formations of Violence: The Narrative of the Body and Political Terror in Northern Ireland*, University of Chicago Press, Chicago, 1991, p. 69.

and the Internet. As package, payload or packet, these presuppositions are complicated, and all refer to one another as part of a cultural understanding and causo-contextual regress in which border security has already been taking place; yet they're almost never explicitly referred to. Like instructions shipped with a product, 'sending a message' supposes its way into the packages it sends, with the knowledge of what to do with it tucked away in the packaging.

The addressees of Australia's border security communications were and are also referents *made* – in and through communication. And further: illegals and evil people smugglers are socially constructed categories of person and group agents whose message-receiving existences were communicated to a second set of audiences, all of whom were attending events with conjuncturally specific communicative purposes in the introductory section. This second set of audiences consisted in variously interested publics with differing degrees of cultural understanding, people who knew what was being talked about, what it meant, and why it was of political importance. These interested publics were *there*, with varying degrees of physicality, investment and attention, 'receiving the giving of the message'. These include(d) but aren't limited to:

- talkback radio hosts and their audiences;
- thinktank audiences and their entourage of interests and supporters;
- journalists, experts, pundits, op-ed writers;
- voters responsive to the sovereign prerogative;
- critical observers – including here – retrieving, analysing and conveying re-described understandings of these traces from cultural memory.

Notably, unlike 'illegals' and 'evil people smugglers', these sets of audiences are assumed to be on the inner side of national boundaries, or they can 'enter' into 'Australia' as a topic without the relevant authorisation and travel arrangements that a physical arrival is required to have in order to arrive and remain 'in the country' lawfully (section I.9). Without this second set of audiences, necessarily present yet habitually unindicated when sending the message happens, each of the above 'messages' of border security would have passed unwitnessed, unrecorded, unremembered, the scuttled hull of a smuggler's boat falling to the sea floor of the Sunda Trench.

Taken as individuals and groups, this second set of audiences comprises the densest web of Australian border security's most invested publics. These are publics with definite addresses within the nation, people in the know and in the border continuum. As most are voters, they can also be push polled by Gallup, Morgan, Galaxy and Newspoll, letterboxed by Labor and Liberal, and swayed by the persuasive force speech acts and the 'forceless force' of better policy proposals.[12]

12 Habermas, Jürgen, *Legitimation Crisis*, Beacon Press, Boston, 1975, p. 108.

These publics invested in border security can be activated into believing that border security is effective based on the knowledge that 'the message has been sent', just as they can be physically united as a nation through the representative materiality of enforcement operations.[13]

This dense web of invested publics is crucial for border security's societal integration, including the integration of the idea that 'border security is sending the message'. Without some admixture of these audiences attending to border security's severances in society, 'the message of border security' would never 'arrive' at its intended offshore addresses, regardless of the presence or absence of a technical infrastructure capable of delivering it. Enfolded within the secured nation whose spaces they circulate within, the above publics can all be observed as nodal points along the border continuum, their smoothed mobility and convinced subjectivity – or just their vote or the prevention of their cynical disaffection – as important for the legitimacy of operations as the disruption of people smugglers in Java, the interdiction of asylum seekers in the Indian Ocean and the design and servicing of enforcement assets' engines that prevents breakdowns during rescues in turbid water full of debris. Yet this dense network of invested publics, the people most interested in the sending and successful delivery of the message of border security are not listed as one of Border Force's dot points (section I.2): they are not formal parts of the framework of movement, though they are within the border continuum as threats from global space who must be impeded, detained and removed to secure circulation (section I.11). Alongside working through an understanding of border security as communication, a further purpose of this chapter is to consider the Australian emergence of this second set of putatively onshore and habitually unindicated audiences as receptive publics 'shoring up' border security's integration in society.

2.3 Observing Border Force sending 'the message': re-thinking the 'sending the message' theory with Luhmann's assumptions

In order to better observe these publics for the message of border security, in this section I accept Luhmann's invitation to emphasise communication's emergence.[14] Along these lines, communication is an improbable, social, recursive process where nothing is transmitted, but where "communication creates a memory that can be called on by many persons in quite different ways," so that "the system pulsates . . . with a constant creation of overflow and selection".[15] Observed in this way, border security is neither a dead letter nor something done

13 See: Chambers, Peter, 'The Embrace of Border Security', *Geopolitics*, 20: 2, 2015, pp. 20–21.

14 Luhmann, Niklas, 'What is Communication?' *Communication Theory*, 2: 3, 1992, p. 254.

15 Op.cit., p. 254 and Luhmann, Niklas, *Theory of Society 1*, Stanford University Press, Stanford, 2012, pp. 251–358.

upon receipt of delivery. As emergent communication, border security is a social process that lives in charged and nuanced language triggered by selective activations of cultural memory understood as meaningful. Over time, as its meanings stabilise and the severances of border security's world are taken as integral to Australia, border security is remaking Australia, just as 'Australia' is remaking its shores of politics and horizons of justice for border security.

As something that becomes understood *in* communication perpetuated *through* communication, border security is a unilateral projection of national sovereignty that only continues to exist to the extent that it's continually woven back in to the political life of 'the people'. 'Nations of border security' continue to live on the secured side of the boundary: by experiencing the border continuum as meaningful; by knowing their identity is secured through its operations. Border security's 'postal workers', 'bombardiers', 'servers' and 'clients' may understand their work as 'sending of the message', but if we follow Luhmann and observe this work, 'active with action',[16] as

1 something improbable that emerged as and in communication,
2 punctuated by understanding as a condition of connection with further communication, with every selection, plucked from the overflow, as the basis for the next,

then 'the message of border security' is never a mere duplication, nor is it just the delivery of a finished product, nor a commodity exchange that could be completed when transferred, 'signed, sealed, delivered'. As communication that continually adds to cultural memory wherever it is meaningful, that drags society into the currents of its selection and overflow wherever it is pursued or followed, border security is an iterative social process whose selections don't just cause transnational smuggler audiences to 'get the drift' about – for example – how evil they really are and why they're being punished. *A society of border security lives in the drift of border security's meaning as its agents trawl the seas for threats.* As these meanings constrain possibilities that shape the conditions of action, they move the shores of politics and constrain horizons of justice. This also means they are important systemic aspects of power in transformation.

As a theory of communication and a theory of border security as communication, the 'sending the message' theory maps on to my interpretation of Luhmann's systems theoretical assumptions in the following ways.

Border Force's communication strategy enacts the 'message sending' theory of communication, transforming Border Force's agents into 'deliverants' sending the package to its rightful recipients. On this level, actions *are* attributed to

16 Pottage, Alain, 'Power as an Art of Contingency: Luhmann, Deleuze, Foucault', *Economy and Society*, 27: 1, 1998, p. 23.

individuals, and this produces what we might describe as 'subjectivating objectivations' as key political effects, as in the ways explored by Foucault in his later work.[17]

To observe this as an emergent social process punctuated by understanding: as all involved go about 'sending the message' and get invested in their work of enacting border security, *their message changes the reality it describes.*[18] This is also their reality *in* the world of border security, just as it is 'the world in becoming' *of* border security, which, as an observing system that exists socially, perpetuated by operations whose medium is meaning, is something that continues – exists? –[19] beyond and thus transcends the lives and control of the individuals whose intentions and unconscious language it moves through. We thus already have two 'levels' of communication in play throughout this chapter, and indeed throughout *Border Security.*

Luhmann's account of communication demands that we accord theoretical primacy to his assumptions as a closer account of what's actually going on, but without jettisoning the idea that those involved think about themselves as human subjects involved in the subjectively meaningful communicative action of sending the message – even though, on his assumptions, they are the environment of communication, not its system (scrambling Habermas' action-based account and the system/lifeworld distinction used to critique Parsons).[20] I now explicate each of these levels side by side.

On the first level of communication – 'sending the message' – communication *is* the simultaneity of transmission, reception, object, load and meaning. Through communication operations, the government responds by 'delivering the goods', or promises to do so, if elected: "[a] Coalition government will restore real policies that live up to" the decisionist prerogative, policies for which Labor has neither the heart nor the resolve.[21] Observed on this first level, border security *is* a kind of discursive payload, and communication is the relay of transmissions delivering it *and* the knowledge that delivery reliably takes place when messages are sent.

Consider Figure 2.1.

17 Foucault, Michel, 'The Subject and Power', *Critical Inquiry*, 8: 4, 1982, pp. 781–782.

18 Paraphrasing a famous catchphrase of Philip K Dick. See: Dick, Philip K., *Flow, My Tears, the Policeman Said*, Mariner Books, Boston, 1974, p. 130.

19 Borch, Christian, 'Social Systems', *Niklas Luhmann*, Routledge, Abingdon, 2011, p. 19 and Rasch, William, 'Luhmann's Ontology', in LaCour, Anders and Philippopoulos-Mihalopoulos, Andreas (eds.), *Luhmann Observed: Radical Theoretical Encounters*, Palgrave Macmillan, London, 2013, pp. 38–60.

20 Habermas, Jürgen, *The Theory of Communicative Action Vol. 2: Lifeworld and System: A Critique of Functional Reason*, Beacon Press, 1992.

21 'The Coalition's Operation Sovereign Borders Policy', *SIEVX.COM*, 2013. http://sievx.com/articles/OSB/201307xxTheCoalitionsOSBPolicy.pdf, p. 4.

Figure 2.1 'No Way' campaign poster

Source: Australian Government, Department of Immigration and Border Protection, Creative Commons[22]

22 'No Way: You Will Not Make Australia Home', Department of Immigration and Border Protection, www.border.gov.au

The measure of success of 'missives' such as the above leaflet is deduced in relation to the entelechy of border security as a message understood in this way: Australia, a secured space of orderly circulation in which "the rules apply to everyone", even "unaccompanied children",[23] is a place 'you' have no way of ending up 'in', or ever making home. Border security's horizon of perfect communication *is* the unreachability of Australia.

Notably, this schema produces a circle of enforceable reasoning in which the message arrives that asylum seekers cannot arrive. As a consequence of successful transmission, actual asylum seekers cannot arrive – which is 'proof' that the message was received. This projection of *Terra Australis ignotum* produces Australia as totally 'continent', a fully secured space in which the following factors are, ideally, perfectly congruent and achieved:

- all risks are pre-empted: no departures or routes escape knowledge;
- surveillance is total: all would-be arrivals are detected;
- operational control is effective: no vessels (can) arrive un-interdicted;
- circulation is secured: in the full realisation of strategic goals only the authorised arrive, and they do smoothly in their millions, but only within secured circuits, and only by plane (section I.9); the unauthorised never arrive.

Looking at these points as means and ends within the border continuum, we can also observe that 'no way' means 'no boats', which also means 'no asylum'. As 'the message', the 'no, no and no!' of border security *means* the absence of boats, the indefinitely detained bodies of all would-be boat arrivals, and the resulting resilient integrity of the 'framework of movement'. When 'no, no and no!' remains observed as the sent message, deterrence and control are accepted onshore as having been achieved, with the further concluding inference: border security works.

As the dystopian flipside implied by these intrasystemic goals, the 'absence of the security-procured absence' would generate something like the 'undermining power of uncontrolled movement' evoked by Mr Turnbull.[24] This darkening shadow loads the message with urgent importance, because it means that, but for the absence-producing power of sending the message, Australia would cease to be sovereign. These several tensioning points in the corners of the imaginary web of reference of border security's world co-produce the necessary and integral presence of the message of border security in Australian society.

23 Luhmann, Niklas, 'What is Communication?' *Communication Theory*, 2: 3, 1992, p. 256 and Foucault, Michel, 'The Subject and Power', *Critical Inquiry*, 8: 4, 1982, pp. 786–787.

24 Colgan, Paul, 'Malcolm Turnbull talks up Australia's Border Protection as "The Best in the World" Ahead of UN Talks', *Business Insider Australia*, September 18, 2016. www.businessinsider.com.au/malcolm-turnbull-talks-up-australias-border-protection-as-the-best-in-the-world-ahead-of-un-talks-2016-9

By way of further opening a critical space, shifting emphasis to the second level of communication while observing 'No Way', following Luhmann, means paying closer attention to the factors that are assumed. These include the factors only hinted at as border security's 'deliverants' attend to the distinctions they're making in the course of sending the message from border security's world, the blindspots, background conditions and values involved in drafting, packaging, transmission and delivery. As I do, I observe the following meanings emerging in the course of sending the message.

In the above pamphlet, Border Force attributes *operational success* to its agents' ability to achieve the ends of communication through their actions. Sending the message 'to them' achieves unreachability, an absence accorded a very high normative value because sending the message 'secures us', delivering the nation from evil and illegality. This sets up a dialectic of politics and its invisibility, in the following ways. The pamphlet attributes operational success (which is not political) to absence. It co-attributes *political failure* (which *is not* operational), to any resistance to operational success,[25] including the presence of asylum seekers: 'there are noncitizen children on our beach again, we are not sovereign once more' – crisis, national emergency. This hypothetical, normatively loaded situation, tinged with hysteria, is then accorded status as: the ineffectiveness of border security, the ongoing presence of 'the boats' and the stubborn undeniable realisation that 'they' 'still haven't got the message yet' – including agents who believe this as political opposition and any other dissenting voices. These last points will become central in the final section of this chapter dealing with the *Operation Sovereign Borders* briefings (sections 2.10–2.12).

Seen as 'an emergent reality and state of affairs *sui generis*',[26] the message of border security functions as a conceptual unity within border security's world, one gratefully received and given a stable place in the lives of those for whom it is hosted as meaningful. To the extent that it achieves metastability as meaningful, 'border security' becomes capable of maintaining a tight and politically vital congruence between otherwise disparate elements. This is its societal dividend for the invested, and speaks to its power and wonder as a way of achieving sovereignty for the nation. For after all, what have Afghani asylum seekers, Indonesian fishermen, Norwegian fishing lines, Filipino sailors and the Australian Navy got to do with one another? Before Tampa and ordinarily, nothing; in the border continuum and operationally, everything. This speaks to the 'big somehow' raised earlier (section 2.2): *somehow* operations brought them together; *somehow* they're observed as holding together; *somehow* all of this is 'within' the border continuum.

Zooming out to connect our focus back to this chapter's focus on Australian border security's broader societal emergence, the conditions in which 'border security' is a sensible 'message' *came into existence*; they did not always exist.

25 Luhmann, Niklas, 'What is Communication?' *Communication Theory*, 2: 3, 1992, p. 251 and Borch, Christian, *Niklas Luhmann*, Routledge, Abingdon, 2011, pp. 32–25.

26 Luhmann, Niklas, 'What is Communication?' *Communication Theory*, 2: 3, 1992, p. 252.

A society capable of 'sending the message' of border security is a state of affairs that emerged. As the former head of Military Public Affairs, Brigadier Gary Bornholt, recalled, the asylum seekers on board *Tampa* were not observed as a threat in the last week of August, 2001:

> In Defence it wasn't a big deal, because these numbers of people were very, very small and that's why they didn't represent a security threat.[27]

People seeking protection by trying to arrive in Australia aboard boats only days after arrivals were 'not a big deal' *came to be* observed as categorical threats, and this situational definition, which shapes how operations are conducted and continues to 'say' why interdiction and indefinite offshore detention are necessary, holds to the time of writing.

As communication, at the most diffuse level border security absorbs uncertainty about global space (section I.2). It does so by responding to it in ways that secure national sovereignty[28] (Chapter 1). Yet in the course of sending the message border security secretes as much uncertainty as it absorbs, building itself into its global spaces in ways that from then on mean border security and global space are systemically co-dependent. To integrate key points from the previous chapter for this section's purposes, the operational treatment of historically disparate entities as *decisively* 'alike' – for a nation whose sovereignty is 'from then on and therefore necessarily' threatened by their likeness – adds an important political futurity to border security and the nation, because it necessitates the perpetual 'sending of the message' as an integral way of responding to restore sovereignty. This also bears upon a polity's understanding of its past, because it tends to preclude a critical public discussion of the historical and political conditions by which this contingent state of affairs came to be, which in turn obscures the context operations nonetheless rely upon. It also enforces the operationally necessary recognition that vulnerable people are threats (sections 1.10–1.12). This gathers toward a critical normative point, an 'island' (section 1.7) in *Border Security* we will keep returning to.

As communication that consists in 'sending the message', border security indicates itself. The circularity of operations precludes an easy understanding of its own self-made, self-securing situation as anything but an urgent situation that requires the intensification and promotion – of border security. This means avoiding hesitation that would impede the continuation and expansion of the ambit of operations. It also means avoiding critical reflection that might jeopardise Border Force's future, which is then held to the future of the nation and sovereignty as integral, technical, and necessary (sections 4.1–4.2).

27 Raschella, Adrian, 'Former SAS Commander Breaks Silence on Tampa', *abc.net.au*, updated July 8, 2013. www.abc.net.au/news/2011-07-07/former-sas-commander-breaks-silence-on-tampa/2785164

28 Luhmann, Niklas, *Theory of Society, Volume 1*, Stanford University Press, Stanford, 2012, pp. 185, 235.

By observing border security as emergent communication enacted in a reality it makes a difference to, I hope to open thinking beyond the enforced shores of politics of border security's world, toward other possible horizons of justice. With these theoretical and normative points about 'sending the message' as our background and observational position, this chapter's analytic foreground now shifts into the empirical.

2.4 April 9, 2013: 'We want to go to New Zealand please help us'

On February 16, 1969, a group of West Papuans arrived near Thursday Island; the first recorded 'boat arrival' of asylum seekers in Australia.[29] Seen from border security's world, the arrival of 'raft men' would expose an absence of sufficient coastal surveillance around Australia, with the drastic implications we can draw from the key dot points in the 'No Way' pamphlet. Yet the lack of surveillance 'exposed' by the arrival of the raft men was not raised as a worrying issue: the absence was absent. This shows how contemporary Australian expectations about coastal surveillance are normative, while exposing the occluded contingency and contested political valence of such norms. By its own terms, read from the 1969 mainland, the arrival of the West Papuan raft men was a non-event.[30] Australia had been reached without anything being 'breached'.

Forty-four years later, around midday on Tuesday April 9, 2013, a vessel sailed in to Geraldton Harbour, Western Australia.[31] The fishing boat, visibly crowded with people standing on deck, dropped anchor only a few hundred metres away from amazed locals onshore at the Dome Café.[32] Curiously, the boat had Deutsche Bank's logo painted on the port and starboard sides of the hull just above the waterline, and was flying the New Zealand flag. But this was neither an off-course expedition nor a misguided venture, and these unexpected visitors were neither Kiwi fishermen nor German bankers.

Over the course of the day the following became clear: those aboard were Tamils fleeing Sri Lanka[33]; they had been at sea for forty-four days, having sailed more

29 'Eight Men in Raft Ordeal', *Sydney Morning Herald*, February 18 1969, in Neuman, Klaus, *Across the Seas: Australia's Responses to Refugees*, Black Inc, Melbourne, 2015, p. viii, n.332.

30 The synchronous point is that Haitians were problematised as 'boat people' from 1972, though their asylum claims were negated from September 1963 (section 3.8–3.10).

31 Taillier, Sarah, 'Asylum Boat Spotted Day Before Geraldton Arrival', abc.net.au, April 11, 2013. www.abc.net.au/news/2013-04-11/asylum-boat-first-spotted-at-kalbarri-day-before-geraldton-arri/4623238

32 Mullany, Ashlee, 'Asylum Boat Carrying 66 Sri Lankan Passengers Sails into Geraldton', news.com.au, April 10, 2013. www.news.com.au/national/asylum-boat-carrying-72-sri-lankan-passengers-sails-into-geraldton/story-e6frfkp9-1226615986980

33 Renshaw, Catherine, 'The Problems With Recognising Sri Lankan Boat Arrivals as Refugees', *The Conversation*, May 3, 2013. http://theconversation.com/the-problems-with-recognising-sri-lankan-boat-arrivals-as-refugees-13895

than 5,400km across the Indian Ocean; and they intended to sail for Auckland, New Zealand, nearly as far again.[34] Even for an experienced navigator with GPS, sailing a wooden hulled coastal fishing boat east toward New Zealand through the wild oceans south of Australia is almost certainly a suicide mission. Yet the implications of the foolhardy journey signalled by the arrival – like the professed intentions of those aboard – were studiously ignored and selectively negated by news media and campaigning politicians, in favour of border security. It's therefore worth placing the 2013 Geraldton arrival side by side with the 1969 Papuan raft men as two heuristic end points of the Australian emergence of the message of border security: at one end, the 'absence of the absence' of coastal surveillance, at the other, the 'obvious immediate harm' of this boat arrival in 2013, and the enforced necessity of doing whatever was necessary to re-produce the mainland absence of asylum seekers, as follows.

From Wednesday April 10, 2013, the arrival of the 'Deutsche Bank'[35] was framed as a 'serious breach of border security' and 'an urgent matter of national security'.[36] This 'breach' became the pretext for crisis talk led by politicians and journalists in Perth and Canberra, including calls for legislative review, more surveillance, and further and stronger enforcement measures. In news reports published that Wednesday, the Premier of Western Australia, Mr Colin Barnett, characterised the arrival as "shocking", a "game changer" and "a serious, unprecedented and unacceptable breach of Australia's border security". Barnett also asserted that the arrival was a security threat to local grain export and was connected to "crime gangs, crime syndicates, whatever else, drugs and the like".[37] Variants of the above quote were disseminated widely through national news media without critical scrutiny or references to historical cases where unprepared governments faced genuine crisis numbers (such as the Indochinese Exodus), or where the government of the day had to deal with an unprecedented or complex situation during an election season (such as the Mariel boatlift) (section 3.9). It bears repeating: the Deutsche Bank was *one* boat carrying sixty-six people *who professed to be attempting to get to New Zealand*.[38] As of writing, no other similar

34 'Asylum Seekers Return to Sea After Mistakenly Arriving in Australia', *The Civilian*, April 10, 2013. www.thecivilian.co.nz/asylum-seekers-return-to-sea-after-mistakenly-arriving-in-australia/

35 This is my chosen name for the vessel, which remained unnamed by news media.

36 Paddenburg, Trevor and Mullany, Ashlee, 'War of Words Over Geraldton Arrivals as Cyclone Victoria Stops Flights', *The Australian*, April 10, 2013. www.theaustralian.com.au/news/asylum-boat-carrying-72-sri-lankan-passengers-sails-into-geraldton/story-e6frg6n6-1226617279185

37 'Boat Carrying Asylum Seekers Pulls into Geraldton', abc.net.au, updated April 10, 2013. www.abc.net.au/news/2013-04-09/boat-carrying-asylum-seekers-pulls-into-geraldton/4618844

38 McCluskey, Ian, 'Boat Arrivals on the Mainland: What Difference Does It Make?' *Parliament of Australia*, posted April 12, 2013. www.aph.gov.au/About_Parliament/Parliamentary_Departments/Parliamentary_Library/FlagPost/2013/April/Boat_arrivals_on_the_mainland_what_difference_does_it_make

vessels have arrived in Geraldton or attempted a comparable journey on this route, nor does it have a relation to Gillard's 'evil trade that must be punished' like vessels attempting to arrive from Java (section 2.1).

As a boat arrival, the crucial point was that Deutsche Bank was a genuine anomaly, but this was studiously missed by the politicians and journalists involved in discussing its arrival and uncritically disseminating Barnett's assessment. To anyone attending to the details, the Deutsche Bank wasn't even properly speaking a 'boat arrival': just as failing implies trying, *arriving* by boat would ordinarily imply an intention to 'arrive in Australia' on the part of those aboard. And yet, in the months leading up to the 2013 federal election, the presence of *one* boat, even one attempting to arrive in New Zealand, was immediately framed by politicians and news media as a border security 'breach' significant enough to merit further policy measures costing billions of dollars.

On the same day the Deutsche Bank arrived in Geraldton, the opposition leader took the 'border security breach' framing and wove it in to his election campaign narrative. Mr Abbott described the Geraldton arrival as a 'disaster' and sign and signal of the Gillard Labor government's 'surrender':

> It just gets worse and worse all the time and I think effectively the Government has kind of surrendered. . . . And the problem with surrendering on boat people is that in the end it discredits the whole of our immigration program.[39]

Labor ministers protested that Coalition spokespeople were "acting hysterically", but Home Affairs Minister Jason Clare dutifully ordered an investigation into the event.[40] By the 2013 election – the *Operation Sovereign Borders* election – the electoral necessity of not getting wedged on national security meant that the incumbent Labor government was incapable of contending with a situational definition that, by this time, the Coalition were using to own them, day after day. During the week in which the Geraldton arrival was leveraged as a 'national breach' and 'surrender', representatives from the Greens were the only spokespeople of political parties who raised questions about the arrival's status and significance and expressed concern about the fate of those who'd been at sea for forty-four days, and who faced detention, rape and torture if they were sent home[41] (section 6.3).

In a radio interview on Thursday April 11, opposition defence spokesperson Senator David Johnston elaborated upon a statement issued to news media by

39 Griffiths, Emma, 'Abbott Accuses Government of "Surrender" on Boat Arrivals'. www.abc.net.au/news/2013-04-10/abbott-accuses-government-of-'surrender'-on-boat-arrivals/4620160

40 Op.cit.

41 Lane, Sabra, 'Greens Push for Legal Guarantees for Geraldton Boat Arrivals', *The World Today, ABC Radio National*, April 11, 2013. www.abc.net.au/worldtoday/content/2013/s3734670.htm

the campaigning Coalition stating that the Geraldton incident highlighted the need for its policy of introducing seven surveillance drones, at a cost of 1.5 billion.[42] In the course of the interview, Johnston went further: "*obviously* given the threats at the moment and the fact that we've had a boat come all the way down to Geraldton, *obviously* seven might need to be rethought".[43] Instead of questioning the obviousness of Mr Johnston's in-the-moment 'rethinking', or his slippery pluralisation of the anomaly as 'threat*s* at the moment', the next question was: "[o]nce the unmanned air aerial aircraft detect suspected asylum seeker boats, what would then happen next?"

The news coverage of the Geraldton arrival ended that week in an op-ed in the *Sunday Telegraph* entitled 'Illegal boat's mainland arrival should alarm all'. Here, Piers Akerman, in an opinion piece that deployed the rhetorical tropes of 'human cargo' and 'flood',[44] descried the Geraldton arrival in the following terms:

> the threat exposed by this dramatic breach of the nation's border security is massive. At the most alarming level, it is not beyond the bounds of speculation to contemplate what could have occurred had a terrorist group chosen to create chaos by landing an armed cell onto the streets of the sleepy ocean-side city, just as a small body of terrorists was inserted into Mumbai on November 29, 2008, killing 164 people and wounding at least 308. The menace posed by the illegal arrival of such a vessel goes well beyond that of obvious immediate harm. The threat posed to the nation's rural economy by the introduction of exotic plant and animal diseases carried even unknowingly by crew and passengers on such illicit craft is inestimable.[45]

In the months leading to the 2013 federal election, what's culturally striking about news media coverage on boat arrivals is not that pieces such as the above op-ed were written – as they have in so many places for so long (sections 2.5, 5.5) – so much as it is that most serious journalists did not typically question such assertions when they related to border security during this time. The politicians and pundits most active in making the strongest claims were politically aligned ideologues with skin in the game whose careers stood to gain by boosting threats. Yet like Premier Barnett and Senator David Johnston, no one making assertions was held in any way responsible for what they said, which news agencies for the

42 This figure refers to Air 7000 phase 1B, intended to replace Australia's Orion surveillance capabilities with a combination of manned and unmanned systems.

43 Lane, Sabra, 'Greens Push for Legal Guarantees for Geraldton Boat Arrivals', *The World Today, ABC Radio National*, April 11, 2013, italics mine.

44 Garland, David, 'On the Concept of Moral Panic', *Crime Media Culture*, 4: 1, 2008, p. 11 and Martin, Greg, 'Stop the Boats! Moral Panic in Australia Over Asylum Seekers', *Continuum: Journal of Media & Cultural Studies*, 29: 3, 2015, pp. 304 –322.

45 Akerman, Piers, 'Illegal Boat's Mainland Arrival Should Alarm All', *The Sunday Telegraph*, April 14, 2013. www.dailytelegraph.com.au/news/opinion/illegal-boats-mainland-arrival-should-alarm-all/story-e6frezz0-1226619898855

most part just reticulated, linking to one another's links, linking to press releases, op-eds and recorded interviews with politicians. Nor were those making claims involving the expenditure of billions in public funds, such as Mr Johnston, questioned about the reasoning and costs implied in the further measures they were calling for. That the 'obvious immediate harm' of a group of Sri Lankans sailing for New Zealand could pass as a reasonable description of the Geraldton arrival indicates the extent to which the distinctions of border security's world transformed what was sensible to say and possible to contend about vulnerable people seeking protection by boat.

The further politically significant effect is that by 2013 border security *itself* had ceased being a political topic or object of contention among those most actively involved in communicating its message in Australia. By the time of the 2013 federal election, border security had become so obviously necessary as to require no comment about full support for it, while a single boat trying to reach New Zealand was representable by the opposition leader as 'a total surrender that discredited Australia's immigration program in its entirety'. By 2013, the Geraldton arrival was *just* 'a failure of border security' and an absence of coastal surveillance to which the immediate, urgent, and *only* proper response could be: an intensification of border security.

In the remainder of this chapter I seek to show how this came to be. What's involved in the formation of the message border security, to the point where border security's distinctions about people arriving and national sovereignty in Australia had so transmuted that it was no longer necessary to consider the most basic facts about 'their' seeking protection 'here'? We need to consider how 'the very idea' of border security became obvious enough to 'the Australian people' that by 2013 *Operation Sovereign Borders* made unassailable popular sense, while any direct contention with this state of affairs was electoral suicide.

2.5 April 1976–December 1977: "No one believes that these refugees should suddenly be coming to Australia"

In 1976 boat arrivals became politically legible as a *potential* problem of Australia's national sovereignty: on the horizon, but not yet within the shores of federal parliamentary politicking around the issue. The first five Vietnamese 'boat people' arrived in Darwin Harbour in April 1976, and small groups[46] continued to arrive in Darwin throughout that year. In December 1976, a Melbourne tabloid, the Sun-News Pictorial, "warned of a 'tide of human flotsam' lapping the shores of northern Australia, and speculated about an invasion of

46 UNHCR puts the total number of *re-settled* Exodus refugees as 1,311,183 in the years 1975–95. '4 Flight From Indochina, The State of the World's Refugees', *www.unhcr.org*. www.unhcr.org/3ebf9bad0.pdf

Australia's far north 'by hundreds, thousands and even tens of thousands of Asian refugees' ".[47]

In 1977, the phenomena of 'boat people' arriving in Darwin was politicised as an election issue in the federal election of that year. On November 20 and 21, 1977, six vessels arrived in the vicinity of Darwin Harbour, carrying 218 people in total. In contrast to the 'raft men' of 1969 (section 2.4), by 1977 asylum seekers arriving by boat were visible – to *some* onshore – as a worry meriting a decisive political response. Immediately, Australian news media were handling the worry by drawing on a reservoir of rich metaphors, emotive adjectives and cultural memory, such as those above, representing the issue as a worryingly growing problem meriting a decisive response from elected officials of the federal government. One newspaper report dubbed these Darwin arrivals "the second fleet"[48] (sections 1.2–1.3).

On November 26, 1977, shortly after the 'arrival' of 'The Second Fleet' in news media rhetoric, Gough Whitlam, then leader of the opposition was campaigning in Darwin. In a radio interview, Mr Whitlam responded to the issue of arrivals. Whitlam is reported as saying that, if elected, he would cancel the purchase of a "costly new frigate and replace it with many more new patrol boats to watch Australia's coastline". The report goes on to paraphrase and quote Mr Whitlam as follows:

> (Whitlam) said the boats were needed to control the influx of refugees from countries such as Vietnam, to counter widespread drug-running and to prevent animal and human diseases entering Australia.
>
> 'We don't know enough about the sudden influx of people from sea,' he said.
>
> 'No one believes that, two-and-a-half years after the Vietnam War these refugees should suddenly be coming to Australia'.[49]

This quote is historically significant for two reasons. First, it rates as a very early mention made by a senior Commonwealth official – perhaps the first – of a need for increased coastal surveillance and a militarised approach to boat arrivals in Australia. These arrivals were not yet a 'breach of border security', but unlike the Raft Men eight years earlier, the absence of surveillance *was* noted as a lack, and therefore something that could be and ought to be developed and implemented.[50] Second, the quoted comment shows Whitlam breaking a settled agreement made

47 Neuman, Klaus, '"Queue Jumpers" and the Perils of Crossing Sydney Harbour on a Manly Ferry', *Inside Story*, October 1, 2014. http://insidestory.org.au/queue-jumpers-and-the-perils-of-crossing-sydney-harbour-on-a-manly-ferry

48 Op.cit.

49 Steketee, Mike, 'Refugees: Asians May Be "Twisting Our Tails"', *Sydney Morning Herald*, November 26, 1977, p. 2.

50 Luhmann, Niklas, 'What is Communication?' *Communication Theory*, 2: 3, 1992, p. 256.

and held by the major parties from the postwar period on that politicking around this issue – especially during 'crises' and elections – would release the xenophobic genie from the bottle.[51] As I will explore later in this chapter (sections 2.6–2.9), this was not the last time a campaigning politician broke this gentlemen's agreement in postwar Australia, but in this case, the ramifications were minor, and as follows.

The 1977 'need for boats to control the influx' was, arguably, an isolated piece of opportunistic political improvisation on Whitlam's part. It was tailored to the only national audience where the issue had any traction, Darwin. As Klaus Neuman's careful archival work notes, the issue is significant precisely because it failed to resonate.[52] Outside Darwin, 'the nation' didn't yet care about 'stopping the boats' in an electorally significant way.

By way of linking in to broader dynamics, we might glance at synchronous conjunctural factors, conspicuously the persistence of the Cold War and broad public support for variants of a Keynesian social compact among a national citizenry of equal locals. This sat alongside the discursive absence of any societally legible 'globalisation', let alone 'globalisation backlash'.[53] Sufficed to say, Whitlam lost the '77 federal election – but 'stopping the boats' wouldn't have elected him, or even boosted his prospects as it did Abbott's in 2013. Whitlam might have dog whistled, but outside Darwin, no one barked.[54] After its election, the Fraser government held to a liberal internationalist, multilateral approach to boat arrivals, consonant with Australia's obligations under international law – as they were recognised internationally.[55] Between 1976 and August 1981, 2059 Vietnamese people arrived seeking asylum by boat.[56] Between April 1975 and June 30, 1981, the Fraser government resettled 51,780 erstwhile 'boat people' in Australia, selecting them from camps in southeast Asia and landing them in the territory – by plane[57] (section I.9).

51 Neuman, Klaus, *Across the Seas: Australia's Responses to Refugees*, Black Inc, 2015, pp. 282–286.
52 Op.Cit., p. 286.
53 Bigo, Didier, 'Security and Immigration: Toward a Critique of the Governmentality of Unease', *Alternatives* 27, 2002, p. 66.
54 'Under the Radar: Dog-whistle politics in Australia', The Australia Institute. www.tai.org.au/node/1290
55 Section I.5, 3.12, 6.1–6.
56 Phillips, Janet and Spinks, Harriet, 'Boat arrivals in Australia since 1976', *Parliament of Australia*. www.aph.gov.au/About_Parliament/Parliamentary_Departments/Parliamentary_Library/pubs/rp/rp1314/BoatArrivals
57 The 1975–1995 Total is 137, 543. See: '4 Flight From Indochina, The State of the World's Refugees', *www.unhcr.org*, www.unhcr.org/3ebf9bad0.pdf and York, Barry, 'Australia and Refugees, 1901–2002: An Annotated Chronology Based on Official Sources', *Parliament of Australia*. www.aph.gov.au/About_Parliament/Parliamentary_Departments/Parliamentary_Library/Publications_Archive/online/Refugeess3

2.6 April 1999–August 2001: 'illegals', 'queuejumpers' and the Howard government's role in the emergence of the message of border security

In describing the lead up to the Tampa Affair and the late 90s spike in asylum seeker boat arrivals that pre-tensioned it, it's critical to note the cultural mood of late 90s Australia. Australia's proponents and representatives represented themselves and their country bullishly as a place of buoyant openness, confident diversity, and brightly growing multicultural futures. In 1999, the understanding of Australia that predominated was in so many ways *unlike* the US in 1979–1980 or Europe in 2013–2015: 1999 Australia was not read by most as a nation-state in apparent decline suffering 'impotence' or 'being held hostage' as the 1980 US was framed during Mariel (section 3.9). Nor was the federation of colonies that had come through the dusty bush-dreaming years of White Australia as a multicultural Commonwealth a failed political project comprised of formerly strong-states losing privilege and living standards and 'falling apart' in the face of uncontrolled globalisation and unwanted migration, such as 2015 Europe was observed as.

Australia's pre-millennium wave of cultural confidence came as the economy sailed unscathed through the Asian Monetary Crisis that rocked neighbouring ASEAN countries in 1998. Meanwhile, the Howard government had convincingly represented Australia a good international citizen that had shepherded East Timor to largely peaceful post-Soeharto independence after the referendum in 1999.[58] At the turn of the millennium, the bursting of the dotcom bubble had little to no effect on Australia's national economy. The 'millennium bug' (Y2K) proved to be a vaguely disappointing nonevent, and the massive post-Seattle protests against the World Economic Forum on September 11, 2000 in Melbourne (the S11 protests) were overshadowed in the dominant public imagination by the Sydney Olympics, which opened on September 15, 2000.[59]

The peak moment of the Sydney 2000 Opening Ceremony provides a cultural condensation point for the particularities of this moment of buoyant, optimistic

58 Clifton, Tony, 'Fields of Dreams: The Battle for the Timor Sea, Home of Oil, Gas, Hot Air and Hope, *The Monthly*, July 2005. www.themonthly.com.au/monthly-essays-tony-clifton-fields-dreams-battle-timor-sea-home-oil-gas-hot-air-and-hope-63 and McGrath, Kim, 'Oil, Gas and Spy Games in the Timor Sea', *The Monthly*, April 2014. www.themonthly.com.au/issue/2014/april/1396270800/kim-mcgrath/oil-gas-and-spy-games-timor-sea

59 Neilson, Brett, 'Bodies of Protest: Performing citizenship at the 2000 Olympic Games', *Continuum*, 16: 1, 2002, pp. 13–25.

Iveson, Kurt and Scalmer, Sean, 'Contesting the "Inevitable": Notes on S11', *Overland*, 161, Summer 2000 and McCulloch, Jude, 'Paramilitary Surveillance: S11, Globalisation, Terrorists and Counter-Terrorists', *Current Issues in Criminal Justice*, 13: 1, pp. 23–35.

openness.[60] After an audio-visual hagiography trumpeting 'the multicultural society we have today', represented as emerging *from* 'Australia's generous post-war reception of refugees fleeing war', the dancers in the middle of the stadium formed the shape of the mainland coastline, facing outwards. At the crescendo, the performers – filmed fading to a closeup of an indigenous man in ceremonial dress – threw out their arms to the global simulcast audience, while the compere asserted: "vibrant, brilliant – Australia".[61]

A little less than a year later, in August 2001, Australia appeared to still be basking in the golden afterglow of Sydney 2000: a young, medium-sized nation-state at peak confidence, embracing the 'challenges and opportunities' (sections 4.6–4.9) of Asia-Pacific globalisation with 'open hearts and open arms' (section 3.9). But polling from 1998 revealed a dark counterpicture. A "poll in 1998 showed the average Australian overestimated by 70 times the number of boat people arriving each year in the country",[62] meaning the 'average Australian' (in *these* polled samples) anxiously imagined 14,000 were arriving in a calendar year in which 200 actually did, aboard seventeen vessels. Ongoing polling, from 1998, also revealed community sentiment about boat arrivals was consistently very strong and very negative.[63] If the Sydney 2000 Opening Ceremony was a crafted projection of 'vibrant, brilliant Australia' confidently celebrating globalisation and multiculturalism in a way unthinkable a century earlier at Federation and the inception of White Australia, polling among key voter groups showed an unexpected and undeniable desire for hardened hearts and closed borders on the matter of boat arrivals.

To fully understand the cultural pre-tensioning that gathered around this time, we have to jump back to 1996 for just a moment. On September 10, 1996, Pauline Hanson gave her maiden speech to the House of Representatives (section I.9). Like the S11 protests focusing on global justice and corporate greed in September 2000, Hanson's speech was deeply critical of the lived effects of what passed under the banner of globalisation:[64]

> Immigration and multiculturalism are issues that this government is trying to address, but for far too long ordinary Australians have been kept out of any debate by the major parties. I and most Australians want our immigration

60 As noted by Perera, Suvendrini, *Australia and the Insular Imagination: Beaches, Borders, Boats, and Bodies*, Palgrave Macmillan, New York, 2009, pp. 15–17.

61 *Leaky Boat* (documentary), *abc.net.au*. www.abc.net.au/tv/programs/leakyboat.htm; and Fitzsimmons, Peter, '15 Years Ago Today, the World Watched in Awe as the Sydney 2000 Games Began', *Sydney Morning Herald*, September 15, 2015. www.smh.com.au/nsw/15-years-ago-today-the-world-watched-in-awe-as-the-sydney-2000-games-began-20150915-gjmx7p.html

62 Marr, David and Wilkinson, Marian, *Dark Victory*, Allen and Unwin, Melbourne, 2004, p. 48.

63 Op.cit., pp. 44–49.

64 McCulloch, Jude, 'Paramilitary Surveillance: S11, Globalisation, Terrorists and Counter-Terrorists', *Current Issues in Criminal Justice*, 13: 1, p. 23.

> policy radically reviewed and that of multiculturalism abolished. I believe we are in danger of being swamped by Asians. Between 1984 and 1995, 40 per cent of all migrants coming into this country were of Asian origin. They have their own culture and religion, form ghettos and do not assimilate. Of course, I will be called racist but, if I can invite whom I want into my home, then I should have the right to have a say in who comes into my country.[65]

Those Australian audiences living with this cultural memory perhaps remember Hanson's speech for the phrase that triggered them either way: "I believe we are in danger of being swamped by Asians". But closer retrospection on the fuller texture of the speech shows a critique of the marginalisation of ordinary Australians from the discourses and policies affecting their lives and lived experience-based concerns about the pernicious effects of globalisation on the former 'centres' of rural and regional Australia, White Australia's declining heartland. It is this critique and the way it was ignored, rather than the racism that was rightly noted, that speaks to its cultural significance. Reading forward and outward, we can note the striking consonance of Hanson's words with synchronous speech acts of the new xenophobic nationalist right *across* the White Atlantic, from Le Pen to Fortuyn to Brexit and Trump.

From at least April 1999 the Howard government was actively responding to the 'community feeling'[66] powerfully captured by Hanson, shaping it as an electoral issue that could work in the Coalition's favour. Howard's art was his ability to present his responsiveness to community feeling as a democratic honouring of 'the will of the people'. The Howard government used immigration and asylum seekers to sideline Hanson while subsuming tinges of One Nation's xenophobic nationalist rhetoric into Coalition policy. The magic trick was that they did so while pushing GDP and population growth, with the latter using the massive expansion of skilled temporary migration as an integral tactic (sections 5.4, 5.7), as well as driving neoliberalisation through further, deeper and wider privatisations, corporatisations, outsourcing and offshoring. The Howard government appeared to be offering some of its 'globalisation anxious' constituents a subject position that said the following: 'As long as you hate migrants politely, you can express support for the forces you benefit financially from that bring them here, and provided you studiously avoid making the connection between these two factors, you can still regard yourself as a decent person who is rightly concerned for the country they love'.

65 Hanson, Pauline, 'Pauline Hanson's Maiden Speech in the House of Representatives', September 10, 1996. http://australianpolitics.com/1996/09/10/pauline-hanson-maiden-speech.html

66 Howard's own retrospective phrasing describes it as an 'honorable community feeling'. See: *Leaky Boat* (documentary), www.abc.net.au/tv/programs/leakyboat.htm and also Howard, John, *Lazarus Rising: A Personal and Political Autobiography*, Harper Collins, Sydney, 2011.

With the benefit of hindsight, the following factors percolating through the Howard government in the late 90s have become clearer for the role they played in formulating of the message of border security.

In 1999 key cabinet ministers in the Howard government knew:

- the rough numbers of asylum seekers who'd arrive in 2000 and 2001,[67]
- the regions they where they were coming from,
- the smuggler networks involved, and
- the situations people were fleeing.

In sum: a few thousand a year fleeing war and persecution in Afghanistan and Iraq; availing themselves of smuggler networks in Java; that the Australian Federal Police knew well, because they were actively disrupting them. By most reasonable measures and accurate estimates, at least 90% of these people were UN-definitional refugees, known populations comprising part of a larger regional and global problem. On November 15, 1999, Mr Ruddock, when the Minister for Immigration and Multicultural Affairs, was quoted as saying that "as many as 10,000 people could be packing up now in the Middle East with a view to trying to access Australia",[68] he knew – with quite a high degree of accuracy – what he was talking about.

Mr Ruddock formed a publicly expressed intention as a governmental response to boat arrivals at this time. It was developed with the full knowledge of the conditions just listed, and in consultation of all other members of cabinet. Mr Ruddock was explicit: "[M]y important objective is to ensure that they know before they start on that path that any objective that involves permanent residency in Australia will not be met".[69] Temporary Protection Visas (TPVs), introduced on October 20, 1999, were an explicit measure intended to achieve Ruddock's objective, whose essence was to prevent seeking asylum by boat from being a viable 'migration pathway'.[70] From what we know about Ruddock's explanation of his rationales,[71] this was about maintaining support for the integrity of the migration program, specific measures taken with regard for the system as a national whole. What's also notable is the way that speech acts around boat arrivals during this time smoothly connected a rhetoric loaded with stereotypical

67 See: Phillips, Janet and Spinks, Harriet, 'Boat Arrivals in Australia Since 1976', *Parliament of Australia*. www.aph.gov.au/About_Parliament/Parliamentary_Departments/Parliamentary_Library/pubs/rp/rp1314/QG/BoatArrivals

68 But what he did not say was: "*no more* than a maximum of about 10,000 Afghanis and Iraqis, who are fleeing war and persecution, intending to seek asylum by arriving in Australia". See: Sara, Sally, 'Govt Struggles to Stop Flow of Illegals', *PM, ABC Radio National*, Monday November 15, 1999. www.abc.net.au/pm/stories/s66365.htm

69 Sara, Sally, 'Govt Struggles to Stop Flow of Illegals', *PM, ABC Radio National*, Monday November 15, 1999. www.abc.net.au/pm/stories/s66365.htm

70 See section 3.8–3.10.

71 Palmer, David, 'The Values Shaping Australian Asylum Policy: The Views of Policy Insiders', *Australian Journal of Public Administration*, 67: 3, 2008, pp. 307–320.

metaphorics – "flow", "record influx", "illegal immigrants", "packing their bags preparing to set sail", "stem the flow", "pipeline" – to what was *already* a deterrence policy. That is: a policy designed to deter arrival, not to offer protection. We can see a clear, explicit, intentional, executive-led shift toward deterrence-based policies from November 1999.[72]

From 1999 the Howard government was well aware of the smuggling networks operating between Java and Ashmore Reef, because the Australian Federal Police were actively disrupting them, in cahoots with their Indonesian counterparts, often using very murky means, and reporting progress on these matters back to cabinet. There were also five Indonesian National Police 'strike teams' "funded and directed by the AFP to 'disrupt and dismantle' the syndicates" who surveilled passengers, attached tracking devices to boats, and recruited spies among the crews and customers".[73] Certain groups of Indonesian authorities were working with and even *for* certain smugglers,[74] and Commonwealth-funded disruption agents were likewise actively (and in individual cases profitably) involved in the game. The murky disruption of people smuggling was well known – and in some cases well organised by – the Howard government, two years and more before the Tampa Affair.

These Commonwealth instructed AFP-led people smuggling disruption efforts coincided with the assent, on July 16, 1999, of *Migration Legislation Amendment Act (No. 1) 1999*, which for the first time explicitly used the phrase 'people smuggling', in the course of making it an offence. In part this happened because Max Moore Wilton[75] – appointed by Howard in late 1996 to drive cultural change in the public sector by pushing through a whole-of-government governance approach – was personally "driving Canberra's efforts for the previous two years . . . to crack down on boat people and people smuggling".[76]

From 1999–2001, senior ministers in the Howard government[77] were also massaging boat arrivals as an electoral issue by reframing boat arrivals as 'a problem of illegal migration' (section 3.10). From this time, asylum seekers were routinely referred to as 'queuejumpers' who 'come here illegally'.[78] The daily

72 Hugo, Graeme, 'From Compassion to Compliance? Trends in Refugee and Humanitarian Migration in Australia', *Geojournal*, 55, 2001, pp. 27–37.

73 Marr, David and Wilkinson, Marian, *Dark Victory*, Allen and Unwin, Melbourne, 2004, p. 53.

74 Op.cit. See the passage on Kevin John Enniss, p. 53.

75 Brough, Jodie and Millett, Michael, 'The Axeman Cometh', *Sydney Morning Herald*, November 1, 1997. http://australianpolitics.com/1997/11/01/the-axemen-cometh.html

76 Marr, David and Wilkinson, Marian, *Dark Victory*, Allen and Unwin, Melbourne, 2004, p. 32.

77 Conspicuously the Prime Minister, Defence Minister Peter Reith and Minister for Immigration, Multiculturalism and Indigenous Affairs Phillip Ruddock.

78 Pickering, Sharon, 'Common Sense and Original Deviancy: News Discourses and Asylum Seekers in Australia', *Journal of Refugee Studies*, 14: 2, 2001, pp. 169–186, Saxton, Alison, 'I certainly don't want people like that here': the discursive construction of "asylum seekers"', *Media International Australia*, 109: 1, 2003, pp. 109–120 and Walsh, James P., 'Border Theatre and Security Spectacles: Surveillance, Mobility and Reality-Based Television', *Crime, Media, Culture: An International Journal*, 11: 2, 2015, pp. 201–221.

reference to asylum seekers as 'illegals' throughout 1999–2000 – especially over talkback radio and via sympathetic outlets in print media and broadcast newsmagazines, whose most invested audiences sat in marginal seats – worked to demonise and dehumanise boat arrivals in the spaces where the greatest electoral advantage could be gained from doing so.

The social construction of 'illegals' and 'queuejumpers' also worked to refigure social relations via expectations: the 'denouncer of illegality' was encouraged to feel righteous in their condemnation of 'illegals' presence and behaviour, while encouraging politicians, shock jocks and columnists stood by ready and willing to respond to the righteously aggrieved by making an empathic connection that stressed that their grievance was genuine, proper, serious and only dismissible by the politically correct, for three substantive reasons.

- 'Irregularity' *per se* was represented by Howard government ministers as undermining the integrity of the immigration program as well as public support for and perception of its successes, and the nation's proud commitment to multiculturalism.[79]
- The persistent presence of 'illegals' themselves, both as a stubbornly problematic population and as wily, manipulative individuals with criminal proclivities and associations as their 'baggage', undermined Australia's 'generous commitment' to the humanitarian program, (and thus)
- *any* perceived 'softness' would send the message that 'we' tolerated the presence of 'the kind of people' who would 'jump the queue'.

Notably, all three substantive points carry the implicit vision of a good society as regular, legal and orderly – and call for punitive tactics as part of a strategy of control in order to 'restore' this vision of the good.[80]

The three substantive points also gather resonance because they draw fuel from a witches brew of socio-cultural triggerpoints that are culturally peculiar and systemically observed as subjectively meaningful. For these sensitised, responsive audiences, 'boat people' evinced a disrespect for 'process' *and* the socially agreed sequences of people who rightly wait their turn: as stubborn presence, as governmentally worrying problems, and as people whose arrival renders them capable of making undeniable and burdensome demands for welfare and services. Second and speculatively, their presence upset a fragile social compact between diffuse

79 Hugo, Graeme, 'From Compassion to Compliance? Trends in Refugee and Humanitarian Migration in Australia', *Geojournal*, 55, 2001, pp. 27–37 and Palmer, David, 'The Values Shaping Australian Asylum Policy: The Views of Policy Insiders', *Australian Journal of Public Administration*, 67: 3, 2008, pp. 307–320.

80 Garland, David, *The Culture of Control: Crime and Social Order in Contemporary Society*, Oxford University Press, Oxford, 2001.

sentiment, international image and self regard: if the national 'we' welcomed the stranger in our midst, if 'we' were vibrant, brilliant, open Olympian Australia, how was it that 'we' also 'were *forced* to respond so harshly' toward desperate people fleeing difficult situations? Perhaps 'ordinary Australians' were prepared to commit to accepting 11,000 or so 'real' refugees each year as the limit of national hospitality, but 'a bunch of boat people just rocking up' – uninvited – and making demands for care and support was 'taking the piss'.

More than anything, the irregular and illegal nature of 'boat people' played into a supreme cultural value, conception of justice as fairness as 'the fair go'. 'Illegals' didn't' just violate the 'fair go' by 'jumping the queue'. In coming uninvited *and then* engaging in parasitic behaviour by appropriating scarce resources rightly the property of citizens, just by arriving by boat, they:

- undermined the value of citizenship,
- appropriated and spent scarce, unrecoverable cultural resources, and
- redirected resource-limited care facilities away from marginalised, vulnerable – but more worthy – intra-national populations.

Playing a precisely voiced cultural performance of this admixture of concerns to a primed set of publics, well known through polling, allowed the Howard government to reap electoral gain – and/or stem losses to Hanson and the xenophobic right – by being seen to be 'getting tough' while simultaneously avowing that 'we are generous nation' that has always shown compassion for (real) refugees.

To summarise the inter-action of these shifts, then: for a few years before Tampa the Howard government had been actively engaged in a precise executive-led policy shift toward a deterrence policy. This began with murky disruption of people smuggling and institutional re-alignments, then was fed by a broader and recursively re-worked rhetorical platform, backended by broad cultural change within the public service pushed by Howard and lead by 'Max the Axe'. The refined platform referred in very precise ways to topical global issues calibrated to be expediently effective and nimbly responsive to what was known through polled sentiment *and* earlier electoral support for explicitly xenophobic policies. The condensed position engendered by this shift between 1999–2001 held that, *as a nation* (on this side of the national boundary):

- 'we' should never look as though 'we are being pushed around',
- 'we' are not a soft touch,[81]
- 'we' don't like 'illegals' 'coming here and queuejumping', 'in defiance of our laws'.

81 Mcleod, Shane, 'Federal Government Turns Back Asylum Seekers', *PM, Radio National*, August 27, 2001. www.abc.net.au/pm/stories/s353164.htm

And added the following reasons for the *urgent* necessity of the policies (to be enforced on *that* side of the national boundary):

- as many as ten thousand of 'them' could be packing up now
- if 'they're' going to come here illegally, what will 'they' do when they get here??.[82]
- "what is a sovereign government, if you can't decide who's gonna come in and who's not?"[83]

An inner circle of cabinet ministers worked together to pressurise the public sphere for electoral gain using this condensed position. The further cabinet-led shift I observe is that these meanings were actively attached to the sovereign nation as the only proper responder, with the villainous and irrepressible 'illegality' of 'queuejumpers' the transgressive quilting point necessitating a decisive 'drawing a line'. By 2001 it was as if the restoration of law itself depended on drawing a bright, hard line, as if asylum seekers would threaten the lawful order of multicultural Australia, unless someone took a stand.

Once in play, this admixture of factors was recursively refined between regular polling, community sentiment and senior government officials, who continually and reflexively readjusted the detail of speech acts with great fidelity over the course of years. The Howard government played (to) its publics, played with fear, and played upon the most deeply held national values just described, knowing as they did which notes and tone to take, based on the nation's pulse as it was taken and re-taken. In all these ways, the Howard government's refined position had already fully emerged by late August 2001 when *Tampa* rescued *Palapa*'s occupants: *just as* numbers increased, *in* an election year, *one month* before 9/11. If, to paraphrase Seneca, luck is when preparation meets opportunity, *Tampa* was Howard's lucky break.

2.7 Queuejumpers, 'illegals' *and* the societal absence of border security in 2001

And yet, in August 2001 'border security' was not routinely spoken of. Notwithstanding broader societal shifts such as those just canvassed, border security would not be possible without a coalescence and concatenation of state-institutional elements. If we think of the 'border continuum' as a contemporary observation made from border security's world in its Border Force becoming in 2014 (section I.2), we have to consider how the continuum became observable

82 Simon, Jonathan, 'Refugees in a Carceral Age: The Rebirth of Immigration Prisons in the United States', *Public Culture*, 10: 3, 1998, pp. 577–607.

83 Paraphrasing ex Howard government minister Peter Reith, in *Leaky Boat* (documentary). www.abc.net.au/tv/programs/leakyboat.htm

in this way via a new conceptual unity that from then and to the time of writing governs them.

In Chapter 1 I used Foucault's concept of *statifications* to follow how sovereignty can be observed as working towards the emergence of border security as an observing system whose agents construct its state-attached difference as a unique, daunting, new task of state work and national necessity whose existence was not properly recognised or prepared for until 'this urgent now'. The threat environment 'we' now see *necessitates* a further and tighter integration of elements as border security, now.

Modern state-based attempts to screen the arrival, regulate the presence and ensure the orderly expulsion of people and things have encompassed institutionalised variants and combinations of the following:

1 the coast, navigation and safety (coast guarding);
2 import *qua* disease (quarantine);
3 import and export *qua* trade, tariff and tax (customs and excise);
4 arrival on the level of population (immigration);
5 the dynamic relation of international and global mobility and individuals attached to nation-states through forms of citizenship (residence).

As institutions concatenated so that they receive their proper place within the border continuum – for Border Force's defined border security purposes – coast guards, quarantine, customs, immigration and passports somehow have to be drawn in to a state-led but not state-dictated refiguration – not just of security, but also of the border – for there to be or become something like the 'continuum concept', a protect-able border and border security.

Ruddock's explicit intention to prevent asylum seeking by boat from becoming a 'migration pathway', shows us one clear and ramifying point where the Howard government shifted to a deterrence-led policy: formed little by little from 1996, then very clearly articulated from 1999 onward. The synchronous measure of temporary protection visas (TPVs) sat alongside this, and intentionally placed a Migration-department issued intensification on top of the stress already borne by already arrived asylum seekers with the introduction of mandatory detention from November 1992 – in turn legibly influenced by the 70s–80s policies of humane deterrence prosecuted by ASEAN nations[84] and the US' post Mariel shift to 'deterring illegal migration' (section 3.10). Australia's immigration detention centres were privatised in 1997,[85] but all were still onshore (sections 3.9–3.12). There was talk of increasing coastal surveillance led by Moore-Wilton from his

84 Simon, Jonathan, 'Refugees in a Carceral Age: The Rebirth of Immigration Prisons in the United States', *Public Culture*, 10: 3, 1998, pp. 583–584.

85 Phillips, Janet and Spinks, Harriet, 'Immigration Detention in Australia', *Parliament of Australia*. www.aph.gov.au/About_Parliament/Parliamentary_Departments/Parliamentary_Library/pubs/BN/2012-2013/Detention

appointment on May 13, 1996, to complement the disruption of people smuggling actively underway in Indonesia from that time. But definite talk of 'using military assets' to 'control the influx' – as Gough Whitlam had mentioned when he tested the waters of Darwin Harbour in the 1977 election – remained a radical position right into the millennium. That is, the idea that 'we' must 'stop the boats' *using navy assets* (let alone 'to restore a national sovereignty imperiled by their arrival') was dismissed as a nonstarter by the people with the greatest operational understanding of the dangers and hazards it entails as an on-water operation.

When Moore-Wilton made the first well-documented governmental suggestion of using the Navy to blockade boats attempting to arrive at Ashmore Reef, in 1999, and formally requested a report to canvas its viability, the Commander of the Defence Forces response was as follows,

> No one at that stage thought it was worth a candle. . . . You say you're going to mount this wonderful naval operation, but the boat still gets through. You all look like a bunch of dills. . . . In the public service you do have a problem of understanding just what the limits on force are . . . we are not there to use force (but) to make absolutely sure this never happens. We are there to exercise our rights and responsibilities, and the first premise is that no one loses their life.[86]

So although the carefully orchestrated, patiently executed, executive-led discursive shift toward 'illegals' and 'queuejumpers' was very clear from 1999, I note it alongside the significant societal absences of the obviousness of the militarised frontline approach and its threats that was so visible by 2013 (section 2.4). At the stage at issue in this section, around the turn of the century, there was no public and direct mention of 'stop the boats', *a la* the key phrase of the 2013 federal election. Nor was there the publicly expressed necessity of recognising boat arrivals as a categorical security threat and a threat to national sovereignty and national security, as they would be operationally from 2001, and again in 2006: nor were they considered as such by the military or the Office of National Assessments.[87]

This point is empirically and theoretically important because it indicates that securitisation came *after* the executive-led shift toward deterrence and the attendant discursive re-workings that saw the emergence of the 'illegal' and the 'queuejumper'.[88] Notably, this also fits with Joseph Nevins' overall account of

86 Marr, David and Wilkinson, Marian, *Dark Victory*, Allen and Unwin, Melbourne, 2004, p. 51.

87 Marr, David and Wilkinson, Marian, *Dark Victory*, Allen and Unwin, Melbourne, 2004, p. 50. Office of National Assessments (ONA) is a – fairly unusual – statutorily independent intelligence agency that provides assessments and analyses on topics to the Prime Minister and senior ministers.

88 Bigo, Didier, 'Security and Immigration: Toward a Critique of the Governmentality of Unease', *Alternatives*, 27, 2002, and Vogl, Anthea, 'Over the Borderline: A Critical Inquiry into the Geography of Territorial Excision and the Securitisation of the Australian Border', *UNSW Law Journal*, 38: 1, 2015, pp. 114–145.

the order of events in California from 1994.[89] Finally, the idea that anyone, including a baby or a child, is rightly *permanently* denied access to Australia for attempting to arrive there by boat in order to seek asylum, and *ought* to be intentionally subjected to indefinite offshore detention in squalid, dangerous, unsafe conditions in order to deter others (sections 3.11–12), policy from mid-June 2013 in Australia – was nowhere to be found.

2.8 Boat arrivals by August 2001: "the figures tell a clear story . . . there was a growing feeling that Australia had lost control of its borders"

The passengers boarding *Palapa* who became embroiled in the Tampa Affair were described in the introductory chapter as partaking of a crisis of global space. This crisis of global space remained in the background during our examinations of sovereignty, just as the orange hull of *MV Tampa* remained in clear sight at least twelve nautical miles from the shores of Christmas Island in the final days of August, 2001, where it was visible onshore to the Island's population of Australian citizens. In this section, I zoom right in on the time-sensitive communicated elements of the Tampa Affair once more for what it can tell us about the emergence of the message of border security from 'the growing feeling that Australia had lost control of its borders'. In this section, I do not observe Tampa as the ship, *Tampa*, nor for its passengers, the 433 people rescued from the *Palapa*, but as a political crisis observed from onshore Australia. As we zoom, I give attention to more precise mediation factors and the texture of their agency in communication, in ways that seek to open productive encounters with the theoretical ways of observing communication developed earlier (sections 2.2–2.3). But first, a look at the numbers of arrivals *and boats* leading up to the arrival of the ship that demanded Australia 'stop the boats', because it was the 'the numbers' that were represented by John Howard and the Howard government as necessitating an urgent 'drawing of the line' as a matter of sovereignty.

- In 1998, the number of boat arrivals sat at 200;
- in 1999, it increased to 3,721;
- in 2000, it decreased slightly to 2,939:
- then in 2001 it roughly doubled, to 5,516.

The fluctuations and net increase in individual boat arrivals does not track neatly with the number of vessels:

- 17 vessels in 1998,
- 86 vessels in 1999,
- 51 vessels in 2000,
- 43 vessels in 2001.

89 Nevins, Joseph, *Operation Gatekeeper and Beyond*, Routledge, Abingdon, 2010.

The ratio of individuals to vessels presents an interesting correlation that helps us consider some possible effects of the murky disruption of people smuggling in late 90s Java, and can also be used to read Prime Minister Howard's recollections of the significance of the numbers critically (of which more shortly).

The ratio of individuals to vessels, year to year, shifted as follows:

- In 1998 there were 200 people travelling on 17 vessels, roughly 12 people per vessel;
- in 1999 there were 3,721 people on 86 vessels, roughly 43 people per vessel;
- in 2000 there were 2,939 on 51 vessels, roughly 57 people per vessel;
- and in 2001 there were 5,516 aboard 43 vessels, *roughly 128 per vessel*, or approximately 10 times the number of people aboard each vessel as compared 1998 (section I.9).

If the Commonwealth's primary response to the issue in the late 90s through its smuggling disruption efforts in Indonesia was to some extent effective as intended, it stands to reason they would have reduced the number of *departing vessels* – and the figures bear this out. But if this is the case, then what the above figures co-indicate is that this didn't affect the numbers of *departing people*, and they increased. The inference I draw is the following.

As fewer vessels became available, the smugglers packed more people aboard each boat.[90] Whatever the actual mixture of factors in play, somewhere between what was known to be going on – murky disruption, official corruption among Indonesian officials, and the unscrupulous actions of profit-seeking people smugglers – a situation of grave danger had been co-created by pursuing a disruption and deterrence strategy by August 2001. Deterrence-led policy and profit-seeking smuggler operations had co-produced a chronic SOLAS situation whose essence was the regular departure of unseaworthy vessels carrying hundreds more people than they should have. Moreover: *on the open ocean*, where such coastal fishing boats are not seaworthy with any number of people aboard, let alone capable of carrying children aboard without lifejackets (section I.9). *Palapa*, the fishing vessel carrying the Tampa rescuees we met in the introduction, was a typical of vessel of the co-produced deadly conditions of 2001 (sections i.7–i.10).

In his autobiography *Lazarus Rising*, Prime Minister Howard drew the following conclusions from the figures, which I quote in full (and notably, the following can be read back against points detailed in sections 2.5–2.6):

> The figures tell a clear story. The number rose quite suddenly to 3721 in 1999, remained high at 2939 in 2000 and almost doubled to 5516 in 2001. The dramatic rise in 2001 put the issue on the front pages. Every day, so it

90 'The boats' are a scarce and precious resource for Javanese fishermen, and that many of these assets must be exposed to loss through sinking or scuttling to risk the profit that comes from a successful smuggling voyage.

> seemed, another boat had arrived. The sheer size of our coastline led Australians to feel particularly vulnerable to the unchecked arrival of scores of boats. Visa-holders who came by air had to present valid documentation to arrive here in the first place; even if they overstayed they were not viewed in the same light as people who came here in the first instance without documentation. That is why the alarm about the rise in the number of unauthorised boat arrivals was understandable.
>
> By July and August 2001, there was genuine concern in the Australian community about the flow of asylum-seekers. There was a growing feeling that Australia had lost control of its borders. No matter how logical the arguments the Government had employed to date might have been, there was intensifying public unease. In the process, public support for orthodox immigration and an orderly humanitarian refugee program began to erode. This was apparent to me from extensive talkback radio sessions, comments from MPs and random encounters with members of the public. Politicians are rightly exhorted to 'keep in touch' – no MP doing that would have missed the strength of community feeling.[91]

Howard's account is from 2010, and as the two paragraphs published in his political autobiography they should be read as his own crisp 'on record' version, long after the dust had settled. Yet Howard's account is consistent with how 'the figures' and 'community feeling' were interpreted by the Howard government in the heat of the crisis, as well as how they've congealed to become the Turnbull government's line at the time of writing. The following further factors we can see upon closer examination are notable.

Howard's on-the-record account fails to draw the SOLAS correlation from the ratio of vessels to individuals. Rather, the pertinent correlation he observes is the one between the numbers and their news media effect "[t]he dramatic rise . . . *put the issue on the front pages*".[92] The social fact Howard observes was not that 'boat arrivals' had appeared 'on our coastline' or 'in our territorial waters': they'd appeared 'in our newspapers'. Howard's account also places emphasis on the relation between a repetitive seeming "[e]very day, so it seemed, another boat had arrived", given relevance by a relation between coastline and entry that is largely imaginary. The inference Howard drew from this dwells on in the strong feelings this generated *among 'Australians'*: "[t]he sheer size of our coastline led Australians to feel particularly vulnerable". The overall conclusion adds a sympathetic evaluation to these raised feelings: *understandable* alarm (section 2.4).

Howard has consistently cashed out his position of 'understandable alarm' as being politically responsive and personally sympathetic to an "honourable community feeling" that ought to be respected even by those who disagree with it

91 Howard, John, *Lazarus Rising: A Personal and Political Biography*, Allen and Unwin, Melbourne, 2011, p. 394–395.

92 Op.cit., italics mine.

(section 2.6). Yet it is also full of lacunae that were agentic in bringing forth the message of border security: spaces of dark imagination where anxieties and fears rushed in to fill the void with tensing discourse and ever stronger calls for decisive 'drawing the line'. Nor is there any mention of the shadowy background, both the Howard government's active involvement in the AFP's disruption efforts, and the possibility that these tactics had the unintended but statistically legible effect of making an already hazardous trade far more dangerous. The final key point speaks to the asymmetries of vulnerability and regard generated in the emergence of border security. No Australian has ever died from 'feeling vulnerable' about 'the size of our coastline'; thousands of people have died seeking protection in Australia by boat.

2.9 August 26, 2001 to September 1, 2001: "We are a humane people. Others know that and sometimes they try and intimidate us with our own decency"

On Monday August 27, at 2.04pm,[93] the Prime Minister took a question from Ms Teresa Gambaro,[94] who asked:

> There have been reports of a boat foundered in international waters necessitating a rescue at sea. Does this have any implications for Australia?

Mr Howard's response was a comprehensive and complicated combination of as many as a dozen considerations, all of which were in live play that Canberra afternoon. After describing his government's positions in relation to them one by one, Mr Howard offered the following synthesis of a decision – this is crucial – that *he had already taken*, after scrambling to respond the night before (Sunday August 26), and after extensive crisis discussions with cabinet and the People Smuggling Taskforce. The following is the origin of the later and much more widely disseminated pronouncement "we will decide" (section 1.2), but note as well how, as of 2pm on Monday August 27, Howard's position was still a nuanced balance of international law and humanitarian impressions – ***and*** 'sending a message':

> We have taken this decision based on a proper understanding of our rights under international law. It is the right decision to take in Australia's national

93 All times in this section Australian Eastern Standard Time (AEST) unless specifically mentioned.

94 Gambaro, Teresa, 'Skilled Migrants Need to Be Taught About Hygiene, Says Liberal Teresa Gambaro', *www.news.com.au*, January 10, 2012. www.news.com.au/finance/migrants-dont-know-how-to-wear-deodorant-or-queue-up-say-liberal-teresa-gambaro/story-e6frfm1i-1226240418996

> interest. I hope that, amongst other things, it sends a message to people smugglers and others around the world that, whilst this is a humanitarian, decent country, we are not a soft touch and we are not a nation whose sovereign rights in relation to who comes here are going to be trampled on.[95]

Later that same day, Dagbladet[96] and the BBC[97] repeated variants of Howard's comments, with the equal emphasis on international relations, international law and the Commonwealth's sovereign right to decide who can enter Australia. On the first day that this crisis of global space and mobility emerged in the Indian Ocean, the shape that the Tampa Affair would take on the following day was still not yet well defined. But the Howard government had already played its hand when the prime minister spelled out the government's position on sovereignty in the House of Representatives on the afternoon of August 27: "we are not a soft touch and we are not a nation whose sovereign rights in relation to who comes here are going to be trampled on" (section 2.6). Absent active co-operation from Norway or Indonesia, Howard would have to throw international relations niceties and international humanitarian law commitments overboard if *any* development occurred that could be seen to be a 'trampling' of 'sovereign rights', so declared.

In this seeming to be, we might consider the political geography of the seeming appearance as Howard observed it retrospectively in *Lazarus Rising*, because here is a space of border security *in nuce*. Recall: an issue 'on' the front pages, generating "understandable alarm", *because* "the sheer size of Australia's coastline" led 'Australians' to "to feel particularly vulnerable to the unchecked arrival of scores of boats". Having patiently loaded the socius with a layercake of speech acts and iced it with a public avowal of his determination to make a decision and take a stand, Howard's role was then to fulfill his office by publicly performing his vision of a desirable resolution.[98] To respond to key scholarly claims around this *topos*, as a moment animated by a shared understanding of this 'vision of national social life and social order',[99] activated recursively through years of massaged apprehension and tuned anxiety about boat arrivals, Howard's response could not *just* be 'the

95 'Questions Without Notice, Illegal Immigration: MV Tampa' (Hansard), *Parliament of Australia*, Monday August 27, 2001. http://parlinfo.aph.gov.au/parlInfo/search/display/display.w3p;query=Id%3A%22chamber%2Fhansardr%2F2001-08-27%2F0051%22

96 'Trøstesløs situasjon om bord i "Tampa"', *Dagbladet*, August 27, 2001. www.dagbladet.no/nyheter/2001/08/27/277706.html

97 'Norway Pressures Australia Over Refugee Ship', *bbc.co.uk*, August 27, 2001. http://news.bbc.co.uk/2/hi/asia-pacific/1511202.stm

98 Charlton details that Howard had just returned from a visit to Britain where met Thatcher (final days of July), who had given him a lecture on "willpower and principle". This draws a possible connection with the Falklands. Charlton, Peter, '*Tampa*: The Triumph of Politics', in Solomon, David (ed.), *Howard's Race: Winning the Unwinnable Election*, Harper Collins, Sydney, 2002, p. 81.

99 Jasanoff, Sheila, 'Future Imperfect: Science, Technology, and the Imaginations of Modernity', *Dreamscapes of Modernity: Sociotechnical Imaginaries and the Fabrication of Power*, University of Chicago Press, Chicago, 2015, p. 4.

strategy of an individual' playing with unease,[100] nor was it just 'symptomatic of unconscious wishes held by the nation'.[101] Howard's response was a thoroughly social event that transpired through the pulsation of communication (section 2.3), governing everyone involved without being reducible to the intentional actions of individuals, explicated governmental strategies or unconscious desires.

By the morning of Tuesday August 28 (AEST), *Tampa* was page-one news in Australia, and was receiving ongoing prominent coverage by the BBC and Dagbladet. Throughout most of this day the topic was framed two ways:

1 as an impasse generated by legal uncertainty and political disagreement about whose international responsibility the rescuees were;
2 as a live humanitarian situation for the rescues, crew and captain.

'Three nations cast refugees adrift', read the *Sydney Morning Herald's* page one coverage[102]; 'Refugees stranded at sea – Boat people get refuge in containers, PM sends a message to the world', read *The Age*[103]; EXILED AT SEA – 'We have a lot of sick people on board. These people are in really bad shape' read page one of the *Daily Telegraph*.[104]

By the end of the day on Tuesday August 28 there were a number of developments: rising tensions on board; a diplomatic roundabout "travelling in ever-decreasing circles"[105]; the announcement that "Indonesia's ambassador told Foreign Minister Downer his country did not want them"; the arrival on CI of "a small Australian army force"[106] (section 2.1) and the departure from Fremantle of HMAS Arunga. "Apart from bringing food and medical supplies, the military mission still remains undefined," reported ABC's *Lateline* that evening in Australia.[107] The 'small army force', as it would shortly transpire, was the counter-terrorism unit of the SAS.

That night in Canberra, Mr Howard was repeating the congealing government line, which was condensed further during his appearance on *Lateline*, as follows:

IAN McMINN: Government sources are now saying if there is not a breakthrough soon there's likely to be a high level mission sent to Jakarta because the PM will not back down.

100 Bigo, Didier, 'Security and Immigration: Toward a Critique of the Governmentality of Unease', *Alternatives*, 27, 2002, p. 73.
101 Brown, Wendy, *Walled States, Waning Sovereignty*, Zone Books, New York, 2010, p. 133.
102 'Three Nations Cast Refugees Adrift', *Sydney Morning Herald*, August 28, 2001, p. 1.
103 Dodson, Louise, Mann, Simon and Taylor, Kerry, 'Refugees Stranded at Sea – Boat People Get Refuge in Containers, PM Sends a Message to the World', *The Age*, August 28, 2001.
104 Tsavdaridis, Noula, 'TURNED AWAY 'We Have a Lot of Sick People on Board: These People Are in Really Bad Shape', *The Daily Telegraph*, August 28, 2001, p. 1.
105 'Asylum Seekers in Limbo at Sea', *ABC Lateline*, August 28, 2001. www.abc.net.au/lateline/stories/s354039.htm
106 Op.cit.
107 Op.cit.

JOHN HOWARD, PRIME MINISTER: We have come to the conclusion as a government that we just can't continue sending a signal to the rest of the world that this is a nation of easy destination.

IAN McMINN: Meanwhile, it is beyond dispute that the majority of the Australian public feels exactly the same.

PETER MAHER, REHAME NATIONAL MEDIA MONITORING: A lot of these callers are now saying perhaps Pauline Hanson was right, perhaps all this immigration that she talked about will end up completely overrunning Australia.[108]

On the same evening on *A Current Affair*,[109] Howard *actively* shifted the debate – and here we *do* clearly see an individual strategically governing with unease.[110] In an interview made to this program's audience, the Prime Minister accused asylum seekers of making use of Australia's humanitarian norms to further their own ends – by going on hunger strikes and threatening suicide.

> We are a humane people. Others know that and sometimes they try and intimidate us with our own decency. On the other hand, we cannot surrender our right as a sovereign country our right to control our borders and we cannot have a situation where people can come to this country when they choose.[111]

The international nuance of Howard's position of a day earlier was falling away, and with the winnowing out of a balance of multilateral, humanitarian concerns and responsibilities was the increasingly stark, strong assertion of the decisionist prerogative to decide who can arrive, expressed as the quintessence of national sovereignty. It was as if the nation would stand or fall, based on Howard's ability to remain firm.

As an overarching description, I observe a winnowing out of concerns in play, day by day. To integrate and summarise this sifting narrowing so far:

- On Monday August 27, Howard had presented a dozen considerations when questioned in parliament (see footnote 113);
- on the morning of Tuesday 28, representatives from the Howard government and global news media were presenting the issue as an international

108 Op. cit. I direct the reader's attention to the person of Mark Textor, pollster, whose role in this for the Coalition is discussed in a footnote on pp. 417–418 *Dark Victory*. Textor learned his political trade in the US in the early 1990s (section 3.10), where he must have been well acquainted with Bush Snr. and Clinton's responses to post-Aristide Haitian arrivals in 1992–1993. Textor was providing his services to the Coalition from the late 1990s.

109 Marr, David and Wilkinson, Marian, *Dark Victory*, Allen and Unwin, Melbourne, 2004, pp. 85, n.405.

110 Bigo, Didier, 'Security and Immigration: Toward a Critique of the Governmentality of Unease', *Alternatives*, 27, 2002, p. 73.

111 Marr, David and Wilkinson, Marian, *Dark Victory*, Allen and Unwin, Melbourne, 2004, p. 85. Also: 'Canberra Preview – Wednesday', *RN Breakfast, ABC Radio National*, August 29, 2001. www.abc.net.au/radionational/programs/breakfast/canberra-preview–wednesday/3492086

relations impasse and a humanitarian situation, with the additional onshore Australian caveat that 'our sovereign rights will not be trampled on'.

- By the evening of Tuesday August 28, the SAS counter-terrorism unit had been scrambled, and Howard shifted the illocutionary force of his assertions away from the governments of Norway and Indonesia, toward asylum seekers, national sovereignty, staking his reputation on his conviction.
- By first reports on Wednesday August 29, Tampa was re-framed as a full-blown domestic political crisis with the Howard government at its centre, a 'make or break' stand off between 'the asylum seekers trying to intimidate the nation with its own decency', and the Australian Prime Minister prepared to interpose himself, act decisively and 'restore' national sovereignty.

Captain Rinnan entered Australia's territorial waters at 11.39am Canberra time on Wednesday August 29, 2001.[112] When he did so, he could not have known quite how spectacular the reaction would be, nor could he or any of those aboard easily imagined its implications for people seeking asylum in Australia by boat. At 11.45am, the Prime Minister ordered the Chief of Defence Admiral Chris Barrie to order the SAS to board and secure *MV Tampa*; at 1.15 pm, Admiral Barrie informed the Prime Minister that "the ship had been secured by 18 SAS troops with full co-operation from ship's crew"; at 1.45pm, just before question time, Mr Howard briefed Opposition Leader Kim Beazley; then at 2pm, Wednesday August 29, 2001, Prime Minister Howard informed the House of Representatives that "the ship has been secured".[113]

On the publicly voiced accounts of a number of parliamentarians on Thursday 30 of August, voters – *especially* voters in marginal electorates – inundated their local members with phonecalls. Those who rang Coalition members offered glowing congratulation for Howard and the Liberal party's hard stand. The phonecalls to Labor members are remembered for their bristling outrage: life-long Labor voters vowed to vote for the Coalition unless something was done immediately. The sentiment that then appeared via telephone from polled publics suggested a thumping victory for the Coalition, and howling fury at the Labor party's betrayal of its loyal supporter's wishes.

2.10 Evaluating the nascent message of border security: from "we will decide" to "deliberate deception motivated by political expedience"

As the summary of 'A Certain Maritime Incident' puts it, the Tampa Affair was a crisis "generated by the Government's rhetorically charged insistence that no

112 At 9.39am *CI time* that day.

113 'Ministerial Statements, Illegal Immigration: MV Tampa, *Parliament of Australia*, Wednesday, August 29, 2001. http://parlinfo.aph.gov.au/parlInfo/search/display/display.w3p;query=Id%3A%22chamber%2Fhansardr%2F2001-08-29%2F0067%22

asylum seeker aboard the Tampa was to set foot on Australian soil".[114] This aligns Howard's voicing of national sovereignty, pursued in Chapter 1, with this chapter's focus on the message of border security. In line with the overarching contention of this chapter, Tampa triggered the formation of a new regime of border security, a fully implemented apparatus with a number of different inter-active elements that concatenated previously distinct institutional functions as border security (section 2.7). But as we've explored, for the trigger to function – in the way that 'trigger warnings' pre-empt their audience's complexes in order to reduce the unleashed force when 'triggering' occurs – a large and complex array of tensions had to be pulled into focus and dialed up until they resonated in sympathy. As we imagine the hard twangs of aggrieved Australian voters emanating from the telephones of local members across the desks of the nation on those days in August 2001, what I observe is how the recursive interaction of polled sentiment and the careful discursive massage of primed publics over a number of years played through a crisis where the Howard government used improvised political rhetoric that was superbly timed, and culturally attuned. When Beazley called Howard on this, the latter demonstrated an unblinking willingness audaciously to throw out the playbook, and 'all of this' then interacted in a way that enabled the emergence of the message of border security in communication – but how exactly? The time sensitivity of the moment itself is also an agentic factor.

The emergence of border security in Australia would not have happened as it did without the way in which the Howard government observed and took advantage of the precise arrangement of ambient conditions of unease as they appeared to key publics *at that precise moment.* Howard gathered the darkening atmosphere into the thunderclap of 'we will decide'. At the same time, Howard's carefully polled and addressed comments wouldn't have resonated in the cultural context of the federal election of 1977 (see section 2.5), nor would 'drawing the line' with such determination have played well in September 2000, during the Olympics. Cultural changes on the level of 'the nation', such as the analysis of Brown and others direct us toward, are surely factors in play 'somehow'.[115] But in turn, they would not have condensed as they had by the mid-90s – in Australia as elsewhere – without globalising structural transformations. These structural changes were *engendered* by a quarter of a century of privatisation, offshoring and – most notably for rural, regional, ageing, white, working-class Australians and their resonators, like Hanson – the destruction of the Keynesian social contract (section 2.6). But the further point returns us to Seneca's aphorism 'luck is where preparation meets opportunity'. The Howard government artfully massaged an opportunity of their own partial making, and they were

114 'A Certain Maritime Incident', Commonwealth of Australia, October 23, 2002. www.aph.gov.au/Parliamentary_Business/Committees/Senate/Former_Committees/maritimeincident/report/index, p. 3.

115 See: Brown, Wendy, *Walled States, Waning Sovereignty*, Zone Books, New York, 2010, p. 133.

also fully prepared with a 'ready to go' policy response crafted along the lines of Max Moore-Wilton's people smuggling disruption and Ruddock's deterrence-led model, which emerged as the result of concentrated effort at cultural and institutional change within 'Canberra', from Moore-Wilton's hiring in 1996, and with great focus to the matters of people smuggling and asylum seeking, from 1999. Without overdetermining its agency, it is crucial to note the cultural shift engendered by the pivot toward a deterrence-led policy model. As we'll return to – and this is a point with global and topical relevance for North America and Europe as of writing – much follows from the contingent choice of deterrence as a strategic path (section 3.10).

Two months after the Tampa Affair, on *October* 28, 2001, three weeks after Australia had cast its lot in with the US' invasion of Afghanistan and become a member of the Coalition of the Willing, and two weeks after the towing and sinking of *SIEV 4* by *HMAS Adelaide* (sections 1.11–1.12), Howard proclaimed the following speech act, which we have already encountered: "we will decide who comes to this country and the circumstances in which they come".[116] This is the iteration of the decisionist prerogative most often quoted; it leaves out the many iterations prior to this, which began with much more nuance, such as the twelve concerns in Howard's response to the House of Representatives on August 27 (see section 2.9). In the wake of Tampa, the message was distilled even further, to the following:

- October 29: "[w]hat I am asserting is the right of this country to decide who comes here".
- October–November: "[w]e will decide who comes to this country".[117]

In retrospect, Howard claims the widely disseminated phrasing of October 28 was "unscripted", and that "*because* it captured the mood of the public it resonated".[118] In his account, the mood of the public comes first; a resonant speech act is one that captures a mood *because* it was already there. We've encountered this causal order of reasons with Howard's account of 'understandable alarm' and 'honourable community feeling'. There as here, Howard successfully painted himself as a led leader, a vessel through which the will of the nation passed, vibrating. In this sense, Howard was: action, system, node, conduit, transmission, subject, object, package, message, receipt, process *and knowledge of this putative totality as* effective (section 2.2–2.3). As we are considering how the message of border security came to be seen as almost unassailable common sense in and through communication, what should we make of this, empirically and theoretically?

116 Howard, John, 'Delivered at Sydney, NSW, October 28, 2001', Museum of Australian Democracy. http://electionspeeches.moadoph.gov.au/speeches/2001-john-howard

117 The latter phrasing is from a television advertisement broadcast in October and November of 2001. www.abc.net.au/lateline/content/2001/s422692.htm

118 *Leaky Boats*. . .

For Howard to call his 'we will decide' unscripted belies the deftness of his government's handling of the script he co-wrote; it disavows its patiently polled development over two years and the persistent diligence of cabinet ministers in shaping it using news media; and it passes over the fact that the Howard government were deferential toward a 'community feeling' that they intentionally co-built on talk-back radio, and by feeding gossip to favoured op-ed writers. This *coalesced* during Tampa, but it continued *after 9/11*, overcoded by the Global War on Terror in a way that the Howard government took ruthless electoral advantage of, to the point where, with Children Overboard[119] a communicative dynamic emerged that is described nowhere better than in the official report into the matter:

> genuine miscommunication or misunderstanding, inattention, avoidance of responsibility . . . [a] public service culture of responsiveness and perhaps over-responsiveness to the political needs of ministers, and deliberate deception motivated by political expedience.[120]

And yet, even this depiction is too unambiguous, especially to the extent that it accords agentic mastery to the actions of key cabinet ministers and their staff. Recalling Tampa nearly a decade later, Howard recalls being surprised by the surging intensity of public feeling in June–July and the rushing emergence of border security from the crisis by September 2001: this is borne out in Hansard, especially the repeated mention of 'being inundated' with phonecalls to electorates, especially marginal electorates. If Howard knew on some level he was unleashing the xenophobic genie from the bottle, even he was surprised by the atmospheric force of its release. How should we evaluate this, in line with this chapter's focus?

Was this inundation a predictable response to the tricky use of Hanson's dog whistle on being 'swamped'; was 'we will decide' apiece with the governmentality of an unease, or did something darker than "deliberate deception motivated by political expedience" emerge from the depths of the national unconscious and surface through the speaking person of the Prime Minister? Even those most responsible for bringing border security's world ashore into Australian political life were not fully in control of it or its significance. Border security's emergence was profoundly social: it pulled all those involved into the undertow of its meanings, and swept the nation into the swirling currents of the border continuum, and its expansive world of on-water operational matters. Border security's emergence in communication contains so much responsibility distributed among

119 This involved cabinet ministers knowingly falsely accusing asylum seeker parents of throwing their children into the water *on purpose* – based on information from the Navy – then refusing to promptly clarify or fully correct the record, once this was publicly falsified.

120 'A Certain Maritime Incident', *Commonwealth of Australia*, October 23, 2002. www.aph.gov.au/Parliamentary_Business/Committees/Senate/Former_Committees/maritimeincident/report/index, p. xxii.

so many agents; yet now, as a social fact and piece of national infrastructure, it appears to be beyond most political agency, let alone individual control.

2.11 *Operation Sovereign Borders* and the societal integration of border security via "on-water operational matters"

At this point, a full historical account of Australian border security would dwell on the wake of Tampa: the Pacific Solution, *Operation Relex I* and *II*, Children Overboard and so forth. I forgo this treatment here, both because these events have been very well explored, and because they speak to the national detail of border security, rather than its societal message. With the emergence of the message of border security as our objective, and with theories of communication as our background focus and way of understanding the message (sections 2.2–2.3), I return analytic attention to the months after the Coalition won the 2013 federal election by promising to deliver *Operation Sovereign Borders.*

What I wish to do here is stage a contrast: between border security as politics, as just explored above in the late months of 2001, and the extrapolitical domination of border security, in 2013, as explored via the arrival in Geraldton of the Deutsche Bank (section 2.4). From the contested complications of August 2001, so full of compounding complications, tensioned uncertainties and passionate contestation, this section brings us to a moment more than a decade later when the societally integrated message of border security became culturally dominant, evincing a societal shift from the message of border security as something contingent and improbable, to border security observed – by those operating using its distinctions – as something undeniable and unassailable.

2.11a September 23, 2013: 'shipping news to people smugglers'

On Monday September 23, 2013, five months after the Deutsche Bank arrived in Geraldton, five days after the Coalition's 'stop the boats' election victory, Mr Morrison elaborated his approach to information flow under *Operation Sovereign Borders* as the new Minister of Immigration *and Border Protection.*

> This government is going to stop the shipping news by ensuring that those boats aren't coming to report. That's our focus. . . . The Government was not operating an operation such as this. The Government was running a welcoming service. . . . It is the Government that sets the framework as to how information is to be dealt with. The Government previously set those rules and the Opposition responded to the environment that the government set for themselves.[121]

121 'Transcript: Press Conference – Operation Sovereign Borders', September 23, 2013. http://sievx.com/articles/OSB/20130923OSBPresser.html

In this setting, 'stopping the shipping news'[122] was fully integrated into the government's campaign intention to 'stop the boats'. *Operation Sovereign Borders* was no longer about 'sending the message' of border security, *it was* border security.

In integrating 'stop the boats' and 'stopping the shipping news', Morrison explicitly and intentionally intensified border security as *Operation Sovereign Borders*, transforming it, briefing by briefing, operation by operation, from a policy with a communication strategy into a communication strategy policy with an enforcement arm doing its onshore-unobservable work in a great oceanic beyond 'out there somewhere'. With its re-arrival as *Operation Sovereign Borders*, border security was made into an integrated communicative array where deterrence freely shifted between medium and form:[123] message, warning, interdiction; punishment, briefing, reassurance.

If we observe Morrison's communicated distinctions in their immanent web of reference, following our theoretical assumptions (section 2.3), they imply that political agency as border security is observed as possible, based on the choice of a communication strategy. If a government 'operates the operation' in a certain way', 'the shipping news' will cease, and the message of border security will have been effectively delivered. So then: border security *is* a message, but it only works if delivered in a certain way. The political choice of an information handling framework – border security 'packaged' as a weekly briefing – is capable of transforming the Indian Ocean, either into:

- a secured threat environment (as operated by the Coalition) or
- an 'unsafe smuggler's harbour' (as operated by the Labor party).

'Operating the operation' through Morrison's information handling framework retains border security's integrity by sending the following notably paradoxical message. Morrison's briefings excluded people smugglers from communication, via weekly announcements that loudly announced their excommunication from communication.[124] The further presumption, which is what renders the paradox operative for border security as communication, is that people smugglers are listening, paying attention and 'get the message'.

In early October, only weeks after the beginning of the ending of 'shipping news to people smugglers', prominent journalists were interpreting Mr Morrison's border security communications as secretive.[125] This was generalised to evaluate the novelty of the Abbott government, and to distinguish its style of

122 Shipping news refers to news conveyed by ship or news of a ship's arrival.
123 Luhmann, Niklas, *Theory of Society, Volume 1*, Stanford University Press, Stanford, 2012, pp. 113–120.
124 Luhmann, Niklas, 'Speaking and Silence', *New German Critique*, 61, 1994, pp. 25–37.
125 Horn, Eva, 'Logics of Political Secrecy', *Theory, Culture and Society*, 28: 7–8, 2011, pp. 103–122.

executive authority from the predecessor cabinet ministry.[126] The presence of 'secrecy' and 'distrust', 'so soon after the election', were seized upon by news media agents as way of characterising a emergent, dangerous, 'disturbing new trends'. The nub of these critiques concerned the public sphere. On the matter of border security, concerned *publics* were 'not being informed'; journalists could not get at 'the whole truth'.[127]

2.11b November 2013: of loose lips and on-water operational matters

By early November 2013, nearly two months after the election and the first briefing, *Operation Sovereign Borders'* paradoxes began to multiply.[128] This time, they were offered to the public as explanations for how operations were rightly proceeding. To wit: Mr Morrison began using the briefings to tell the electorate that he had nothing to tell the electorate about border security – and that this was the best proof that *Operation Sovereign Borders* was working, and that the government should be trusted *and* left alone to 'get on with it' on this basis.[129]

On Friday November 8, 2013, Mr Morrison fronted that week's briefing. It must have been the usual full hour, at least: the transcript runs to over seven thousand words. But if it is remembered, the Eighth Briefing will most likely be remembered for two things: for what the minister and General Campbell repeatedly refused to say, and for the stated reason they refused to say it: 'on-water operational matters'.

To pre-empt a point about onshore/offshore that will be developed in detail in the following chapter, we can see the form of offshore re-entering Morrison's observation of border security's operations (section 3.2). In his own rare words, offered in an earlier briefing, General Campbell drew a distinction between 'on-water operational matters' and "off-water reception and processing of illegal maritime arrivals under the control of the Department of Immigration and Border Protection".[130] In what follows I parse this as the distinction between "on-water operational matters" and 'off-water observational matters'. In the context of the *Operation Sovereign Borders* briefings, I interpret on-water as offshore and

126 Grattan, Michelle, 'Liberal Secrecy a Flawed Strategy', *The Conversation*, October 21, 2013. http://theconversation.com/liberal-secrecy-a-flawed-strategy-19406

127 Habermas, Jürgen, *Legitimation Crisis*, Beacon Press, Boston, 1975 and Luhmann, Niklas, 'What is Communication?' *Communication Theory*, 2: 3, 1992, p. 255.

128 Luhmann, Niklas, 'The Paradoxy of Observing Systems', *Cultural Critique*, 31, 1995, pp. 41, 42 (italics in original).

129 Luhmann, Niklas, *The Reality of Mass Media*, Stanford University Press, Stanford, 2000, pp. 40, 42–43.

130 'Transcript: Press Conference – Operation Sovereign Borders', Friday November 1, 2013. http://sievx.com/articles/OSB/20131101OSBPresser7.html

off-water as onshore, and employ these in the background as shores of politics to analyse this section from the transcript of the Eighth Briefing:

JOURNALIST: Minister, this is an issue of great public interest, and where the boat goes – the plight of these people is part of that. Why can't you be more forthcoming?

SCOTT MORRISON: Because that would go to our conduct of on-water operations, and I, and the Commander, are not going to put our operations at risk through a public commentary on those operations. Now, when we announced before the election – let's go back to then – and I announced with the leader of the then-Opposition, now the Prime Minister, and Major General-retired Molan, that we were going to put in place Operation Sovereign Borders. It would be a military-led, border security operation. That has significant implications for how matters under such an operation are handled in the public sphere.

Now, I was quizzed during the election campaign about these sorts of communication issues, and I was very up-front about it. So Operation Sovereign Borders, and the way information is being managed under Operation Sovereign Borders is as the Coalition represented it to the Australian people during the last election. And I have been pleased with the reaction I have had from people as I have moved around Australia, about the effectiveness of this operation, and the fact that we are just getting on with the job.

After a short digression onto international relations between Australia and Indonesia, the following:

JOURNALIST: So when this particular overnight operation is over, will you explain the full story to us?

SCOTT MORRISON: Well again, I will go into as much detail as would not compromise any of our on-water and ongoing operations.

We have been crystal clear about that in all of our eight briefings. So you've have had eight briefings on this issue, and we have made the rules about how we convey information on these operational matters, I think, crystal clear. And we will continue to conduct ourselves that way.

JOURNALIST: So you will tell us where the boat goes?

SCOTT MORRISON: Well I have given my answer to that question.

Let us enter the hermeneutic circle Morrison's reasoning for a moment, following the Luhmannian assumptions about communication guiding my observations of him sending the message of border security (section 2.3). Morrison consistently remonstrated with journalists that the electorate had communicated a 'mandate' to institute *Operation Sovereign Borders* that had emerged when 'the people' elected the Abbott government. The electorate, in bestowing its 'mandate',[131] had been given sufficient indication that they could and should expect 'the communication of silence' about on-water operational matters.

The significant implication of the electorate's bestowing its 'mandate' upon a 'military-led border security operation' is that no discussions about border security in the public sphere could rightly refer to what was actually happening, from the moment of the election onward. A discursive lacuna formed around the mandate, whose essence was the displacement of any positive political discussion of the detailed operations of its politics: done well, border security *meant* not talking about border security, 'just getting on with operating the operation', in off-water silence. 'What goes on water, stays on water'. Echoing Howard's deference toward honourable community feeling, this was represented as Mr Morrison's obedience to public opinion, while the proof that the Abbott government was delivering was that he was 'just getting on with (not talking about getting on with) it'. As the weekly briefings evolved into punctuated silence about on-water operational matters, communicating a space of opacity in the name of security was elevated into the effective delivery of the will of the nation as it expresses its sovereignty through border security.

Mr Morrison draws a significant and categorical public implication 'for how (offshore) matters are handled in the public sphere' (see sections 2.2–2.3) from which we can extract a further point about border security as off-water communication about on-water operational matters, and the way this severs the public/private distinction anew in a space of border security. Reading his comments, *any* public discussion of offshore conduct carries the potential to compromise operations, endangering national sovereignty by increasing the likelihood of the kind of 'dramatic breach' that would come once people smugglers are 'in receipt of the shipping news' and resume penetration of Australia's vulnerable coastline (section 2.4). This implication is further loaded *because* of the way the Abbott government hystericised the Deutsche Bank's meaning: if a vessel seeking to arrive in New Zealand could be framed as 'national surrender' and 'a total discreditation of the migration program', then it follows that, by November 2013, the border continuum had been sensitised to the point where even the murmur of a boat could burst the circuits of secured circulation, be read as a loss of sovereign control, discredit the 'orderly framework of movement' and engender a crisis of faith in the migration program and multiculturalism *tout court*. 'Stop the boats' loaded the decks in all these ways. For Morrison, the mere implication of what *might* happen if the public discusses on-water operations is sufficient evidence for prosecuting a staunch *absolute refusal* to communicate about the offshore conduct referred to as on-water operational matters. With a strange twist, this

131 Rundle, Guy, 'Rundle Mythbusts Abbott's Victory, crikey.com.au, September 10, 2013. www.crikey.com.au/2013/09/10/rundle-mythbusts-abbotts-victory/

arguably draws upon a reservoir of wartime cultural memory in which 'loose lips sink ships' (see sections 1.7 and 5.5).

Finally, the muted presence of a living emblem of military authority and national duty at the weekly briefings is striking. That Mr Morrison's absolute refusal to discuss on-water operational matters was made standing beside one of Australia's most senior uniformed military officials is significant; moreover, an ex SAS platoon commander (section 2.1). General Campbell's silence on operational matters was rendered as the carrying out of an unquestionable duty above public scrutiny. As General Campbell made the career choice to take this political decision, he donated the rhetoric of operational space and the dignity of national service and sacrifice to the Abbott government.[132]

On November 16, 2013, Mr Morrison removed General Campbell in response to increasing news media criticisms that his silent presence at Morrison's briefings was politicising the military.[133] However, when "[a]sked on Friday if he was aware of concerns within the Defence Force that his role was being politicised, General Campbell replied, 'I am unaware of those'" The same article went on to report that "General Campbell also gave detailed reasons why revealing too much information could work to the benefit of people smugglers trying to sell passage to Australia to asylum-seekers". The report did not include any of those details.

In April 2014, five months after he eventually reported feeling uncomfortable with his political role in *Operation Sovereign Borders*, General Campbell starred in the Abbott government's YouTube version of the 'No Way' commercial[134] (sections 2.2–2.3). Aside from respecting its own belief in the chain of command by obediently carrying out the wishes of the people as ordered by the executive, we may well question what the Australian Defence Force gains by being enfolded into the executive-led delivery of a political policy, as well as the dignity of office and public trust it risks losing. On February 24, 2015, it was announced that General Campbell was made Chief of Army;[135] as of writing, he has not broken his silence on his silences.

132 Grattan, Michelle, 'Morrison Reacts to Heat Over Politicising the Military', *The Conversation*, November 13, 2013. http://theconversation.com/morrison-reacts-to-heat-over-politicising-the-military-20325 and Wadham, Ben, 'Operation Sovereign Borders: Dignified Silence or Diminishing Democracy?' *The Conversation*, January 8, 2014. http://theconversation.com/operation-sovereign-borders-dignified-silence-or-diminishing-democracy-21294

133 Wroe, David and Snow, Deborah, 'Minister Takes General Out of the Political Fray', *Sydney Morning Herald*, November 16, 2013. www.smh.com.au/federal-politics/political-news/minister-takes-general-out-of-the-political-fray-20131115-2xmmu.html

134 Laughland, Oliver, 'Angus Campbell Warns Asylum Seekers Not to Travel to Australia by Boat', *guardian.com.au*, April 11, 2014. www.theguardian.com/world/2014/apr/11/angus-campbell-stars-in-videos-warning-asylum-seekers-not-to-travel-by-boat

135 Wroe, David, 'Angus Campbell to Become Australia's Next Chief of Army', *The Sydney Morning Herald*, February 24, 2015. www.smh.com.au/federal-politics/political-news/angus-campbell-to-become-australias-next-chief-of-army-20150224–13nng7.html

2.12 The politics in the message of border security, from conflict to integration, and the 'ring of steel' of 'a migration superpower'

By March 2014, six months' worth of 'stopping the shipping news', and by extension *Operation Sovereign Borders*, was declared victorious.[136] "This operation is working, Chair," said Mr Morrison. "The boats are stopping. The way we manage information is an important part of this operation".[137]

Morrison's absolute refusal to discuss any on-water operational matters carries the message sending theory to its final point of delivery (sections 2.2–2.3). Normatively, it also bears with it a set of assumptions about the politics of communication that I have been tracking throughout this chapter. The 'victory' of the assumptions carried into society with the enaction of *Operation Sovereign Borders* can bring us to some provisional conclusions about the message of border security: both as settled public opinion and 'bottled' policy drifting away from Australia as a hopeful policy model for Europe,[138] and as what is then integrated as necessary from then on in the polities to which it attaches indefinitely.

Operation Sovereign Borders integrated Australian border security in society. It has done so to the point where – anywhere onshore 'in' Australia, anywhere 'within' the border continuum – border security can appear meaningful as form, message, warning and punishment, without most questioning this shapeshifting state of affairs itself as improbable, or unnecessary, or resisting it as nonsense or a basic violation of the most important ethical horizons (section 6.6), something 'not worth a candle' like militarised interdiction had been to most, in 1999 (section 2.7).

I observe the emergence and intensifying reiteration of the message of border security traversed in this chapter as a movement from conflict to integration. By extension, I characterise the message of border security as something that came to the centre of political contestation in Australia by 2001, but that since this time as been offshored, buried, negated, then quietly reinstalled as national infrastructure, a set of severances placed as far beyond the shores of politics as the nation can imagine – and still recognise itself and its interests. From 1996, alongside a growing critical awareness of globalisation, people seeking asylum in Australia by boat became politicised in the true sense. This followed the gradual emergence of these factors from 1977 (a focus of the coming chapter): a contentious phenomenon provoked a number of problems and responses and engendered conflicts

136 'Operation Sovereign Borders: The First Six months', *abc.net.au*, March 26, 2014. www.abc.net.au/news/interactives/operation-sovereign-borders-the-first-6-months/

137 'Passengers Describe Drama of Turning Asylum Seeker Boats Back', *ABC 7.30 Report*, March 17, 2014. www.abc.net.au/7.30/content/2014/s3965617.htm

138 Frum, David, 'Closing Europe's Harbors: The Urgent Case for Stopping the Flow of Illegal Migrants Across the Mediterranean', *The Atlantic*, July/August 2015. www.theatlantic.com/magazine/archive/2015/07/closing-european-harbors/395321/

that continue to ramify through institutions, jumping across scales, and forcing critical reflection – and its silencing – about global mobility, sovereignty, identity, rights and justice.

The Australian emergence of the message of border security involved a maritime re-thinking of state and nation as a twenty-first-century sovereign entity that courts the coursing, vibrant dynamism of global mobility *while* repelling its recognised risks and threats – we will return to this moment from its second decade of routine operations by way of global logistics, in Chapter 4. As this re-thinking of state and nation happened, border security moved from a radical, marginal idea to something broadly appealing and *intensely desired* by electorally significant publics by August 2001. Yet by the middle of 2013 border security *itself* had become almost unthinkably necessary infrastructure protecting the nation from the 'obvious immediate harm' of the 'dramatic breach' (sections 2.4, 2.11). And with the election of the Abbott government, *Operation Sovereign Borders* fully integrated border security into society by emphasising that its operations were so important they could no longer be discussed.

In an unusually clear and direct address of the political implications of his theoretical construction, Niklas Luhmann addressed a crucial co-relation between conflict and integration:

> Usually, when speaking of integration, sociologists imagine a well-oiled machine, something pleasant and harmonious. If everyone is well integrated, the future and cooperation will be secure, one will get along, and there will be peace. But what exactly is integration? If we define this concept, too, in more formal terms and say that integration is the limitation of the degrees of freedom that components have, then it is obvious that conflict has a strong integrative effect. Components are integrated to the degree that the options, states, and qualities that a system can have are reduced. . . . A theory of conflict must also be a theory of too much integration in a social system and of the tendency to regain additional options and introduce them into the conflict. This tendency is a sort of cancer. There is rampant growth in the system because it is too integrated.[139]

As a movement from conflict to integration, the message of border security transformed from something that pressurised the national political atmosphere until it burst with the thunderclap of the decisionist prerogative, to on-water matters buried beneath contention and outside visibility, metaphorically like the Internet's undersea cables. As a social system whose medium is meaning, border security's communications are never as well blanketed from their environmental irritants as the biological and physico-technical counterparts their metaphorical

139 Luhmann, Niklas, 'Double Contingency, Structure, Conflict', in *Introduction to Systems Theory*, Polity Press, Cambridge, 2013, pp. 250–251.

employers dream they'll become. Retaining the integration of the message of border security makes a percentage of its human proponents work hard for their wage (Max Moore-Wilton), their integrity (Peter Reith) and their promotion (Scott Morrison, Angus Campbell), while its severances remain apparent to others as violent nonsense and needless cruelty (section 6.5). This comes full circle with the following communicated moments, which bring us out of the post Operation Sovereign Borders 'victory' to this moment of writing, and this chapter's conclusion.

On September 20, 2016, the Minister for Immigration and Border Protection declared that Australia was a 'migration superpower'.[140] This phrase was made to fit the Prime Minister's comments to the UN just two days earlier, where border security was represented as integral to any properly functioning multiculturalism, and described as the ideal underpinning of a society open to globalisation (sections 2.1, 4.6–4.7). In a piece of advertorial published just a week later, on September 24, 2016, The Daily Telegraph, Australia's most deferentially pro-Coalition, anti–asylum seeker tabloid, became 'the first media organisation allowed to the frontline of Operation Sovereign Borders'. In their advertorial, Daniel Meers and Simon Benson proudly reported the following[141]:

> AUSTRALIA is creating a ring of steel around our borders, escalating air surveillance and sea patrols *in response to the worsening refugee crisis in Europe.*[142]

Seen from border security's world, the future vision of multicultural Australia is a migration superpower, open to migration and globalisation, yet wedded to a negation of asylum, carried to its dystopian horizon by the message of border security, symbolised by the crowning ornamentation of a ring of steel.

140 'Minister for Immigration and Border Protection – Address to the Australian Strategic Policy Institute', *Liberal Party of Australia*. www.liberal.org.au/latest-news/2016/09/20/minister-immigration-and-border-protection-address-australian-strategic

141 Meers, Daniel and Benson, Simon, 'Ring of Steel to Protect Our Borders', *The Daily Telegraph*, September 24, 2016. www.dailytelegraph.com.au/news/nsw/sea-and-air-patrols-are-securing-australian-borders-like-never-before/news-story/135aea6297f4eb50744867245c980763

142 Op.cit., italics mine.

Part II

Border security's international lineages and global alignments

Chapter 3

You will never see the shores of Australia

Offshore's form, offshoring detention for border security

3.1 Introduction: the pivotal location and paradoxical function of offshore in global spaces of negated politics and justice

Border security's unilateral projection of Australia's national sovereignty relies on offshore and offshoring. This reliance on offshore upholds and integrates the distinctions of border security's world so that off-water observational matters can be kept from perturbing on-water operational matters (sections 2.10–2.12). Australian border security's reliance on offshore also means that its national sovereignty is now secured in the global spaces produced through the two-sided form of offshore we'll direct theoretical focus toward throughout this chapter. Offshore also opens a way to considering the international and the global in border security, our framing in this second of the three parts of *Border Security*.

In order to locate and explicate the pivotal location and paradoxical function of offshore centres as global spaces of negated politics and justice, this chapter moves away from the Australian spaces where border security emanated – through sovereignty, in communication – the analytic foreground in section one. Here, I enquire into the form of offshore and the observable features of offshoring processes in colonising imperial *statifications* here and there, then and now. I look at the emergence of maritime interdiction in the US Caribbean and consider key aspects of the US' vanguard use of offshore detention at Guantánamo Bay. I then return to Christmas Island (CI) once again to directly consider offshore detention, as well as offshore processing on Nauru, and Manus Island (sections 3.11–3.12). Empirically, this chapter seeks points of global emergence and greater analytic precision responsive to oft-made historical and international comparisons between Guantánamo and CI, between islands and offshore sites. This chapter points beyond then back to contemporary Australia, allowing us to apprehend general global dynamics and observe comparable international political relations at work in the production of offshoring processes and sites through offshore's form, with a view to the fate of asylum seeking by boat in the Mediterranean in the political present of the time of writing.

As we will explore in this and the following chapter's exploration of global logistics, the fact that offshore sites are *nebulous* global spaces that are *operable in specific ways* shows us two key things that help us understand border security as global infrastructure working to secure circulation (section I.2, i.6, i.9, i.10). First, it shows us that the national is no longer distinct from the international or global in ways 'we' might conventionally understand. Second and relatedly, it shows us how knowledge of this nebulous state of affairs is leveraged by group agents working as observing systems – which, to return to key points raised via the crab bridge, gives a way to think normatively about contingent selections enacted as durable designs with existential consequences, both inflicted and unintended (section I.2, i.10). The production of offshore sites as black boxes placed beyond the shores of politics,[1] beyond horizons of justice, is reflexive and agentic; offshoring processes are *statifications* (section 1.1). Restoring sovereignty, holding people offshore, strengthening the border continuum, retaining the integrity of the framework of movement, sending the message of border security: offshoring further integrates border security *in* society, *on* islands, 'out there' in the open ocean, in the interest of certain peoples, via a further and deeper investment in border security's increasingly societally integrated world.

By offshoring *detention*, the 'the state' seeks to contain 'itself' and its discontents, integrating its contradictions through the selective use of paradox applied to categories of person.[2] As a practiced understanding, enacting border security by detaining people offshore produces spaces where sovereignty is *and is not*, just as it secures detainable categories of people kept *as if* they are not people. We will encounter this legally fictioned paradoxical figure under the names 'Cuban-Haitian entrant' (section 3.9), 'offshore entry person' and 'unlawful noncitizen' (section 3.12), phrases that denote individuals and populations who must be warehoused indefinitely, even though evidence keeps arriving onshore that this destroys their lives. To connect a key claim I develop here with the substantive explorations of the implicit normativity of global logistics in the next chapter, the dedifferentiation of jurisdiction over persons, rights and things[3] produced by the warehousing of people offshore is legible through its alignment to the norms and goals of global logistics. By way of furthering our global focus in section two of *Border Security*, this shows us how what appear as particularly American, Australian or Anglophone political phenomena and peculiar national-cultural symptoms – which in other senses they also definitely are – are also local instantiations of a fundamental general problem

1 MacKenzie, Donald, 'Opening the Black Boxes of Global Finance', *Review of International Political Economy*, 12: 4, 2005, pp. 555–576 and Barry, Andrew, *Political Machines: Governing a Technological Society*, Athlone, London, 2001.

2 Luhmann, Niklas, 'The Paradoxy of Observing Systems', *Cultural Critique*, 31, 1995.

3 Mussawir, Ed, *Jurisdiction in Deleuze: The Expression and Representation of Law*, Routledge, Abingdon, 2011.

of the political present. Offshore sites are political spaces that disclose negated horizons of global justice.

I note, finally, the politics *opened* by the aspirational 'closures' and actual expulsions of offshore and offshoring.[4] Responding to 'threatening' instantiations of globalisation by offshoring detention doesn't simply shut out asylum seekers; nor are their contentions ended or erased when they are muted and negated. This chapter offers a critical reading of the politics in offshore detention that suggests it is not best understood as being about 'exclusion of the Other', 'unity of the nation', or even just 'total domination' (although diligent and reflexive attempts in these directions have all been diligently made by onshore Australian agents, as explored in chapters one and two). Attuning to the operational centrality of paradox in the two-sided form offshore opens politics *through* asylum's closure which prompts implicating questions about the (im)possibility of *global* politics and justice. Why is global justice *impossible* for detainees? Why is border security *necessary* for Australia?

Pursuing these questions, a further normative purpose of this chapter is to locate the location and function of offshore detention centres as replicant global spaces of injustice, and repossess our implication in the expansion of their securing operation. Though I do not wish to foreground this in the study that follows, on a theoretical level I am exploring ways to apply Luhmann's systems theory to socio-spatial problems,[5] in ways that, further do not shy away from the normative. Luhmann's redescription of Spencer-Brown's *Laws of Form*, and the paradoxical ways in which two-sided forms can be skilfully applied to effectuate offshoring processes that are and are not here and there, are and are not sovereign, where suffering does and does not happen, show us a way toward a dark heart beating in the political present. Offshore sites are *our* dystopias, and offshoring processes are our dystopian negations of utopian possibilities, other possible justices and polities (section 1.1). I consider what this means, nationally and globally, for offshore's integration as elements of Australian border security spread to Europe as a 'best practice' response to global mobilities judged *so threatening* by Australia's former prime minister that 'the future of Europe' is at stake.[6]

4 Luhmann, Niklas, *Theory of Society, Volume 1*, Stanford University Press, Stanford, 2012, p. 34.

5 Borch, Christian, 'Spatiality, Imitation, Immunization: Luhmann and Sloterdijk on the Social', in LaCour, Anders and Philippopoulos-Mihalopoulos, Andreas (eds.), *Luhmann Observed: Radical Theoretical Encounters*, Palgrave Macmillan, Basingstoke, 2013, pp. 150–168 and Jacobs, Joren and Van Assche, Kristof, 'Understanding Empirical Boundaries: A Systems-Theoretical Avenue in Border Studies', *Geopolitics*, 19: 1, 2014, pp. 182–205.

6 'Transcript: Tony Abbott's controversial speech at the Margaret Thatcher Lecture', *The Sydney Morning Herald*, October 28, 2015. www.smh.com.au/federal-politics/political-news/transcript-tony-abbotts-controversial-speech-at-the-margaret-thatcher-lecture-20151028-gkkg6p.html and Neuman, Klaus, 'Boat People and Gunships in the Mediterranean, *Inside Story*, May 12, 2015. http://insidestory.org.au/boat-people-and-gunships-in-the-mediterranean

3.2 'No man is an island': offshore's form, offshore as a global norm in 'the age of offshore' and offshore and offshoring as form and process

The terms offshore and offshoring ordinarily refer to drilling platforms, tax havens and transfers of socially secured and politically unionised manufacturing across national borders to zones 'elsewhere' in which 'the same work' can be performed 'at a reduced cost'. In this chapter, I follow a growing archive of critical explorations of offshore sites and offshoring processes to where these detailed explorations draw analytic attention.[7] I do so with the political intent just introduced (section 3.1), by attending to designed attempts to negate questions of justice, and the ways that many different offshoring processes implicate us as they work differentially for the production of global class relations.

The key bridging claim underpinning this political and normative concern is that offshoring processes are diverse and specific *but not disparate*, and this is how we get a first critical 'in' to understanding one of offshoring's salient political effects. Offshore doesn't *just* produce categories of person who *must be* detained, *can be* warehoused and *can never* arrive and be protected and cared for – as this chapter details it at length. It also works toward securing *smoothed* circulation and *screened* mobility for onshore enclaves, 'we', the people who remain, for the most part, the unexamined beneficiaries of that which is (and those who are) offshored through offshoring – the focus of the two chapters to come. Whether in detention or banking, offshoring is about border security *as well as* global finance. As a coda that will become an explicit focus in Chapter 4, this also shows that Australian border security isn't *just* about Australia – or border security.

In recent decades the application of offshore has become a global norm, while practices of offshoring have been central to recent transformations of labour and capital. Offshore is also how the global rich moved and kept 22–33 trillion in assets after 2008[8]; offshore is why Amazon and the Book Depository are so cheap – for global middle-class consumers, for now – and offshore is among the reasons why Apple became the most profitable corporation in history so far, in 2015.[9] Off-

7 Brittain-Catlin, William, *Offshore: The Dark Side of the Global Economy*, Farrar, Strauss and Giroux, New York, 2006, Deneault, Alain, *Offshore: Tax Havens and the Rule of Global Crime*, The New Press, New York, 2011, Mountz, Alison and Loyd, Jenna, 'Transnational Productions of Remoteness: Building Onshore and Offshore Carceral Regimes Across Borders, *Geographica Helvetica*, 69, 2014, pp. 389–398, Palan, Ronen, *The Offshore World: Sovereign Markets, Virtual Places, and Nomad Millionaires*, Cornell University Press, Ithaca, 2003, Shaxson, Nicholas, *Treasure Islands: Tax Havens and the Men who Stole the World*, Vintage, London, 2012, and Urry, John, *Offshoring*, Polity Press, Cambridge, 2014.

8 Allen, Frederick E., 'Super Rich Hide $21 Trillion Offshore, Study Says', *www.forbes.com*, July 23, 2012. www.forbes.com/sites/frederickallen/2012/07/23/super-rich-hide-21-trillion-offshore-study-says/#73c8623873d3

9 'Apple Now Most Profitable Corporation in History of World', *People's Pundit Daily*, January 28, 2015. www.peoplespunditdaily.com/news/economy/2015/01/28/apple-now-most-profitable-corporation-in-history-of-world/

shoring processes have been key to the transfer of unionised blue-collar jobs out of the OECD, and the sending of a fair portion of the world's industrial proletariat – the political subject of the communist international – to south-eastern China. The ensuing destruction of the post-war Keynesian social contract, and its replacement with neoliberalisations and economic globalisation (sections 2.6, 4.6, 5.4, 5.7–5.9), all banking with/on the seamless, borderless operation of unconstrained finance capital – whose central ideological claim was that 'a rising tide lifts all boats' – would not have transpired as they have without specific applications of offshore's form. We are now at the point where all accumulative processes refer to or rely on the form of offshore or move through offshored sites. As the Panama Papers show,[10] offshore is not 'corruption within the game' or 'the corruption of the game', it has become the game. It might be no exaggeration to call the first decades of the twenty-first century the age of offshore, yet almost nobody would recognise the name of their age in this form.

In what follows I explore *offshore as form* and *offshoring process(es)*. To say that offshore is a form is to emphasise the way that offshoring processes rely on differential applications of the form of offshore – a circular construction. To speak of form after Plato is, perhaps, to be accused of taking refuge in the serenity of the immutable by distaining the phenomenal mess of process.[11] But this is not what is meant by form in way I express it here. Form doesn't preclude or exclude process, it enables the operations that procure it as a difference. Nor is the form of offshore an immutable identity remaining the same over time and in space. Rather, as an iterative form enacted anew with every operation, and that involves repeatedly crossing its own boundary (which *takes* time and *makes* space), offshore is the engine of its own difference.

I parse offshore and offshoring, form and process, as follows. All offshoring processes seek to produce 'some form of offshore', and all offshore sites are offshore in certain and often highly specific ways, though no two offshore sites can be identical, and *many are not physically offshore*. This last point is crucial, especially as it complicates Alison Mountz' influential insights on islands and offshore detention,[12] which rely on the background fact that islands *are* (physical islands),

Ockenden, Will, 'Apple Pays $193m Tax in Australia on $27b Revenue as Federal Government Vows to Capture Lost Taxes', *abc.net.au*, March 7, 2014. www.abc.net.au/news/2014-03-06/tax-expert-explains-how-apple-pays-193m-tax-on-27b-revenue/5303426

10 'The Panama Papers: Politicians, Criminals and the Rogue Industry that Hides Their Cash', *The International Consortium of Investigative Journalists*. https://panamapapers.icij.org/

11 Plato, 'Part VII: The Philosopher Ruler', *The Republic*, Penguin, London, 2007, pp. 189–249.

12 Mountz, Alison and Briskman, Linda, 'Introducing Island Detentions: The Placement of Asylum Seekers and Migrants on Islands', *Shima: The International Journal of Research into Island Cultures*, 6: 2, 2012, pp. 21–26 and Mountz, Alison and Loyd, Jenna. 2014, 'Transnational Productions of Remoteness: Building Onshore and Offshore Carceral Regimes Across Borders', *Geographica Helvetica*, 69, pp. 389–398.

even as the analysis focuses on the spatio-temporal stretching of state authority via sovereignty and 'enforcement archipelagos'. The tack I take, in contrast, follows Carey McWilliams by insisting that islands are never natural facts, but rather ways that we construe separation where there is also always relation: hence the way that, for him, southern California is an 'island on the land'.[13]

In order to clarify this, consider the social fact that the City of London is physically onshore in the city in London, but that one of its key roles in global finance is the provision of offshore banking services, and that it is itself complexly offshore.[14] Consider how 'the island continent' Australia is onshore, yet that, to foreshadow a consequential trajectory I will explore (see section 3.11–3.12), it has been made an offshore excised place[15] *for asylum seekers.* As I explore these and other examples of offshoring, I dwell on how the desired political effects of offshore's form are produced through its continual application to a space over time. This is skilled, organised, creative labour undertaken in real places[16]: imaginatively, in communication, often (but not always) on literal-physical islands, with a whole heavy materiality and implicit normativity as its entourage. The production of dystopias is work done by actual people whose utopian imaginings become actual places of profit and suffering.

Offshor*ing* refers to sets of social processes applied to capital and labour, unfolding via the form of offshore in space over time. We can see that this is a circular construction that keeps pointing back to offshore without saying how 'it' works or what 'it' is (other than an overly self-referential, circular construction). Like many of the avowedly, intentionally circular theoretical constructions in *Border Security*, the orbit of offshore operations can also be described as elliptical. In this first gloss, I beg the reader's patience while I draw along the wobble in the formal path of offshore's orbital ellipses by considering the constitutive role of paradox in its operation, flagged above (section 3.1).

In the construction of sovereign spaces as 'elsewheres', offshoring processes operate via the paradox inherent in offshore's form. That is, the ways in which offshore 'is and is not' a form produces spaces that 'are and are not' offshore: are and are not *de jure* sovereign (section 1.10–1.11, 2.11), are and are not *de facto* elsewhere (section 3.7, 3.11). This names a key benefit of the form's use: the application of offshore enables a conjugation of benefits and costs via the 'is

13 "Walled off from the rest of the country by mountain ranges and desert wastes, Southern California is an island on the land, geographically attached, rather than functionally related, to the rest of America". McWilliams, Carey, *Southern California: An Island on the Land*, Peregrine Smith, Utah, 1980, p. 14.

14 Palan, Ronen, *The Offshore World: Sovereign Markets, Virtual Places, and Nomad Millionaires*, Cornell University Press, Ithaca, 2003 and Shaxson, Nicholas, *Treasure Islands: Tax Havens and the Men Who Stole the World*, Vintage, London, 2012.

15 'Migration Amendment (Unauthorised Maritime Arrivals and Other Measures) Act 2013', Commonwealth of Australia, 2013. www.legislation.gov.au/Details/C2013A00035

16 Sassen, Saskia, *Territory, Authority, Rights: From Medieval to Global Assemblages*, University of Chicago Press, Chicago, 2006 and Ziegler, Garrett, 'The City of London, Real and Unreal', *Victorian Studies*, 49: 3, 2007, pp. 431–455.

and is not'. Is offshore processing undertaken in and for Australia? It is *and* it is not; it *is* where it *is not*.

This conjugation I'm describing indicates how offshore's form reproduces itself in the process of its operation, in a way that stabilises operations. Offshore operations *remain* indefinitely offshore: enemy combatants in GITMO cannot be easily brought onshore or released into the world (section 3.4–9); detainees on Nauru cannot be reached by legal counsel or journalists, but they are freely dominated by guards and routinely exposed to the threat of physical and sexual abuse.

Recalling Mr Morrison's signature announcement about on-water operational matters (sections 2.10–2.12) offers one instance that gathered offshore's auto-replication *in* the conjugation of costs and benefits *for* border security, a kind of off-water performance of offshore *as* on-water. Recall that the Minister for Immigration and Border Protection was 'consistently insistent', week after week, that the Abbott government 'was not here to operate the operation in this way'. As Mr Morrison re-drew these distinctions, tightening the circle of and integrating the ring of steel briefing by briefing, this meant the impossibility of talking publicly to the public about border security – during public briefings about border security. Mr Morrison's 'announcement' was offered as proof that the Abbott government was, as he said, "operating the operation" effectively, and this, in turn, was taken to mean that the Abbott government alone could be trusted by the public,[17] in contrast to the 'surrender and failure' of the nation's borders by their party-political opponents.

Returning to summarise the distinction between offshore as form and offshoring processes: offshore is a form, not a place; but offshoring processes can only take place through the application of offshore to specific places. Applications of the form of offshore turn them into specific offshored places, producing offshoring processes and offshored effects that are not reducible to the form of offshore, insofar as they vary so much.

- Offshore *banking*, offshore *drilling*, offshore *detention*: each and all of these processes remain anchored in their immanence, distinct problems and activities of their worlds.
- Yet after offshoring has begun, and to the extent that operations continue, these are offshore places hosting an offshoring process, thus they are also all offshore: *offshore* banking, *offshore* drilling, *offshore* detention.

In these ways: offshore is a form without which the specific places offshoring takes place wouldn't make sense as described, and offshoring refers to specific

17 Luhmann, Niklas, *The Reality of Mass Media*, Stanford University Press, Stanford University Press, 2000, pp. 40–43 and Karnitschnig, Matthew, 'Cologne Puts Germany's "Lying Press" on Defensive: Media's Timidity on Refugees Prompts Charges of Bias', *Politico.eu*, January 20, 25, 2016. www.politico.eu/article/cologne-puts-germany-lying-media-press-on-defensive-migration-refugees-attacks-sex-assault-nye/

places subjected to applications of the form of offshore, whose offshoring histories make them distinct in certain ways: both from their onshore others *and* from the places they 'once' were before they were offshored.

Christmas Island (CI), for example, is no longer 'the island it once was' prior to its becoming an offshore excised place. The application of offshore's form is truly paradoxical, and not merely contradictory,[18] because when offshore is a form it is not a place, and when it is a place, it is not the form – the form it yet cannot 'be' without and still be offshore. But only for the time in which *we* observe these distinctions as meaningful – and this breaks out of these elliptical orbits by referring back to us drawing this distinction as observers. 'No man is an island': John Donne, and Martin Luther King Jr evoking him,[19] raise the choice to see separation where there is also relation as *the* fundamental ethical choice, in both cases as a way of indicating the universality of Christianity and all of humanity's equal, loved and meaningful place in Christ. In a more systems theoretical vein, each enaction of offshore via an offshoring process involves our choice to uphold offshore as a worldmaking distinction where another set of relations and severances are also always possible.[20] Our islands are ours alone to make together.

3.3 Circumventions within circulation: 'minimise, hide, protect, escape': four descriptors of general political effects sought through offshore's form

Having apprehended offshore's form and the distinction between offshore and offshoring, I now focus on common and societally prevalent political effects sought through its application. Offshore is a two-sided form that includes things by excluding others. Offshore can be applied in many settings, for a number of purposes. The most common contemporary applications of the form of offshore enable offshoring processes that:

- *minimise* the fiduciary risks and costs associated with taxation and regulation (multinationals and profit shifting);
- *hide* harmful practices from environmental and labour practice oversight and critical scrutiny (export processing zones and waste disposal);

18 Borch, Christian, *Niklas Luhmann*, Routledge, Abingdon, 2011, pp. 62–63.

19 Donne, John, *Devotions Upon Emergent Occasions and Death's Duel*, Vintage, London, 1999, p. 103 and 'Martin Luther King Jr.'s 'Letter From Birmingham Jail', *The Atlantic*, April 16, 2013. www.theatlantic.com/politics/archive/2013/04/martin-luther-kings-letter-from-birmingham-jail/274668/

20 Poerkson, Bernard, 'At Each and Every Moment, I Can Decide Who I am. Heinz von Foerster on the Observer, Dialogic Life, and a Constructivist Philosophy of Distinctions', *Cybernetics & Human Knowing*, 10: 3–4, 2003, pp. 9–26.

- *protect* organised group agents (especially multinational corporations, governments, oligarchs and the most powerful of the most organised criminals) from the political and ethical impedance that 'the same work' would attract onshore, and;
- *escape*, by finding a place *a sylon* (beyond theft or pillage – see below), a haven or asylum: a fiscal paradise, or just a place where one might live.

The common factor is that all these applications of the form of offshore produce what I describe as 'circumventions within circulation' (see section I.10) as their most generally observable political effect: systemic efforts toward *minimising* risks, *hiding* harms and hazards, and *protecting* group agents from politics and ethics, and by extension exposure to justice as fairness and responsibility, or just escape and safety from harm.

These applications of the form of offshore are, with varying degrees, intentionally and reflexively assembled by skilled workers on behalf of their clients to achieve such effects, where a system is observed as a difference that needs to be 'worked around'. This not only implies a reflexive understanding that systems exist[21] (section I.8), it means that we can – to return to a key point (section I.10) – attribute degrees of responsibility to the group agents who co-ordinate with one another to secure recognised benefits through their formation, cultivation, and defence.[22]

Culturally prevalent uses of offshore, such as offshore banking centres and offshore detention centres, are constructed around 'counterforms' whose nebulous existence is proven by the necessity of their artful negation. That people go to such lengths to program exploits[23] into the systems in which they are thereby agents indicates a fuzzy logic of systems in play, as just mentioned; but it also means that we can trace the contours of some kind of 'something' that was there such that it had to be gotten around.

Circumvention within circulation is produced by a degree of conspiration (see section 2.12), which relies on an admixture of plausible deniability and the ability to avoid or evade costs and responsibilities. This is part of what makes offshore an intense global object of private interest *and* an intense subject of global public concern. I see this 'counterform' as one way of understanding the spied necessity of *offshore* detention: an interposition whose 'standing between' prevents two separated groups from relating to one another in other possible ways *also* shows us that other ways must be prevented because they are possible. Tax evasion presumes taxation, and by extension the state and its secured publics; border security presumes the asylum seeking it negates, and by extension people

21 Borch, Christian, *Niklas Luhmann*, Routledge, Abingdon, 2011, p. 56.

22 Pettit, Philip, 'Responsibility Incorporated', *Ethics*, 117: 2, 2007, pp. 171–201 and Marion Young, Iris, *Responsibility for Justice*, Oxford University Press, Oxford, 2011.

23 Exploits are codes that take advantage of a network's vulnerabilities, or program such vulnerabilities in, in such a way they can then be used to the programmer's advantage.

rendered stateless and insecure as they flee war, political terror and the destruction of homes and liveable situations, for a better life.

To compound the normative and political implications, tax evasion and asylum seeking are attempts at evasion and capture that show an understanding that those involved might escape *or be held responsible* for what they're attempting through their circumventions. With very different motivations, tax evaders and asylum seekers are trying to escape something via an elsewhere: this shows us a common utopia of our time as the island haven, a place *a sylon* (section 6.6). As Neuman notes,

> The word 'asylum' is derived from the Greek *asylon*, which denotes the absence of sylon (robbery; theft; pillage), and refers to a sacred site from which people or objects must not be removed. Thus, anyone who fled to such a place was safe from those pursuing her. The ancient Greeks extended this concept by applying it to non-citizens seeking protection from the clutches of their home state. Similar practices can be found in other societies.[24]

Seen from these utopian shores, offshore keeps another politics and justice beyond a horizon offshoring processes nevertheless navigate in relation to. If a horizon of perfect justice or the freedom of total escape *couldn't* exist as a ramification of an offshoring process, it wouldn't be necessary to avoid, evade and negate it. But to the extent that I observe this as profoundly unjust – because of the unfairness and irresponsibility with which it operates or implies, without which it couldn't operate or wouldn't happen – offshore's closures open onto another justice.

3.4 September 27, 2013: "You will never see the shores of Australia"

Among the Commonwealth's stated purposes of using offshore for border security is that it deters arrival and enables indefinite detention and offshore processing – which, in circular fashion, is insisted upon because it deters arrival. Control is the desired effect; deterrence is the stated purpose. The use of offshore in Australia's area of maritime interest circles its way toward a harsh assertion that says to asylum seekers: 'do not arrive, 'no way', 'go back to where you came from' (section 2.2–2.3). Offshore "includes some things by excluding others".[25] More specifically, Australia's use of offshore for control and deterrence includes people in the space of border security *by* excluding them from spaces of asylum, *by* including their bodies in the thing-like space of detention that seeks to permanently

24 Neuman, Klaus, *Across the Seas: Australia's Responses to Refugees*, Black Inc, Melbourne, 2015, p. 9.

25 Luhmann, Niklas, *Theory of Society, Volume 1*, Stanford University Press, Stanford, 2012, p. 56.

exclude them, as claimants for protection.[26] These carefully designed political effects are what would accompany most adapted policy variants of the Australian model, should its emigration back to Europe be welcomed by policymakers.

Since May 2013, boat arrivals *can never* arrive in Australia. As an inflicted consequence of their attempt to arrive by boat seeking asylum, everyone who has attempted this journey, including babies and children, is permanently barred from settling in Australia – for the term of their natural lives.[27]

Since the inception of *Operation Sovereign Borders*, Maritime Border Command has gone further than the *Operation Relex* measures detailed in Chapter 1 (section 1.11–1.12), by seeking to prevent arrival by forcibly turning around and towing back interdicted vessels. 'Turnarounds and towbacks' have raised a number of questions about violations of maritime and human rights laws and Indonesia's sovereignty,[28] and have also involved documented cases of refouled Sri Lankans being tortured and detained[29](section 6.3). All those who have not been turned around or towed back, who have been interdicted for attempting to arrive by boat, are processed offshore: anyone found to be a refugee is to be settled in a third country (Papua New Guinea and Cambodia); everyone processed whose claims are rejected must 'go home'; as all unlawful noncitizens do not have a visa and cannot arrive, all those being processed, rejected or who are unwilling to accept resettlement, remain in detention as of writing. With the full emergence of this suite of political effects of 2013-onward offshoring for border security, thousands of would-be arrivals have been caught in an indefinite space of offshore detention, forever barred from administrative processes where their vulnerability can be recognised in Australia as asylum. Australia no longer offers protection for boat people; in all the ways just listed, it punishes them for trying to arrive,[30] in order to achieve deterrence and control.

26 "[B]orders are no longer the shores of the political, but have indeed become . . . *things* within the space of the political itself", in Balibar, Étienne, *We, the People of Europe? Reflections on Transnational Citizenship*, Princeton, 2003, p. 92, italics in original.

27 The final legality of this is still unclear as of writing. Conifer, Dan and Anderson, Stephanie, 'Refugee, Asylum Seeker Lifetime Visa ban "Extreme", "Evil", "Sick", Labor MPs Say', *abc.net.au*, updated October 31, 2016. www.abc.net.au/news/2016-10-31/asylum-seeker-refugee-lifetime-ban-extreme-evil-sick:-labor/7980686 and McIlroy, Tom, 'Government-Dominated Committee Finds Lifetime Visa Ban Pointless and Cruel', *The Sydney Morning Herald*, November 22, 2016. www.smh.com.au/federal-politics/political-news/lifetime-visa-ban-pointless-and-cruel-parliamentary-committee-20161122-gsv78j.html

28 Dastyari, Azadeh, 'Explainer: The Legal Implications of 'Tow-Backs', *The Conversation*, January 20, 2014. http://theconversation.com/explainer-the-legal-implications-of-tow-backs-22151 and 'Is it illegal to turn back boats in international waters to Indonesia?' *ABC Fact Check*, updated November 17, 2014. www.abc.net.au/news/2013-09-26/government-turn-back-boat-policy/4979898

29 'Torture Claims Emerge From Sri Lanka', *ABC 7.30 Report*, April 24, 2013. www.abc.net.au/7.30/content/2013/s3749532.htm

30 This in line with Amnesty International's 2016 assessment. 'Australia: Island of Despair: Australia's 'Processing' of Refugees on Nauru', Amnesty International, October 17, 2016. www.amnesty.org/en/documents/asa12/4934/2016/en/

Nine days after entering office, the new Minister for Immigration and Border Protection, Mr Scott Morrison, was flown the 3700km distance from Canberra to Australia's offshore detention centre on Manus Island[31] to deliver the message of border security by making an announcement. Mr Morrison's on-the-record recollection is as follows:

> At the centre, I delivered a clear message to those who are in that centre, including to those who had just arrived. . . . I gave them a very clear message, and it was this; they will not be getting what they came for. They would remain there at that centre until they went home or were settled in a country other than Australia. I confirmed that the new government had implemented a more comprehensive and strengthened set of measures that we would not be putting up with people coming to Australia illegally by boat, and that they should warn others not to follow them. I also advised that we'd be seeking to identify and arrest anyone who sought to support or facilitate someone coming to Australia illegally by boat, including if they were family members, and offered a warning in that regard.[32]

Martin Appleby, an Australian contractor-employee of British multinational security corporation G4S, was present at Mr Morrison's address. On Appleby's recollection, the minister got up on a platform and "addressed one of the compounds", cast his hands out, and said:

> "you will never see the shores of Australia".[33]

I would like to dwell on what it means for Australia's minister of Immigration and Border Protection to stand on a platform in an offshore detention centre on a remote island in Papua New Guinea, cast out his hands, and say precisely such a thing as 'you will never see the shores of Australia'. If the Tampa Affair, in Prime Minister Howard's words, placed border security "on the horizon of Australian politics",[34] 'you will never see the shores of Australia' proclaimed an *intention* to place boat arrivals not just "outside Australia's refugee protection system",[35]

31 Manus Island is part of Papua New Guinea. The island is located to the northeast of the mainland, a little more than 818km from Port Moresby.

32 'Transcript: Press Conference – Operation Sovereign Borders', Update, Monday September 30, 2013. http://sievx.com/articles/OSB/20130930OSBPresser2.html

33 Laughland, Oliver, Bennett, Christian and Code, Bill, 'Scott Morrison Visit Sent Manus Tension Soaring, Says G4S Whistleblower', *www.theguardian.com*, Monday 28 April, 2014. www.theguardian.com/world/2014/apr/28/scott-morrison-visit-sent-manus-tension-soaring-says-g4s-whistleblower

34 Howard, John, *Lazarus Rising: A Personal and Political Autobiography*, Allen and Unwin, Melbourne, 2010, p. 393.

35 Op.cit., p. 403.

but beyond the shores of politics, beyond any horizon of justice. Morrison's was knowingly a message of damnation.

Onshore, 'you will never see the shores of Australia' staged the political paradoxes and lived contradictions of *Operation Sovereign Borders* at a peak of intensity between September 2013 and March 2014, as explored via the declared silence of on-water operational matters (section 2.11–2.12). Intentionally at least, Morrison's is the terminal speech act of the dominant onshore narrative of Australian border security, an offshore proclamation of the end of asylum 'in' Australia for boat arrivals, and sign and signal of an effort to totally dominate a category of person, made by a victorious government as the delivery of an electoral mandate and the message of border security. As a phrase that figuratively stood atop the shoulders of the transformations examined in the previous two chapters, as the restoration of nation sovereignty and the full and final delivery of the message, 'you will never see the shores of Australia' crowns the achievement of border security as the ring of steel, an offshoring process capable of producing permanent and total nonarrival and perfectly smooth secure circulation in one. At stake is a shift from border security as a policy whose explicit purpose as deterrence and control toward the nascent vision of a global enclave constituted by a category of person's permanent denial of the shores of Australia, based on the mode of transport they attempted to employ to arrive.

In thinking about Morrison's *mise on scène* for his staging of the terminal speech act of *Operation Sovereign Borders*, the final place where 'the boats' were stopped 'for good', we also need to dwell on how offshore detention keeps opening politics through its closure of asylum and the shutting down of an invitation to care for vulnerable humans.[36] Over the course of fifteen years, a political project has emerged among Australian border security's architects and avatars that has aligned the intentional action of group agents toward the ideal of border security as an operationally closed system of national sovereignty truly and *totally* capable of *flawlessly* screening global space of mobility by 'stopping the boats'. A border continuum tightly coupled to the executive and captive news media, capable of silencing all critical scrutiny (section 2.12). In the previous chapter, we saw by looking at the No Way pamphlet (section 2.2) that this is a political project aspiring to *total* control over vast maritime spaces and people's entire lives that constructs Australia as a *fully* secured space, answering key electorates' anxieties about coastlines (section 2.8) with a multi-billion dollar a year militarised projection of sovereignty where all risks are pre-empted via 'blanket' surveillance, where operational control is effective and circulation is secured. The complete success of 'you will never see the shores of Australia' is the utopian vision of Australia imagined by border security's world, the full integration of a totally effective societal securing process: total control, complete deterrence.

36 "All openness is based on the closure of the system". Luhmann, Niklas, *Theory of Society, Volume 1*, Stanford University Press, Stanford, 2012, p. 34.

Yet in spite of the *almost* complete success of this political project as of writing, at certain moments such as Morrison's triumphal damnation of Manus detainees, Australian border security keeps opening back onto horizons of justice. This opens points of observation where border security operations are no longer merely or plausibly about border security, and where law, ethics, the stench of smuggling and the inveterating indignity of detention, bring the border continuum's architects back to shores of politics they would deny detainees. Morrison's message presents us with the sight of a bully burnishing his electoral prospects and career trajectory atop a milk crate, flown in to lord it over a bunch of men warehoused in shipping containers, losing their minds in the maddening swamp heat as they're denied a future by way of receiving the message of border security – because Australia's commitment to a particular way of practicing sovereignty prevents them from ever seeing the shores of Australia. Yet this state of affairs too has its history; the following section traces its key international antecedents and global lineages.

3.5 Guantánamo, GWOT, G(I)TMO: imperial colonisations of the US Caribbean

In 2016 Guantánamo is perhaps still seen as a creature of the US-led Global War on Terror. But this 'GWOT and G(I)TMO' history[37] are of secondary importance here, for two reasons. First, GITMO was a subsequent variant of offshoring detention practices that built on the earlier US colonisation of Spanish, Cuban Guantánamo without which the Bay's US detention facilities would not have been readily available for their Global War on Terror re-deployment.

These offshored detention practices, in turn, leveraged early twentieth-century imperial and regional *statifications* that sought to solve an object of onshore political worrying central to this book: the attempted arrival by boat of asylum seekers. That these arrivals emerged in the 70s and came to a head as early as 1980, provoking maritime interdiction and eventually offshore detention as deterrence-led policy responses – *fully two decades before Australia by 2001*, and fifteen years before the US/Mexico border came to the foreground scholarly understanding of border security, from roughly 1994 – makes US responses in the Caribbean globally innovative and therefore crucial for scholars trying to understand how recent iterations of border security such as Australia's emerged under the influence of US policy. By extension, it also ties in to the genealogy of deterrence policies state-based agents are seeking to emulate when they gesture

37 Agamben, Giorgio, *Homo Sacer: Sovereign Power and Bare Life*, Stanford University Press, Stanford, 1998, Agamben, Giorgio, *State of Exception*, University of Chicago Press, Chicago, 2005, Butler, Judith, *Precarious Life: The Powers of Mourning and Violence*, Verso, London, 2004, Derrida, Jacques, *The Beast and the Sovereign, Volume 1*, University of Chicago Press, Chicago, 2009, pp. 93–95 and Lemke, Thomas, *Biopolitics: An Advanced Introduction*, NYU Press, New York, 2011, pp. 53–65.

toward Australian border security as “a hopeful model for Europe”.[38] With these already tangled lines in mind, the historical details in this and the following two sections can be most easily read through by noting the analytic emphasis I put on temporal sequence and time sensitivity in order to apprehend the enabling conditions and causal irreversibility of the complex social processes named by offshoring detention – known in *Border Security* by pursuing the nontrivial effects of the recursive production of distinctions of observing systems (section I.2, i.11). To distill how I understand historical agency, purpose and causality here:

- *agency* gathers in a precise moment, assembled from disparate elements;
- sets of elements gathered agentically for one specific *purpose* are later selectively re-purposed for others which would have been functionally improbable, and even impossible to imagine, in earlier political spaces;
- *causality* in conditions of complexity is nonlinear, and moreover, when attempting to apprehend the dynamics of historical phenomena, we must attend to context-dependent constraints, and inter-actions which jump scales.[39]

The complex historical development of immigration detention camps around Guantánamo Bay, and its succession of uses, purposes and effects, is also globally significant in the earlier and less noted *maritime* emergence of border security that later influenced the strategic framing of US homeland security's strategy of ‘prevention through deterrence’,[40] published in August 1994. Considering Guantánamo in its US Caribbean from these perspectives is a way of re-thinking the US' geopolitical role in relation to the Cold War *and* its own post–Cold War security practices and globalisation-era symptoms (section 3.8). In geopolitical terms whose most significant crisis event for border security we'll touch upon (section 3.9), the 1980 Mariel Boatlift can be read as an untimely end to the Cold War that evinced several *already* post–Cold War – but not yet *quite* border security – policy responses to maritime asylum seekers. It can thus be read alongside the Australian points of emergence traced in this and the previous two chapters, both as international comparisons, and as global points of emergence.

An examination of the Cold War complications that attended these US imperial offshoring processes responding to asylum seeking is also helpful for

38 Balogh, Stefanie, ‘Europe ‘Needs an Asylum Solution’: Jim Molan’, *The Australian*, April 21, 2015. www.theaustralian.com.au/national-affairs/immigration/europe-needs-an-asylum-solution-jim-molan/story-fn9hmlgu-1227312738365 and Frum, David. 2015. ‘Closing Europe's Harbors: The Urgent Case for Stopping the Flow of Illegal Migrants Across the Mediterranean’, *The Atlantic*, July/August 2015. www.theatlantic.com/magazine/archive/2015/07/closing-european-harbors/395321/

39 Connolly, William E., *The Fragility of Things: Self-Organizing Processes, Neoliberal Fantasies, and Democratic Activism*, Duke, Durham, 2013 and Juarrero, Alicia, *Dynamics in Action: Intentional Behaviour as a Complex System*, MIT Press, Cambridge, 2002.

40 Rosenblum, Marc R., ‘Border Security: Immigration Enforcement Between Ports of Entry’, *Congressional Research Service*, 2012, p. 4. fpc.state.gov/documents/organization/180681.pdf

nuancing scholarly claims explored and developed in the conclusion of the previous chapter (section 2.12). Mariel 1980 didn't *just* 'usher in' the carceral age discussed by Jonathan Simon[41] and redeveloped by others responding to Simon's Foucauldian framing.[42] The wake of Mariel, like the wake of Tampa, enabled a security field-generating label 'illegals' to pass onshore into communication via the offshore realm of maritime space, a point not covered in Nevin's terrestrially located examination of *Operation Gatekeeper* in '94. Thus it offers important nuance about the role of the political in preventing the emergence of post–Cold War security fields than Bigo covers[43]; it tracks Nevins' pivotal figure of 'the illegal' to a place where it emerged nearly a decade and a half before *Operation Gatekeeper* in 1994[44] (and nearly four decades before Trump); and it shows how borders moved to the centre of political contestation *at* the limit of sovereign power.[45] Following these adjustments, we can also take points from the following to re-frame Brown's political theory of walling as a rather US-centric narrative: sovereign walling is not quite as portable an example as Brown needs to casts it as in order to describe sovereignty's waning[46] in the face of globalisation's erosive flows. This brings us to the US-centric *maritime* narrative of imperial control over Guantánamo.

To prepare the reader, this and the following sections (3.7–3.10) are heavy on historical details that, as they interact and jump scales, not only produce time-sensitive spaces of political agency, they also produce complications in the telling. Although I've attempted to rescue only those elements necessary for a schematic re-telling that pinpoints the lineages of offshoring detention in border security, in line with scholarly necessity and methodological commitments, there are still many details to contend with. Readers who wish to avoid this rough passage

41 Simon, Jonathan, 'Refugees in a Carceral Age: The Rebirth of Immigration Prisons in the United States', *Public Culture*, 10: 3, 1998, pp. 577–607.

42 Bosworth, Mary and Kaufman, Emma, 'Foreigners in a Carceral Age: Immigration and Imprisonment in the United States', *Stanford Law and Policy Review*, 22: 2, 2011, pp. 429–454, Loyd, Jenna, 'Carceral Citizenship in an Age of Global Apartheid', *Occasion*, 8, 2015, pp. 1–15, Moran, Dominique, Gill, Nick and Conlon, Dierdre (eds.), *Carceral Spaces: Mobility and Agency in Imprisonment and Migrant Detention*, Routledge, Abingdon, 2013, Mountz, Alison and Loyd, Jenna, 'Transnational Productions of Remoteness: Building Onshore and Offshore Carceral Regimes Across Borders', *Geographica Helvetica*, 69, 2014, pp. 389–398, Pickering, Sharon, 'Floating Carceral Spaces: Border Enforcement and Gender on the High Seas', *Punishment and Society*, 16: 2, 2014, pp. 187–205.

43 Bigo, Didier, 'Security and Immigration: Toward a Critique of the Governmentality of Unease', *Alternatives*, 27, 2002, pp. 64, 73, 76.

44 Nevins, Joseph, 'The Ideological Roots of the Illegal as Threat and the Boundary as Protector', in *Operation Gatekeeper and Beyond*, Routledge, Abingdon, 2010, pp. 118–155.

45 Balibar, Étienne, *We, the People of Europe? Reflections on Transnational Citizenship*, Princeton University Press, Princeton, 2003, Garland, David, 'The Limits of the Sovereign State: Strategies of Crime Control in Contemporary Society', *The British Journal of Criminology*, 36: 4, 1996 and Bosworth, Mary, 'Border Control and the Limits of the Sovereign State', *Social and Legal Studies*, 17: 2, 2008, pp. 119–215.

46 Brown, Wendy, *Walled States, Waning Sovereignty*, Zone Books, New York, 2010.

across the US Caribbean can skip to where the moment this chapter returns to CI (section 3.11). With the just-introduced points about agency, purpose and causality in mind, I now dive in.

3.6 Imperial control via 'legislated ambiguity': effective jurisdiction and control, not sovereignty

In 1898, during the Spanish-American War, the United States occupied Cuba. US occupation was framed by the US as its noble assistance of heroic Cuban efforts to oust the Spanish. But a more accurate description of its significance is that the occupation of Cuba was about a transfer from Spanish *Imperial* domination to US *imperial* domination.[47] I observe the distinction between Spanish Imperialism and US imperial domination as follows.

Where Spanish Imperialism had been about the mass religious conversion and total government of enslaved or subject populations accompanying the direct exploitation of mineral resources and commodities, US imperialism, to combine key points made by Amy Kaplan and Deborah Cowen,[48] sought to dominate precisely *without* salvational, territorial and governmental commitments to the living. The US sought to colonise and dominate the region through supply chain security and the strategic control of space *in the absence* of direct conversion, exploitation and government.[49]

At the turn of the century, the overarching purpose of occupying Guantánamo Bay was logistical. The US government's vision of twentieth-century imperialism was predicated on naval power, and at this precise time, this meant coal power. As a logistical matter, retaining access to Guantánamo through the lease was about providing a coaling station for the US Navy strategically located in the Caribbean. An antecedent of the arrival of the ghost flight is the coaling of the naval destroyer.

With leasing for coaling, we can see how a highly time-sensitive *statification* developed by a large jurisdiction was used to solve a geopolitical problem by using a small jurisdiction.[50] By 1909, less than a decade after the signing of the

47 Johnson, Chalmers, *The Sorrows of Empire: Militarism, Secrecy, and the End of the Republic*, Metropolitan Books, New York, 2005.

48 Kaplan, Amy, 'Where is Guantánamo?' *American Quarterly*, 57: 3, 2005, pp. 831–858 and Cowen, Deborah, 'From National Borders to Global Seams: The Rise of Supply Chain Security', in *The Deadly Life of Logistics: Mapping Violence in Global Trade*, University of Minnesota Press, Minneapolis, 2014, pp. 53–91.

49 Foucault, Michel, *Security, Territory, Population: Lectures at the Collège de France*, Palgrave Macmillan, London, 2007, Foucault, Michel, *The Birth of Biopolitics: Lectures at the Collège de France*, Palgrave Macmillan, London, 2008, Foucault, Michel, *The Government of the Living: Lectures at the Collège de France*, Palgrave Macmillan, London, 2014.

50 Palan, Ronen, 'International Financial Centers: The British-Empire, City-States and Commercially Oriented Politics', *Theoretical Inquiries in Law*, 11: 1, 2010, pp. 152–153.

lease, "the Navy had converted from sails and coal to 'black oil,' powering their ships with unrefined crude oil".[51] As Erik Dahl notes, "[t]he first oil-burning American destroyer, USS Paulding, was commissioned in 1910, and by 1911 the USS Nevada-class battle-ship was planned for solely oil as fuel".[52] The USS Texas, the last coal-fired American battleship to be commissioned, joined the fleet in 1914.

Between 1898–1903, Guantánamo Bay was: a spoil of colonial war; a political laboratory and test site for the Caribbean expression of newly formulated culturally patterned vision of imperialism; and a prudent strategic site for a Navy with an appetite for a fuel that, less than a decade later, it would no longer need in logistically significant quantities at geopolitically strategic points.[53] These ways of constructing Guantánamo had their own materiality, and – importantly, where we imagine islands (section 1.7, 3.2) – they also relied upon the contextually constrained ability to co-imagine Cuba, the Caribbean, America and imperialism as the environment in which the enaction of a number of creative, worldmaking political projects was possible, prudent and necessary. Agency was gathered here for a very specific purpose, with political effects unforeseeable at that time, that would later be used in offshoring detention.

Control of space and supply chain security – and by extension *this* time-specific practiced understanding of imperial domination and logistics – was enacted on Guantánamo at the turn of the century by asserting effective jurisdiction and control *while* remonstrating that 'ultimate sovereignty' lay with Cuba. As Amy Kaplan phrases it, US authorities 'legislated an ambiguity' by inserting the Platt Amendment into Cuba's new constitution, which we can think of by analogy as a programmed vulnerability, like a Trojan or exploit. Through the insertion, the US reserved a right to intervene militarily, and to control Cuba's economy and international relations. It also demanded a guarantee on "the lease or purchase of coaling and naval provisions".[54] To integrate some key contentions of this chapter (see section 3.3), this was creative work involving skilled group agents, people working for institutions with very precise know how and agentic ways 'in' to the structures of the state sovereignty of those polities. The skilful ability to observe a constrained operability 'there' enabled agents of US domination to build a robust imperial *statification* that could operate in what would otherwise – in other times, for other people – be unworkable conditions. Finally, what's significant about the insertion of the Amendment is the way it effectuated what I describe as an 'operable nebulousness' (see sections 3.1, 3.3) that continues to exist into the political present, a vagueness you can do politically creative things with *if you*

51 'Office of Fossil Energy', *energy.gov*. http://energy.gov/fe/about-us/our-history

52 Dahl, Erik J., 'Naval Innovation: From Coal to Oil', *Joint Force Quarterly*, Winter 2000–2001, p. 54.

53 With the switch from coal to oil operating range increased by 70%, from 2,800 nautical miles to 4,000 nautical miles.

54 Kaplan, Amy, "Where Is Guantánamo?" *American Quarterly*, 57: 3, 2005, p. 835.

know how, that moreover were and are points of operability that are neither clear nor workable to 'outsiders'. In these ways, post-Amendment Guantánamo, more than a century from this point of writing, was already a global space in formation (section I.1).

3.7 US policy responses to asylum seeking in the 1970s: triangulating the Cuban and Haitian Cold War Caribbean via the friend–enemy distinction

Guantánamo's US imperial, colonial and labour history[55] unfolded over the early decades of the twentieth century shaped most strongly by the evolving political relations of the imperial US and its Caribbean: conspicuously Haiti and Cuba. In a strange counterpart to the boat-disappearing Bermuda Triangle, it was 'the boats that suddenly appeared' in 1972 that caused the biggest issues for authorities in the US. These boats emerged from continual triangulations generated by political tensions within and between the US, Haiti and Cuba.[56]

Following key points from critical scholars re-examining the boat-producing triangulation that came to a head with Mariel, most accounts foreground US-Cuba and place US-Haiti in the background. This is regrettable, because offshore detention on Guantánamo was first imposed on Haitian asylum seekers in November 1991, as I'll return to (section 3.9–3.10), notably *a full decade before post-Tampa Australia*, and a year before Australia made its first moves toward deterring boat arrivals through the imposition of mandatory detention, in 1992.

However, to connect these lineages of offshore detention and border security to their enabling conditions in prior historical contexts and constraints, Haitian asylum seekers only came to be detained offshore on Guantánamo because of what had transpired with Mariel in 1980, mostly between US-Cuba, where Cuba and Castro certainly comprised Mariel's attentional foreground. And yet, to complicate this further, the Reagan administration's post Mariel responses, from 1981, built a novel deterrence-led trajectory upon interlocking US immigration 'crises' that began arriving by boat from Haiti, *eight years before* Mariel, in 1972. *Three years after* the West Papuan Raft Men exposed 'the absence' of maritime

55 Hansen, Jonathan M., *Guantánamo: An American History*, Hill and Wang, New York, 2011 and Lipman, Jana K., *Guantánamo: A Working-Class History Between Empire and Revolution*, University of California Press, Berkeley, 2008. Also: Maurer, Noel and Yu, Carlos, *The Big Ditch: How America Took, Built, Ran, and Ultimately Gave Away the Panama Canal*, Princeton University Press, Princeton, 2010.

56 Lipman, Jana K., ' "The Fish Trusts the Water, and It Is in the Water That It Is Cooked" The Caribbean Origins of the Krome Detention Center', *Radical History Review*, 115, 2013, pp. 115–141, Loyd, Jenna, 'Carceral Citizenship in an Age of Global Apartheid', *Occasion*, 8, 2015, pp. 1–15 and Paik, A. Naomi, 'Carceral Quarantine at Guantánamo Legacies of US Imprisonment of Haitian Refugees, 1991–1994', *Radical History Review*, 115, 2013, pp. 142–168.

surveillance in Australia in 1969 (section 2.5), *three years before* the Indochinese Exodus ramped up, from 1975, 'the boats' first appeared in 1972 as a political problem that US authorities sought to stop.

As with other jurisdictions, US policy responses to asylum seekers in the postwar period were ad hoc and served Cold War foreign policy ends.[57] Where asylum seeking is concerned, this pivoted around a properly Schmittian expression of the political as the distinction between "friend and enemy".[58] Throughout the 1970s – indeed, until Mariel – whenever Cubans arrived in the US seeking asylum, US government officials and news media read Cuban arrivals as causal, political and unproblematic. Along such lines: 'Cubans are arriving in the US *because* they are fleeing communist oppression'.

As a paradigmatic speech act in this postwar, Cold War vein, in October 1965, President Lyndon Johnson declared that,[59]

> those who seek refuge here in America will find it. The dedication of America to our traditions as an asylum for the oppressed is going to be upheld. . . . The lesson of our times is sharp and clear in this movement of people from one land to another . . . it stamps the mark of failure on a regime when many of its citizens voluntarily choose to leave the land of their birth for a more hopeful home in America. The future holds little hope for any government where the present holds no hope for the people. And so we Americans will welcome these Cuban people. For the tides of history run strong, and in another day they can return to their homeland to find it cleansed of terror and free from fear.[60]

In glaring contrast to the open welcome given to Cuba's 'innocent victims escaping communist oppression for a life of American freedom' from the Cuban Revolution *until* Mariel 1980, Haitian asylum claims had been systematically foreclosed and negated by the INS from the moment the first claimant applied, in September 1963.[61] Here we can 'intensify' one of Luhmann's key points about

57 Stepick, Alex, 'Haitian Boat People: A Study in the Conflicting Forces Shaping U.S. Immigration Policy', *Law and Contemporary Problems*, 45: 2, 1982, pp. 163–196. Also: Australia didn't really have a 'refugee policy' as we would understand it until 1977. See: Hugo, Graeme, 'From Compassion to Compliance? Trends in Refugee and Humanitarian Migration in Australia', *Geojournal*, 55, 2001, pp. 27–37 and Neuman, Klaus, *Across the Seas: Australia's Responses to Refugees*, Black Inc, Melbourne, 2015.

58 Schmitt, Carl, *The Concept of the Political: Expanded Edition*, University of Chicago Press, Chicago, 2007, p. 26.

59 Section I.8. Ten years after Rolling Thunder, the US then had to deal with the Indochinese Exodus – the correlations bear exploration and reflection.

60 'Remarks at the Signing of the Immigration Bill, Liberty Island, New York', October 3, 1965, *LBJ Presidential Library*. www.lbjlib.utexas.edu/johnson/archives.hom/speeches.hom/651003.asp

61 Stepick, Alex, "Haitian Boat People: A Study in the Conflicting Forces Shaping U.S. Immigration Policy", *Law and Contemporary Problems*, 45: 2, 1982, p. 178.

operational closure – "[a]ll openness is based on the closure of the system"[62] – through an encounter with Schmitt's concept of the political. The degree of intensity of the US' enmity with Cuba enabled an inversely warm, open, friendly and unproblematic reception of the Cubans who (thus) fled it. As a tragic irony, the US' openly friendly and supportive relations with the staunchly anticommunist Duvalier regime, in contrast, precluded US openness to the claims of Haitian asylum seekers and by extension placed all Haitians beyond the horizon of asylum – in the following significant ways, later of great significance in the emergence of border security and offshore detention.

In 1972, when 'Haitian boat people' started crossing the Caribbean and arriving in the US in numbers read as problematic by US officials, they were initially framed as refugees. But as the years wore on, their reasons for departing were increasingly read as economic, rendering their reasons for arriving as illegal and their wishes to stay illegitimate.[63] *Cubans* may have been leaving "the land of their birth for a more hopeful home in America" consistent with President Johnson's remarks a decade earlier in '65, but Cold War political distinctions meant that they did so in a way that arrival itself 'proved' that 'they're here' for political reasons.[64]

Haitians, on the other hand, had left Haiti *because* of 'personal disputes', and they were arriving in America *because* they were 'economic migrants'. Cuban boat arrivals came in from the cold under the cover of the geopolitical intensity of the age; Haitian boat arrivals were correspondingly rendered illegible as political, jailed for entering illegally and read as a problematic and parasitic population. On the level of population, Haitian motives were uncovered as economically motivated; and as individuals they were denounced for having 'no more than personal reasons' for coming. Nineteen-seventies Haitian boat people were framed as a category of persons without legitimate political, legal, prudential and moral grounds for claiming asylum. The added implication here – always implicit, seldom absent – is that because Haitians were nonetheless making claims for protection (formulated as bureaucratic demands on resource-constrained, taxpayer funded institutions), the suspicion of manipulation stuck to them: 'who else but conmen would rort a system intended for the world's most desperate people?'.[65] We can see a contemporary counterpoint to this with the causal order of reading in Peter Dutton's response to a detainee who set himself alight on Nauru: 'people have self immolated to get to Australia'.[66]

62 Luhmann, Niklas, *Theory of Society, Volume 1*, Stanford University Press, Stanford, 2012, p. 34.

63 Maley, William, *What is a Refugee?* Scribe, Melbourne, 2016.

64 'Beware the Supermarket Shopping Asylum Seekers', *Crikey*, March 29, 2010. www.crikey.com.au/2010/03/29/theyre-heeeeeeeere/

65 Pickering, Sharon, 'Common Sense and Original Deviancy: News Discourses and Asylum Seekers in Australia', *Journal of Refugee Studies*, 14: 2, 2001, pp. 169–186, and Saxton, 'I Certainly Don't Want People Like That Here': The Discursive Construction of "Asylum Seekers"', *Media International Australia*, 109: 1, pp. 109–120.

66 Kelly, Sean, 'Things Peter Dutton Has Said Since May: The Words of the Nation's Minister for Immigration Tell Their Own Sad Story', *The Monthly*, August 18, 2016. www.themonthly.com.au/today/sean-kelly/2016/18/2016/1471504197/things-peter-dutton-has-said-may

These framings of asylum seeking as economically and personally motivated – and *therefore* illegitimate, selfish or suspicious – were imposed as a way of understanding the motivations of Haitian boat people *a quarter of a century before* homologous framings of Afghan and Iraqi asylum seekers were developed by the Howard government, from 1996, which culminated in Australian scenes like the Deutsche Bank's arrival in Geraldton in 2013[67] (sections 2.4–2.8). There is of course nothing new about xenophobic prejudice toward *migrants* based on suspicion of them, based on a causal-economic motive. Californian and Victorian responses to Chinese migrants in the second half of the nineteenth century are a case in point. What is novel about this political constellation is that it's responding to instances of boat-borne *asylum seeking* that became politically problematic onshore in the West just as Keynesian mass migration (by boat) declined and civil aviation was set on its trajectory toward middle-class ubiquity (section I.9).

Specifying Bigo and Balibar's reading of these elements as possible signs and signals of the *new* racism, "a racism of the era of 'decolonization', of the reversal of population movements between the old colonies and the old metropolises, and the division of humanity within a single political space",[68] I also read these US Caribbean points as antecedents of efforts by the office-seeking xenophobic right of the OECD West, from roughly 1994, to discredit asylum seekers as 'migrants' and 'illegals' by metonymically enchaining economic motivations with selfish, manipulative, unstoppably criminal behaviour, culminating in the 2015 resonance of Katie Hopkins' claim that 'migrants are like cockroaches . . . who deserve to be drowned, but in a way that cannot provoke care'.[69]

The counter-loading of 'the economic' also indicates the symbolic hegemony of the political in the Cold War context of the 70s US Caribbean, because a description of Haitian motivations as *merely* economic and personal is so at variance with what even the following glance at the empirical record of 70s Haiti shows. The Doc Duvaliers were tyrants, and under their rule Haiti was a country where state terror was a normal technique of government. In 70s Haiti political

67 Mountz, Alison, 'Embodying the Nation-State: Canada's Response to Human Smuggling', *Political Geography*, 23, 2004, pp. 323–345.

68 Balibar, Étienne, 'Is There a 'Neo-Racism'?' in Balibar, Étienne and Wallerstein, Emmanuel (eds.), *Race, Nation, Class: Ambiguous Identities*, Verso, London, 1991, p. 21 and Bigo, Didier, 'Security and Immigration: Toward a Critique of the Governmentality of Unease', *Alternatives*, 27, 2002, p. 65.

69 "Once gunships have driven them back to their shores, boats need to be confiscated and burned on a huge bonfire. . . . Drilling a few holes in the bottom of anything suspiciously resembling a boat would be a good idea, too, just for belt and braces". This was married to a tweet that said "[s]how me bodies floating in water, play me violins and show me skinny people looking sad. I still don't care". Hopkins, Katie, 'Rescue Boats? I'd Use Gunships to Stop Migrants: You May as Well Set Up a Libya to Italy P&O ferry', *The Sun*, April 17, 2015. www.thesun.co.uk/news/1541491/rescue-boats-id-use-gunships-to-stop-migrants/ and 'Why Did Sun Delete Katie Hopkins' 'Gunships to Stop Migrants' Tweet?' *The Guardian*, September 4, 2015. www.theguardian.com/media/mediamonkeyblog/2015/sep/03/why-did-sun-delete-katie-hopkins-gunships-to-stop-migrants-tweet

opponents were beaten in broad daylight by *tonton macoutes*, abducted in the night, subjected to torture; they turned up dead or broken, or they never turned up.[70] Poverty and inequality aside, by any reasonable political measure, Haiti was an island of terror and fear,[71] which means that those escaping their homeland were doing so *because* they had 'a well-founded fear of persecution for reasons of membership of a particular social group, or political opinion'.

Yet however authoritarian, the Duvalier regimes were 'friendly' anticommunist regimes, not those victims of the US' socialist enemies, fleeing Cubans. Papa Doc was notable for his skill in playing the US by framing his oppression of political opponents and critics as anticommunist, with the spectre of 'a second Cuba' repeatedly used as the threat horizon. So enmeshed, *any* US admission of a Johnsonesque situational definition in which Haitians were 'fleeing the land of their birth for a more hopeful home in America in the future hope that they can return to their homeland to find it cleansed of terror and free from fear' would have also been a criticism of the friendly Duvalier regimes, and by extension a repudiation of the support elements of US anticommunist involvement in Haiti. As in so many 'third world' countries during this period, anticommunism – which, on the ground, so often meant the suppression of democracy through state terror – earned the Duvalier regimes perennial carte blanche and political, economic and military support.[72]

For our purposes, we can see the salient effect of the friend/enemy distinction by noting the following 95:5 ratio. As Stepick notes, during 1975–1976 "the United States granted asylum to 5% of those fleeing rightist regimes and 95% of those fleeing Communist countries".[73] This 95:5 ratio pinpoints a crucial factor in play that helps explain the Cold War conditions constraining the post–Cold War co-emergence of offshoring detention and border security in the grip of the shift toward deterrence and control.

The 95:5 ratio also complicates arguments that give causal primacy to race as a factor in this context. Notwithstanding the manifest presence of anti-black racism raised by the spectre of – to recast Johnson's '65 rhetoric – a 'human tide pouring forth' into Florida, throughout this period the overwhelming majority of Cuban boat arrivals were paroled in, and their arrival didn't trigger politicisation, the securitisation of migration and the generation of 'illegals' in the way that Haitian arrivals were already beginning to, but in ways that had not quite clarified into current metastable framings. This does not amount to contending that race

70 Heinl, Robert Debs and Heinl, Nancy Gordon, *Written in Blood: The Story of the Haitian People 1492–1995*, UPA, Lanham, 2005. For a work focusing on Haiti from the 90s to the present, see: Hallward, Peter, *Damming the Flood: Haiti and the Politics of Containment*, Verso, London, 2007.

71 Dernis, Martin M., "Haitian Immigrants: Political Refugees or Economic Escapees?" *University of Miami Law Review*, 10: 1, 1976, pp. 27–41.

72 Indonesia, Chile, Egypt, Iraq, Pakistan, Argentina, Algeria, etc.

73 Stepick, Alex, 'Haitian Boat People: A Study in the Conflicting Forces Shaping U.S. Immigration Policy', *Law and Contemporary Problems*, 45: 2, 1982, p. 173.

was not always a powerful factor in play, which it was – and this nuances simple periodisations eliciting concern about 'the *new* racism', in turn urging us to think with greater critical acuity about 'facile conceptions we may have about race and class'.[74] But it does show us how the conditions border security actually emerged in didn't coalesce until post–Cold War political constellations, via globalisation. This refigured the status and locus of the political: in relation to the nation-state; and the duties wealthy, powerful states and citizens owe(d) to noncitizens claiming to be fleeing armed conflict, state terror and unworkable situations.[75] The 95:5 ratio names a set of Cold War rationales that, counterfactually, pinpoint a constraint that begs us to consider the complex emergence of border security in our post–Cold War, globalised worlds. Border security and offshore detention – like the shift toward deterrence in the culture of control[76] – constitute our shores of our politics, our horizons of justice. Islands of offshore detention are worlds of our making, constructions of our political present.

Haitian arrivals in north America in the 70s also prompted the US government's generation of three governmental conditions for offshore detention:

- maritime interdiction,
- offshore detention, and
- excludable categories of person.

The first two of these will be covered in the following section (3.9). But to begin with the third of these, the routine and systemic negation of Haitian asylum claims, over time, produced a *de facto* category of person, the asylum seeker as *non arrivée*. By way of the brutal banality of routine negation, the whole of Haiti's population, barring its airborne elite and conspicuous political 'exiles', were made incapable of arrival, protection or recognition, either as refugees or as migrants who could stay, dream and work until they became Americans.[77] Those who wish to understand the plight of those on Manus and Nauru who will 'never see the shores of Australia' in this chapter, the thousands of Sri Lankans refouled by Australia, where they face torture (section 6.3), or the millions of Syrians currently in camps around the Mediterranean, should look back to the fate of Haitian boat arrivals seeking asylum in the US in the 1970s.

The negation of Haitians asylum claims was formalised through the Haitian Program, the INS-led effort to integrate expulsion of Haitians through the denial of their asylum claims with maximal procedural efficiency, which concretised in 1977.

74 Loyd, Jenna, 'Carceral Citizenship in an Age of Global Apartheid', *Occasion*, 8, 2015, p. 3.

75 "We are living through an epochal transformation. . . . We have come to call this transformation globalization". See: Sassen, Saskia, *Territory, Authority, Rights: from Medieval to Global Assemblages*, Princeton University Press, Princeton, 2006, p. 1.

76 Garland, David, *The Culture of Control: Crime and Social Order in Contemporary Society*, Oxford University Press, 2001.

77 Hugo, Graeme, "From Compassion to Compliance? Trends in Refugee and Humanitarian Migration in Australia", *Geojournal*, 55: 2001, p. 28.

The Haitian Program worked to deny Haitian claimants access to lawyers, and it sped up exclusion-enabling processing through mass hearings, eventually held in secret.

The Haitian Program is also hugely significant for Guantánamo, which had been laying fallow 'in' Cuba, unspied as an 'island' for conducting offshore detention, and more recently interrogative torture. For the Haitian Program is the first context in which Guantánamo's use was explicitly suggested as a way of transforming the US' legislated ambiguity into a way of holding and keeping asylum seekers: *beyond* civil rights and the courts, *yet still under* US domination. August 20, 1978 is a precise and momentous date where we can pinpoint the emergence of offshore detention. On this day, an INS official, Mario Noto, bent his attention toward the political problem of boat arrivals.[78] When he did, Noto conceived of offshoring detention on Guantánamo as a way of solving the problem of Haitian asylum *by stopping the boats* – twenty-one years before the Australian Commonwealth saw to use CI in this way.[79]

3.8 US Caribbean triangulations of the 1980s and 1990s: Mariel and the US shift toward interdiction and offshoring

The boat-producing triangulations of the 70s US Caribbean, just traced, reached a tense and untimely post–Cold War climax with the Mariel Boatlift of 1980. As recent scholars have noted, echoing Simon's influential work, Mariel is a globally significant event invaluable for understanding shifts in postwar migration policy and the handling of asylum seekers.[80] Given the Australian emergence of border security that was the focus of first section of this book, 'the numbers' in 1980 can be productively placed alongside Australia in 2001 and 2012, the two calendar years in which the Coalition led shrill declarations of 'national crisis' over boat arrivals (section 2.8). During Mariel, as many as 125,000 Cubans and between 10–25,000[81] Haitians arrived in Miami, Florida.[82] In the years of crisis that triggered the emergence of border security in Australia two decades later, 5,516 and

78 Hansen, Jonathan M., *Guantánamo: An American History*, Hill and Wang, New York, 2011, p. 276.

79 "Send them to Guantanamo" was culturally legible as a solution by Mariel in 1980. The phrase appears in video footage of a TV news broadcast in the section of *Cocaine Cowboys* covering the Mariel Boatlift. See: Corben, Billy, *Cocaine Cowboys: Reloaded* (documentary). www.imdb.com/title/tt3845960/?ref_=nm_flmg_prd_5

80 Loyd, Jenna, 'Carceral Citizenship in an Age of Global Apartheid', *Occasion*, 8, 2015, p. 7.

81 The former is Lipman's figure, the latter is Gutekunst's. See: Lipman, Jana K., '"The Fish Trusts the Water, and It Is in the Water That It Is Cooked" The Caribbean Origins of the Krome Detention Center', *Radical History Review*, 115, 2013, p. 117 and Gutekunst, Claire P., 'Interdiction of Haitian Migrants on the High Seas: A Legal and Policy Analysis', *Yale Journal of International Law*, 10: 151, 1984–1985, p. 154.

82 Copeland, Ronald, 'The Cuban Boatlift of 1980: Strategies in Federal Crisis Management', *Annals of the American Academy of Political and Social Science* 467, 1983, pp. 138–150, Engstrom, David Wells, *Presidential Decision Making Adrift: The Carter Administration and the Mariel Boatlift*, Rowman & Littlefield, Lanham, 1997 and Simon, Jonathan, 'Refugees

5,459 individuals arrived.[83] A year of crisis in Australia in 2001 was a peak day of Mariel in 1980.

In thinking about Mariel as a pivotal event for the co-emergence of offshore detention and border security that happened in 1980, it's worth noting a shift in cultural mood at the precise turn of the decade.[84] In line with theoretical points about communication developed in the previous chapter (section 2.2–2.3), this helps us append key points about agency, purpose and causality in history (section 3.6) by considering the time sensitivity of political resonance, how and why it is that certain things, people and events, but not others, resonate with broad publics at particular moments.[85] Mariel coincided with a seachange in US cultural life, an atmospheric shift that Reagan and his entourage of 'Neos' were attuned to and feeding off.[86] The broader point for this chapter is threefold, as follows.

First, Mariel *in 1980* was not only a quilting point in a US-specific cultural shift, it's legible as an untimely post–Cold War event with global ramifications for asylum seekers that took place during a year when relations between the US and USSR were as tense as they had been in 1962. That is to say, what seemed to many influential commentators at the time as a quintessentially 'Cold War stoush between Cuba and America' can be read retrospectively as untimely and full of portentous factors heralding the dynamics of the political present central to this book: yet how could anyone at that time have known such a thing? Second, Mariel transpired just as Reagan began ushering in the American-style neoliberalism that, among so many other political effects, contributed to how asylum seeking has come to be understood and responded to, especially by the governments of the Anglophone world 'in today's globalised world', especially from 1994. Third, Mariel – in 1980 – *already* signified a number of global 'crises' of mobility, migration and asylum. These came into scholarly focus by the late 90s[87] were fully legible to broader publics of the rich West after September 2001, and have become an obsessive focus of the populist xenophobic right as of writing. The difference is that in 1980, the conceptual frames and rhetorical readymades

in a Carceral Age: The Rebirth of Immigration Prisons in the United States', *Public Culture*, 10: 3, 1998, pp. 577–607.

83 In the period 1976–2012, a total of 37,113 people arrived in Australia by boat seeking asylum. See: Phillips, Janet and Spinks, Harriet, 'Boat Arrivals in Australia Since 1976', *Parliament of Australia*. www.aph.gov.au/About_Parliament/Parliamentary_Departments/Parliamentary_Library/pubs/rp/rp1314/BoatArrivals

84 Didion, Joan, *Miami*, Simon and Schuster, New York, 1987 and Schlosser, Eric, *Command and Control*, Penguin Allen Lane, London, 2013, pp. 12–17.

85 Connolly, William E., 'The Evangelical-Capitalist Resonance Machine', *Political Theory*, 33: 6, 2005, pp. 869–886.

86 We can read forward and see another attuned apprehension to cultural mood played by the Howard government in 2001 (section 2.8–2.9).

87 See also: Harding, Jeremy, 'The Uninvited', *London Review of Books*, 22: 30, 2000. www.lrb.co.uk/v22/n03/jeremy-harding/the-uninvited

(such as deployed with the Deutsche Bank's arrival in Geraldton) were notably absent – as was border security's world. Agency, purpose, causality: the past is both the font of the present and incommensurable with it.

The fate of Haitian asylum seekers in *this* 1980 triangulation – in the following ways thoroughly unlike the US Caribbean of the 1970s – helps us pinpoint the time sensitivity of Mariel. On March 15, 1980, a month before Mariel, the US' Refugee Act became law, intending to replace Cold War expediencies and ad hockery (section 3.8) with uniform, nondiscriminatory principles grounded in multilateral internationalism and human rights. Then, on July 2, 1980, handing down his ruling in a class action filed on behalf of Haitian claimants who alleged their asylum applications had been systemically negated throughout the 70s, Judge King found that the Haitian Program had involved the systematic denial of asylum over a protracted period, and that race had been a factor in play[88]:

> Those Haitians who came to the United States seeking freedom and justice did not find it. Instead, they were confronted with an Immigration and Naturalization Service determined to deport them. The decision was made among high INS officials to expel Haitians, despite whatever claims to asylum individual Haitians might have. A Program was set up to accomplish this goal. The Program resulted in wholesale violations of due process, and only Haitians were affected. This Program, in its planning and executing, is offensive to every notion of constitutional due process and equal protection. The Haitians whose claims for asylum were rejected during the Program shall not be deported until they are given a fair chance to present their claims for political asylum.[89]

Alongside the Refugee Act, King should have resulted in a resounding and durable legal and political victory, opening a restorative horizon of justice for wronged Haitians opening onto an open shore of asylum for all noncitizens, from that moment into the future. Indeed, it contained this futurity of legal responsibility and care toward vulnerable noncitizens. But King was handed down at almost the exact historical moment when Haiti and the Haitians had been pushed into the background of a bilateral stoush between the US and Cuba. Seen from the political present, we can observe that King's judgment had come precisely seventy days too late to matter to any future Haitians who might have been affected by it, Guantánamo's first offshored detainees – a decade later, from November 1991 – conspicuous among them. When the Mariel Boatlift (Mariel) began on April 20, 1980, it erased any context in which King's judgment, and the Refugee Act, could matter to boat people seeking asylum from that time.

88 'Haitian Refugee Ctr. v. Civiletti, 503 F. Supp. 442 (S.D. Fla. 1980)', *Justitia US Law*. http://law.justia.com/cases/federal/district-courts/FSupp/503/442/1467096/
89 Op.Cit.

The numbers and the rate of arrival in Mariel bear emphasis.[90] Mariel, recall, involved the arrival in Miami[91] of 125,000 Cubans and between 10–25,000 Haitians: *during* the Iran Hostage Crisis, *in the year* of a bitterly fought Presidential nomination campaign, and *in a matter of months.* According to Copeland's figures, when the crisis peaked in May–June 1980 more than 5,000 people a day were arriving at the docks at Key West, Florida. US officials faced an event horizon with potentially several million arrivals,[92] where the 'people smugglers' were wealthy Miami Cubans chartering seaworthy ships hundreds of feet long that ferried several hundreds at a time across the Caribbean.[93] The US government confronted this without a plan or a precedent, and with the semantic weight of Johnson's Cold War expressions of 'openness' and Walter Mondale's recent excoriation of ASEAN leaders' responses to the Indochinese Exodus complicating matters.[94]

However, in the US of 1980, on the cusp of Reagan's America, the idea that Mariel signified sovereign loss of control over *the* border is not conspicuous in the patterns of discourse Simon draws from the archives.[95] Mariel was regarded as an 'unprecedented crisis' and in defeat President Carter conceded it "hurt us badly" when he had been "made to look impotent" by accepting "those refugees from Cuba".[96] But Mariel was widely read four ways in the United States, as:

1 an 'immigration crisis';
2 a socio-political crisis in Miami, for Florida, and

90 The following from Dernis, which indicates that the scale of the problem in the mid-70s was more akin to that faced by Australian authorities in the 2000s. "The Haitians have frequently arrived in South Florida by way of overloaded sail and fishing boats, in one case undertaking the hazardous 800-mile voyage with 38 people crowded into a 20-foot boat. . . . On August 29, 1976, more than 150 Haitians sailed into Miami on a boat of only 50 feet". Dernis, Martin M., 'Haitian Immigrants: Political Refugees or Economic Escapees?' *University of Miami Law Review*, 10: 1, 1976, p. 27.

91 The population of the city of Miami in 1980 was 346,880; the population of greater Miami in the same year 1.6 million, 70% of whom were of Cuban descent.http://scalar.usc.edu/hc/sites-that-speak/miami-1959–1980-socio-historical-overview

92 This rate continued over the course of a year would have meant 1.8 million boat arrivals in Key West, approximately one in five of whom (3.6 million) would have been Haitian. Cuba's population was 9.8 million in 1980, roughly the same as the state of Florida in that year – Haiti's was 5.6 million.

93 A distance of 254 nautical miles (470km), a day's sailing at 10 knots.

94 Mondale, Walter, 'Speech to the U.N. Conference on Indochinese Refugees at the Palais de Nations', July 21, 1979. http://nakbaeducation.com/wp-content/uploads/UNSpeech19MONDALE.pdf

95 Simon, Jonathan, 'Refugees in a Carceral Age: The Rebirth of Immigration Prisons in the United States', *Public Culture*, 10: 3, 1998, pp. 577–607.

96 "The refugee question has hurt us badly. It wasn't just in Florida, but it was throughout the country. It was a burning issue. It made us look impotent when we received these refugees from Cuba". Carter, Jimmy, '1980 Presidential Election Remarks With Reporters on the Results of the Election', November 5, 1980. *The American Presidency Project.* www.presidency.ucsb.edu/ws/?pid=45463

3 a humanitarian crisis for the detainees[97]; and later,
4 an object lesson for policy makers in how not to handle a federal crisis.[98]

Mariel was so notably not a crisis of 'the border', national sovereignty and national security in the way that boat arrivals were framed in pre-millennium Australia. In the latter case, a far better prepared government, armed with historical precedents – Mariel looming large among them – confronted perhaps 3% of the *actual* numbers involved in Mariel, with an infinitely smaller horizon of possible arrivals (sections 2.6–2.8). This directs us to a disjuncture between 'the numbers' and the emergence of border security: the two do not even vaguely correlate, let alone 'tell the clear story' Howard read back from them in hindsight (section 2.8). To recall: the Howard government's response was to:

1 first establish a deterrence approach (1996 onward, with clear focus from 1999),
2 then re-frame the facts and numbers in definite and interested ways (1998–2001),
3 in order to play to the shifting addressees of the message of border security, for electoral gain, which coalesced when *Tampa* appeared (August 2001).

But for this order of causal-effects to be gathered agentically and purposed politically, deterrence, maritime interdiction and the use of offshore detention had first to emerge. In Mariel in 1980, from which they emerged, they had not yet appeared. As a projection of national sovereignty, border security doesn't 'just' respond to problematic instances of human mobility, as its proponents claim; it is a societal response to a problem that becomes visible when arrivals appear in global space observed as a threat environment.

Mariel is conventionally understood as beginning when Castro opened the ports on April 20, 1980: and here is an empirical example where we can see, once again, a co-constitutive movement between openness and closure that, via crossing, opened a political space. The decisive moment of Mariel came when Castro was reported publicly as having 'opened the *jails*' four days later, on April 24. This was read as a tactical masterstroke by the *New York Times* on the day,[99] but from our perspective we can observe that 'opening the jails' escaped Castro's intentions and opened the way for institutional securitisation and the societal

97 Lipman, Jana K., ' "The Fish Trusts the Water, and It Is in the Water That It Is Cooked" The Caribbean Origins of the Krome Detention Center', *Radical History Review*, 115, 2013, pp. 115–141.
98 Engstrom, David Wells, *Presidential Decision Making Adrift: The Carter Administration and the Mariel Boatlift*, Rowman & Littlefield, Lanham, 1997.
99 Thomas, Jo, 'Castro Turns the Tables', *New York Times*, April 25, 1980, p. 1. http://query.nytimes.com/gst/abstract.html?res=9803EEDD153BE732A25756C2A9629C94619FD6CF&legacy=true

production of 'illegals' (which was neither his intention, nor could it have been known), in part because it inverted the US' openness to Cuban asylum claims by foreclosing the horizon of the Cold War political. Opened jails presented US authorities, and the Coast Guard as the frontline institutional responder, with the arrival of a no-longer-at-all-political and suddenly all-too-suspicious 'bunch of criminals'. The Cold War effectively ended nine years ahead of schedule in Miami, because opening the jails opened a passage out of the triangulations of the Cold War US Caribbean toward the dynamics of the 'carceral age'.[100]

Opening the jails had immediate further political effects emanating from the United States that co-operated via rhetorical resonance and the norms of international law, enabling a discursive shift. Paralleling the semantic shift in the meaning of asylum seekers as 'boat people' during and after the Indochinese Exodus in the five preceding years,[101] from the open jails of Mariel on it was no longer a simple, easy thing for campaigning politicians such as President Carter to score rhetorical slam dunks with the 'innocent victims of communism', as President Johnson might have fifteen years earlier, backgrounded by the Statue of Liberty, Ellis Island, the Manhattan skyline and the choppy waters of Upper Bay. On the contrary, in the wake of the 1980 Presidential election, what was retrospectively visible as the 'winning move' – still with us, more than ever – was Reagan's promise to 'get tough on illegality'.[102]

In relation to the UN-based norms of the Refugee Act, opening the ports meant that anyone who wished to leave was free to do so, thus nobody was 'fleeing' – effectively removing grounds for UN-definitional asylum claims. Opening the ports and the jails meant that anyone released from prison was free to go to America: this presented US authorities with an inherently contentious, politically ambiguous and potentially destabilising mass arrival immediately made legible through the prism of 'illegality and criminality coming uncontrollably ashore'.

On May 5, 1980, President Carter famously made a public comment about Mariel during a campaign speech. Carter's remarks may just as well have been Johnson's, but they were fifteen years ***and an epoch*** wide of the mark:

> We'll continue to provide an open heart and open arms to refugees seeking freedom from communist domination and from economic deprivation, brought on primarily by Fidel Castro and his government.[103]

100 'Refugees in a Carceral Age: The Rebirth of Immigration Prisons in the United States', *Public Culture*, 10: 3, 1998, pp. 582–583.

101 Robinson, W. Courtland, *Terms of Refuge: The Indochinese Exodus and the International Response*, Zed Books, London, 1998.

102 'Refugees in a Carceral Age: The Rebirth of Immigration Prisons in the United States', *Public Culture*, 10: 3, 1998, p. 583.

103 Copeland, Ronald, 'The Cuban Boatlift of 1980: Strategies in Federal Crisis Management', *Annals of the American Academy of Political and Social Science*, 467, 1983, p. 147.

Openness and closure. 'Open hearts and open minds' only works in the absence of open ports and open jails: the co-presence of the latter functioned as a kind of portal into an (as-yet-unnamed) threatening future in which the refuse of the world poured in to Miami, as Johnson might say, "in one mighty and irresistible tide". Where in 1965 the mere fact of Cuban arrival 'proved' the failure of the Castro regime *and* arrival's coveringly political cause and nature, now *the very same fact* uncovered an unstoppable, surging mass 'sturdy enough to make the journey, strong enough to make land, enduring enough to make a home in the land of freedom, and cunning enough to kill and steal if it became necessary to do so'. Nine days after 'open hearts and open minds', Carter backflipped, and – in a global first, twenty-one years before Howard – ordered the Coast Guard to stop the boats.[104]

3.9 'The simple truth of national survival': post-Mariel Reagan era innovations in deterrence

Two innovations in deterrence, crucial to the emergence of border security, were developed by the Reagan administration in 1981 in response to Mariel in 1980: maritime interdiction, and indefinite offshore detention. These two planks of Australia's 2001 Pacific Solution[105] – integrated as the ring of steel by 2016 after the full onshore victory of *Operation Sovereign Borders* – were deployed as fully articulated deterrence measures by the US from September 1981, in no small measure based on the perception that the Carter administration had failed in its response to Mariel in 1980.

Maritime interdiction was announced on September 29, 1981, via a Presidential Proclamation and Executive Order. 12324 was ordered "in view of the continuing problem of migrants coming to the United States, by sea, without necessary entry documents, and in order to carry out the suspension and

104 They initially refused to do so, on Safety of Life at Sea grounds. Copeland, Ronald, 'The Cuban Boatlift of 1980: Strategies in Federal Crisis Management', *Annals of the American Academy of Political and Social Science*, 467, 1983, p. 147.

105 In a time when John Howard, as treasurer, was a cabinet minister in the third Fraser government. As a cabinet minister Howard would have been routinely briefed on Mariel, the Carter administration's handling of it, and would have been well appraised of post-Mariel responses in the Reagan administration. As a cabinet minister in the Fraser government during the Indochinese Exodus, Howard was also routinely exposed to Fraser's (later praised) response to 'Vietnamese boat people'. As a conservative, and a canny learner capable of learning from and incorporating the policies of others (section 2.6–2.8), it's also not unlikely that Howard would have celebrated Reagan's victory and sought to learn and gain electorally from the GOP's campaign tactics and policy strategy on this issue, just as he may well have done from Margaret Thatcher's decisive stand on the Falklands. On the latter possibility, see: Charlton, Peter, '*Tampa*: The Triumph of Politics', in Solomon, David (ed.), *Howard's Race: Winning the Unwinnable Election*, Harper Collins, Sydney, 2002, p. 81.

interdiction of such entry". Its explicit purpose was "preventing *illegal* migration to the United States by sea".[106]

Consider the following complicated causal interlocking of the post-Mariel 1981 Caribbean triangulation (distilling key points from the previous two sections):

- maritime interdiction was a post-Mariel, Reagan administration response,
- developed bilaterally with the Haitian government to prevent Haitians arriving in Florida, from September 1981,
- that did away with the Cold War-based differential political treatment of Cubans and Haitians that had endured until Mariel via the political paroling in of Cubans, and the systematic negation of asylum claims under the Haitian Program[107](section 3.8).

Post-Mariel, the US government also developed a 'non-discriminatory' category of person. The 'Cuban-Haitian entrant' was both the conceptual unity and the living, detainable instantiation of post-Mariel norms. The ***'entrant' enabled exclusion*** (the paradox of openness and closure, once more), by allowing US authorities to apply the non-discriminatory principles written into the Refugee Act, so that nonarrival and the negation of asylum could be applied equally to all.

Maritime interdiction was the continuation of the Haitian Program on the high seas, because its carefully designed purpose was deterring arrival, preventing asylum. After Executive Order 12324 – in contrast to the crisis days of Mariel – the Coast Guard would board vessels suspected of attempting to approach the US and 'screen' those aboard, bringing ashore only those "few 'screened-in' Haitians found to have" – notice the insertion of UNHCR language here – "credible fears of political persecution".[108] As practiced in the 80s Caribbean, maritime interdiction was widely criticised on human rights grounds: as legally extraterritorial, as procedurally opaque and as opening the way to routine refoulement, especially where on-water interviews, whose credibility cannot be critically scrutinised, were used to ascertain the credibility of asylum claims.[109] These critiques

106 'Executive Order 12324 – Interdiction of Illegal Aliens', *The American Presidency Project*, September 29, 1981. www.presidency.ucsb.edu/ws/?pid=44317, italics mine.

107 Simon, Jonathan, 'Refugees in a Carceral Age: The Rebirth of Immigration Prisons in the United States', *Public Culture*, 10: 3, 1998, p. 594–595.

108 Koh, Harold Hongju, 'Refugees, the Courts, and the New World Order', *Utah Law Review*, 3, 1994, p. 999.

109 Taylor, Savitri, 'Sri Lankan Boat Arrivals: Enhanced Screening, Diminished Protection', *The Conversation*, November 1, 2013. http://theconversation.com/sri-lankan-boat-arrivals-enhanced-screening-diminished-protection-19601, Evershed, Nick, Farrell, Paul, and Laughland, Oliver, "In' or 'out': What We Know About 'Enhanced Screening' of Asylum Seekers', *The Guardian*, July 3, 2014. www.theguardian.com/world/2014/jul/03/asylum-seekers-may-be-subject-to-speedy-on-water-screenings and 'Maritime Interception and Screening of Asylum Seekers at Sea', *Kaldor Centre for International Refugee Law*, July 1, 2015. www.kaldorcentre.unsw.edu.au/publication/maritime-interception-and-screening-asylum-seekers-sea

accord with the evidence, but they don't countenance design intent – and here I observe the centrality of deterrence. Maritime interdiction and on-water screenings do what they're designed to: 'when used as intended', they prevent arrival. Deterrence is their purpose, and they are effective in procuring this as a political effect, something that any critique of their effects must first reckon with.

As a deterrence policy, maritime interdiction has been extraordinarily successful by its own measure. As Claire Gutekunst noted in the mid-80s, "the number of undocumented Haitians apprehended entering the United States dropped from approximately 1000 per month in the summer of 1981 to 134 in all of 1982".[110] Of the 22,000–24,600[111] Haitians interdicted over the decade to '91, "only 11 were screened in and brought to the US to pursue asylum claims".[112] From the 95:5 ratio that obtained in the Cold War 70s (section 3.8), in the US Caribbean of the 1980s interdiction program asylum seekers had a 0.05% (1 in 2,000) chance of acceptance. The same fate has befallen asylum seekers trying to arrive *in Australia* by boat since June 2013 (section 3.5); in 2015–2016 the Coalition trumpeted this as the greatest proof of the policy's success and the best reason why its wholesale adoption by European states should be adopted.[113]

A further and categorical difference between on-water screenings post 1981, as compared to the Haitian Program in the 70s, was that they took place beyond the territorial reach of US civil rights, law and the courts.[114] This 'extraterritoriality by design' was put in place because it allowed return to be expedited as efficiently as it had in the years of the Program, but via a new pretext that was defensibly legal *and* seemingly in line with human rights norms that *also* secured returns from enforceable accusations of refoulement *and* conspicuous public criticisms of policy such as might emerge from prominent and drawn out US court cases, such as in King. Here's where these '81 onward points, gathered from elements that emerged in the 70s, swerve back to the more explicit and direct use of the form of offshore for offshoring detention. Through the US' innovation with maritime interdiction we can see a commitment toward generating offshore-like deterrence effects; but through its imperfections or incompleteness we can also

110 Gutekunst, Claire P., 'Interdiction of Haitian Migrants on the High Seas: A Legal and Policy Analysis', *Yale Journal of International Law*, 10: 151, 1984–1985, p. 167.

111 The former figure is Gutekunst's, the latter is Ratner's. Ratner, Michael, 'How We Closed the Guantanamo HIV Camp: The Intersection of Politics and Litigation', *Harvard Human Rights Journal*, 11, 1998, p. 190.

112 Koh, Harold Hongju, 'America's Offshore Refugee Camps', *University of Richmond Law Review*, 29, p. 139.

113 Balogh, Stefanie, 'Europe "Needs an Asylum Solution": Jim Molan', *The Australian*, April 21, 2015. www.theaustralian.com.au/national-affairs/immigration/europe-needs-an-asylum-solution-jim-molan/story-fn9hml1gu-1227312738365

114 Gutekunst, Claire P., 'Interdiction of Haitian Migrants on the High Seas: A Legal and Policy Analysis', *Yale Journal of International Law*, 10: 151, 1984–1985, p. 167 and Kaplan, Amy, 'Where Is Guantánamo?' *American Quarterly*, 57: 3, 2005, pp. 831–858.

read a plausible impetus toward a further and final offshoring solution through the application of offshore's form (of which more shortly).

Alongside interdiction and screening, note the commensurate discursive presence of a concern with '*illegal* immigration' in Executive Order 12324. The figure of the illegal emerged in this space,

- *without* the force of anticommunism sheltering asylum seekers under the strange umbrella of potential nuclear annihilation;
- *with* the novel presence of 'the global' as a new and disquieting space from which threatening, ambiguous entities were 'suddenly' emerging.

As in other political spaces, this figuring of illegal arrival via an executive-led interdiction against crossing and entering engendered a new dialectic of global space, with its own contradictions, disjunctures and hierarchies, which remain ours to the time of writing. The seeming 'suddenness' with which the illegal emerged in the post-Mariel Reagan era helps us think about Nevins' account of how the appeal of walling along the US/Mexico border coalesced around 1994,[115] as well as how the discursive reframing of asylum seeking led by the Howard government from '96, then with increasing intensity from '98, got electoral traction by November '01, post-*Tampa*, post 9/11 (section 2.6–2.10). Once the 'illegal' becomes yoked to deterrence policies involving routine mistreatment beyond care, a political space can open where 'the border' can then be cast as the supreme stake in a polity's existence. Thus by June 14, 1984, President Reagan could easily and directly say the following: "the simple truth is that we've lost control of our own borders, and no nation can do that and survive".[116] In 1980, the semantic loading in the pattern, where deterrence addressed 'the simple truth of national survival', was absent from Carter's recollections of Mariel.

Reagan-led commitment to the interdiction and deterrence of mid-80s 'illegals' can also be read forward against late 90s Australian Defence Force incredulity that an interdiction policy that was about preventing arrivals and deterring arrival *could be* safe and practicable (section 2.7). It also sits across the political history of deterrence policies and their ethical horizons. As with critiques of interdiction on moral and human rights grounds, what we have to countenance from post-Mariel policy developments canvassed above: the durable lesson that 'deterrence works'. This was the 80s lesson the US took from ASEAN leaders' responses to the Indochinese Exodus with 'humane deterrence', which in turn influenced the deterrence policies applied in 1990s Europe based on US experiences in the 1980s.[117] We've

115 Nevins, Joseph, 'The Ideological Roots of the Illegal as Threat and the Boundary as Protector', in *Operation Gatekeeper and Beyond*, Routledge, Abingdon, 2010, pp. 118–155.

116 'The President's News Conference, June 14, 1984', *The American Presidency Project*. www.presidency.ucsb.edu/ws/?pid=40049

117 Simon, Jonathan, 'Refugees in a Carceral Age: The Rebirth of Immigration Prisons in the United States', *Public Culture*, 10: 3, 1998, p. 584.

explored how the Howard government, synchronous with other polities, shifted to deterrence around 1996. 'Deterrence works' is also the lesson that Tony Abbott encouraged the leaders of Europe to take as he toured Europe boosting the Australian policy model in 2015, and this has been the increasingly strong claim mirrored back by the North Atlantic right in recent years, with reference to Australian policy, and its 'great whacking gunships',[118] as an ideal.

The ethically disquieting yet politically consistent reading from deterrence-led policies, a reading that becomes more plausible in the light of *Operation Sovereign Borders*' broadcasted success and clear eyed bipartisan, mainstream support in contemporary Australia, is as follows. If you're willing to manipulate human rights rhetoric and ignore the letter and spirit of humanitarian law and expose people to the risk of drowning at sea and torture upon return, you can stop the boats and secure electoral victory in the process. A policymaker or politician willing to 'go there' ***knows*** that the US' pioneering of maritime interdiction from '81 achieves deterrence. As Mr Abbott commented on August 5, 2013, "the US coast guard turns around boats between America and Cuba. It's standard naval practice to intercept and turn around boats on the high seas".[119]

Indefinite offshore detention in Guantánamo began in November 1991 with the fall of Aristide.[120] The particular conditions in this case are full of tragic irony: co-armed with the possible use of Guantánamo lodged in institutional-cultural memory since the Noto Memo proposed its use in '77 ***and*** the legally defensible means of stopping, boarding and turning boats around via maritime interdiction, from '81, from 1991 the Coast Guard began transferring ***screened-in*** detainees to Guantánamo, under the pretext of providing safe haven. As with the application of UNHCR-like language toward Cuban-Haitian entrants to deny them protection, providing 'safe haven' to the 'screened in' worked toward importing the semblance of human rights ideals into offshore detention, in a way that ensured that people could be detained ***indefinitely***, ***and*** sent back if need be. Offshoring detention provided a way for onshore governments to mobilise an offshore population by impeding, detaining and returning it, as a deterrence policy that would serve the simple truth of national survival.

We can sit this alongside consistent Commonwealth government defences that offshore processing is consistent with Australia's commitments to international law. Those who'd arrived at Guantánamo's camps were 'only there as a temporary measure', they would and should be re-settled in their homeland, and they would

118 Hopkins, Katie, 'Rescue Boats? I'd Use Gunships to Stop Migrants: You May as Well Set Up a Libya to Italy P&O ferry', *The Sun*, April 17, 2015.

119 Marszalek, Jessica, Scarr, Lanai and Tin, Jason, 'Scrapping Carbon Tax 'My First Act' Says Opposition Leader Tony Abbott', *news.com.au*, August 5, 2013. www.news.com.au/national/federal-election/scrapping-carbon-tax-8216my-first-act8217-says-opposition-leader-tony-abbott/story-fnho52ip-1226691201649

120 Dailey, Peter, 'Haiti: The Fall of the House of Aristide', *The New York Review of Books*, March 13, 2003. www.nybooks.com/articles/2003/03/13/haiti-the-fall-of-the-house-of-aristide/

return there, as soon as *US authorities decided* it was 'cleansed of terror and free from fear'. Strangely, the admission of the necessity of safe haven implied after-the-fact what had been 'known to be known'[121] about Haiti for three decades, from 1957: Haitians manifestly did have credible fears of prosecution, because state terror was a decades-old norm whose exception was the brief glimmer of Aristide's first rule.[122]

On May 24, 1992, President Bush signed Executive Order 12807, the so-called Kennebunkport Order, "which directed the Coast Guard to intercept *and immediately return* all refugees to Haiti *without any asylum screening process*".[123] The Kennebunkport Order is an unambiguous antecedent of Operation Relex and *Operation Sovereign Borders.* The on-water operational realities generated by both these punitive intensifications of deterrence and control have produced situations where people have been exposed to the risk of drowning at sea via militarised interdiction and the realised threat of torture on return based on perfunctory on-water screening. That both of these deadly horizons accord with Katie Hopkins' wish that asylum seekers be drowned in a way beyond care[124] indicates that we should look to speech acts like executive orders and Howard's decisionist prerogative for privileged places where the fantasy of deterrence is voiced sovereignly, noting the political and societal effects this generates and the ungrievability of what then transpires.[125] For on documented occasions, "[w]hen the Coast Guard encountered intransigent refugees who refused to disembark into the hands of their persecutors, it drove them off its ships with fire hoses".[126] The 'simple truth' of deterrence enabled as routine what had been morally abhorrent to the Coast Guard little more than a decade earlier, because of its primary responsibility to Safety of Life at Sea. As with Operation Relex, the interposition of security on the high seas generated a double vision, with the vulnerability of the human threats as its constitutive blindspot (section 1.11–1.12).

During the '92 election campaign, Bill Clinton condemned the Kennebunktport Order and Bush's responses as cruel.[127] But in office, the Clinton administration continued substantive support for deterrence-based policies, nuancing rhetoric while holding to deterrence, and fighting challenges in the court. Deterrence held: in 1998, *Sale v. Haitian Centers Council* effectively granted presidential

121 Luhmann, Niklas, *The Reality of the Mass Media*, Polity Press, Cambridge, 2000, pp. 13, 20.
122 The 1990 election was held on December 16; Aristide was deposed as a result of the *coup d'etat*, on September 29, 1991.
123 'Executive Order 12807 – Interdiction of Illegal Aliens', *The American Presidency Project*, May 24, 1992. www.presidency.ucsb.edu/ws/?pid=23627
124 Hopkins, Katie, 'Rescue Boats? I'd Use Gunships to Stop Migrants: You May as Well Set Up a Libya to Italy P&O ferry', *The Sun*, April 17, 2015.
125 Butler, Judith, *Frames of War: When Is Life Grievable?* Verso, London, 2009.
126 Paik, A. Naomi, 'Carceral Quarantine at Guantánamo Legacies of US Imprisonment of Haitian Refugees, 1991–1994', *Radical History Review*, 115, 2013, p. 150.
127 Koh, Harold Hongju, 'Refugees, the Courts, and the New World Order', *Utah Law Review*, 3, 1994, p. 1003.

authority "to interdict refugees on the high seas and summarily return them to their oppressors".[128]

Of the 40,000 or so Haitians who fled after the Aristide coup, 30,000 were returned to Haiti by US authorities.[129] By 1993, the only Haitians who remained in offshore detention camps at Guantánamo were 310 HIV positive men, women and children, held in Camp Bulkely. On June 8, 1993, Judge Sterling Johnson Jr. ordered the closure of "what he called 'nothing more than an HIV prison camp.' The remaining 142 Haitians were flown to the United States".[130] Less than a decade later, on January 11, 2002, the first detainees were brought to GITMO.

3.10 Christmas Island, both onshore and off: from Australia's most profitable gambling enclave to its first purpose-built offshore detention centre

18,931 km away on CI, around the time Camp Bulkeley was ordered closed, construction on a boutique casino on CI was nearing completion. The boutique luxury resort was a joint venture between a West Australian businessman named Frank Woodmore and an Indonesian with very close links the Suharto regime, Robby Sumampow.[131] The Christmas Island Casino and Resort operated from 1993 until 1998, with its true boom years around the mid-90s.[132] Its establishment is intelligible in a broader socio-cultural context of strong Australian government support for casino building from this time onward: Melbourne's Crown Casino opened in 1994, Sydney's Star City in 1997. The development of all these casinos, oriented toward high net worth individuals and 'Asian high rollers' (section 5.7) involves a realignment of the task of government over the two decades to the time of writing: on neoliberal lines in neoliberal times. Alongside the shift toward deterrence, moral crusades against illegals and the rise of border security and offshore detention and banking, casino construction has been a carefully designed, artfully calibrated way of responding to 'today's globalised world' by securing circulation in favour of a definite set of political interests. All of these political constructions and their elaborate projects and projections necessarily

128 Ratner, Michael, 'How We Closed the Guantanamo HIV Camp: The Intersection of Politics and Litigation', *Harvard Human Rights Journal*, 11, 1998, p. 220.

129 Sewell, Dan, 'Haitians Escape Guantanamo, Not HIV Shadow: Miami: Immigrants Infected With Virus That Causes AIDS Fight to Build New Lives in United States, a Country That Has Made Them Feel Unwanted, Deeply Suspicious', *LA Times*, December 12, 1993. http://articles.latimes.com/1993-12-12/news/mn-1026_1_united-states

130 Op.cit.

131 Neighbour, Sally, 'The Christmas Party', *4 Corners*, July 1, 2002. www.abc.net.au/4corners/archives/2002b_Monday1July2002.htm

132 This section reprises and develops points made in Chambers, Peter, 'Society Has Been Defended: Following the Shifting Shape of State through Australia's Christmas Island', *International Political Sociology*, 5, 2011, p. 26.

involve offshore finance in various ways; all of them tell us how globalisation actually works.

CI's casino was established in years when the status and locus of CI's residents was supposedly finalised (sections 1.8–1.9). As I've examined in Chapter 1, after significant legal ambiguity and political contestation, by 1993 Christmas Islanders were Australian citizens living in Australia like anyone else, earning its wages, paying its taxes and subject to its laws and invested in its political projects. The Casino contributed $11 million per year to this local Australian economy,[133] while its successful operation in the final declining years of phosphate mining made it the island's major employer by the mid-90s. A tiny island was being re-worked by a larger jurisdiction to secure financial circulations from adjacent Indonesia, just as broader political reconfigurations of the task and purpose of the Commonwealth government and the newly clear central role of global cities re-placed the casino as an ideal post-industrial strategy in this new constellation of Australian interests – a topic we will return to, via citizenship and migration, in Chapter 5 (section 5.4–5.7).

The Casino generated huge profits, especially considering its size. An ex-employee described it as "an orgy of cash", turning over $15 million profit in a weekend.[134] At its peak, the tiny casino's annual turnover was $5 billion per year.[135] Back in Canberra, the Australian government charged an annual license fee of $1 million and took 8–10% of gross profits. The casino's time-sensitive success can be attributed to a finely calibrated combination of discrete distanciation and cozy connections co-operating with the collusion, corruption and nepotism through which Soeharto's New Order (ORBA) regime stabilised its three decades long pillage of Indonesia's rich mineral, animal and human resources, and the violent repression of political dissent – which begun, like Haiti under Papa Doc, under the cover of anticommunism. The majority of the casino's clientele were members of the ORBA elite, cronies and their families and guests who flew in to dispose of millions in cash with secure *Gemütlichkeit.* CI's casino made sense as a business model because pressure from rising Islamist interests made gambling impossible in Jakarta, since roughly 1982. The casino was physically close to Java so it could be easily reached by plane, but its clients would 'still benefit from the rule that the Australian government had ultimate say and control over any gambling that took place within the territory'.[136] This meant that gambling was not happening where it was *haram*, in increasingly Islamist Indonesia.

133 Op.cit., p. 26.

134 Neighbour, Sally, 'The Christmas Party', *Four Corners*, Australian Broadcasting Corporation, 2002. www.abc.net.au/4corners/archives/2002b_Monday1July2002.htm

135 Wright, Tony and Narushima, Yuko, 'Casino for Asylum Housing', *The Sydney Morning Herald*, July 1, 2009. www.smh.com.au/national/casino-for-asylum-housing-20090630-d43h.html

136 Re-casting John Yoo's *explanans* as to why the US constructed GITMO on Guantánamo.

In 1997 the Asian Monetary Crisis hit; by May 1998 Indonesia was suffering from riots and instability, and on May 21, 1998 Soeharto was forced to resign. With the fall of Soeharto the orgy of cash ended, the high rollers disappeared. Without the shady millions of Indonesian high rollers washing through it, the money dried up and the casino was left profoundly insolvent. For Christmas Islanders, the 1993–1998 success of the casino had profoundly restructured CI's economy, while allowed its Australian citizen residents a imagine a different island horizon in which their place was to be a future-making engine of profit and a niche site for eco tourism, or perhaps an ideal place for a spaceport.[137] The rendering inoperative of the casino, a physically tiny but massively profitable turbine of circulation, threw the Islanders' future direction and purpose into doubt. By dawn on the morning of August 29, 2001, as an SAS piloted helicopter hovered over the huge orange hull of *MV Tampa*, its thrusters keeping it just outside territorial waters, CI and its population had effectively become wards of the state, and their island future was an open question and an unsolved Commonwealth problem.

The CI casino was *effectively* offshoring billions of dollars of Indonesian money and rinsing it back ashore through Australian channels. But was the casino therefore offshore – in the formal and effective senses developed throughout this chapter (sections 3.1–3.4)? Observed from Java, CI's casino *was* an island enclave where an inner circle of cronies could gamble a percentage of their loot, away from Islamist critics, but in this way it was like dozens of islands in the Indonesian archipelago that fulfill niche tourism needs. Like the applications of offshore's form discussed so far, the stable operation of the casino *did* open a space of circumvention within circuits of accumulation. Yet when the gamblers came to the island, they simply 'came to Australia' as noncitizens, and they came to gamble at a resort that, though small and inaccessible in comparison to Melbourne's Crown Casino,[138] was for most intents and purposes no different.

The free admission of high rollers *by plane* provides a counterfactual against the political necessity of indefinite offshore detention for asylum seekers attempting to arrive *by boat*: both pivot around the totality of authorised admission in Australia, while showing how this is politically contingent (sections i.8–i.9). Since 1980, all noncitizens must carry a passport to enter Australia, and since 1992, any noncitizen seeking to enter Australia must additionally have a visa in order to do so. As explored in the introduction (section I.9), the contingent political choice of a universal visa system means that any noncitizen who does not have a visa and is recognised as seeking to enter, or who is attempting to remain, is an 'unlawful noncitizen'. It is this government-generated category of person, alongside the association of boat borne asylum seeking with people smuggling, criminalised by

137 Chambers, Peter, 'Society Has Been Defended: Following the Shifting Shape of State through Australia's Christmas Island', *International Political Sociology*, 5, 2011', p. 26.

138 Leys, Nick, 'No Expense Spared for High Rollers' New Home at Crown Casino', *Herald Sun*, September 10, 2010. www.heraldsun.com.au/news/no-expense-spared-for-high-rollers-new-home-at-crown-casino/story-e6frf7jo-1225916687016

the Howard government in 1999 (section 2.1), that has generated the political resonance of the 'illegal' in Australia.

The resonance of 'illegal' has to be seen side by side with SIEVs and SUNCs (sections 1.10–1.12). Since September 2001, people seeking protection in Australia by boat are recognised as travelling aboard Suspected Illegal Entry Vehicles (SIEVs), while they are recognised and referred to as Suspected Unlawful Non Citizens (SUNCs). Indonesian high rollers at the Casino between 1993 and 1998, flying to CI on chartered flights, were issued a rubber stamp visa upon arrival. The Commonwealth government welcomed these noncitizens to the island, even though they hadn't queued and submitted their carefully compiled, meticulous travel arrangements and given detailed and complete reasons for travelling prior to their departure. Likewise, the Commonwealth's agents did not regulate their entry or presence by 'detaining' them for any time longer than was necessary to extract a portion of the wealth they spent – by securing their Indonesian wealth as Australian dollars.

This is one point we can use to observe deterrence in operation with boat arrivals: it would be simpler, safer and much cheaper to issue asylum seekers a rubber stamp visa upon arrival by plane, bring them ashore, then process their claims, or issue them at airports in Indonesia. This would cripple extortionate and profoundly unsafe seaborne smuggling economies by depriving smuggler networks of demand and remove the desperation that leads asylum seekers to seek smugglers out, without the need to spend billions of dollars annually on militarised interdiction and offshore processing. But these measures, so much cheaper, so much safer, technically trivial in a twenty-first century that flies a million Australians to Bali each year (section I.9), would not stop them coming, nor would it make asylum seekers' lives uncomfortable enough to send the message of border security. Speculatively, then:

- Australians want Asian gamblers to arrive because they spend money, then leave;
- Australians do not want asylum seekers to arrive, because they make demands for protection, then stay.

Border Security's shores of politics and horizons of justice must reckon with this cultural norm, its lines of desire, its boundaries of care and how this sits atop deterrence, secured by offshore processing.

To return focus to the key theoretical point of this chapter on the form of offshore and offshoring processes (sections 3.2–3.4): was CI *formally* offshore in the sense developed, an operative paradox? As an engine of profit for Australia that was also an island-sized, weekend-long loophole in which its clientele could dwell and play, the casino leveraged the fact that CI was onshore Australia during the years of the casino's 'orgy of cash'. It was the co-incidence of CI's physical proximity to Indonesia and its legal status as a territory of the Commonwealth of Australia made the island an attractor for asylum seekers, from 1998. The further point is that, like high rollers between 1993–1998, Afghani and Iraqi asylum seekers from 1998 came to CI *because it was Australia*, because it wasn't offshore. Until the wake of Tampa, if you could get to CI, you had made it ashore. CI, an offshore island, was onshore Australia (section 1.7). This is of course effectively a kind of physico-political paradox, but it was one whose very contradictions prompted the implementation of another formal and societal one that aligned with the tightening circles of border security's world, along with the following key measures.

3.11 "Powers to move people": the application of offshore's form via maritime interdiction, offshore excised place, offshore entry person

In response to Tampa, the Commonwealth enacted three related pieces of legislation, all driven by the societal force of the expressed need to restore Australia's national sovereignty and send the message of border security, as surveyed in chapters one and two. The first of these, which validated the Howard government's militarised response to Tampa and reinforced the provisions authorising interdiction, is also worth considering comparatively as a variation and development from Reagan's Executive Order 12324 (section 3.10).

The Border Protection Act[139] gave authorised officers 'powers to move': to detain people, to 'bring them in' to the Migration Zone, or to "take the person, or cause the person to be taken, to a place outside Australia", including by placing or restraining them on – and/or removing them from – ships and aircraft. In the language of section 3AA, these are "powers to move *people*", but they also transform people into thinglike objects who *can be* moved around, detained and warehoused indefinitely[140]: dedifferentiating persons, rights and things *in the extension* of nebulous yet domineering jurisdiction over them.[141] The logistical aspects of the Border Protection Act, and how they align with the global project of securing circulation, will become a key focus in the following chapter; here I focus on humans, authorised officers and categories of person.

139 'Border Protection (Validation and Enforcement Powers) Act 2001', *Federal Register of Legislation*. www.legislation.gov.au/Details/C2004A00886

140 The indefinite nature of offshore mandatory detention is a contentious legal issue that has never been settled. The Commonwealth maintains that mandatory detention is not indefinite; yet detainees, including children, have remained in existential limbo for many years (in 2014 detainees spent an *average* of 274 days in detention). Staged appearances like Mr Morrison's 'you will never see the shores of Australia' (section 3.5), indicate that detention is punitive and that it also seeks to collectively punish in order to send a deterring warning to another population. Ting, Inga, and Walters, Conrad, 'Asylum Seekers' Time in Detention Soars', *The Sydney Morning Herald*, May 2, 2014. www.smh.com.au/federal-politics/asylum-seekers-time-in-detention-soars-20140503-zr3eg.html

141 Mussawir, Ed, *Jurisdiction in Deleuze: The Expression and Representation of Law*, Routledge, Abingdon, 2011.

Like Executive Order 12324, the Act granted authorised officers powers of interdiction when they have "reasonable grounds for believing" that people appearing on boats had an "intention . . . to enter Australia ***unlawfully***". This clarified moves made with the criminalisation of people smuggling to Australia in 1999, while also making the absence of a visa – 'not having' a document indicating authorisation to enter and remain, a document that can only be given by the entity refusing to issue it – synonymous with 'unlawfulness'.

The co-construction of border security's world via the Commonwealth's semantic alignment of undocumented arrival with unlawfulness was effectuated in an onshore rhetorical context where the same groups of people were routinely called 'illegals' and 'queuejumpers' by the most senior elected officials of the land (sections 2.6, 2.7). As with Executive Order 12324, we see a post–Cold War, deterrence-typical insistence on an *illegality* of intention, rather than asylum seeking's relation to survival: fleeing and removing families and children from armed conflict, politics, poverty, inequality and an attempt to fulfill basic human needs. This is a precise point where we can note a nascent observing system in operation through the contingent political choice to reduce the complexity of human arrival by regarding it unilaterally in a way that rightfully authorises extremely harsh treatment – ***because*** sovereignty is threatened, ***in order to*** send the message of border security.

The embrace of the illegal is extrasystemically vexing, as the ***no one is illegal*** campaign indicates.[142] If observed through the distinctions of international humanitarian law and norms, the overwhelming majority of these 'illegals' seeking asylum in Australia by boat in the late 90s were Afghan Hazaras and Iraqi Christians, religious and ethnic minorities fleeing persecution by the Taliban and Saddam Hussein. More than 90% of these groups were later found to be UN-definitional refugees (section I.7 – i.9). But whereas twenty years earlier in the 80s, US interdiction-meriting illegality was framed in relation "the continuing problem of ***migrants coming to the United States***, by sea, ***without necessary entry documents***",[143] post-Tampa the object of worry was not undocumented migration *per se* – and this is very telling of a particularly Australian aspect of border security's world expressed by the Border Protection Act.

Post-Tampa, authorised officers – thousands of people – were given extremely broad powers to move, stop, detain and warehouse people offshore ***because*** of an Australian iteration of Reagan's 'simple truth of national survival' (section 3.10): 'the borders of Australia', and by extension 'the border itself', came to be recognised – onshore – as a threaten-able 'thing' that could and must be protected.[144] Like Howard's electorally sensitive and seemingly empathic responsive-

142 'No One Is Illegal', no one is illegal. www.nooneisillegal.org/

143 'Executive Order 12324 – Interdiction of Illegal Aliens', *The American Presidency Project*, September 29, 1981. www.presidency.ucsb.edu/ws/?pid=44317, italics mine

144 Burke, Anthony, 'A Fantasy Debate, Disdainful of Basic Facts', *The Drum*, *abc.net.au*, September 2, 2011. www.abc.net.au/news/2011-09-02/burke-a-fantasy-debate-bereft-of-basic-facts/2867052

ness to the way 'the sheer size of Australia's coastline had led Australians to feel particularly vulnerable to the unchecked arrival of scores of boats' (section 2.8), this is a reification of *the* border. It relies on a political relationship with maritime geography that is experientially distant and emotionally charged. As those who live to tell of attempts to cross the open ocean on overloaded and unseaworthy coastal fishing boats testify, a coastal fishing boat on the open ocean lists and heaves in the swell, the ocean roils and spits spray, swells rise and the wind howls, and the smell of bilge water, diesel and vomit sloshing around in the leaky, overcrowded hull makes you nauseous – even if you do not suffer from seasickness. You cling to the slippery wooden skin and skeleton of a floating boundary (section I.8), the only thing that keeps you from a vast, cold, wet space that can kill even a strong swimmer in minutes; and there are sharks. You can't swim, your children are screaming, they don't have lifejackets. Such routine situations that arise in the navigation of global space have not led great numbers of Australians to feel particularly vulnerable about the vulnerable. Instead, Howard, the major parties and most of news media have led *Australians* to feel particularly vulnerable about themselves, via a coastline most never visit and live many thousands of kilometres away from. The Timor Sea is not easily cognisable as a 'thing' if you are actually crossing it. We can note the following shift, then.

By late 2001 the Commonwealth's use of maritime interdiction was not just meant 'to stop people coming by sea without the proper documents' – above all it was meant to "protect Australia's borders".[145] More than in the post-Mariel US Caribbean of the Reagan era, in the wake of Tampa maritime interdiction – between Indonesia and Australia, between Iraqis, Afghanis and Australians – was loaded with national significance and territorial force. Out of this loading co-emerged the contemporary Australian cultural norm that 'the border' is some*thing* that could and should rightly be *totally* protected and that people seeking protection by crossing it are threats, *all of whom* have to be interdicted and deterred.

Through the Border Protection Act, stopping asylum was refigured triply as a way:

1 of *deterring* the arrival of 'illegals',
2 of *defending* national sovereignty, and
3 of *thinking* about 'the border' as a thing rightly protected from the protection-seeking arrivals who (from then on and forever) arrive by boat to threaten it.

It is in the sustained cultural grip of this onshore island imagining – a very parochial tightening apprehension of global space, and the unilateral projection of 'no way!' that follows from it – that we can observe the border continuum instantiated

145 'Executive Order 12324 – Interdiction of Illegal Aliens, *The American Presidency Project*, September 29, 1981. www.presidency.ucsb.edu/ws/?pid=44317

as a 'ring of steel' represented as the goal and jewel of a 'migration superpower', an Australia more secured than it has ever been (section 2.12).

The second piece of post-Tampa legislation, the Excision Act,[146] removed certain territories from the Migration Zone, re-specifying them as 'offshore excised places'. This is the moment we can see the application of offshore's paradoxical form to CI.

The excision of CI allowed the Commonwealth a legally defensible way of claiming that asylum seekers who had reached the Island hadn't arrived in Australia in a way they, like the Indonesian high rollers, had been smoothly capable of in the 90s. But excision effectively circumscribed the ambit of its effects by only being applicable to unlawful noncitizens, because in this context it meant that boat-borne asylum seekers could not arrive – for the purposes for which they had sought to. When boats after the excision made it to CI without foundering or being interdicted, Commonwealth agents still treated people brought ashore to CI as bodily 'there', and detained them on the island. The nonapplication of the Migration Act via the excision meant that asylum claims could not be initiated, and that – in every effective way like post-Mariel Caribbean moves against Cubans-Haitian entrants – access to journalists, lawyers and the courts was precluded. Detainees were still expected to be compliant and not attempt escape,[147] but they were no longer legal persons able to apply to become refugees or gain access to the courts to protest the fairness of the conditions they were subjected to or question the rightful application of the procedures that kept them there.[148] In these ways, excision effectuated a circumvention within circulation that unilaterally imposed conditions whose reciprocal applicability to the dominator was unthinkable (section 3.3).

For excision has a simultaneous and less noted onshore Australian meaning: it allowed authorised agents of the Commonwealth to remain in Australia when they travelled to CI. This is why the role of paradox in offshore's form is pivotal, especially the way it can be interposed as a relation of political, legal and ethical separation. Any Australian flown 5,000km from Canberra to deal with unlawful noncitizens lands in territory as sovereignly Australian as the airports they've departed from and return to. Australians after the excision 'never left Australia' when flying to CI to administer and enforce the detention of asylum seekers. Asylum seekers after the excision could never arrive, though they remained in

146 'Migration Amendment (Excision from Migration Zone) (Consequential Provisions) Act 2001', *Commonwealth of Australia*. www.legislation.gov.au/Details/C2004A00888

147 'Detainees have "no right to escape"' *The Sydney Morning Herald*, August 6, 2004. www.smh.com.au/articles/2004/08/06/1091732062324.html and Perpitch, Nicolas, 'Yongah Hill Detainees Face Transfer to Christmas Island After Failed Escape Attempt', *ABC News*, June 3, 2015. www.abc.net.au/news/2015-06-03/yongah-hill-detainees-fail-in-escape-attempt/6517866

148 Mussawir, Ed, *Jurisdiction in Deleuze: The Expression and Representation of Law*, Routledge, Abingdon, 2011.

detention on the island. As earlier (section 3.2), this raises questions of comparisons with other detention islands and how we should understand them theoretically, which I will return to in the conclusion.

The third main plank of post-Tampa policy, the Consequential Provisions Act[149] introduced a new category of person, the 'offshore entry person' (since 2013 'unlawful maritime arrival'),[150] and two new categories of offshore visas. We should observe the homology with the category of person 'Cuban-Haitian entrant', as well as the offshore handling and asylum negating screening-out purposes it fulfils. The Consequential Act enables Commonwealth authorities to deal with people in offshore excised places; it's a way of matching a category of person with their rightful political space and treatment: *offshore* excised place, *offshore* entry person, *authorised* officer. As with the operational necessity of recognising asylum seekers as security threats in the space of security, an 'offshore entry person' *is* the consequential entity produced by necessity of governing SUNCS aboard SIEVs when they are interdicted and transferred to offshore excised places.

What closes the circle between these three related pieces of post-Tampa legislation is the unilateral recognition of an authorised officer, specifically their on-water operational suspicion, cast through the idea(l) of reasonableness, that the person is an 'unlawful non-citizen':

> If an officer knows or reasonably suspects that a person in an excised offshore place is an unlawful non-citizen, the officer may detain the person. . . . If an officer reasonably suspects that a person in Australia but outside the migration zone . . . is seeking to enter an excised offshore place; and . . . would, if in the migration zone, be an unlawful non-citizen; the officer may detain the person.[151]

Routine absolves authorised officers of a need to exercise reasonableness on their own, or enter the hesitating space of true critical thought where one might think otherwise about the human one is grappling with in the fullness of her complexity.[152] Suspicion is included into the acronym SUNC, it is already a distinction made by

149 'Migration Amendment (Excision from Migration Zone) (Consequential Provisions) Act 2001', *Federal Register of Legislation, Commonwealth of Australia*, www.legislation.gov.au/Details/C2004A00888

150 'Migration Amendment (Unauthorised Maritime Arrivals and Other Measures) Act 2013 (No. 35, 2013) – Schedule 1', *austlii.edu.au*. www.austlii.edu.au/au/legis/cth/num_act/mamaaoma2013683/sch1.html

151 'Migration Act (1958), section 189', *austlii.edu.au*. www.austlii.edu.au/au/legis/cth/consol_act/ma1958118/s189.html

152 See: Pickering, Sharon, 'Floating Carceral Spaces: Border Enforcement and Gender on the High Seas', *Punishment and Society*, 16: 2, 2014, pp. 187–205.

border security as an observing system. Everyone aboard a SIEV *is* a SUNC.[153] Suspicion and reasonableness, together – unobservable, unmeasurable, placed offshore, beyond critical scrutiny or review – give authorised officers the power to move people without operational impedance or critical hesitation, shifting the burden of complexity[154] back on to the interdicted and out into the operating environment from which threat objects keep emerging.

SUNC has the societal effect of further integrating border security's severances into the way vulnerable people can be perceived. The normative implication of this is an escalation of asymmetries of recognition, harm and infliction, insofar as it produces a situation where the least vulnerable feel the most justified for their total commitment to maximal securing, while the most vulnerable are the least justified for protesting and resisting their treatment. Since roughly 2013 this escalation of asymmetries of harm and recognition has created a defensible onshore speaking position where people bringing documented allegations of physical and sexual abuse, attempted suicide and mental breakdown have been accused by responsible Commonwealth officials of causing outrage by bringing claims, in turn 'justifying' personal attacks on the bearers of the information, with the treatment in question relegated to the background or flipped into 'proof' of manipulative behaviour intended to outrage the nation and 'shake our conviction'. To quote Mr Abbott's advice for Europe from border security's world, which takes this framing and generalises it into an expression of 'national resolve':

> This means turning boats around, for people coming by sea. It means denying entry at the border, for people with no legal right to come; and it means establishing camps for people who currently have nowhere to go.
>
> It will require some force; it will require massive logistics and expense; it will gnaw at our consciences – yet it is the only way to prevent a tide of humanity surging through Europe and quite possibly changing it forever.
>
> We are rediscovering the hard way that justice tempered by mercy is an exacting ideal as too much mercy for some necessarily undermines justice for all.
>
> The Australian experience proves that the only way to dissuade people seeking to come from afar is not to let them in.[155]

As with the notion that boat arrivals *are* a threat to '*the* border', the human consequences of the Consequential Provisions Act, voiced in Abbott's 2015 rhetoric,

153 Chambers, Peter, 'The Embrace of Border Security: Maritime Jurisdiction, National Sovereignty, and the Geopolitics of Operation Sovereign Borders', *Geopolitics*, 20: 2, 2015, p. 21.

154 Luhmann, Niklas, 'What Is Communication?' *Communication Theory*, 2: 3, 1992, p. 256.

155 Transcript: Tony Abbott's controversial speech at the Margaret Thatcher Lecture', *The Sydney Morning Herald*, October 28, 2015. www.smh.com.au/federal-politics/political-news/transcript-tony-abbotts-controversial-speech-at-the-margaret-thatcher-lecture-20151028-gkkg6p.html

are, we might say, *very* consequential. Alongside the other factors and elements explored in this section, the Consequential Provisions have worked to push boat arrivals back to the point where people seeking asylum *are* recognised *as* 'unlawful *people*' by the authorised officers interdicting them. Embodiment in its fullness is a suspicious intention. This deinviduation of people also shores up the secured border through a co-productive reification abiding in the simple truth of national survival: just as the border *is* (and must survive); so too illegals *are* (and must be deterred). Just as the border is rightly secured; so too illegals are rightly exposed to cruelty, for the sake of deterrence – and as this 'gnaws at *our* consciences', for senior ministers like Mr Abbott, Mr Dutton and Mr Morrison, somehow this too is an opportunity for national self regard.

3.12 May 5, 2013 – April 25, 2016: excision of the mainland and offshore detention in Australia's border security colonies, Manus Island and Nauru

In 2002, one year after the above post-Tampa measures became Australian law, the Commonwealth began work on the detention centre on CI, Australia's first purpose-built offshore immigration detention centre. Between 2001 and 2007, the Coalition government also operated offshore detention centres on Nauru and Manus Island as part of the Pacific Solution[156]: the former *de jure* the world's smallest republic, the latter an island part of Papua New Guinea. We can see imperial *statifications* (section 1.1, 3.6) at work here by attending to disparities of size and scale, relations of dependency, and time-sensitive hegemony.[157]

A central substantive claim of this chapter has been that offshore processing is about achieving deterrence and control through the negation of asylum; as these strategic objectives are pursued through the application of offshore's form, warehouse-able categories of person are produced who can be moved, detained, destroyed and discarded with relative ease. I've also observed how the application of offshore's form to detention opens a space of domination beyond the shores of politics, a low-risk arena in which the agents of states can push asylum seekers and Pacific leaders around in 'their' geopolitical backyards. With Nauru and Manus, Australia can enlarge its pretensions toward regional hegemony without the risks of escalation and pushback that might emerge in, say, a stoush over a contested island with a neighbouring nation-state with a large and powerful military, such as Indonesia or China. Australia can safely 'punch down' in the Pacific with offshore

156 Phillips, Janet, 'The 'Pacific Solution' Revisited: A Statistical Guide to the Asylum Seeker Caseloads on Nauru and Manus Island', Parliamentary Library of Australia. http://parlinfo.aph.gov.au/parlInfo/download/library/prspub/1893669/upload_binary/1893669.pdf

157 Palan, Ronen, 'International Financial Centers: The British-Empire, City-States and Commercially Oriented Politics', *Theoretical Inquiries in Law*, 11: 1, 2010, pp. 152–154.

processing, while border security's world, and the colonies it imposes, loom as large as fate for some of these tiny 'ex-colonial' Pacific political spaces.

How might we think about these brutal social facts of Australia's political present in light of what was also explored by way of historical international antecedents? As with the US Caribbean, these are fundamentally relations of domination and dependency. This is laid bare by the durable social fact of offshore detention centres themselves, which have transformed the economies of whole islands into island-sized solutions, worlds of American homeland and Australian border security. In the contemporary Australian constellation at issue in this and the previous two sections, these dominations and dependencies are concretised and literalised by the acceptance of aid and bank transfers. In the case of the Republic of Nauru, offshore processing is what keeps the lights on. This dependency ties systemic abuse and the destruction of children's mental health[158] to the bidding of the Australian nation and the island future of the world's smallest republic: 14,000 thousand people's lives made dependent upon support for the infliction of cruelty to children.[159] As with the infliction of torture in GITMO, and the negation of Haitian asylum claims under the Haitian Program, maritime interdiction and safe haven, these conditions are all systemic features that emerge in these different applications of offshore's form to the problem of those who seek to arrive by crossing the national boundary and entering the nation. In sum, applications of offshore's form produce circumventions within circulation that effectuate deterrence and control by dominating vulnerable noncitizens as threatening things.

Onshore in Australia, and especially where public critics of offshore processing level their claims against the Commonwealth and its agents of domination, CI, Manus Island and Nauru are treated as 'the same', or part of the same moral abyss. This is true in important senses, but there are important distinctions and contrasts. A glance at the texture of these strong relations and slight incongruities allows concluding observations about the form of offshore, national sovereignty and a tropical geopolitics of border security taking place in dark and far-flung parts of Australia's Pacific backyard.

Unlike Manus and Nauru, CI remains a territory of the Commonwealth of Australia and an offshore excised place. CI is Australia; an offshore island legally onshore for all but one legislated purpose. The purpose-built detention centre constructed there is as secure and Australian as the medium security prison whose design it was based on, and its use is as politically durable as Australians' onshore commitment to border security, and taxpayers' willingness to keep paying to conduct detention on the Island, which raises costs by a factor of ten: the cost per

158 'Australia: Island of Despair: Australia's 'Processing' of Refugees on Nauru', Amnesty International, October 17, 2016. www.amnesty.org/en/documents/asa12/4934/2016/en/

159 Sparrow, Jeff, 'What's the End Game for Australia's Border Policy – A World of Walled City-States? *The Guardian*, May 6, 2016. www.theguardian.com/commentisfree/2016/may/06/whats-the-end-game-for-australias-border-policy-a-world-of-walled-city-states

offshore detainee was revealed in 2016 as sitting at $573,100[160] (AUD) per person per year.[161] As discussed (section 3.12), post excision CI's political economy abides in the paradox of offshore's form (section 3.1–3.4): it is Australia for Australians who travel to and from there *and* it is not Australia for asylum seekers who cannot arrive when they are detained there, unlawful noncitizens in an offshore excised place.

On May 17, 2013, federal parliament excised the mainland from the Migration Zone. Australia is now an offshore excised place.[162]

The excision of the mainland passed *almost* unnoted; it was conspicuous as a news media nonevent, a thing of little or no tension or moment in onshore political life. What it meant was that even people aboard boats who arrived in Australia's territorial sea or coastal waters, like those Sri Lankans aboard the Deutsche Bank only a month or so prior to the announcement – could be interdicted and transferred offshore for processing. In the years since the mainland's excision, as CI's purpose has shifted to detaining unlawful noncitizens pending determination of deportation and exclusion claims, most of the weight of processing would-be boat arrivals has been borne by Nauru and Manus Island.

Nauru and Manus Island are not Australia, but as offshore processing centres they exist for border security's world, which on these islands secures onshore Australia in its sovereign identity. Nauru and Manus Island are colonies of Australian border security, penal colonies of a certain kind. Offshore processing on both sites has endured[163] because of an interacting combination of the following three factors:

1 The co-emergence of maritime interdiction, offshore excised places and offshore entry person (now unlawful noncitizen) means that asylum seekers no longer 'arrive' when they seek or get to 'Australia', and they can be transferred to a third country for processing;
2 informal bilateral arrangements and formal contractual arrangements have been developed and agreed to between senior elected officials from Australia, Nauru and Papua New Guinea, eventuating in the establishment of detention facilities for offshore processing; and,

160 444,324 USD, 403,362 EUR.

161 Gordon, Michael, 'Revealed: The Cost of Stopping the Boats Put at $9.6 Billion', *The Sydney Morning Herald*, September 13, 2016. www.smh.com.au/federal-politics/political-news/revealed-the-cost-of-stopping-the-boats-put-at-96-billion-20160912-grea35.html and Martin, Peter, 'The Extraordinary Cost of Keeping Asylum Seekers in Detention: Over $500,000 Each', *The Sydney Morning Herald*, September 14, 2016. www.smh.com.au/comment/the-extraordinary-cost-of-keeping-asylum-seekers-in-detention-over-500000-each-20160914-grftcj.html

162 Barlow, Karen, 'Parliament Excises Mainland From Migration Zone', *Radio Australia*, May 17, 2013. www.radioaustralia.net.au/international/2013-05-16/parliament-excises-mainland-from-migration-zone/1131736-0

163 Dyett, Greg, 'The Day the Nauru Centre Was Closed', *sbs.com.au*, August 26, 2013. www.sbs.com.au/news/article/2013/02/08/day-nauru-centre-was-closed

3 publicly avowed respect for the supremacy of state sovereignty by Commonwealth ministers, stabilised arrangements through rhetorical appeals to the supremacy of state sovereignty and the commensurate necessity of international noninterference, so that, to quote Mr Morrison, "[a]s the individuals and the (Manus) centre are located in PNG territory, it has primary responsibility".[164]

As Commonwealth colonies of border security, political spaces dominated by the severances of border security's world, Nauru and Manus are islands of Australian domination. They are in effect secondary sites of detention[165] enabled by the suite of policy measures enabling maritime border security, centrally: the offshore excised nature of CI and the mainland; the Commonwealth's powers to move people; and the 'unlawful noncitizen' as a moveable, warehouse-able category of person whose suffering merits an infinitesimal degree of critical scrutiny or care compared to onshore Australian lives. Nauru and Manus produce circumventions within circulation; offshoring procures deterrence and control that secures onshore Australia's sovereign anxieties by exposing living people to the ordeal of offshore processing and the protracted anguish of mandatory detention while this processing is taking place.

The nuance of these points, taken together, help us avoid the seductive neatness of assertions like 'Nauru is Australia's Guantánamo'[166] or 'Manus Island is a state of exception'.[167] Neither of these phrases is untrue as an overarching evaluative description. Nauru and Manus are both violent hellholes beyond the rule of law where deterrence and control is predicated on opaque domination with near impunity and Australian officials punching down in the Pacific while leaning on expedient arrangements agreed to by the political elite of relatively small and highly dependent colonies. Nauru and Manus are, by most descriptions, camps where the infliction of cruelty is systemic, and the effects on human health have been observed by the UN as deplorable, inhuman and degrading,[168] by Amnesty

164 'Is Australia responsible for asylum seekers detained on Manus Island?' *ABC Fact Check*, updated February 28, 2014. www.abc.net.au/news/2014-02-27/who-is-responsible-for-asylum-seekers-detained-on-manus/5275598

165 Benton, Lauren, 'Island Chains: Military Law and Convict Transportation', in *A Search for Sovereignty: Law and Geography in European Empires, 1400–1900*, New York University, New York, 2010, pp. 162–222.

166 Isaacs, David, 'Nauru and Manus Island Are Australia's Guantanamo Bay', *The Sydney Morning Herald*, February 29, 2016. www.smh.com.au/comment/nauru-and-manus-island-are-australias-guantanamo-gay-20160228-gn5qtg.html

167 Boochani, Behrouz, 'Australia, Exceptional in Its Brutality', *Overland*, April 25, 2016. https://overland.org.au/2016/04/australia-exceptional-in-its-brutality/

168 'Children in Immigration Detention: Statements by the United Nations', *Australian Human Rights Commission*. www.humanrights.gov.au/our-work/asylum-seekers-and-refugees/publications/children-immigration-detention-statements-united

as punitive and torture,[169] and by expert observers as worse than war zones.[170] The post–Pacific Solution Commonwealth does not exterminate the people it sends to Manus and Nauru as was done during the Final Solution, it keeps them alive until many of them break.[171] This involves the ruination of lives, including the physical, mental and future destruction of babies and children, which we can see clearly from innumerable cases of self harm, and a suicide pact between a group of children.[172]

Nauru and Manus all point back to the boundaries of Australia they enforce as impassible for boat-borne asylum seekers. As nebulous yet operable global spaces producing deterrence and control in a way that helps anxious voters in marginal Australian seats feel less anxious about their coastline, immigration and globalisation (section 2.8), Nauru and Manus work, as island colonies of Australian border security, to produce these circumventions within circulation, which minimise Australian risk, hide harmful Australian practices and protect group agent beneficiaries onshore in Australia. Nauru and Manus' existence is entirely relational, and implicates all of the Commonwealth and its citizens, both as a political formation responsible for border security and as a parliamentary democracy where the actions of elected officials are representative of the will of the people.

Manus and Nauru, second, are border security colonies imposed on small, dependent jurisdictions in Australia's imperial backyard. In line with these reasons, a more appropriate comparison with Guantánamo is 'safe haven': the temporary shelters and US military constructed camps agreed to by Panama, Honduras and other countries when post-Aristide, Clinton administration Guantánamo was deemed full.[173] 'Safe haven' lacks the denouncing force that Guantánamo has come to signify on its own by this second decade of the Global War on Terror. Safe haven is also a framing less likely to merit headlines, receive op-ed go ahead or elicit action-spurring outrage from concerned publics. Yet

169 'Australia: Island of Despair: Australia's 'Processing' of Refugees on Nauru', Amnesty International, October 17, 2016. www.amnesty.org/en/documents/asa12/4934/2016/en/

170 'Mental Trauma on Nauru Worse Than War Zones: Neistat', *ABC RN Breakfast*, October 18, 2016. www.abc.net.au/radionational/programs/breakfast/refugee-mental-trauma-worse-than-war-zones/7941392

171 Section I.3, 1.12, Foucault, Michel, 'Right of Death and Power Over Life', in *The History of Sexuality, Volume One*, Penguin, London, 2008, pp. 133–160, Vaughan-Williams, Nick, *Border Politics: The Limits of Sovereign Power*, Edinburgh University Press, 2009 and Lemke, Thomas, *Biopolitics: An Advanced Introduction*, New York University Press, 2011.

172 'Trauma on Nauru and Manus', *RN Late Light Live*, July 4, 2016. www.abc.net.au/radionational/programs/latenightlive/paul-stevenson/7557752

173 Koh and Loyd, 'Antigua, Dominica, St. Lucia, Suriname, and the Turks and Caicos'. Loyd, Jenna, 'Carceral Citizenship in an Age of Global Apartheid', *Occasion*, 15, 2015, p. 10. As Koh documents, there were nearly '40,000 Haitians and Cubans . . . being held on Guantanamo by fall 1994', and in late "October 1994. . . 30,000 Cuban refugees (were) being indefinitely detained on Guantanamo and in Panama". In: Koh, Harold Hongju, 'Refugees, the Courts, and the New World Order', *Utah Law Review*, 3, 1994, p. 1008.

'safe haven' was not haven, nor was it safe[174]: like indefinite detention on Nauru and Manus, it was about the negation of asylum,[175] which destroys people's mental health by removing the horizon of a viable future – which is not 1:1 carceral, punitive or exceptional, but contains its own particular societal toxin and aftertaste. The destruction of children is not 'the same' as torture conducted ostensibly to elicit information, nor is it the sexualised abuse and degradation of Abu Ghraib, Baghram and other black sites where low value detainees were tortured, beaten, raped and humiliated. Such policy-level intentions are absent on Manus and Nauru, although beatings and rapes are common and have gone unpunished. These points all direct us toward distinctions of intention, conduct, trauma and political effect: ours is the choice to consider the extent to which they matter when such treatment is systemic.

A further substantive distinction that emerges from the comparison returns to the limits of sovereign power. As with the US' use of 'safe haven' in its imperial backyard in the early 90s, recourse to Nauru and Manus *in 2012* was less the production of bare life through the expression of sovereign power[176] than a symptom of limit, weakness and failure,[177] between 2009–2012. Unlike the explicit deterrence effects intended in the Pacific Solution in 2001, the Commonwealth's transfers of interdicted detainees to Nauru and Manus, and the revivification of detention on those islands in 2012, was more to do with expediency and panic: a sign of reactive capitulation in the face of mass drownings, underwritten by deference to the findings of a panel of experts,[178] rather than hardline determination and decisive dominance. The Gillard government caved to the Coalition's framing (Chapter 2), they implicitly accepted that the Howard government stopped the boats with offshore detention ('deterrence works'), and so they re-opened facilities senior ministers had wholeheartedly condemned on moral grounds, only years earlier.

At this point we also note the interaction of electoral contingency, the absence of political courage and path dependence resulting from prior commitments to carefully designed effects. As a result of the 2002–2003 design choice of a medium security prison and a location remote even on CI, the half billion purpose-built

174 Morin, Karen, '"Security Here Is Not Safe": Violence, Punishment, and Space in the Contemporary US Penitentiary', *Environment and Planning: D*, 31, 2013, pp. 381–399.

175 Loyd, Jenna, 'Carceral Citizenship in an Age of Global Apartheid', *Occasion*, 8, 2015, p. 10.

176 Agamben, Giorgio, *Homo Sacer: Sovereign Power and Bare Life*, Stanford University Press, Stanford, 1998.

177 Garland, David, 'The Limits of the Sovereign State: Strategies of Crime Control in Contemporary Society', *The British Journal of Criminology*, 36: 4, 1996, Bosworth, Mary, 'Border Control and the Limits of the Sovereign State', *Social and Legal Studies*, 17: 2, 2008, pp. 119–215.

178 Spinks, Harriet, 'Breaking the Deadlock? The Report of the Expert Panel on Asylum Seekers', *Parliament of Australia*, August 13, 2012. www.aph.gov.au/About_Parliament/Parliamentary_Departments/Parliamentary_Library/FlagPost/2012/August/Breaking_the_deadlock_The_Report_of_the_Expert_Panel_on_Asylum_Seekers

detention centre could not securely hold the interdicted people brought to CI when numbers increased, from 2009.[179] The capacity of the built centre is hard to interpret, but a regular capacity of 420 may mean that: the Coalition never anticipated large surges in numbers, such as faced by the Rudd and Gillard governments between 2009–2012; the centre was a constitutively inappropriate design, or that; the centre could not hold because it was designed to overflow. When CI could no longer accommodate the numbers arriving, the Gillard government then arrived at the position of actively seeking to re-open facilities and explore 'solutions' that Rudd government officials had earlier described as a "cynical, costly and ultimately unsuccessful exercise".[180] Weakness and failure, expediency and panic, and agency in the hands of systemic momentum and designed constraints.

Of Australia's four offshore detention islands,[181] CI does merit a formal comparison with Guantánamo. But with sovereignty and jurisdiction as our pivots, and national security and its store of continually emerging global threats as the 'operating environment' whose observers we are observing, Guantánamo is in the following senses the opposite or inverse of CI – and brings us to an overarching comparison that offers a concluding point on offshore and offshoring.

Guantánamo's camps, then and now, are spaces of US domination kept under jurisdiction and control while being kept outside sovereignty, rights and the courts. Guantánamo provided an expedient way to hold people beyond the constitution, rights and the flag – in a political formation where those elements are accorded the highest normative value. As one of the Neocons' lawyer architects, John Yoo, summarised his work in the legal construction of GITMO:

> I think what the policy makers (were) trying to do was to try and find a place that was physically close to the United States so it can be well-protected but still would benefit from the rule that the United States Military has ultimate say and control over any prisoners held outside the country.[182]

The way GITMO's camps are 'kept under and outside' the United States, but in a way that detainees are still under effective US domination, relies on *de jure* respect for a second sovereignty which is *de facto* disrespected by the fact the Americans are still detaining enemy combatants there, *in Cuba*, several decades after the Cubans began returning the cheque for the lease. Simultaneously, Guantánamo's camps are enabled by the time-sensitive historical contingency of the

179 By calendar year: 2009: 60 boats, 2,726 people; 2010: 134 boats, 6,555 people; 2011: 69 boats, 4,565 people; 2012: 278 boats, 17,202 people; 2013: 407 boats, 13,108 people.

180 Dyett, Greg, 'The Day the Nauru Centre Was Closed', *sbs.com.au*, August 26, 2013. www.sbs.com.au/news/article/2013/02/08/day-nauru-centre-was-closed

181 I include the post-excision mainland in this description.

182 Quoted in: Gibney, Alex (director), *Taxi to the Dark Side* (documentary). www.imdb.com/title/tt0854678/

Platt Agreement examined earlier (section 3.6–3.7), which remains because the structure of strict territoriality and state sovereignty has a more than rhetorical authority, especially where the US is the dominant claimant.

In contrast to the way Guantánamo is kept 'under and outside' the United States (territory, rights, flag, law), as an excised territory of the Commonwealth CI is a 'beyond within', a 'beyond' for asylum seekers that remains securely and sovereignly 'within' the Australian Commonwealth for whom its excised status is integral for maintaining secured circulation inside the border continuum. This directs us toward the legally important point that the United States and Australia are very different political formations, and that this makes any easy comparisons or moral denunciations on the basis of 'states of exception' or 'camp' tricky, at best, and simply wrong, at close range. I leave this to the jurisprudes, while also noting that this redounds to a key theoretical point about the social construction of islands and 'islands' where the paradoxical form of offshore is applied (section 1.7, 3.2): Guantánamo is an 'island' in Cuba and an island in the US Caribbean; CI is an Australian island no different to the island mainland, unless you are an asylum seeker attempting to arrive there by boat in order to seek protection.

To sum up, then. Offshore is a two-sided form whose paradoxical logic is capable of producing circumventions within circulation (section 3.3–3.4): expediently useful, metastable structures that avoid the cost, risk and loss effects of what they produce. People on Manus go mad, they riot and are murdered; women on Nauru are raped and set themselves on fire; children are paralysed with depression and plot suicide together. The minister says this is their fault, or proof they want to get to Australia so much, or is read as damning evidence of an essentially manipulative nature, or, at least, regrettable yet never quite systemic instances that do not diminish the 'nonetheless': that this is still a best practice policy that the Turnbull government still promotes as a response Europe would do well to emulate. Deterrence and control are *desired* for these immediate benefits, for the way offshore secures circumventions within circulation, for the way offshore processing stabilises spaces of infliction beyond any horizon of justice – this is what any normative critique of offshore detention must countenance. Large numbers of people desire deterrence and control above all; if people suffer terribly as a consequence of 'the simple truth of national survival', so be it.

Chapter 4

Ships in the night

Border security in the normative order of global logistics

4.1 Introduction: the alignment of border security with global logistics

In this chapter I explore the alignment of Australian border security with the goals and values of global logistics. Pinpointing the homologies of this normative alignment – which is also a dis-and re-assembly of the national and the global[1] – gives us a way to specify how national sovereignty interacts with global space through border security, alongside offshore. It also weaves the theoretical account given so far into recent discussions examining globalisation as a transformation of power and political space,[2] adding in insights from recent critical explorations of logistics.[3] At the same time, this chapter presents a more open and speculative set of observations as ways of thinking otherwise by giving border security's backgrounded elements direct and sustained attention.

Global logistics, already encountered at the crab bridge and the migration of the red crabs (i.10) is ordinarily imagined and represented as the technical management of supply chains put at the business world's disposal as an ideally

1 Sassen, Saskia, *Territory, Authority, Rights: From Medieval to Global Assemblages*, Princeton University Press, Princeton, 2008.

2 Galli, Carlo, *Political Spaces and Global War*, University of Minnesota Press, Minneapolis, 2010, Sassen, Saskia, *Territory, Authority, Rights: From Medieval to Global Assemblages*, Princeton University Press, Princeton, 2008, Sassen, Saskia, *Expulsions: Brutality and Complexity in the Global Economy*, Belknap Press, Cambridge, 2014 and Sloterdijk, Peter, *In the World Interior of Capital*, Polity Press, Cambridge, 2013.

3 Cowen, Deborah, *The Deadly Life of Logistics: Mapping Violence in Global Trade*, Minnesota University Press, Minneapolis, 2014, Gregson, Nicky, 'Logistics at Work: Trucks, Containers and the Friction of Circulation in the UK', *Mobilities*, 2015. http://dx.doi.org/10.1080/17450101.2015.1087680, Kanngeiser, Anja, 'Tracking and Tracing: Geographies of Logistical Governance and Labouring Bodies', *Environment and Planning: D*, 31: 4, 2013, pp. 594–610, Mezzadra, Sandro and Neilson, Brett, 'Extraction, Logistics, Finance: Global Crisis and the Politics of Operations', *Radical Philosophy*, 178, pp. 8–18, Neilson, Brett and Rossiter, Ned, 'Still Waiting, Still Moving: On Labour, Logistics and Maritime Industries', in Bissell, David and Fuller, Gillian (eds.), *Stillness in a Mobile World*, Routledge, London, 2011.

seamless service.[4] Ogilvy's *16 Ways to Benefit from Logistics*, produced for UPS, describes logistics as "the art and science of getting things exactly where and when they need to be there"[5]: global transport, *borderlessness*, planetary unimpedence, safe, timely and precise arrival.

So on first glance, global logistics appears in almost every way the opposite of border security, which we might imagine as national negations of global space securing sovereignty trough screening, impedance, stoppage, interdiction, non-arrival. Using Ogilvy's parsing of global logistics, border security could even be read as 'the art and science of stopping things exactly when they try to arrive and preventing them from getting to where they say they need to be'. It is also as far away as possible from the hazardous actualities of open ocean boat travel aboard profoundly unseaworthy vessels like the *Palapa* and all other SIEVs that reckon with global space as exposure, vulnerability and deadly hazards (section I.7–I.10). In line with a key contention, this is to do with the politics of border security (section 2.12), not the logistics of global mobility (section I.9–10). Yet curiously, as I explore, the two have become systemically related in border security's world, producing a fundamental dialectic of the political present that meets in the disjunctive making of enforceable boundaries *and* the limitless, expansive pursuit of profit.

In this chapter I undertake an analysis of where global logistics' normative understandings of people, things and space are imported into border security operations, revealing the outlines of Australian border security's alignment with a global normative order with an ecumenical jurisdiction[6] underpinned by an idealist metaphysics. On a theoretical level, this is a concrete way of thinking through practices and implications of 'actually existing globalisation'; on a normative level, it indicates a 'foreign presence' within these systems of national sovereignty and secured circulation, a global horizon of operations kept working in the national background, ordering the evaluation of risks and benefits, activities and security threats. This is one sense in which border security is no longer about borders, or security or the unilateral projection of national sovereignty, but rather the apprehension of global space as threat *and* opportunity.

In Border Force's key documents, logistical norms are applied that posit the movement of objects as 'activity', and imagine 'seamlessness' as the ideal state of motion for objects of interest.[7] Meanwhile, a morally loaded differentiation between good and bad activities provides a fundamental orienting binary for cognising legitimate

4 UPS' tagline is 'synchronizing the world of commerce'; DHL's is 'Excellence. Simply delivered'; FedEx's is 'Whatever it takes' and 'The World on Time'.

5 '16 Ways to Benefit From Logistics', *UPS*. http://thenewlogistics.ups.com/guide/UPS-16Ways-Guide-PDF-US.pdf

6 Hannerz, Ulf, 'Notes on the Global Ecumene', *Public Culture*, 1: 2, 1989, pp. 66–75. The background reference, here as throughout *Border Security* and Donne, John, *Devotions Upon Emergent Occasions and Death's Duel*, Vintage, London, 1999 (section 1.7, 3.2).

7 This and other related points in this chapter reprise and develop contentions made in: Chambers, Peter, 'The Embrace of Border Security: Maritime Jurisdiction, National Sovereignty, and the Geopolitics of Operation Sovereign Borders', *Geopolitics*, 20, 2015, pp. 13–16.

activities in Australia's area of maritime interest (section 4.6–4.7). Legitimate activities *must be* kept in smooth motion; illegitimate objects *must be* impeded and interdicted. Enacting these evaluations via the good/bad activities binary enables intervention on technical grounds in the name of security: securing the expansion of the legitimate-and-good while impeding the course of the illegitimate-and-bad as a necessary task, both for Border Force, and for 'the whole inhabited earth'.[8]

The normative implications of border security's alignment with global logistics bear upon how we might understand the political and moral status of offshore detention and the suffering it inflicts (sections 3.10–3.12), based on the unstated, implicit background reasons ordering it in very basic yet subtle ways. These background reasons are all observable in Border Force's key documents, but mostly they pass unobserved by border security's critics: like ships in the night.

To inaugurate the argument with a critical observation whose normative implications I pursue later in this chapter: Border Force, and the Commonwealth government, supports the unlimited expansion of secured circulation above all. This 'total global situation' – 'today's globalised world' – is understood by Border Force as:

- threatened in *increasingly sophisticated ways* by the forces of informal movement and organised criminal activity;
- in an institutional context of increasing circulation (invited) *and* decreasing institutional resources[9] (regretted), and, thus;
- the urgent need for securing through *evermore integrated* means.

As a further Australian loading of these general dynamics of compounding threat, intensifying urgency *and* the need to manage increasing circulation with fewer resources each financial year, I also indicate how global logistical norms and values have been imported into Border Force's peculiarly Australian iterations of border security's world, and how they can be understood alongside the rise to cultural dominance of Customs in its Border Force becoming. Indeed, it was the recognised interaction of these factors that served as the governmental impetus for the formation of Border Force on July 1, 2015 through amalgamation of Immigration and Customs, in which the empowerment of Customs' norms and

8 Playing on the etymology of ecumenical in 'oikoumenē', the whole inhabited earth. The samizdat question is whether global logistics might be regarded as the new *nomos* of the earth, a utopia of distribution, rather than production (Soviet Socialism) or consumption (neoliberal capitalism) – or at least 'that which delivers it unto us'. See: Schmitt, Carl, 'The New Nomos of the Earth', in *The Nomos of the Earth in the International Law of Jus Publicum Europaeum*, Telos Press Publishing, New York, 2006, pp. 351–357.

9 Australian Border Force, 'The Future of Border Protection', *Australian Government Immigration and Border Protection Portfolio*, 2014. www.ibrarian.net/navon/paper/The_future_of_border_protection.pdf?paperid=23143312. Notably, like many key pdf files this document is no longer held by Border Force.

culture and the paramilitarisation of the amalgamated entities has loomed large[10] (section I.3). The following aspect of this amalgamation – just a month after Immigration's seventieth birthday – is notable.

Immigration remains a department committed to people as humans and legal persons, however much they are caught in the slow teeth of its administrative grinder. Customs, in contrast, has always been about screening 'entering entities', crossings whose complexity its agents handle by reducing them to objects that may pass or must be seized. Through its promotion to the position of institutional primacy, and through Border Force's alignment with global logistics, border security's most basic commitment in its second decade of operation is not at all to the people on the move most intensely secured by it, whether onshore citizens or offshore asylum seekers. In *The Future of Border Protection* Border Force observes no humans,[11] only a system of circulation whose ideal is secured seamlessness and those objects its observers are capable of regarding as threats and opportunities.

Attending to the alignment of border security with logistics, finally, is about apprehending the short circuits and scalar jumps implied in the 'global locations' and 'global identity', two global points that return us to national sovereignty, the message of border security and offshore detention via a detour that explicates the global background of the *prima facie* national, domestic and peculiarly Australian aspects of border security's emergence examined in Part I. Redounding to the 'evermore urgently secured nation' living in the secured circulations of the border continuum *and* transcending it in one identity-and-crisis-inducing stroke, the national project of Australian border security works as part of an avowed, reflexively understood global strategy seeking to secure the expansive movement of the legitimate and the profitable. By way of what we might regard as its 'contrajection', border security pulls its agents and entities in two directions. Border Force's logistics-aligned activities don't simply tighten the nationally sovereign space 'Australia' now off limits to boat arrivals, they do so as reflexive contributors to the expansive global space of logistics. For those critical of border security and offshore detention, this final point is important to note. Border Force's alignment with global logistics is neither secret nor a conspiracy, rather it is something its architects are publicly proud of. The fully integrated Australian model

10 McCulloch, Jude, *Blue Army: Paramilitary Policing in Australia*, Melbourne University Press, Melbourne, 1997 and Finnane, Mark, *Police and Government: Histories of Policing in Australia*, Oxford University Press, Oxford,1994.

11 This is literally the case: the only human face in 'The future of border protection' is that of the minister. Also: 'The Future of Border Management: Maintaining Security; Facilitating Prosperity', *www.pwc.com*. www.pwc.com/gx/en/industries/government-public-services/public-sector-research-centre/publications/future-border-management.html; www.pwc.com/gx/en/psrc/pdf/the-future-of-border-management.pdf and 'Reimagining the Border: A Functional View of Border Management', *www.boozallen.com*. www.boozallen.com/content/dam/boozallen/media/file/Homeland-Security-Articles-Functional-Border.PDF

has a logistical heart; an open announcement that very few concerned about border security have given any attention to – not because it is hidden in plain sight, but, perhaps, because concerned voices focus on human suffering, while logistics is nonhuman.

In the 'tightening expansion' of these dynamics we can, perhaps, hear the new *nomos* of the earth breathing, as others struggle to circulate and breathe freely in the differential tightenings of its grip. *The Future of Border Protection* we will encounter is set up so that its most privileged clients do not notice this mobility-supporting background taking place. Ideally, as a business traveller you would not even notice the deported asylum seekers on your flight, let alone be delayed by them in an unseemly struggle with Border Force officials. At the horizon of this chapter border security and people disappear into *The Future of Border Protection*, within whose utopian, dystopian horizons there is only smooth passage and the comforting, orienting embrace of hitech equipment.

4.2 Global logistics: from the metaphysics of 'moving stuff around' to 'the ultimate background of human existence in contemporary capitalism'

As I've just introduced, on first glance global logistics is about 'moving stuff around' efficiently. Within its ordinary spectrum of meanings and activities, global logistics refers to the globally competitive use of hardware and software, transport infrastructure, and management processes and practices to 'deliver the goods' to *very precise* locations that *could be anywhere*. In these ways, global logistics is both a societally diffuse physico-technical pragmatics of organising people and things and a set of well-known, concrete and teachable measures for the management of locatable, deliverable mobile objects – in what is observed as a global system whose ideal state is one of quickened circulation: smooth, rapid, ceaseless, seamless movement.[12]

In systems theoretical terms, global logistics is an observing system that makes its difference by rendering global complexity operable for the purposes of getting something very precisely to someone, anywhere, at any time. In these ways, sitting alongside its relation to globality, transport systems and its ideal of borderlessness, it also has affinities to border security as an observing system of 'delivering the message', as well as mobilisations effectuated by offshoring measures (section 2.2–2.3, 3.12). To the extent that border security operations become aligned with its norms, wherever such operations take place, the message of border security is delivered logistically – and this, as I'll explore, is increasingly the desired mindset and operational ideal of Border Force. To the extent

12 Cowen, Deborah, *The Deadly Life of Logistics: Mapping Violence in Global Trade*, University of Minnesota Press, Minneapolis, 2014 and note 3.

that any institutional agent imports aspects of the Australian model, logistics is part of the package, as well as the method and philosophy of its rightful delivery (section 2.2–2.3).

As pragmatics and measures practiced in relation to an imagination of 'the whole world' and its ideal state of being, global logistics is already a metaphysics.[13] It is predicated on an abstract and ideal way of thinking about *objects* that become operable to the extent they're handled via standardised referents that mobilise them. In most of the contexts at issue in global logistics' world, objects are rendered operable-mobile-located via a regress of standardised,[14] networked, mediating interfaces: the smartphone and tablet, the USB stick, the box and barcode, and the shipping container are all parts of this world picture. On one remonstration, such reifications of 'the whole world' are as old as means of containment using amphoras, caves and inventories, by some measures is as old as writing itself: what's so new or global about this that it merits this re-description and analytic attention in *Border Security*?

What's particular to *global* logistics is that it's a metaphysics practiced as a pragmatic relation the whole inhabited world, predicated on the idea that anyone anywhere *can* have anything delivered to right to anyone at any time for any reason. This speaks to its self-propagating ecumenical jurisdiction: global logistics is an effective way of conceiving the whole world that enables the complex immanence of people and things to be reduced to operable objects that can be moved around, screened, stopped and stored (see section 3.12). Global logistics also refers to *effectively ubiquitous* and *standardised* procedures that render complexity manageable by proving capable of sending it everywhere in a controlled, precise way: these standards exist and are enforced, because without them intermodal operability would be impossible.

The further point is that global logistics actually exists. Global logistics isn't a dream, or: it is a dream come true *and delivered on time*. The fact that global logistics really works – for those who can afford its services – brings potentially every 'thing' in the world *into* the difference that it makes to the world as a global logistical system. Global logistics is truly global and truly a system, set up for societally accepted communicative purposes that can deliver the message, regardless of what it is. Global logistics has spread with globalisation as surely as proxy wars, intercontinental ballistic missiles and the threat of mutually assured destruction spread during the Cold War. This has transformed potentially everything into

13 Heidegger, Martin, 'The Age of the World Picture', in *The Question Concerning Technology and Other Essays*, Garland, New York, 1977, pp. 115–155, Marcuse, Herbert, 'Social Implications of Technology' in Arato, Andrew and Gebhardt, Eike (eds.), *The Essential Frankfurt School Reader*, Continuum, New York, 1982, pp. 138–162 and Stiegler, Bernard, *Technics and Time, 1: The Fault of Epimetheus*, Stanford University Press, Stanford, 1998.

14 'Standards catalogue: 55.180.10: General purpose containers', *www.iso.org*. www.iso.org/iso/iso_catalogue/catalogue_ics/catalogue_ics_browse.htm?ICS1=55&ICS2=180&ICS3=10

systemically operable referents, controllable objects that are 'merely' locatable, moveable, stoppable and storeable. This final point speaks to the quality of its embrace.

Global logistics' ability to reach around the whole world is commensurate with the bare nature of its embrace – which is less about 'bare life' than 'bare stuff', less about sovereign power than the systemic injunction to secure circulation.[15] By transforming 'everything' into 'something transferable', by rendering everything a locatable, moveable, stoppable, storable object, global logistics' operators turn global complexity into the operability of controllable objects, visible and located, trackable and traceable within its agents' systems.[16] When the objects in question are asylum seekers, living people, this raises profound political and ethical questions – that global logistics' metaphysics is resistant to handling, incapable of observing. The norms and techniques of global logistics can deliver asylum seekers over to their fate *and* deliver us a book on the ethics of this with equal efficiency and indifference. But global logistics is an observing system whose severances tend to repel a questioning of *its* position and agency in this web of reference as an ethical matter, let alone as something highly normative with an implicit politics that becomes clearer through its reappearance in alignment with the task of Border Force. There are already implicit injunctions in this repelling of questioning, and it is the strong undertow of occluded normativity in global logistics' embrace I am especially interested in getting at. It is an injunction that 'says': *Don't shoot the messenger; don't question the messenger's purely technical role; do not foreground unconditional support for the supporting background of the profitable foreground.* Global logistics, then, is about more than moving stuff around efficiently, or it indicates that 'moving stuff around efficiently' is much more thoughtful, complex, politically entangled and ethically fraught than its promoters wish it so seem.

As an ultimate background of human existence in contemporary capitalism, like the physical limits of the nitrogen cycle, the temporality of photosynthesis, bee colony collapse disorder and the subjectively observed horror of global scale industrial meat production, global logistics' shores of politics and horizons of justice are as in need of critical exposition as they're resistant to it.

4.3 From navigation and discovery on Possession Island, 1770 to "stations of a limitless traffic": the 'epochal difference' of 'location-spatial thought'

If Australia's border security is a unilateral projection of *its* national sovereignty in global space, the interaction of all the terms in that phrase was made possible

15 See section 3.12–3 and note 43 and 211 chapter three.

16 Kanngeiser, Anja, 'Tracking and Tracing: Geographies of Logistical Governance and Labouring Bodies', *Environment and Planning: D*, 31: 4, 2013, pp. 598–605.

as the direct, cascading, ongoing consequences of Cook's 'discovery' of what is now known as Australia, on the basis of his taking possession of the east coast of New South Wales in the name of His Majesty George III at Possession Island, on August 22, 1770.

A genealogy of European Australia carried back to 1770, instead of 1788, opens an oceanic, Antipodean history that ties the emergence of Australia and New Zealand to the Age of Discovery, the Pacific, the land appropriation of the new world and the emergence of the British Empire based in part on the enormous technico-cultural head start that Cook's voyages afforded.[17] But as we have explored, the nationalist culture of Australia Day now prefers to look to a point seventeen years after Cook's arrival, encounter and appropriations – the British establishment of a penal settlement in what Cook had called New South Wales – for a contemporary way of celebrating national identity (sections 1.2, 1.3).

Cook's first voyage aboard *Endeavour* is a founding moment of Britain's colonisation of the Antipodes, one that has had an incomparable impact on the patterns of European land appropriation and the civilisations and peoples brought into contact with it and conflict from it. What I wish to emphasise for this chapter by mentioning this opens the following temporal distinction that helps us understand the emergence of global logistics and globalisation. Cook and *Endeavour* – with Banks, Hollander, Spöring, Parkinson, Tupaia and others aboard – sit on the other side of an epochal transformation. The voyages of the *Endeavour* are also seeding events in the emergence of global logistics: but just as the caterpillar undergoes a profound metamorphosis in its butterfly becoming, global logistics is a total transfiguration of the world of discovery that enabled it. Our political present, in turn, looks back at the age of discovery as upon another world, which, in many ways, it was.

At stake in the transformation from Cook's world of discovery to the 'global world' of logistics is what Peter Sloterdijk calls 'location-spatial thought'. With Sloterdijk,

> it makes an epochal difference whether one measures an idealized orb with lines and cuts, sails around a real orb with ships, or lets aeroplanes and radio signals circulate around the atmospheric casing of a planet.[18]

With Sloterdijk's 'difference that makes this epochal difference' in mind as our guide, following a few key moments from *Endeavour*'s first voyage provides excellent counterfactuals for clarifying the momentous transformation between this global 'then and now', which will help us locate their incommensurable normative visions and, in turn, the constitutive blindspot of global logistics' world. This

17 Earlier iterations of White Australia looked more to Cook than to the First Fleet, although the contention still taught to primary school children until very recently was that 'Captain Cook discovered Australia'.

18 Sloterdijk, Peter, *In the World Interior of Capital*, Polity Press, Cambridge, 2013, p. 10.

draws a large and important arc of power in transformation that broadens our globalising understanding of logistics and border security, in the following ways:

- The 'activities' of global logistics' mobilities are
- a set systemically observable, operable, located, controllable objects
- moved between precise locations along supply chains,
- outside whose boundary is an observed environment of operations.

Following Sloterdijk's epochal difference a little further, global logistics' way of observing the world in order to render 'all of this' operable makes *locations* "*stations* of a limitless *traffic*".[19] Yet because this 'station-punctuated world of traffic between locations' is impossible as it's now practiced without GPS and its predicates, the normative order of global logistics only became possible through what Sloterdijk describes as 'location-spatial thought':

> the routine mastery of the symmetry of outward and return journeys that is constitutive for the modern concept of traffic can only be established in a generalized locational space that gathers together points of equal value in a field to form timetables and images of routes. . . . The precondition for what we call world traffic is that the discovery of marine conditions and terrain in geographical and hydrographical terms can be considered complete. Authentic traffic can only come about with a network that makes a given zone accessible, whether as *terra incognita* or *mare cognitum*, for routine crossings.[20]

Cook was a pioneering master in the development of location-spatial thought. But – to return to and build upon the above point about incommensurability – our located world of traffic and circulation that his innovations in maritime navigation contributed so much toward making would have been unrecognisable to him, let alone available to him as a technical resource *in routine use* capable of getting *Endeavour* back to Plymouth with almost thoughtless safety. In this context, it's less the case that 'the past is another country'. Cook 'did things differently' because he inhabited a world that knew nothing of what we conventionally rely on and take for granted as the background conditions supporting our safe, comfortable existences as the globally mobile, the privileged populations whose circulations are secured by border security.

In a globalising landscape of total operational dependency, observational avoidance and experiential distance, ours is a moment in which our most cherished proximities sit on the other side of epochal distances of which most of us care to know nothing, except that the regress of systems work flawlessly and respond instantly and intuitively when we engage with our control surfaces (section I.11).

19 Op.cit., p. 31, italics mine.
20 Op.cit., p. 35, italics in original.

4.3a June 11, 1770, 11pm: reef and hull

HMB Endeavour and the logistical world *un utero* its crew carried were fortunate to make it back to England on July 12, 1771. Just after 11pm on June 11, 1770, while making a running survey[21] sailing north up the east coast of New Holland,[22] *Endeavour* hit a reef, ran aground, and began taking on water (section I.8).

The ship was unaccompanied and in uncharted waters – which, unbeknownst to Cook or anyone aboard, moved beneath their hull through a field of reefs 2,000km long: what we now know is the world's largest living structure (for now), what Cook later called the Great Barrier Reef, for good reason. Endeavour was 32km from shore, and its crew were more than 16,000km from England. Two and a half centuries on, there is almost no situation on earth so isolated; communication and rescue were impossible. In historical-relative terms *Endeavour* and its crew *were* transiting Venus.

As the tide rose, Cook ordered the crew to throw overboard the ship's cannons, stone ballast, and 40–50 "tuns weight". By 11am the next day around high water

> we try'd to heave her off without Success, she not being afloat by a foot or more. . . . As this was not found sufficient we continued to Lighten her by every method we could think off; as the Tide fell the ship began to make Water as much as two pumps could free".[23]

As the tide continued to fall, the ship took on more water; then as it rose again on the next and much larger tide around 9pm on Tuesday June 12, more still:

> This was an alarming and, I may say, terrible circumstance, and threatened immediate destruction to us. However, I resolv'd to risque all, and heave her off in case it was practical, and accordingly turn'd as many hands to the Capstan and Windlass as could be spared from the Pumps; and about 20 Minutes past 10 o'Clock the Ship floated, and we hove her into Deep Water, having at this time 3 feet 9 Inches Water in the hold. This done I sent the Long boat to take up the Stream Anchor, got the Anchor, but lost the Cable among the Rocks; after this turn'd all hands to the Pumps, the Leak increasing upon us.[24]

21 A running survey refers to the production of a map by taking readings and bearings by hand, from a moving ship. This method was repetitive and labour intensive for the crew, and mathematically demanding for Cook.

22 New Holland is the post-Tasmanian term to refer to 'the whole continent' of Australia that denoted the continent until the middle of the nineteenth century – this can be read back in relation to sections 1.2–1.7.

23 'Cook's Journal: Daily Entries', National Library of Australia, June 11, 1770. http://southseas.nla.gov.au/journals/cook/17700611.html

24 'Cook's Journal: Daily Entries', National Library of Australia, June 11, 1770. http://southseas.nla.gov.au/journals/cook/17700611.html

Cook and the crew were ingenious and fortunate in the face of this 'terrible circumstance'. On the suggestion of Midshipman Jonathan Monkhouse,[25] the hull of the Endeavour was fothered. This involved wrapping the broached starboard side of the hull in a sail under the fore chains, and it worked: an instance of seafaring, navigation and a seaworthy observation of the meaning of a hull (section I.8). With the ship off the reef and no longer sinking, Cook sought a harbour to limp into – which they happened upon in time.[26] The time-sensitive good fortune of the voyage is astonishing. Over the next week, with *Endeavour* beached for repairs, Cook's journal reports the wind consistently blowing a gale. Had Cook stayed just a few days longer at Botany Bay and sailed roughly the same course through the reef, neither the jettisoning of cannons and ballast nor the fothering might have been achieved, and *Endeavour* would have broken apart on the reef and sunk, along with everything and everyone on board.

Yet this doesn't tell us the precise reasons why *Endeavour* crashed into what Cook named the Great Barrier Reef *as* it did, *when* it did. On July 30, 1768, James Cook received the secret instructions[27] that governed the first voyage of *Endeavour*. Circumnavigation of the north island of New Zealand, completed a few months earlier, on March 27, 1770, had disproven the thesis that New Zealand was a single continent, which meant that Cook was free to return to England. The actual existence of what is now called New Zealand[28] and Aotearoa *proved* the metaphysics Cook and the Endeavour harboured among themselves and enacted through the rigorous empirical testing of scientific hypotheses that the voyage in fact was. This, in turn, opened a horizon toward the discovery of *terra australis incognita* – so Cook sailed *Endeavour* west.

In heading west from New Zealand to ascertain 'the location of the eastern coast of New Holland' and to delineate it from Van Diemens Land, Cook was following a hunch based on Abel Tasman's 128-year-old maps and what could be deduced more accurately from the far more precise work he had completed during the circumnavigation. Cook knew approximately where *terra australis incognita* was likely to be, and he knew precisely where it was not. A captain without Cook's disciplined manic intensity might have done no more than the secret instructions ordered and sailed from New Zealand for "some known Port" where he might have procured "a Sufficiency to carry You to England" then found "the Most Eligible way of returning home".[29] It was Cook's personal decision as

25 Monkhouse died of malaria on board *Endeavour* on February 6, 1771.

26 In Guugu Yimithir country, whose present-day European terms are the Endeavour River and Cooktown. See: 'Guugu Yimithir Country', *National Museum of Australia*. www.nma.gov.au/kspace/teachers/endeavour/learning/country

27 'Secret Instructions to Captain Cook, 30 June 1768', Museum of Australian Democracy. www.foundingdocs.gov.au/resources/transcripts/nsw1_doc_1768.pdf

28 Tasman named it *Staten Landt*. Three years later it was changed to *Nova Zeelandia*, which Cook Anglicised after his circumnavigation.

29 Secret Instructions to Captain Cook, 30 June 1768', Museum of Australian Democracy. www.foundingdocs.gov.au/resources/transcripts/nsw1_doc_1768.pdf

master to decide to push further into what was – for Europeans of that time – a completely unknown space. In our world of limitless traffic and secured circulation, where no location is unknown and every object in motion is located, such an act of 'bold going' is unimaginable and impossible, and if observed onshore from contemporary Australia would regarded as a serious breach of border security (section 2.4).

4.4 April 3, 2010, 1705: the Reef rat run of *Sheng Neng 1* and the physics of global logistics

At 1054[30] on April 3, 2010, a 230 metre long bulk coal carrier bound for China, *Sheng Neng 1*, departed its berth at the port of Gladstone, loaded with coal and under control of a harbour pilot. At 1306, the pilot disembarked, with the ship's course set at 000°(T). After the pilot's disembarkation, the second mate altered the passage plan, setting a shorter course: still within the boundaries of the designated shipping area that cuts through what is otherwise a Marine National Park and World Heritage site totally off-limits to shipping. He was trying to save time and fuel, trying to save money. *Sheng Neng 1* taking a short cut; *Sheng Neng 1* was in a hurry.

Local fishermen refer to this practice of taking short cuts as 'Reef rat runs', and it's common enough that the phrase is widely known.[31] The second mate's alteration, made at 1530, meant rejoining the ship's original course further east than the unaltered passage plan, and the altered course added new waypoints that required re-checking, re-fixing and re-plotting positions. When you're cutting corners, most of the time, under most conditions, nothing happens: the upped ante is observed in glancing retrospect as the grateful realisation that nothing bad happened. When you're cutting corners under conditions of systemic complexity and technological dependency, you up the ante in ways that compound risk, creating the immediate possibility of systemic failure, the 'possible possibility' of cascading failure, and the unlikely but still real possibility of unpredictable catastrophe (section I.11). This is a nontrivial difference that global logistics makes to the Great Barrier Reef when routine traffic involves 'Reef rat runs'.

At about 1550, twenty minutes after the alteration of *Sheng Neng 1*'s passage plan, the chief mate came to the bridge to relieve the second mate. He'd had less than three hours sleep over the past thirty-six hours.[32] Just after 1600, the second

30 This section follows the conventions of the report (below) and uses twenty-four-hour clock.

31 Connolly, Ellen and Henley, John, 'Reef Running', *The Sydney Morning Herald*, April 9, 2010. www.smh.com.au/national/reef-running-20100408-rv3y.html

32 'Independent Investigation into the Grounding of the Chinese Registered Bulk Carrier *Shen Neng 1* on Douglas Shoal, Queensland 3 April 2010', *Australian Transport Safety Bureau*. www.atsb.gov.au/media/2478832/mo2010003.pdf#page=0, p. 49.

mate plotted the ship's position and left the bridge, informing the chief mate of two crucial factors as he did so:

1 that the ship's passage plan *had been* changed (at 1530);
2 that new waypoints *had not been* entered into the GPS unit (as of 1600).

However, the second mate failed to mention what time the ship was due to change course, based on the amended plan. For his part, the chief mate did not check the position at 1600, nor did he check the distance between the ship's location and the next alteration position.[33] The chief mate was then working on the assumption that the course alteration was to take place at 1700. He was also using the navigational chart appropriate for the unaltered passage plan, not the one he needed after the alteration that identified a catastrophic hazard just ahead: Douglas Shoal. The exhausted chief mate did not know when he was due to change course; he did not know he was off course in any case; and the charts he was relying on did not show the hazard he was piloting *Sheng Neng 1* straight into.

At around 1630, the chief engineer came to the bridge to ask about the ship's speed. In the independent review, the chief mate attributes this 'distraction' as the key reason why he didn't plot a position at 1630: as he missed this moment, he decided to wait until 1700 to plot the ship's position. As a consequence, the altered course *Sheng Neng 1* was already on was never entered into the GPS. The unit he was relying on to render the world physically operable via control interfaces:

- continued to display the original course (set by the harbour pilot around 1300, and in effect until 1530)
- as the ship moved along its altered course (which it had been doing at 12 knots [22.224km/h] since 1530).

As his electronic equipment was communicating information accurate for the unaltered course, the displays of the ships' control interfaces 'continued to give no warning' of the hazards ahead on the altered course, rendering their monitoring functions moot. A world of trafficking between locations relies upon 'the tracking of tracking', but in the absence of full automation this relies upon the (almost always reliable) input of data by (quite often unreliable) human agents that instruct it *to* track and notify, before which it sits unnoticed and unnotifying, its tracking potential idling. To enfold some of von Foerster's key claims about nontriviality raised in the final paragraphs of the introduction (section I.11), this entire situation is nontrivial, yet we are dependent in such situations on control surfaces, assumptions, habits and norms that operate as if the trivialisations we depend upon for safe operation *are* reality. Most of the time, this proves

33 Op.cit., p. xi.

sufficient; sometimes, the jagged reef of an unobserved reality shows itself, and causality fatefully appears.

Between 1630 and 1700, the first mate was at the bridge, looking out the windows and checking the radar. At 1642, *Sheng Neng 1* crossed the 075° waypoint where the turn to re-join the course was required: at this point, the shoal was five nautical miles (9.26km) ahead, but invisible to radar and the naked eye under prevailing sea conditions.[34] At 1700, the chief mate finally took the ship's position using the GPS unit. As he plotted the located ship's position on the chart, he realised they were right on Douglas Shoal. Five minutes later, *Sheng Neng 1* struck the Great Barrier Reef.

4.5 *HMS Bark Endeavour, Sheng Neng 1*: a tale of two colliers as a difference that makes an epochal difference

Two hundred and forty years and roughly 1,000km separate the impacts of the 32m long *Endeavour* and the 225m long *Sheng Neng 1*. Yet more than this separates the reef encounters of these two colliers. Consider the words 'global', 'position' and 'system' and their co-relation that make GPS an observed unity for routine handling, like SUNCs and SIEVs. To re-cast Sloterdijk's epochal difference and the emergence of traffic through location-spatial thought, without 'the network that makes a given zone accessible for routine crossings', Cook's voyage was not traffic: Cook had no 'location' in its contemporary sense. Cook and the ship's crew were conducting a running survey through uncharted waters, not just without a GPS and nautical charts, but without a ship's chronometer.

On board *Sheng Neng 1*, every single one of the profound navigational problems that confronted Cook had been solved by technical means installed as standard equipment in routine use. Two hundred and forty years after *Endeavour*'s collision, there is no technical reason why a shipwreck need happen, even when seafaring is routinely conducted in an area where hazards are as potentially catastrophic as the Great Barrier Reef. The systems that make global logistics technically possible also make navigation through the reef technically safe for a ship the size of *Sheng Neng 1*, even for merely competent sailors: provided they take adequate precautions, are not in a hurry, do not make unauthorised deviations to the course, and the crew maintain communication. *Endeavour*'s passage out the reef after grazing catastrophe was an astounding feat of navigation and great fortune made by an isolated ship a world away from where the secret instructions sent it there were penned. The *Sheng Neng 1* was a weary nodal point in a tireless global logistical system, undertaking routine navigation through a major shipping lane, and in continual communication with support systems circulating 'the

34 Op.cit., p. 14.

atmospheric casing of the planet' that, but for human error, would have informed it of the hazard to the hull (section I.8, 2.2–2.3).

Sheng Neng 1 hit the reef for two reasons, both of which evince a characteristic relation between the limited agency of human action and the systemic causality that global logistics reckons with as an operating environment and *generates* as normal conditions *and* potentially globally catastrophic event horizons. First of all, *Sheng Neng 1* hit the reef because its commanding crew had decided to take a short cut without attending to what this additionally demanded of them as equipment-dependent seafarers. Had they attended to their task with sufficient diligence and communication, their technical systems would have given them ample and timely information that would have allowed them to recognise the hazard and – most likely – prevent the collision. As this came down to the repeated failure to just enter the position into the GPS unit, in the most immediate sense *Sheng Neng 1* can be characterised as a data entry issue.

Sheng Neng 1 also hit the reef because the chief mate was dead on his feet.[35] This collision is about the labour conditions that increasingly characterise the routines of global logistics.[36] It is *where* that labour took place under *the conditions that it did* that made it so potentially consequential for *Sheng Neng 1*, its hull and of course the Reef.

Consider the chief mate's working day. At 0300 on April 2, the chief mate had supervised weighing anchor; five hours later, at 0820, he was supervising loading and deballasting operations, which he did until around 0100 on April 3: a twenty-two-hour working day. At 0300 on April 3, sleeping for just two hours after that shift, he resumed duties to complete cargo loading, completed at 0540. During this extended period of loading supervision, the chief mate was spending approximately three hours after each watch making and checking cargo and stability calculations "and comparing them to the cargo loading computer calculations".[37] The chief mate "was unfamiliar with the operation and reliability of the ship's ballast system"[38]: this was his first time in charge of loading a ship.

The report also describes the chief mate as *choosing* "to remain on duty for the majority of the time the ship was berthed".[39] Here, we should note a human consequence generated by the systemically-mandated necessity of the perpetual and seamless movement of the system as a whole.[40] The tirelessly smooth, rapid movement of the system outran the toll this took on the abilities of the individual

35 Gregson, Nicky, 'Logistics at Work: Trucks, Containers and the Friction of Circulation in the UK', *Mobilities*, 2015. http://dx.doi.org/10.1080/17450101.2015.1087680

36 Cowen, Deborah, *The Deadly Life of Logistics: Mapping Violence in Global Trade*, University of Minnesota Press, Minneapolis, 2014, pp. 69–72.

37 'Independent Investigation into the Grounding of the Chinese Registered Bulk Carrier Shen Neng 1 on Douglas Shoal, Queensland 3 April 2010', *Australian Transport Safety Bureau*. www.atsb.gov.au/media/2478832/mo2010003.pdf#page=0, p. 8.

38 Op.cit., p. 18.

39 Op.cit., p. 18.

40 Op.cit., pp. 18–19.

human agent *nonetheless* placed in charge of it through a crucial point in its operation. When this human agent came to the bridge to pilot the craft, as one of only eight crew aboard, this meant the entirety of *Sheng Neng 1* was a nodal point in a logistical system placed at the mercy of a human component fatigued to the point of failure by prior operations, then placed in command of a ship taking a rat run through a precious and fragile marine ecosystem that required additional data entry and attentiveness on his part.

This brings us to a final point that reveals the epochal difference between discovery and global logistics, a world in which arrival by boat was a wonder, and a world whose norms profoundly shape why border security stops the boats as well as how interdictees and detainees are observed and handled. Cook took his crews further and for longer than they wished, and he was notorious for working them hard. But although his third voyage sought a way through the Northwest Passage – global logistics' greatest shortcut – he never took short cuts himself. Granted Endeavour had to arrive in Tahiti in time for the transit of Venus, at no moment in his seafaring work was Cook 'in a hurry'. It is this factor more than anything that makes the distance between the audacious boldness of maritime navigation in the age of discovery and the wearying technical routines of traffic and circulation in the world of global logistics mutually unfathomable. The moment "you invent the ship, you invent the shipwreck";[41] but only when you invent global logistics do you invent the endless iterative collision ship and reef, spill and disaster, near miss and on-time delivery.

Seafaring transforms the hull into the constitutive blindspot of all shipping operations (section I.8); a key normative point is that *Sheng Neng 1* rendered 'global logistics' invisible as a responsible agent. This raises a critical observation of systems – *tout court* – as a contemporary impasse for global justice as responsibility. At the time, after touring the collision in a plane, the then Prime Minister Kevin Rudd declared that "[i]f we have any foreign vessel or any vessel violating the proper protection of the Great Barrier Reef they should have the book thrown at them".[42] As it transpired, responsibility for this potentially catastrophic shipwreck was 'sent down' to the level of the individual: the chief mate was imprisoned. Systemic success has many parents; systems failure is an orphan.

4.6 "We seek to make it as easy as possible for legitimate trade and travel": global logistics in *The Future of Border Protection*

In aligning itself to the expansion of shipping throughout Australia's area of maritime interest, including through the Reef, Border Force calls the nation's

41 Virilio, Paul, *Politics of the Very Worst*, Semiotext(e), New York, 1999, p. 43.

42 'Vessel Accused of Entering Reef Area', *The Sydney Morning Herald*, April 11, 2010. www.smh.com.au//breaking-news-national/vessel-accused-of-entering-reef-area-20100411-s09u.html

attention to the integral nature of its task of supporting and serving a world of expanding legitimate shipping and trade. The live and unpredictable interaction of these expansive factors can be observed heuristically as a pair of interactive factors:

1 *a diffuse worldview* that speaks about how global competition is already happening and therefore must be transformed from a threat into an opportunity, and
2 *a definite ship-borne materiality* that routinely moves great quantities of coal through the Great Barrier Reef using diesel engine-propelled steel hulls that move on the ocean's surface, contributing to the expansion of global competition, that ship and its crew and its owning interests' position therein, and global emissions and other environmental risks.

This worldview and its materiality, alongside policy-buttressed broad cultural support for increased shipping and export-led GDP growth: emblematically, in October 2014, at the opening of a the Caval Ridge Coal Mine near Morambah (whose Bowen Basin coal is shipped through the Reef), then Prime Minister Tony Abbott described coal as "good for humanity".[43] The marriage of cultural support and actual mine expansions increases the likelihood of 'Reef rat runs', which become seductive *for* fatigued employee-individuals operating in systemic conditions *that* increase the risks and the consequences of risky errors – whose effects then ramify across what are by now interpenetrated systems. This speaks to another difference in the 'world interior' engendered by the epochal difference of location-spatial thought Sloterdijk pinpoints: had *Endeavour* sunk, the consequences would have been immeasurable.[44] Yet *Endeavour* was not a shipwreck that would have endangered the world's largest living thing. Yet is border security's world capable of observing *Sheng Neng 1* as a security threat according to its distinctions? Border Force aligns its task to global logistics; how does it cognise the risks and threats that then attend its work?

The Future of Border Protection,[45] a May 2014 document assembled to herald and describe the arrival of Border Force, is an emblematic artefact from that cultural moment. By the time it was published, *Operation Sovereign Borders* had been publicly declared successful, over (sections 2.2, 2.11–2.12, 3.5): the boats

43 'Coal 'Good for Humanity', Prime Minister Tony Abbott says at $3.9b Queensland Mine Opening', abc.net.au, Updated October 13, 2014. www.abc.net.au/news/2014-10-13/coal-is-good-for-humanity-pm-tony-abbott-says/5810244

44 Both from the anthropocentric and Eurocentric point of view – from which I observe the influence and importance of Cook's voyages for global logistics – and for the indigenous peoples of Australia and Aotearoa, for whom Cook and his influence are epochal, though with a very different valency.

45 Australian Border Force, 'The Future of Border Protection', *Australian Government Immigration and Border Protection Portfolio*, 2014. www.ibrarian.net/navon/paper/The_future_of_border_protection.pdf?paperid=23143312

had been stopped. In May 2014, around the same time, the following information was also disseminated, strengthening investigative, scholarly and critical political claims over two decades and compounding demands for urgent ethical attention: conditions in detention centres were causing high rates of mental illness and suicide attempts; offshore detention cost roughly ten-times the equivalent of detaining people onshore and caused higher rates of mental health issues to emerge; international comparative numbers indicated that Australia detained people far longer than international standards.

Mr Morrison's public response to these criticisms was to commit to the closure of *onshore* detention centres, and to the formation of a 'super agency', Border Force. To come full circle, *The Future of Border Protection* was what accompanied the speech announcing this[46]: just as the treatment of people in detention increasingly returned to onshore critical attention, Border Force issued a document notable for its almost complete non-regard of the humans who comprise its environment of operations.

Morrison's speech presented a distillation of Mike Pezzullo's 'New thinking about borders', from August 30, 2013,[47] and this is where we see the norms of global logistics being directly announced as and for border security, as follows:

> Australia's border is a national asset; and is fundamental to our national security and our economic prosperity. In today's world the border can no longer be considered a purely physical barrier which separates nation states. The border is a complex continuum which enables and controls the flow of people, and the movement of goods, through dynamic supply chains. This continuum stretches offshore and onshore and includes the overseas, maritime, physical border and domestic dimensions of the border. We call this the Border Continuum. . . . Agencies, such as the Australian Customs and Border Protection Service and the Department of Immigration and Border Protection, work across the continuum of facilitation, regulation and law enforcement supporting legitimate trade and travel. By working effectively across each dimension of the continuum, we are able to control who and what has the right to enter or exit, and under what conditions. To protect the safety, security and commercial interests of Australia, we work with our partner border agencies to employ an intelligence-led model across the border continuum. This includes significant effort in the maritime area to identify and respond to illegal arrivals, and to conduct surveillance of our exclusive economic zone for illegal fishing and other maritime threats. It also means we

46 'The Future of Border Protection', The Lowy Institute, May 9, 2014. www.lowyinstitute.org/events/border-protection-scott-morrison (link dead) and https://soundcloud.com/lowyinstitute/scott-morrison-future-border-protection

47 http://newsroom.border.gov.au/channels/Speeches/releases/ceo-speech-to-university-of-canberra-national-security-lecture-series

> seek to make it as easy as possible for legitimate trade and travel, and focus our efforts and resources where they will have the greatest impact.[48]

What's striking about the pamphlet is the directness with which Border Force avows border security's alignment with global logistics, something that both iterations of GAMSA had only said in context and by implication.[49] By May 2014, after the announced success of *Operation Sovereign Borders*, the Commonwealth's strategic vision of secured circulation came to be less about 'illegals and queue-jumpers' (1998–2001), national sovereignty (2001, 2013) and evil people smugglers (2010), and more about enabling business and supporting global logistics. 'Stopping the boats', then, was refigured as the enforcement component of maintaining the border continuum, a set of tactical responses to specific incidents, where the overall strategy was to "make it as easy as possible for legitimate trade and travel": the ability to control "who and what has the right to enter or exit, and under what conditions", and "the flow of people, and the movement of goods, through dynamic supply chains". By the second decade of border security's Australian operation, the locking up of people smugglers and asylum seekers necessary for 'stopping the boats' was revealed to be actually about the smoothing out of sealanes, air routes and airport queues, in anticipation of 'welcoming the ships and the planes' and the located, controllable 'who and what' securely contained aboard them.

As a risky apprehension of a putative totality, a way of thinking about and encompassing 'the whole inhabited world', *and* a way of looking forward to increased numbers of ships and planes, the operating environment co-observed by border security's agents co-consists of a past, present *and future* 'normal state of things' comprised of:

- the *orientating ideal* of increasing and securing legitimate activity;
- the *operational ideal* of smooth, rapid, ceaseless seamlessness, and;
- the *future ideal* of new operating environments, expanded opportunities and increasing revenues.

Throughout this time-and-space of secured circulation, yoked to a vision and pragmata of global logistics in which 'anyone with systems access could receive anything they wished, anywhere, at any time', the environment is also monitored for signs of inactivity, disruption and risk. Intervention is then organised to prevent, impede, minimise or recover from risks and threats, in order to restore 'the

48 Australian Border Force, 'The Future of Border Protection', *Australian Government Immigration and Border Protection Portfolio*, 2014. www.ibrarian.net/navon/paper/The_future_of_border_protection.pdf?paperid=23143312, p. 2.

49 'Guide to Australian Maritime Security Arrangements (GAMSA)', 2013, *Commonwealth of Australia*. www.border.gov.au/AustralianBorderForce/Documents/GAMSA%202013.pdf

normal state of things', a world in which, ideally, all boats are stopped and all ships and planes continue with the least possible impedance.

The *Future of Border Protection* pamphlet frames the Commonwealth's task of border security in support of global logistics with reference to a forecast expansion of activity:

> we are forecasting significant growth in trade and travellers, and threats to the integrity of our border will increase, and become more sophisticated. Air cargo consignments are expected to increase by 85 per cent between 2012–13 and 2016–17. Sea cargo consignments are expected to increase by 20 per cent between 2012–13 and 2016–17. International travellers are expected to increase by 25 per cent between 2012–13 and 2016–17.[50]

As introduced above (section 4.1), the confluence of 'observed increases' was the stated point of constituting Border Force as a super agency: the expansion of activity and a commensurate rise in threat complexity – including the observation that this situational definition, in turn, has been co-observed by human-based organised threats such as organised crime, industrial visa fraud, and expansive terrorist networks – renders consolidation necessary. In *The Future of Border Protection*, consolidation is offered as an institutional-responsive panacea that "strengthens our border" by 'creating efficiencies, reducing structural vulnerabilities and duplication'; thus 'fostering trade and travel'; thus 'realising economic benefits to our nation'; thus 'improving Australia's national security. The causal tightness and congruence of these implications – all drawn by an inaugural observation of activity – add to observations about the threat environment, the rightly protected border and Border Force's national task, whose elements have already been encountered, and assert the amalgamated co-presence of a combination of the three sets of inter-supportive claims:

1 a compounding threat environment: in 'today's (globalised) world', activity keeps increasing and *therefore* – systemically speaking – the threat environment becomes evermore complex and challenging
2 the border as strategic national asset: 'the border' is not just a thing that can be protected, it is a strategic national asset that must be defended and cherished, and doing so will achieve 'the good': community safety, prosperity and security, giving rise to
3 Border Force's national task and necessary integration: Border Force's national task is to provide a response to the threats and challenges of the border by defending and achieving the good, and the best possible way to organise for this is through integration.

50 Australian Border Force, 'The Future of Border Protection', *Australian Government Immigration and Border Protection Portfolio*, 2014. www.ibrarian.net/navon/paper/The_future_of_border_protection.pdf?paperid=23143312, p. 1.

To emphasise a point just raised, what sets all of the above in motion is the nature of activity as constitutive – an unstoppable systemic fact, desirable yet risky, environmental as a putative totality, intrasystemically 'harness-able', but only through good management in and of the border continuum. As GAMSA is the only place where the Commonwealth defines what activity means for Border Force's agents in the border continuum, I return to GAMSA to consider the function of activity for *The Future of Border Protection*.

The first words of GAMSA's introduction are framed as a pull quote in the foreground of a background stock photo showing the sun shining over a calm sea. They state: "[i]n terms of tonnes of cargo shipped and kilometres travelled, Australia is the world's fifth largest shipping nation".[51] The social fact of shipping is given special value in the cultural foreground of a 'shipping nation' whose operational background is dependency. 'When you invent the shipping nation, you invent national dependency on shipping'. The secondary observation that shipping is increasing implies that dependency is intensifying, and this is what prompted the birth of GAMSA *and* the necessity of integrating border security's world into Customs and Immigration, via Border Force. These points speak beyond logistics, insofar as they provide a politically watertight justification for the continued integration of border security beyond sovereignty (Chapter 1) and its emergence in communication (Chapter 2). But likewise, they also remind us, to return to a coda, that border security isn't just about borders, or security or sovereignty.

Embedded in the following description, GAMSA observes 'activity' in this way:

> legitimate maritime activity is a significant contributor to the Australian economy. Interruption of or interference with international shipping operating in Australia's maritime jurisdiction would have an immediate and detrimental effect on Australia's economy and its export competitiveness, and other consequences for lawful activity within Australia's maritime jurisdiction. Substantial environmental impact to an ecosystem may have flow-on consequences in another area. For example, significant environmental damage to the Great Barrier Reef, through marine pollution, would have a detrimental effect on tourism and fisheries.[52]

GAMSA attributes national significance to activity: by evoking legality and order, and by loading these legal and orderly referents with positive value, because they are co-construed as legitimate. This gives us a triplet with the following

51 This point reprises and develops points made in: Chambers, Peter, 'The Embrace of Border Security: Maritime Jurisdiction, National Sovereignty, and the Geopolitics of Operation Sovereign Borders', *Geopolitics*, 20, 2015, p. 416.

52 'Guide to Australian Maritime Security Arrangements (GAMSA)', 2013, *Commonwealth of Australia*. www.border.gov.au/AustralianBorderForce/Documents/GAMSA%202013.pdf, p. 3.

normative loadings we can thus see working in the metaphysical background of *The Future of Border Protection*:

- legality, order, legitimacy (nouns of observed ideals of activity);
- legal, orderly, legitimate (adjectives describing observable activities).

These loadings provide operationalising binaries,[53] because they protect non-interference and promotion of 'the good' and legitimate, just as they authorise rightful impedance and interdiction of 'the bad'. The implications of this are enormous for border security operations, but before we explore these in full it's important to note a discursive tension already generated by beginning from 'activity'. What happens once activity is observed as constitutive, and legitimate activity is taken as the good when it takes place within the border continuum? In this case, as explored, activity *is* – and when legitimate it must not be stopped. 'Legitimate activity' is in a sense the marriage of the ontological and the normative that underpins the necessarily 'good existence' of the border continuum.

We can add this reification to those drawn from 'threats', 'the border' and 'the illegal' (section 1.10–1.12, 3.10–3.12): just as the border *is*, so too illegals *are* . . . so too activity *is* and legitimate activity *is good*. GAMSA is speaking about shipping as its primary referent context, the inherently mobile activity whose essential business is the ceaseless trafficking of the world's commodities between locations explored via *Sheng Neng 1* – unloading, re-loading, then resuming travel, hopefully – even if those aboard haven't had adequate respite from 'activity'. Global shipping waits for no man on an island; global shipping awaits all further activity it anticipates and promptly undertakes. Threats are, border is, illegals are, activity is good – in perpetuity. These background reifications of the key referents of threat, border, illegals and good activity, co-stabilise the spatio-temporal horizons of the border continuum.

The security aspect of GAMSA's logic, applied to all 'shipping activity' taking place in a shipping nation, involves what we might describe as 'stopping stoppages'. This is the 'negative necessary' of 'good activity'. That is, security work in the maritime area of a shipping nation is about preventing the impedance of a constitutively mobile, legal, orderly, legitimate state of affairs that must be defended wherever it is observed by Border Force as threatened. The conduct of legitimate activity calls for security: the observed unity of these two aspects, within the border continuum, brings us full circle back into border security operations. But following Cowen to push this point a little, these predicates are immediately connected to the interest of the system *as a whole*: 'interruption or interference with shipping activity would have an immediate and detrimental

53 Luhmann, Niklas, *Theory of Society, Volume 1*, Stanford University Press, Stanford, 2012, pp. 132–137.

effect *on the economy* and *export competitiveness*'.[54] These final points show the links to what are iterated as macroeconomic concerns; 'the economy' fixes 'the national'.[55] The expansive good of GDP growth, fostered and enacted through international competition via global logistical systems, is taken aboard by Border Force as the *sine qua non* of a beneficent order of trade and the expansion of 'the economy' and its integrated role in securing it for the Commonwealth. It is commitment to the realisation of this ideal that that renders impedance or interruption of legitimate activities as undesirable outcomes. A rising tide lifts all boats; *so* Border Force must stop the boats.

4.7 'Preventing the impedance of activity by responding to recognised risks and threats within the border continuum': integrating recapitulation

But can Border Force observe activity as a risk? The border continuum can be used to observe activity and screen it for risks and threats. The following slight re-arrangement of elements is also true, and less noted: the irrepressible presence of activity can be used to observe entities as risks and threats that enter or are moving 'within' a 'border continuum'. But this co-activation can only transpire *securely* during moments in which that which passes is screened effectively. Border security is a means of securing circulation that responds to *recognised risks* as objects without ever impeding the putative totality of *activity*. In other words, the border continuum is a way of observing activity as security by giving attention to recognised objects moving within the threat environment. To draw the circle tighter and clearer, border security is a way of operating in this environment to support and secure the continuation and expansion of activity – by screening its risks and threats. Mike Pezzullo, CEO of Border Force, elaborates this very clearly, as follows:

> Border control points, systems and processes sit astride supply chains and travel pathways. The very design of these points, systems and processes can add to economic competitiveness and productivity, by fostering rapid movement and border entry or exit. Or they can detract from competitiveness and productivity by impeding movement, entry and exit, and diminishing the efficiency of our national infrastructure. *Fostering legitimate trade and travel, while remaining vigilant for national security, law enforcement and community protection purposes, while also using border controls as an extension*

54 'Guide to Australian Maritime Security Arrangements (GAMSA)', 2013, *Commonwealth of Australia*. www.border.gov.au/AustralianBorderForce/Documents/GAMSA%202013.pdf, p. 3, italics mine.

55 Mitchell, Timothy, 'Fixing the Economy', *Cultural Studies*, 12: 1, 1998, pp. 82–101.

> *of economic revenue and industry policy, are not contradictory policy objectives. They are intrinsically integrated and connected* ***functions of state.***[56]

The Future of Border Protection – which contains the italicised parts of the above quote verbatim, except for the bolded final phrase – continues as follows:

> Recognising this will improve the collection of revenue and community security and safety through a model which balances facilitation with enforcement. Australia needs to benefit from the welcome increase in trade and travel and better prevent harmful and unlawful activity. Current arrangements with the separation of the Australian Customs and Border Protection Service and the Department of Immigration and Border Protection will not deliver a sustainable approach to this.[57]

The necessary existence of Border Force and its societal inception in and through Australian border security, are fully instituted, direct, reflexive recognitions of what Pezzullo observes as "intrinsically integrated and connected functions of state", "seamless and indivisible tasks".[58] Not only is there no contradiction between border security and global logistics, Australia's ideal future, so observed, involves the full integration of border security. But in turn, border security's rightful future place and state function in and for the Commonwealth involves its full integration within global logistics. Mike Pezzullo defines his rhetorical task as changing our thinking about the border by challenging us to recognise this social fact. The 'simple truth of national survival' is only possible by opening the national to the international and global. Border security's closures are enabling conditions of Australia's openness (section 3.8).

With these theoretical points brought back to the foreground for a moment, a recapitulation is fruitful before we return to on-water operations. In Chapter 2 (section 2.7), I described how five formerly distinct and formally un-integrated functions of state related to the border were concatenated as border

56 Pezzullo, Mike, 'CEO Speech to University of Canberra National Security Lecture Series: New Thinking About Borders', newsroom.border.gov.au, August 30, 2013. http://newsroom.border.gov.au/channels/Speeches/releases/ceo-speech-to-university-of-canberra-national-security-lecture-series and Pezzullo, Mike, 'Pezzullo: Immigration Department Won't Be Trapped by History', *The Mandarin*, June 2, 2016. www.themandarin.com.au/65969-michael-pezzullo-immigration-department-wont-be-trapped-by-history/ and Pezzullo, Mike, 'Keynote Address at Mobility Symposium 2016', *Crawford School of Public Policy*, March 21, 2016. www.border.gov.au/about/news-media/speeches-presentations/keynote-mobility-symposium-2016

57 'The Future of Border Protection', The Lowy Institute, May 9, 2014. www.lowyinstitute.org/events/border-protection-scott-morrison (link dead) and https://soundcloud.com/lowyinstitute/scott-morrison-future-border-protection', p. 10.

58 'Pezzullo: Immigration Department Won't Be Trapped by History', *The Mandarin*, June 2, 2016. www.themandarin.com.au/65969-michael-pezzullo-immigration-department-wont-be-trapped-by-history/

security, becoming an observing system, a difference that makes a difference by re-ordering and governing them thereafter, according to its worldmaking severances. They were:

1 the coast, navigation and safety;
2 import *qua* disease;
3 import and export *qua* trade, tariff and tax;
4 arrival on the level of population;
5 the dynamic relation of international and global mobility and individuals attached to nation-states through forms of citizenship.

Re-figured as border security, any of the many stakeholders nominated in GAMSA (section 1.10) are capable of apprehending any one or combination of the following activities – *activities*, thus mobile *functions*, not fixed, single or unitary people, things, places or territories (section 1.10) – as threat objects within GAMSA's purview, from which an enforceable claim of interest or security response become necessary:

1 illegal activity in protected areas,
2 illegal exploitation of natural resources,
3 marine pollution,
4 prohibited imports and exports,
5 irregular maritime arrivals,
6 compromise to biosecurity,
7 piracy, robbery or violence at sea,
8 maritime terrorism.[59]

We can note how the above two lists do and do not map neatly on to one another (or the territory), as well as how they both express longstanding concerns, consistent within modern state work, to protect, guard, screen and secure. But more than anything, what the eight threat categories – unlike the five related yet distinct state functions – are notable for their strong normative loading, and their attachment to shifting figures of illegitimacy: prohibition, illegality, irregularity and contamination.[60] 'Illegitimate' works as a broad organising principle in the production of Border Force's distinctions in GAMSA and *The Future of Border Protection*, without ever explicitly saying – outside tautology – how or why such-and-such an activity is illegitimate.

59 'Guide to Australian Maritime Security Arrangements (GAMSA)', 2013, *Commonwealth of Australia*. www.border.gov.au/AustralianBorderForce/Documents/GAMSA%202013.pdf, p. 4.

60 Douglas, Mary, *Purity and Danger: An Analysis of Concepts of Pollution and Taboo*, Routledge, Abingdon, 2005 and s of the Australian Nation', *Health: An Interdisciplinary Journal for the Social Study of Health, Illness and Medicine*, 2: 4, 1998, pp. 387–402.

With the above in mind, revisiting *Sheng Neng 1*'s collision via GAMSA's definition of security threat for just a moment can clarify how 'activities' are cognised as illegitimate – or not – where activity is ***first*** accorded primacy ***and then*** border security is implemented as intrinsically integrated and connected state functions securing its passage. What follows re-reads *Sheng Neng 1* through GAMSA's metaphysics of activity, ***with*** the CEO of Border Force's above interpretation of border security's fully societally integrated and logistics-aligned 'mobility *fostering*, threat ***vigilant***' role also in mind.

4.8 Reading the Reef collision of *Sheng Neng 1* through GAMSA: just what kinds of activity are observable as security threats by Border Force?

Sheng Neng 1 is legible as a matter requiring a border security response, using GAMSA. Actions were taken by *Sheng Neng 1*'s crew:

- in a 'protected area' that put 'natural resources in jeopardy',
- that did cause a nationally significant 'maritime pollution' event,[61]
- and this was a 'compromise to biosecurity'.

Further: the toxic lead antifouling paint on *Sheng Neng 1*'s hull is prohibited in Australian waters. The labour conditions aboard, one of the two key factors causing the collision, would be unlawful and breaches of occupational health and safety regulations in all Australian states. Its labour conditions were ***unlawful***, its hull was ***polluting*** and its collision with Douglas Shoal did cause "[s]ignificant environmental ***damage*** to the Great Barrier Reef" which manifestly has ***costly*** "flow-on consequences on tourism and fisheries".[62] Put simply, *Sheng Neng 1* was exploitative and unsafe for its crew and hazardous and threatening to the Reef – and many of these points appear in GAMSA in its descriptions of the many threats confronting Border Force in its defence of Australia's area of maritime interest. But was *Sheng Neng 1*'s collision with the Reef therefore a security threat, an illegitimate activity that merited impedance?

As encountered (section 1.11–1.12), GAMSA defines security threat very broadly as "any action, device or event that has potential to cause consequences adverse to Australia's interests".[63] In the final sections of Chapter 1 I analysed

61 'Grounding of the *Shen Neng 1* on Douglas Shoal, April 2010: Impact Assessment Report', *Great Barrier Reef Marine Park Authority*, June 2011. www.gbrmpa.gov.au/__data/assets/pdf_file/0019/17164/ShenNengGroundingImpactAssessmentReport.pdf

62 'Guide to Australian Maritime Security Arrangements (GAMSA)', 2013, *Commonwealth of Australia*. www.border.gov.au/AustralianBorderForce/Documents/GAMSA%202013.pdf, p. 3.

63 'Guide to Australian Maritime Security Arrangements (GAMSA)', 2013, *Commonwealth of Australia*. www.border.gov.au/AustralianBorderForce/Documents/GAMSA%202013.pdf p. 163.

how asylum seekers could not be observed as threats to national security using the IMO's definition; only GAMSA's wider definition of threat could cognise asylum seekers approaching aboard boats as threats (section 1.10–1.12). *Sheng Neng 1*'s collision is clearly cognisable as a 'security threat', both by GAMSA's broad definition and for the actual harm it inflicted on the largest living entity in the world's marine environment, which is also arguably Australia's single most valuable asset, measured as contributing '$5.68 billion and generating almost 69,000 full-time equivalent jobs' in 2011–2012 alone.[64]

GAMSA describes 'prevention and preparedness' as a key responsibility for all stakeholders in Australia's area of maritime interest, including a broad spectrum of maritime operators as stakeholders. 'Prevention and preparedness' involves "the risk mitigation measures that government agencies and other stakeholders take to either deter, disrupt or prevent security threats, or to minimise the adverse consequences if prevention is unsuccessful".[65] If *Sheng Neng 1* was recognised as a security threat, border security's stakeholders would have had responsibilities: either to deter, disrupt or prevent the collision beforehand (which surveillance operations should have observed), and/or to respond afterward with harm minimising mitigation measures.

At no point were any of Maritime Border Command's response assets marshaled to mitigate the adverse consequences of the collision, nor was public comment sought by journalists on what Border Force's senior agents did to prevent *Sheng Neng 1*'s collision. Though threatening according to GAMSA's definition and harmful in ways that might trigger stakeholder responsibilities, *Sheng Neng 1* was never categorised as a border security matter.

A credulous reading of GAMSA's definitions does not supply consistent reasons why this should be the case, so I offer the following interpretation. Although *Sheng Neng 1* did cause 'significant environmental damage to the Great Barrier Reef' which also carried enormous potential to have 'flow-on consequences on tourism and fisheries', the activity it was engaged in was 'shipping activity', and this is coded *a priori* as legitimate. *Sheng Neng 1*'s movement through the reef would in fact have been recognised by Border Force as a 'significant contributor to the Australian economy'. In a hypothetical future in which local fishermen angry about rat run-caused spills 'turned pirate', it is perhaps they who might have expected interdiction, because Border Force actually deals with what it recognises as recognised risks and threat objects; not only does it only operate where it observes intrasystemic threats, it does not apply its own definition to the world outside the threat environment. This means that activity cannot be a threat; another constitutive blindspot of border security's world. This brings us

64 'Economic Contribution of the Great Barrier Reef March 2013', Department of the Environment and Energy, *Commonwealth of Australia*. www.environment.gov.au/sustainability/publications/economic-contribution-great-barrier-reef-march-2013

65 Op. cit.

to the following reification, which we can add to threats (section 1.10), the border (section 3.12), illegals (sections 2.6, 3.10–3.12) and activity (section 4.6).

Legitimate activities *are not* security threats.[66] Legitimacy confers a circulation-securing blessing upon any activity, one that prevents its recognition as a security threat in perpetuity. As with all worldmaking severances explored in *Border Security*, this is not without its costs. Not only did *Sheng Neng 1*'s collision inflict harm on a sensitive and already threatened ecosystem that is also a source of national profit through fishing and tourism, none of the potential harm it carried could then be linked to like cases. In systems theoretical terms, *Sheng Neng 1* couldn't 'contribute to the ongoing differentiation of the system by producing a condensation of meaning that could make a difference'. In colliding with the Barrier Reef, *Sheng Neng 1* never crossed the boundary into the border continuum.

Stuck fast upon the rocks, leaking oil, *Sheng Neng 1* remained outside the border continuum, an anomalous accident in the maritime environment, an 'unrepeatable element from another situation'[67] – in contrast with SUNCs and SIEVs (section 1.12). This points to how and why systemic failure is an orphan: *Sheng Neng 1* did not and could not produce an actionable category of vessel that could be interdicted in all future like cases, even though hundreds of ships of this kind routinely threaten the Reef as they rat run through it each year, hurrying between stations in their limitless traffic. With these points in hand, we can place *Sheng Neng 1*'s collision with the Reef side by side with the contrasting way in which the arrival of the Deutsche Bank in Geraldton was read:

- *Sheng Neng 1*: a routine mishap of no systemic consequence framed as the responsibility of selected individuals aboard;[68]
- Deutsche Bank: a categorical and urgent threat to border security without requiring further thought or enquiry into the intentions of those aboard, meriting the expansion of drone-based surveillance.

Indeed, as a regrettable mishap that took place within the sphere of legitimate activity, *Sheng Neng 1* had to be cleaned up immediately, not for any love of the Reef, but because not doing so would interrupt or interfere with the continued and seamless expansion of activity as international shipping operations through the Great Barrier Reef. Just as there were unseen dangers and unknown hazards ahead of *Sheng Neng 1*, border security's normative alignment with global logistics means it can see some objects as threats, not others. Just as the chief mate couldn't see Douglas Shoal, GAMSA cannot see *Sheng Neng 1*.

66 The inverse holds: Illegitimate activities *are* security threats.

67 Luhmann, Niklas, *Theory of Society, Volume 1*, Stanford University Press, Stanford, 2012, pp. 38–39.

68 Bolt, Andrew, 'Slickers Inspect Slick', *Herald Sun*, April 10, 2010. www.heraldsun.com.au/blogs/andrew-bolt/slickers-inspect-slick/news-story/a9e5b26d3819b75397bc51205f3f2ce2

4.9 Concluding corollaries: double visions, lasting scars and legal necessities of the normative order of global logistics and border security

Given the almost complete absence of humans in *The Future of Border Protection*, I would like to turn concluding attention to the all too human aspects of this, as pinpointed by Hans Blumenberg:

> [a]s humans our frontal optics make us creatures with a lot of 'back', who have to live under the condition that a large part of reality lies behind us and is something that we have to leave behind us.[69]

Read through Luhmann, the back and front of Blumenberg's expression of the human condition is less to do with the physical position of the human eye, and more to do with the position of the observer.[70] Border Force 'cannot see that it cannot see' that in pursuing border security's severences towards a logistical vision of the good society, its efforts and resources have had the greatest human impact on a population it can no longer regard politically or ethically as people to whom it owes fairness and responsibility. Empirically and normatively, there is no justice in *The Future of Border Protection*.

Border Force's increasingly strong preference for logistical thinking and the commensurate national subordination of religious, cultural, communitarian, regionally based ideals of justice, citizenship or relations to country mean that its agents sensitise maximal surveillant attention to the tiniest boat, when people seeking protection are aboard it, while giving no attention to entities that are security threats by its own definitions, when those entities represent a desired source of profit. Perhaps this only tells us that Border Force's partial vision is *very* partial – to commerce and revenue.

Five years after its collision with the reef, *Sheng Neng 1* has made a lasting and harmful impression on this "globally outstanding and significant entity . . . the world's most extensive coral reef ecosystem",[71] in the form of a scar along Douglas Shoal, a region made lifeless by the toxic lead antifouling paint scraped along the coral. In most recent estimates, cleanup costs have trebled from initial estimates, and sit at 141 million Australian dollars.[72] *Sheng Neng 1* happened to the Reef, yet nothing happened from *Sheng Neng 1*. In the half decade since

69 Blumenberg, Hans, *Work on Myth*, MIT Press, Cambridge, 1986, pp. 175–176.

70 [T]he observer is the nonobservable. The distinction he uses to indicate the one side or the other serves as the invisible condition of seeing, as blind spot. And this can be said for all observation". Luhmann, Niklas, *Theory of Society, Volume 1*, Stanford University Press, Stanford, 2012, p. 35.

71 'Great Barrier Reef', *www.unesco.org*. http://whc.unesco.org/en/list/154

72 Moore, Tony, 'Costs to Remove Toxic Paint From Great Barrier Reef 'Triples' to $141 Million', *Brisbane Times*, May 7, 2016. www.brisbanetimes.com.au/queensland/costs-to-remove-toxic-paint-from-great-barrier-reef-triples-to-141-million-20160506-gooe84.html

its grounding, shipping through the Reef – conducted in the same ways, in the same conditions, using the same equipment, with the same imperatives placing demands on ships and crew – has continued to expand:

> More than 9,600 ship voyages were recorded in the Reef between 2012 and 2013, and 3,947 individual ships called in at Reef ports in 2012. At the current growth rate of 4.8% per annum, the projected increase in ship numbers calling into these ports will exceed 10,000 by 2032.[73]

This routine traffic threatens the Great Barrier Reef, but is not observed as a threat to the border: recall that in contrast, in peak years of national crisis, 2000 and 2010, fifty-one and 134 vessels attempted to arrive in Australia. The figures, as John Howard might say, 'tell a clear story' (section 2.8).

The alignment of border security and global logistics, finally, raises the effects of the politics of all this as a question of global responsibility. But as explored, within GAMSA's metaphysics and normativity, border security's systems, like the ramifications of pursuing location-spatial thought as circulations 'around the atmospheric casing of a planet', are agentic yet placed beyond visibility and cognition as matters of justice, yet alone as easy contentions within the everyday shores of politics. These are all parts of our political present that affect us, but we cannot easily contend with them.

Global logistics answers the ecumenical question with a control response that returns agency to humans by proving reliably capable of delivering the goods anywhere, but it resists cognition of its own operations as political and ethical – nor is this easily visible, to most critical observers of border security, who continue to give most attention to the human effects of detention conditions. The absolute background resolutely remains in the places we have allotted it: in society, on our control surfaces, as our politics. This brings us to a curious impasse of our current predicament: ours is an age in which we live complicity through global systems that are agentic, consequential and beyond responsibility. All of us are the contaminating beneficiaries of the systems damaging our lifeworld, which no 'one' can stop. When you invent global logistics as a life support system, do you then invent the ungrievable[74] ruination of living systems? Such questions are outside the border continuum.

73 Grech, Alana and McCook, Laurence, 'Shipping in the Great Barrier Reef: The Miners' Highway', *The Conversation*, May 25, 2015. http://theconversation.com/shipping-in-the-great-barrier-reef-the-miners-highway-39251

74 Butler, Judith, *Frames of War: When Is Life Grievable?* Verso, London, 2009.

Part III

Beyond border security's shores and horizons

Chapter 5

Boundless planes to share

Border security and the living heart of the global city

5.1 Before entering the global city: a brief recap

So far I have examined border security from the perspectives of sovereignty, communication, offshore and logistics. Looking at border security's alignment to the normative order in global logistics enabled an explication of global background conditions of current operations, which indicated the values driving border security's likely future expansion and integration, the double vision of securing circulation, and the unobservable hazards and dangers of Border Force's partiality toward commerce and revenue. Apprehending border security's alignment with a global normative order seeking seamless circulation within the system as a whole, *Border Security* shifted foreground focus: out of border security's Australian emergence (Part I), away from its international and global lineages (Chapter 3), and toward a possible global politics contained within a mostly unexamined yet fundamental commitment to the limitless expansion of lifeless movement. The compounding implications for the globally living and the planetarily limited raise fundamental political questions about responsibility, agency and justice. As blindspots of border security's world visible through an obsessive yet highly selective focus on threats in order to achieve deterrence and control, but that negate human vulnerability in pervasive and definite ways, I suggest that such questions comprise negated horizons of global justice.

Re-examining the political relations between sovereignty, offshore, logistics and border security has meant re-thinking scales and spaces, in a way that feeds in to scholarly debates about how we should best think about the transformation that globalisation names, especially in its relation to the nation-state.[1] The political scales and spaces of border security's world examined so far concern the seemingly far and other: distant, offshore, alien, terminally inadmissable. Border Force keeps circling objects of interdiction across time and space, out there on the ocean's surface, 'in here' during the weekly briefings, in the name of the nation. But where is this nation now located amongst these political scales and

1 Sassen, Saskia, *Territory, Authority, Rights: From Medieval to Global Assemblages*, Princeton University Press, Princeton, 2008, pp. 1–3.

spaces? By *The Future of Border Protection*, the nation abides in the border continuum as a national asset, and the border is conceived and enacted as and through the unending and inter-scalar operational environments of the continuum. With *Operation Sovereign Borders* and 'border *protection*' as twin cultural indicators (section 3.12), we might say that 'the border' is sovereign; the Australian Commonwealth and its populations and territory have subjected themselves to the authority of their own reification, an enormous space that must then be taken responsibility for as border security, in ways that open onto the imperatives of global commerce by closing out the possibility of justice and asylum.

The border continuum is a 'glocal' scale-space of capital and national sovereignty enacted – thus practiced as threatened, at risk, and in need of urgent securing – wherever the threat environment is observed (section I.2). This is a key task, appearing at any and all points along the border continuum, that Border Force's most senior officials have recognised and prepared for, and that now demand further integration (section 4.6). At the limit, the border continuum offers one internally consistent response to the anxiety inherent in the ecumenical question[2] by securing the interests of Australia and its stakeholders, *wherever* they are recognised, across the whole inhabited earth. And yet: Border Force's operations also scale 'back' to the human referents that are its ineliminable subjects and objects of interest. Border Force can't quite get rid of (the) 'people', and it's this human scale and its everyday political spaces of contestation, expressed through a peculiar moment in the global city Melbourne, to which this final chapter attunes.

Border Force's promotion continues to involve work conducted by group agents working within institutions. Border security involves intentional and organised labour; as its CEO says, the border continuum is "formed and sustained through human agency and practice"[3] (sections i.2, 4.6). Enforcers of interdiction and constructor-promoters of offshore detention have been co-operating to unilaterally assemble direct conduits between the local and the global, short circuits that work to secure circulation in favour of a diffuse yet still coherent set of onshore interests, passages of authority that open a way for national sovereignty to get at human lives on the open ocean. Offshoring detention effectuates a set of conduits I've described as circumventions within circulation (section 3.3); global logistics' de-differentiated embrace of 'who and what' – storable people, screenable objects, moveable things (sections 3.12, 4.6, 4.9) – is another. Yet just as most discussions of offshore presume an 'onshore' that passes unremarked as its unmarked space, many of the claims and efforts made in the direction of border security that we've explored through sovereignty, communication, offshore

2 Hannerz, Ulf, 'Notes on the Global Ecumene', *Public Culture*, 1: 2, 1989, p. 66, Luhmann, Niklas, 'Globalization or World society: How to Conceive of Modern Society', *International Review of Sociology*, 7: 1, 1997.

3 Border Force News Room, 'New Thinking About Borders: ACBPS CEO Michael Pezzullo', August 30, 2013. http://newsroom.border.gov.au/channels/Speeches/releases/ceo-speech-to-university-of-canberra-national-security-lecture-series

and logistics presume or imply a privileged set of secured locations 'back here (onshore)' made up of sets of invested beneficiaries: groups of people, organised activities, highly valuable assets. If border security is a unilateral projection of national sovereignty in global space, where 'in' the nation is such a projection emanating, what are its implied centres[4]?

5.2 Border security's political address in/to the global city

In this chapter I explore how the global city is a replicant spatial form implied by securing circulation. Global cities[5] make up a privileged set of 'global locations' within border security's world. Global cities are the locations where 'the society worth defending' through border security lives and thrives, as well as the actual places where many of its globally mobile secured citizens and residents live and traffic between. Global cities:

- comprise the offices and homes where the goods of society are to be delivered as swiftly, precisely and as smoothly as possible;
- make up the onshore places withdrawn from offshore spaces that support them by screening and storing recognised assets and risks elsewhere;
- house the hard and soft infrastructures and support the lifestyles of the publics whose lives are accorded the highest value within the evaluative hierarchies of global capitalism, instituted at the national scale most conspicuously through trade and immigration policy, represented through the 'simple truth of national survival' (section 3.9) and politicians' populist responsiveness to anxieties about coastlines and arrivals (section 2.4, 2.8).

If Border Force's primary alignment is to the normative order of global logistics, an order that supports the seamless expansion of capital and the securing of its beneficiaries, in other words, it's also because of the *growing* centrality of global cities as the political spaces to which global logistics' goods and services are rightly addressed – within the nation. Global cities are the onshore locations that matter most for border security and global logistics alike; and its denizens, differentially, are the people who count the most.

4 To tie it to Yeats' "centre cannot hold" in 'The Second Coming', in *Territory, Authority, Rights*, Sassen writes that the developments described in the dis-and-reassemblies under analysis entail "a move toward the centrifugal, and away from the centripetal dynamics that have marked the development of nation-states", Sassen, Saskia, *Territory, Authority, Rights: From Medieval to Global Assemblages*, Princeton University Press, Princeton, 2008, p. 390.

5 Sassen, Saskia, *The Global City*, Princeton University Press, Princeton, 1992 and *Global Networks, Linked Cities*, Routledge, Abingdon, 2002, Brenner, Neil, 'Global Cities, Glocal States: Global City Formation and State Territorial Restructuring in Contemporary Europe', *Review of International Political Economy,* 5, 1998, pp. 1–37 and Brenner, Neil and Jessop, Bob, Jones, Martin and Macleod, *Gordon, State/Space: a Reader*, Blackwell, New Jersey, 2003.

As a re-emergent global city, Melbourne is one such global location. By looking at Border Force's abortive 'forced entry' into it (section 5.8–5.11), I show how border security comes ashore as a question of address in the broadest sense: of public address and of jurisdiction; of who can speak, who can stay, and who can live well and move freely in the city. With its implied audiences in mind (section 2.2), this is another way of thinking through the message of border security, where and how it emanates, the sense in which it is always, of course, an onshore imagination. I pinpoint citizenship as a central onshore mechanism that locates the global and the local *as* a border *in* the body of the noncitizen resident. The "continuum of materiality"[6] underpinning operations is located in the Great Barrier Reef, and also 'in' people; 'we' are integrated within the border continuum as its greatest asset.[7]

The general situation of border security's address in and to the global city is unavoidably also a part the societies and cultures of control and the ideological and economic dominance of the global city in this age of globalisation, driven by support – increasingly contested – for immigration and the expansion of GDP. But it also speaks to a very particular cultural moment in Australian political life, and I wish to sit a tension at these two irreconcilable scales. The current institutional-cultural domination of immigration by Customs and the executive as Border Force in Australia, crowned by the introduction of the Border Force Act on July 1, 2015, is part of a resisted push to transform immigration into logistically minded screenings (Chapter 4). The implementation of Customs' logistical vision would seek to see the lightest possible touch for business travellers and their interests (section 4.6); the heaviest possible push against the world's poorest and most vulnerable people. I set this up as a horizon of probable institutional and public contestation likely to unfold in border security's third decade of Australian operation.[8]

At the executive level, the push to dominate some of the world's poorest, most traumatised populations is being led through a populist rhetoric that conflates and enchains crime, immigration, terrorism, deviance and otherness. Like finance capital, neoliberalisations and border security before and with it, it is resonating throughout and beyond the rich West via the grievance-driven populism of Brexit, Trump and growing, strengthening sections of the European right, especially those most vocally suggesting Austria and Denmark's full importation of Australia's border security model. To specify our enquiries here, the expansive pursuit of secured circulation in the global city of Melbourne in border security's second decade of operations is thriving hand in hand with a global-societal 'common sense' that 'knows' the value, necessity and expansion of 'what works':

6 Luhmann, Niklas, *Theory of Society, Volume 1*, Stanford University Press, Stanford, 2012, p. 56.

7 "Being closed is always being enclosed in something which, seen from inside, is outside". Luhmann, Niklas, *Theory of Society, Volume 1*, Stanford University Press, Stanford, 2012, p. 54.

8 McCulloch, Jude, *Blue Army: Paramilitary Policing in Australia*, Melbourne University Press, Melbourne, 1997.

getting tough, cracking down, prudential policing, more CCTV and working collaboratively with stakeholders and clients/communities, but never politically with citizens and justice.[9]

On the ground in 2015 Melbourne, to foreshadow this chapter's analytic incursion (section 5.8–5.10), highly placed Border Force officials observed border security as best effectuated through petty compliance work on public transport, assisted by racial profiling in public space by Victoria Police. With *Operation Fortitude*, to which we will give close attention, visa compliance work sought to secure the global city as part of Border Force's 'societal mission'.[10] *Operation Fortitude* and its implications indicates a very particular relation of authorities, scales and spaces, a definite moment where territory, authority and rights – both in the national, and in the global city[11] – were dis-and-re-assembled. Agents within Border Force sought to use border security to leverage aspects of street policing *into* aspects of global processes where a prudential order of integration and exclusion, privileged access and indefinite banishment, are being worked out.

5.3 Melbourne's emergence as a global city in the nineteenth and twenty-first centuries, and its twentieth-century interregnum in White Australia

Melbourne was founded in 1835, at a safe and calm distance from the taint of transportation that besmirched the penal settlements across Bass Strait[12] in Van Diemens Land and those further up the east coast of New South Wales, in Sydney and on Norfolk Island. These clear bright retrospections of 'free settlers' making the land work and gaining 'wealth for toil', to quote Australia's lateborn anthem once again, are clouded by the facts. The establishment of the Port Phillip District of the Colony of New South Wales[13] was predicated on the overturning of local treaties with indigenous groups, which followed the erasure of the legal pluralism that had characterised Van Diemens Land in the first two decades of

9 Garland, David, *The Culture of Control: Crime and Social Order in Contemporary Society*, Oxford University Press, Oxford, 2001.

10 *Operation Fortitude* was the code name for a deception strategy use by the Allies in 1944 to mislead the Nazis about the timing and whereabouts of the Normandy Landing. As with the Pacific Solution, SIEV and SUNC, border security's worldmakers in the Commonwealth have a gift for naming operations and generating acronyms.

11 Sloterdijk, Peter, *In the World Interior of Ca*pital, Polity Press, Cambridge, 2013, Sloterdijk, Peter, 'Foam City', *Distinktion: Journal of Social Theory*, 16, 2008, pp. 47–59 and Borch, Christian, 'Foam Architecture: Managing Co-Isolated Associations', *Economy and Society*, 37: 4, 2008, pp. 548–571.

12 Named by Matthew Flinders during his circumnavigation of Van Diemens Land in 1788–1789. See: Flinders, Matthew and Flannery, Tim, *Terra Australis: Matthew Flinders' Great Adventures in the Circumnavigation of Australia*, Text, Melbourne, 2012.

13 That eventually become the city of Melbourne (1847) in the state of Victoria (1851).

the nineteenth century.[14] These political negations of what had developed from first contact to the 1820s were neither circumstantial nor accidental. Rather, these organised, reflexive responses to different of ways of relating to the land and one another – as peoples, through promises that had just begun to take hold – were political tactics within a governmental strategy intended to set in motion land-appropriating settlements. From 1835, over the remaining decades of the nineteenth century, the tactics of this strategy used criminal law and private property, armed conflict and local policing, to achieve the conquest of Australia (section 1.4). Melbourne's 1835 foundation is, in this sense, year zero of the intentional conquest of the island continent.[15]

From its foundation, Melbourne was a colonial centre from which the conquest of Australia of emanated. As recent research indicates, this was a synchronous transformation that occurred in communication with the conquest of what later became the United States,[16] and this can also be seen in relation to Carey McWilliams pioneering approach to understanding Southern California as 'an island on the land';[17] for McWiliams, Southern California is much more coherently thought of as a succession of colonies and political projects, many with an explicitly utopian edge, that were only much later integrated into and retrospectively legible as part of 'mainland America'. In apprehending its nineteenth-century emergence as a global city, what I'm emphasising is that – like Australia Day and national sovereignty (sections 1.2–1.7) – describing Melbourne's founding as a settled part of 'Australian history' is a later retrospection made from an Australia that did not exist at that time: this should also be considered in relation to what has been said about Australia's state and national sovereignty (sections 1.2–1.7), and 1770 and 1788 as competing alternative year zeroes for European Australia and its state, nation and capital (section 1.2, 4.3).

Melbourne in its first seven decades is, then, better understood as one of a number of British imperial conquests of the New World, predicated on land appropriation via private property and common law. Melbourne in 1835 was the urban centre of an expansionist colony – as aligned with the normative order of

14 From its inception as a tent city along the banks of the Yarra, this meant that local indigenous groups were dealt with as if they were trespassing on Crown land (August 26 1835). This overturning of treaties and turning out of indigenous inhabitants in turning the lands around the settlement into saleable property immediately preceded Governor Burke's assertion of terra nullius from Sydney, New South Wales, on October 10, 1835. www.migrationheritage.nsw.gov.au/exhibition/objectsthroughtime/bourketerra/

15 Boyce, James, *1835: The Founding of Melbourne and the Conquest of Australia*, Black Inc, Melbourne, 2012.

16 Ford, Lisa, 'Indigenous Policy and Its Historical Occlusions: the North American and Global Contexts of Australian Settlement', *Australian Indigenous Law Review*, 12: 1, 2008 and Benton, Lauren, *A Search for Sovereignty: Law and Geography in European Empires, 1400–1900*, New York University, New York, 2010, and chapter 1, note 29.

17 McWilliams, Carey, *Southern California: An Island on the Land*, Peregrine Smith, Utah, 1980.

British colonialism and imperialism as border security is with global logistics and finance capital. Nineteenth-century Melbourne was an engine of expansion that worked to appropriate land, transform it into property, conquer the continent and ensure the stable prosperity of the British Empire. By its own intrasystemic measures, this project was remarkably successful, within a generation: by 1851, squatters' properties had appropriated nearly all pastureland.[18]

As in California, one of the great engines of transformation was the Gold Rush. By 1855 the Victorian Gold Rush was transforming Melbourne from a colonial outpost of prosperous 'free settlers' looking to a pastoral horizon into one of the rushing hearts of the new imperial circulation.[19] As in California, the Victorian Gold Rush coincided with the development of telegraphy and railroads: the first telegraph office in the southern hemisphere opened for business on March 3, 1854; the Port Melbourne railway line opened in September of the same year. And as in California, the Gold Rush generated anti-Chinese sentiment. The first Chinese arrived by boat in Melbourne in 1853; between 1854–1855 31,000 Chinese people arrived in Victoria and New South Wales; the first anti-Chinese legislation that emerged in the British colonies *An Act to Make Provision for Certain Immigrants* was passed in Victoria in 1855.[20]

As discussed in relation to the emergence of national sovereignty (sections 1.2–1.7), Melbourne was a capital city of the British nineteenth century whose Imperial conquest made Australia the nation-state it became at Federation. From the contradictions and real estate bubble set in motion by the Gold Rush, from 1851, came the contraction of 1890. As described, after a ten-year recession, Melbourne retreated into the federation of British colonies that became the nation-state called Australia; by 1901, Melbourne was the capital city of a protectionist enclave selecting immigrations on a racialist basis (section 1.5–1.6), an imperialist yet nationalist political formation in search of its own European political and cultural identity: within the British Empire, far away in the South Pacific.

Described from the perspective of the capitalist imperialist dynamics that dominated the second half of the nineteenth century,[21] the age of 'Australia, the racialist protectionist nation-state', stands between 'then and now' as a seven decade interregnum. In thinking about Melbourne as a global city that Border Force sought to enter (of which more shortly), what I would like to suggest as a better periodisation of its political history is that White Australia's seven decades

18 'The Squattocracy', State Library of Victoria. http://ergo.slv.vic.gov.au/explore-history/land-exploration/pastoral-practices/squattocracy

19 'Victoria's Historic Population Growth: Annual Population Growth, Victoria, European Settlement to Present, 1836–2011', *Department of Environment, Land, Water and Planning*. www.dtpli.vic.gov.au/data-and-research/population/presentations-and-bulletins/victorias-historic-population-growth

20 'Chinese Immigration Act 1855 (Vic)', Museum of Australian Democracy, www.foundingdocs.gov.au/item-did-82.html

21 Hobsbawm, Eric, *The Age of Capital: 1848–1975*, Abacus, London, 1975 and Hobsbawm, Eric, *The Age of Empire: 1875–1914*, Abacus, London, 1989.

interrupted Melbourne's – so far! – more durable modern identity as a global city: open for investment, driven by migration, thriving on accessible low interest capital, rampant real estate speculation and high levels of immigration. Observed in this way, Melbourne 2016 is more akin to Melbourne 1888 than Melbourne 1956, the year it hosted the Olympics. This makes the postwar period, and especially its end around 1975, a pivot point for describing the transformations between Australian citizenship in the era of strict territoriality (postwar, the Cold War, the Keynesian nation-state) and Melbourne's re-emergence as 'the global city in Border Force's sights in 2015'.[22]

5.4 A tale of two Melbournes, 1975 and 2015: tracing the four decade re-emergence of Melbourne as a global city, via tertiary education

Nineteen seventy-five Melbourne was a continuation of postwar Melbourne, a parochial, insularly Aussie shadow of the heaving, gold-rich, future-facing British Imperial Melbourne of 1875. As Ava Gardner quipped after a spell residing in Melbourne for the filming of *On the Beach* in 1959, Melbourne in those days was 'the perfect place to make a film about the end of the world'. Yet 1975 Melbourne, completely unlike its Victorian ancestor a hundred years prior, was also a city constructed around the nationally defined needs of its Australian citizen residents: in ways no longer possible for all Australians in 2015, and no longer possible *at all* growing numbers of people who live in Australia as of writing. In becoming a global city and onshore space to which logistics and border security are addressed, Melbourne has been transformed into a city which is not 'for' all its people, and can only prosper by fostering relations to the networks and supply chains of global capital, the global locations of routine traffic and secured circulation that its diverse populations are induced to align themselves toward in order to draw a benefit, secure a life, ward off marginalisation, deportation and banishment.

Alongside the construction and boosting of casinos from the early 90s (section 3.11), the *topos* that exemplifies the re-emergence of Melbourne as a global city – imagination, policy, actuality – is the re-making of tertiary education as a mass market, overseas attractor and export product. Tertiary education is a field also integrated into border security via residence and citizenship, both because Border Force regulates the entry and presence of all noncitizen resident populations, and because conducting a mass market that involves international students

22 Two years before the last ship, *Australis* arrived in Melbourne carrying migrants (1977), and the synchronous development of Australia's first refugee policy. See: 'Ships, 1940 – 1970', Museum Victoria. https://museumvictoria.com.au/discoverycentre/websites-mini/journeys-australia/1940s60s/ships-1940s70s/

requires the global city to accommodate and govern noncitizen residents in their hundreds of thousands.

In 1975, the Whitlam Labor government abolished tertiary education fees, removing 'money' as a barrier to university entry *for all citizens.*[23] As Whitlam signalled his government's intention in 1972,"[w]e believe that a student's merit, rather than a parent's wealth, should decide who should benefit from the community's vast financial commitment to tertiary education".[24] The meritocratic opening of tertiary education to all citizens is often cited as the high water mark of social democracy in Australia, yet like Cook's voyages, though on a smaller temporal scale and effective stage, it is of another world – for the following reasons. Universal access on the basis of merit went hand-in-glove with a policy of zero net population growth, 'removing the commitment to expand the immigration program in order to fit immigration needs specific to the capacity of Australia to provide employment, housing, education and social services'.[25] This sat alongside a Keynesian macroeconomic goal of zero unemployment. National goals such as universal access for all eligible citizens on the basis of merit, were thoroughly Keynesian, nationalist and social democratic – synchronous with most countries in the OECD at that time, and completely at odds with contemporary constraints in the wake of four decades of neoliberalisation. In 1975, when Australia's population sat at 13.89 million, there were around 250,000 students attending Australian universities[26] (one person in fifty-five); in 2015, with population sitting at just under 24 million, there were over 1.2 million people enrolled (roughly 800,000 of whom were domestic, one person in thirty). As Australia's population nearly doubled, the tertiary education sector grew nearly fivefold.

To specify this 1975 demographic patterning further, from a civilian population aged fifteen years and over, Australia's 1975 workforce comprised a little less than six million people: 4.36 million of whom were born in Australia, 1.635 million of whom were born outside Australia.[27] Of these, 3.9 million were

23 That is: all citizens *who finished high school*, which effectively excluded the blue collar working class of that time.

24 Knott, Matthew, 'Gough Whitlam's Free University Education Reforms Led to Legacy of No Upfront Fees', *The Sydney Morning Herald*, October 21, 2014. www.smh.com.au/federal-politics/political-news/gough-whitlams-free-university-education-reforms-led-to-legacy-of-no-upfront-fees-20141021-119bws.html

25 Neuman, Klaus, *Across the Seas: Australia's Response to Refugees: a History*, Black Inc, Melbourne, 2015, p. 242.

26 Parr, Nick, 'Who Goes to University? The Changing Profile of Our Students', *The Conversation*, May 25, 2015. http://theconversation.com/who-goes-to-university-the-changing-profile-of-our-students-40373

27 These figures breakdown further, so that of total persons not born in Australia in 1975: 461,700 arrived before 1955; 358,700 thousand arrived between 1955–1961; 334, 600,000 between 1962–1967; 398,100 thousand between 1968–1973, and 82,700 thousand between January 1974–February 1975. Thus in 'the postwar period', Australia was absorbing 60–80 thousand migrants per year, when total population was 13.89 million. These figures can be visualised in relation to Victoria here: 'Victoria's Historic Population Growth:

male, 3.6 million of whom had full-time jobs. Of the 3.9 million males in the 1975 workforce, 890,000 were not in the labour force, but only 144,900 were counted as unemployed, a seasonally adjusted unemployment figure of 3.3%. Of the 4.9 million women aged fifteen and over, a little over two million were in the workforce, 2.8 million out of the workforce, with 1.3 million working full-time jobs, 599,000 in part-time employment and 128,000 unemployed, a seasonally adjusted rate of 5%.[28] Union membership was roughly 50%; average duration of unemployment, about ten weeks.

We have to also consider where and how this 1975 working population lived in pre-global city Melbourne. In 1975, when average full-time earnings were around 8,000 dollars a year,[29] the median house price in Melbourne was 19,800 dollars. A three or four-bedroom freestanding dwelling on a suburban quarter acre (1011 m2) block – synonymous with 'the Australian Dream' – cost a little more than double the annual average wage.[30] But when citizens were still capable of living the Australian Dream without financial strain and cradle-to-grave debt, the housing market was, not coincidentally, not an object of speculation for most 'ordinary Australians'. In 1975, housing was still regarded as a social right, not an individually possessed tradeable commodity valued primarily as an investment for its capital gains. Credit required excellent credentials and substantial savings to access, and mortgage interest rates were around 10%. In 2015, to paint the contrast, average annual earnings sit at around 78,000 (9.7 times higher), while the median house prices in metropolitan and inner Melbourne hover above 725,000 and 1.27 million, respectively[31] – roughly ten and sixteen times the average annual wage. To intensify the contrast further, using the 1975 figures for average earnings and median house price, average residential land was going at roughly $20 per square metre[32] in 1975. By the time of writing, the range within 5km of

Annual Population Growth, Victoria, European Settlement to Present, 1836–2011', *Department of Environment, Land, Water and Planning*. www.dtpli.vic.gov.au/data-and-research/population/presentations-and-bulletins/victorias-historic-population-growth

28 'The Labour Force, February 1975', *Australian Bureau of Statistics*. www.ausstats.abs.gov.au/ausstats/free.nsf/0/BF171A1080225CA2CA2576CC00197D60/$File/62030_02_1975.pdf

29 'Average Weekly Earnings', September Quarter 1975, *Australian Bureau of Statistics*. www.ausstats.abs.gov.au/ausstats/free.nsf/0/5BACEEAF1C7DF296CA25750C00194241/$File/63020_SEP1975.pdf

30 '40 Years of Change: 1975 to Today', *McCrindle*. http://mccrindle.com.au/the-mccrindle-blog/40-years-of-change-1975-to-today

31 Interest rates sit at around 5%. 'Median Prices', *www.reiv.com.au*. www.reiv.com.au/property-data/median-prices

32 Demand for interest-only loans has grown by 80% in the three years to 2015. Frazer, Simon, 'Banks Place Many Interest-Only Home Loan Customers 'at Risk': ASIC Report', *www.abc.net.au*. www.abc.net.au/news/2015-08-20/many-interest-only-home-loan-customers-at-risk/6711784

CBD is 5–10,000 per square metre, though prices well in excess of 10,000 AUD have become common.[33]

Forty years after Whitlam's policy of universal access to tertiary education for all citizens on the basis of merit, tertiary education has become the commodity and service it was designed and promoted to be from the early 90s, and is now global city Melbourne's single largest political economy (this point will be enfolded into this section's 1975–2015 contrast of urban real estate shortly). Tertiary education is no longer 'universally accessible for all citizens regardless of their financial circumstances on the basis of merit', and though subsidised, the Commonwealth government has repeatedly tried to pass legislation enabling it to charge market rates of interest on student debt, in line with 'global best practice'. As with Border Force, Australian tertiary education has become very partial to screening global flows for their observed value as revenue streams.

In the decade between 2005–2015, the component of tertiary education packaged as international education services grew to become Victoria's largest services export industry, with "the onshore component . . . generat(ing) $4.7 billion in services exports for the State. An estimated 30,000 Victorians are employed by the sector",[34] roughly a third of the national estimated total.[35] A university, RMIT, is the CBD's single biggest owner of real estate. By 2015, of the 1.2 million students enrolled[36] in Australian universities, 344,658 of them were enrolled in Victorian institutions, most of which are in Melbourne.

In 1975, very few citizens, let alone noncitizen residents such as international students, lived in what was by this time beginning to be called Melbourne's central business district (the CBD), the heaving centre of 'marvellous Melbourne' in the second half of the nineteenth century. In what will become a key confluence in the following section, by 2015 tertiary education and the global city coincide in Melbourne's CBD, which has been actively re-developed since the early 1990s to accommodate international students, temporary business residents, offshore investors and tourists. CBD resident population increased from 76,000 to 126,000 between 2005–2015, which returns the metropolitan population to Gold Rush levels. As of writing, construction of high-rise CBD residential is

33 In the following reported figures in London's Kensington and Chelsea in 2016 were at a median of 11,000 GBP, or 17,000 AUD. Butterworth, Myra, 'So what's the REAL price of property in the UK? Average is £2,216 per square metre but it's as high as £11,321 in London', *www.dailymail.co.uk*, May 20, 2016. www.dailymail.co.uk/property/article-3599013/Average-price-UK-property-2-216-square-metre-11-321-Kensington.html

34 'Victoria's Future Industries International Education Discussion Paper', *State Government Victoria*. http://yoursay.business.vic.gov.au/futureindustries/application/files/5114/3676/6619/DEDJTR_InternationalEducation_Discussion_Paper.pdf

35 Sydney takes the other third, and the remainder of Australia (six cities, 14.9 million people) the rest.

36 'Record Number of Students in Higher Education in 2015', Department of Education and Training. https://ministers.education.gov.au/birmingham/record-number-students-higher-education-2015

booming, with several hundreds of apartments being added each year. In stark contrast to 1975, most of these dwellings are directed at offshore investors (as investment) and international students (as mid-term accommodation), not local residents (as life-long homes). Rough estimates indicate "13,480 high rise . . . dwellings are in the construction pipeline . . . expected to be completed within the next five years", with the CBD "set to gain the most, adding roughly "6000 dwellings or 44.7 per cent".[37] By 2031, recent projections indicate that Melbourne's current population of 4.4 million will double, to 8.8 million, while tertiary education, which focuses on young people and these offshore markets, is projected to grow by 25% along with "the 18–24 years old population over the next 20 years".[38] In 2016, the hot market of CBD apartment construction and boosting has been observed as a dangerous bubble.[39]

It is *this* Melbourne CBD that Border Force projected its orderly, screened expansion of during *Operation Fortitude*: a global city strategically opened to global investment, that welcomes noncitizen visitors who bring or embody forms of capital recognised as being of value to the Commonwealth, and that routinely regulates and periodically interdicts and ejects others recognised as lacking this.

5.5 "Security from deportation" the instrumental value of contemporary Australian citizenship and the implicit politics of migration ratios

Between 1973–1975, alongside the meritocratic opening of tertiary education to the citizen/high school graduates enclosed within the Australian nation who were eligible to apply for it, the Whitlam government adopted a non-discriminatory approach to migration.[40] As it did so, permanent migration was reoriented away from a setup that courted shiploads of nation-reproducing European bodies, toward family reunion – by plane. In 1977, a year after the first asylum seekers fleeing Vietnam arrived in Darwin Harbour (section 2.5), the Humanitarian Programme was established, along with the distinction between refugees (sourced from the offshore resettlement program) and asylum seekers (directly arriving by

37 'Daily Population Estimates and Forecasts', *City of Melbourne*. www.melbourne.vic.gov.au/about-melbourne/research-and-statistics/pages/daily-population-estimates-and-forecasts.aspx

38 Parr, Nick, 'Who Goes to University? The Changing Profile of Our Students', *The Conversation*, May 25, 2015. http://theconversation.com/who-goes-to-university-the-changing-profile-of-our-students-40373

39 Johanson, Simon, 'Apartment Correction to Cause Australia-Wide Recession: Report Warns', *The Sydney Morning Herald*, September 2, 2016. www.smh.com.au/business/property/apartment-correction-to-cause-australiawide-recession-report-warns-20160902-gr7bce.html

40 Neuman, Klaus, *Across the Seas: Australia's Response to Refugees: a History*, Black Inc, Melbourne, 2015, pp. 240–244.

boat).[41] During the Fraser government's response to Indochinese refugees, 2,059 people arrived by boat, while more than 200,000 were accepted offshore for permanent settlement, and arrived by plane.[42] These numbers should be placed side by side with comparable events discussed in Chapter 3, Mariel 1980 (section 3.9), and the 'years of crisis', 2001 and 2011–2013 (section 2.7–2.9, 3.9).

Between the postwar and the time of writing, the salient transformation between postwar and contemporary Australian migration and citizenship involved a shift from human labour to human capital – with the visa as its pivotal mechanism. From the 'golden soil and wealth for toil' extolled in the '84-onward national anthem *Advance Australia Fair* (section 1.7), toward the bestowal of visas on anyone capable of embodying the forms of capital recognised by the Commonwealth as desirable. Following the severances of Chapter 4 (section 4.6–4.9), we could observe desirable arrivals as embodying or embodied 'legitimate activities'. To parse this transformation on the level of population and its regulation, postwar Australia shifted:

- from a postwar White Australia that wanted *European bodies for their whole lives*, so the nation could expand across the territory,
- to a capitalist Commonwealth that wants *skills for the time in which they remain valuable*: to the nation, in the global city.

This shift from a Commonwealth that desired bodies *en masse*, for life, to one that courts skills in the eye of its own shifting desires shows up very clearly in the Commonwealth's statistics. Consider the increase in total postwar population and the proportion drawn from overseas. Since 1945, "over 7.5 million people have settled" in Australia, and its "overseas-born resident population is . . . estimated to be 28.1 per cent of the population in June 2014".[43] Focusing on this chapter's global city, 34% of Melbourne residents were born overseas, and like exorbitant inner urban real estate prices and gentrification, this is roughly in line with other global cities: New York City is roughly 36%, London 37%, Auckland 39%.[44] In Melbourne, a *further* 20% of people have at least one parent who was

41 Hugo, Graeme, 'From Compassion to Compliance? Trends in Refugee and Humanitarian Migration in Australia', *Geojournal*, 55, 2001, pp. 27–37.

42 Phillips, Melissa and Boese, Martina, 'From White Australia to Stopping the Boats: Attitudes to Asylum Seekers', *The Conversation*, June 21, 2013. http://theconversation.com/from-white-australia-to-stopping-the-boats-attitudes-to-asylum-seekers-15244

43 Phillips, Janet and Simon-Davies, Joanne, 'Migration to Australia: A Quick Guide to the Statistics', *Parliament of Australia*. www.aph.gov.au/About_Parliament/Parliamentary_Departments/Parliamentary_Library/pubs/rp/rp1516/Quick_Guides/MigrationStatistics

44 Ives, Mike, 'New Zealand Property Boom Attracts Overseas Buyers', *New York Times*, May 7, 2015. www.nytimes.com/2015/05/08/greathomesanddestinations/new-zealand-property-boom-attracts-overseas-buyers.html?_r=0 'London: Census Profile', *The Migration Observatory*, May 20, 2013. www.migrationobservatory.ox.ac.uk/briefings/london-census-profile

a migrant:[45]the majority of Melbourne's residents no longer have their lineages purely or in some cases even partially in White Australia.[46] Notably, this ratio is at a 120-year peak, not seen since the Victorian Gold Rush, the last time a large population lived in Melbourne's urban centre.

As introduced earlier (section 5.4), in the four decades between 1975–2015 Australia's population increased by 9.6 million, from 13.9 million to 23.5 million. This tracks approximately with global growth, as world population increased during this time from a little over four to a little over seven billion people. But in Australia's case, increases in migration, not births, have accounted for the largest and fastest growing proportion of the increase during this period. In 1985, net overseas migration accounted for 36.6% of total population growth, which was steady with the 1995 figure of 37.7%. But by 2005 it had reached 49.4%, and by 2015 it was tracking at 55.1%.[47] In the four decades to 2015, 'net overseas migration'[48] increased from 13,515 to 193,100 per annum. By 2015, the majority of Australia's population growth was due to migration, *as* migration itself has increased, *as* it has been directed at global cities.

With these measures and their implied meanings in mind, we have to consider how the semantics of the 'migrant' have been reshaped by the status and ratio of different visa classes within this population of noncitizen arrivals, both permanent and temporary (sections 2.6–2.10, 3.8–3.9). From the mid-80s there has been a shift in the ratio of permanent migrants to Australia: family, skilled and humanitarian. All of these visa categories are capped. This is explicit in the case of skilled permanent, implicit in the case of family (because family reunion is effectively pegged to skilled permanent) and governed via an annual quota, in the case of the humanitarian program. Like the latter, family reunion coincided with the shift toward multiculturalism in Australia. Yet from the political present, with border security's world fully emerged, it is family reunion that appears as a vanishing mediator between the postwar imperative to 'populate and assimilate' and the contemporary migration program's primary focus on skilled and temporary migration.

In the grip of this contemporary focus, the humanitarian program has declined substantially since its inception, just as the intake and proportion of skilled temporary has increased hugely.

- In 1984–1985, there were 44,200 migrants within the family program, 10,100 within skilled and 14,207 within the humanitarian program (68,507).

45 Megalogenis, George, *Australia's Second Chance*, Penguin, 2015, p. x.

46 Huntley, Rebecca, 'How Racist Are We?' in *Still Lucky*, Penguin, Melbourne, 2017, pp. 68–102.

47 Phillips, Janet and Simon-Davies, Joanne, 'Migration to Australia: A Quick Guide to the Statistics', *Parliament of Australia*. www.aph.gov.au/About_Parliament/Parliamentary_Departments/Parliamentary_Library/pubs/rp/rp1516/Quick_Guides/MigrationStatistics

48 Net overseas migration measures departures and arrivals of permanent and temporary entrants, then represents the increase or decrease in the population overall from this.

- In 1994–1995 there were 44,500 family, 30,400 skilled and 14,858 humanitarian (89,758);
- in 2013–14 there were 61,112 family, 128,500 skilled[49] and 13,750 humanitarian (203,362).

During this three decade period, the total population increased by roughly 7 million people, to around 23 million, which means that family migration tracked a little below population growth. In contrast, skilled permanent migrants grew twelvefold as population increased by roughly a third, while Australia's refugee intake remained static at around fourteen thousand, decreasing significantly as a percentage of population.

In the shifting ratio of permanent migrants that took place as border security emerged in Australia we can see policy choices, reflexively made selections, passionately held value commitments – politics. This is worth considering in light of what we've already explored, especially: Howard's publicly disseminated responsiveness to the community feeling that ordinary Australians felt vulnerable about the size of their coastline; in 'years of crisis' in which 5,516 and 5,459 individuals arrived (section 2.8); the phrase 'stop the boats' and its impact on asylum seekers via the policy measures of the 2013 election campaign and *Operation Sovereign Borders* (sections 2.10–2.12, 3.11–3.12); and the expansion and integration of indefinite offshore detention beyond the shores of politics (sections 3.11–3.12). We might also think of all this in relation to the politically un-contentious 'refugees' flown in as part of the humanitarian programs quota, at the rate of 12,000–14,000 a year since 1977.

It's also worth considering the following: a Commonwealth that wished to maintain the humanitarian intake in line with its population growth would have increased the quota above 20,000 per year by the time of writing. Had the many thousands waiting in vain for processing in Indonesia been brought to Australia by plane in this way (homologous to the Fraser government's response to the Indochinese Exodus), this would have deprived Java-based people smugglers of their business model, 'stopped the boats' *and* prevented drowning[50] – without the need for militarised interdiction and indefinite offshore detention (sections i.9–i.10, 2.8, 3.9–3.10). At this point, once again, we hit remonstrations from deterrence and control: counterfactually, this helps isolate the agentic power of a deterrence-led policy and the policy and ethical entailments and societal effects that follow from its predicates (section 2.6–2.8, 3.10). Likewise, an Australia that wished to increase its population through as mass intake of refugees as it did in the postwar period, but with the non-racial predicate supposedly

49 Permanent skilled migration is capped at 180,000 a year. This places a *de facto* artificial cap on family at approximately 60,000 a year, far below actual demand, which means delays getting a family visa as applications above the 60k 1/3rd of the total are rolled over to the following year, and so on.

50 Section 6.4.

instituted with a non-discriminatory immigration policy and a cultural embrace of multiculturalism (1975 onward), could now be welcoming 170,000 refugees per year. The shift in the ratio of skilled, family and humanitarian, alongside the massive increase in overall migration numbers during the years of border security's emergence, implies a whole politics experienced and contested everyday yet seldom expressed in parliamentary politics or by most news media, even though it's indicative of the policy settings and norms that global cities actually live by, and that shape the new logistical horizon of border security and immigration in *The Future of Border Protection* that the Commonwealth is now navigating Australians towards.

In the period of Melbourne's re-emergence as a global city, the most dramatic increase in arrivals skilled *temporary* residents and international students. This impacts on Sydney and Melbourne most, for two reasons. First, these cities are the two places that absorb the greatest proportion – roughly two-thirds – of this nationally counted population, with huge implications for infrastructure, local and state government, and people's place in the city, whether through the direct and pervasive, differential effects of gentrification or through the feeling of being at home in a place one has lived one's whole life. Second, the arrivals have a societal impact, because recursively re-oriented policy settings and other political communication continues to grow in their direction,[51] reaching out and capturing skilled temporary and international students – in the national interest.

Many of these temporary visa categories are courted arrivals, warmly welcomed and incentivised categories of arriving person who sit in an inverse correlation to boat arrivals. In the age of 'stop the boats' – where even one arrival is read as surrender and failure – temporary business and student visa categories are totally uncapped. This resident population moves in and through the city like the consumer objects of global logistics, floating in and out of the areas of Sydney Harbour and Port Phillip Bay on tides of supply, demand and desire. The stable expectation of this inherently fluctuating multiplicity, however, is that they will 'return home' by plane (section 3.11): at some point, in the not too distant future – or apply for PR (permanent residency). Overseas students are one population welcomed and expected on these conditions. In 1996–1997 the number of overseas students in Australia was 113,000, while the number of temporary business (long stay 457) visas was 25,786. In 2014, overseas student visas numbered 292,060 and 457s sat at 98,570. In less than two decades, international students more than doubled, while 457s quadrupled. To specify the relation of these fluctuations with global supply and demand, these numbers are slightly down on the pre-GFC increase between 2004–2005 and 2008–2009, when Australia added more than 140,000 overseas students as numbers grew from 174,786 to 319,632.[52] In that period, 457s doubled from 48,590 to 101,280.

51 Luhmann, Niklas, *Theory of Society, Volume 1*, Stanford University Press, Stanford, 2012, p. 67.

52 'Rudd Welcomes 'Big Australia'', *abc.net.au*, updated October 23, 2009. www.abc.net.au/news/2009-10-23/rudd-welcomes-big-australia/1113752 then Gordon, Josh, 'Rudd flips

To summarise the shift inhering in the avowedly instrumental value of contemporary citizenship and the implicit politics of migration ratios: like Sydney, Melbourne's re-emergence as a global city is about two policy-led demographic changes and the urban dynamic they engender. The first of these is the dramatic and decisive move from family reunion to the expansion of skilled business migration indicated by the ratio within permanent migration,[53] with the humanitarian program as a static orphan witnessing this while patiently queueing in the annual steady quota. This also helps us isolate the longer temporality of the shift from 'postwar bodies for the nation' to 'skilled residents in the global city' (section 5.4).

The second policy-led shift is indicated by the rise of the temporary residents just detailed: during the decades when the Commonwealth began to stop the boats, international students more than doubled and 457s quadrupled. The majority of these new residents were absorbed by Sydney and Melbourne, whose population growth, as mentioned, is now majority driven by net overseas migration and the attendant expansion of economies servicing these populations, side by side with their longstanding residents.[54] For local residents with access to sufficient capital to risk investing in expanding business and real estate opportunities, this has been an enormous opportunity for prosperity and a driver of gentrification; for locals without access to substantial amounts of capital at relatively low interest, and large numbers of people who can't hold on to their neighbourhoods as rents increase and the provision of social housing and affordable declines,[55] these very same processes *mean* marginalisation and poverty, in ways that would most likely be of grave concern to Melbourne in 1975 and 1901, but that are analogous to the worldmaking expropriations of the period of conquest.[56]

5.6 Who is Australia for? Observing the meaning of contemporary citizenship through the rise of the SIV and PIV in the wake of SIEVs and SUNCs

Considering this gloss on demographic and migration policy factors in relation to citizenship and border security, a clear sense emerges of who Australia and its

on 'big Australia'", *abc.net.au*, April 4, 2010. www.smh.com.au/national/rudd-flips-on-big-australia-20100403-rkvo.html

53 As family reunion increased by a third from 44–61,000, skilled business quadrupled from 30–128,000 while humanitarian declined from 14–13,000.

54 Sydney and Melbourne are Australia's two demographic centres. With slightly more and slightly less than 20% of Australia's total population living in each, their combined population accounts for slightly less than 40% of the total – yet they absorb around 66% of migration.

55 Skelton, Russell, 'Massive Decline in Affordable Housing Adding to Number of Homeless in Melbourne', *www.abc.net.au*, Updated October 19, 2016. www.abc.net.au/news/2016-10-19/affordable-housing-decline-adds-melbourne's-homeless/7946800

56 Hobsbawm, Eric, *The Age of Capital: 1848–1975*, Abacus, London, 1975, pp. 143–294.

global cities have been designed for, and the differential effects that state who can enter, live and stay in them. If you:

- are a tourist or a temporary business or student resident, come as you wish, hopefully with your millions, and invest in property.
- are skilled and wish to stay permanently, come in your hundreds of thousands, and pay to apply to bring your families.[57]
- are a processed UN-definitional refugee from a distant camp, come by plane as part of the annual quota, or do not arrive.
- come by plane on a tourist visa *then* claim asylum, please fill in this form and we will add you to the annual quota.
- are an asylum seeker attempting to arrive by boat, go back to where you came from, or we will detain you until you 'take the package' (section 6.4) that means you agree to be sent there – and 'you will never see the shores of Australia' (section 3.5).

Apprehending the social sorting effects generated by these policy settings gives a clearer sense of the differential beneficiaries intentionally produced in the course of securing circulation through immigration policy, and the global class relations worked out, reinforced and enforced in the process. It also discloses aspects of Border Force's logistical norms and goals: a key task of Australian government at all scales involves using the global city as an attractor-destination for capital *while* the using border security to screen out those considered of no use or value within this normative order – as authorised arrivals expand (section 4.6, 4.9). This returns us to the question of the place and meaning of the 'undeportable, unshippable, undetainable' – the citizen – in all of this.

Points covered in the previous section indicate that a contemporary citizen is a person defined by their relation to mobility and states. More precisely, 'an Australian citizen in 2015' is a person who is undeportable from an Australia they can securely return to after freely departing from by plane, and who can choose to live in any of its locations, subject to their ability to afford Australian real estate within commutable distance of places of employment. Citizenship forms a fixed address a citizen relies on as somewhere to depart freely from and return safely to. Contemporary citizenship is a differential mechanism that secures the un-deportable international mobility of permanent residents and citizens *by* screening the attempted international mobility of deportable, temporary others. Like maritime interdiction, this performs the following triplet of co-enabling functions (section 3.12). It co-produces:

- deportable people (a durable, legally embedded process of social sorting),
- authorised deporters (authorised social sorters attached to institutions),
- a secured population (a 'jet civis' enjoying seamless mobility [section I.9]).

57 $6,865 (AUD) base application charge, $3,435 per additional application 18+, $1,720 per application <18 years. See: 'Fees and Charges for Visas', *Department of Immigration and Border Protection*. www.border.gov.au/Trav/Visa/Fees

If logistics is about effectuating the smooth, rapid movement of people and things between precise, secured locations, then citizenship's enmeshment in logistics via border security can be described as its transitive technology of privileged human mobilisation.

Expressed in its contemporary governmental language, the value of Australian citizenship is as follows: "[t]he instrumental advantages of citizenship for migrants are security from deportation, an Australian passport and eligibility for permanent government employment (including in the armed services)".[58] To redescribe this in the critical theoretical language developed in *Border Security*, citizenship is a governmental mechanism that pivots around deportation, silently presupposing a world of locations and agents of states regulating the porting between them as the unexplicated background of operations.

The 'common ground' of contemporary Australian citizenship is deportation.[59] This is a general condition of the political present, and should give us pause to consider what citizenship actually means, outside its ideological loadings and relation to belonging and cultural memory. Contemporary nationality 'belongs' elsewhere, and is not meaningful in the way many Australian citizens suppose. It's worth placing the recentness of this occluded social fact side by side with its incommensurable yet adjacent imperial past, and the open political meaning of indigeneity 'in Australia', just as it makes understanding the resonance and dissonance of militarist nationalism in the contemporary Australia of global logistics, global cities, mass migration, multiculturalism and endless GDP growth all the more vital.

The co-relation between contemporary Australian citizenship and the capital-aligned state brings us to the following description. An Australian is someone who continually works and pays in order to remain freely within the economy and the national infrastructure – including the border continuum – that supports their life, and whose expansion secures their future as a return on an investment. These relations are liberated from the normative loadings of shackles and ships past: no one need be of a certain race or skin tone, loyal to a queen, prepared to die in a war, pass a dictation test,[60] have citizen parents who gave birth onshore or even speak English. Contemporary Australian citizenship is unencumbered by the discriminatory practices Australian identity still contends with as the weight of its past. But to someone from White Australia – whether in 1901 or in 1975 – contemporary citizenship might seem a coldly instrumental thing, like the ring of steel that supports it, the disquieting vision of a society fully integrated into

58 Klapdor, Michael, Coombs, Moira and Bohm, Catherine, 'Australian Citizenship: A Chronology of Major Developments in Policy and Law', *Parliament of Australia*, September 11, 2009. www.aph.gov.au/About_Parliament/Parliamentary_Departments/Parliamentary_Library/pubs/BN/0910/AustCitizenship

59 The claim has a general applicability, though with all due caution: US, Israeli, Japanese and French citizenship all have their specificity, tying them in to a people, a book, revolutions and empires.

60 Under the White Australia policy, noncitizens were required to pass a dictation test in a European language *randomly chosen* by a migration officer.

secured circulation that has abandoned the communal treasure gained through the sacrifices and exposure to injury, where stories told in a certain accent could be transformed into life-and-death meanings, beating a unity out of the actual and imagined sharing of vulnerability. When sovereigns issued the death command, they also provided subsidised housing to veterans who survived the battlefield. In the contemporary period, all such conditions have been rendered conditional and transient.

With the development of the Significant Investor Visa (SIV) and Premium Investor Visa (PIV), the Commonwealth has elevated the pathway to permanent residence and citizenship into a realm beyond any risk of the sacrifices and exposure expected in earlier communities of unified national citizens and loyal imperial subjects. The SIV, introduced on November 24, 2012, was developed by the Commonwealth to attract High Net Worth Individuals (HNWIs) and their skills, networks and capital to Australia with the lure of a smoothed pathway to permanent residency. As an SIV applicant, deposit five million in government-selected investments and you're guaranteed permanent residency in four years. On May 17, 2013, one day after the Commonwealth passed legislation to excise the mainland from the Migration Zone, the first HNWI-cum-SIV, a Chinese toy manufacturer "who invested $5 million in Victorian state government bonds"[61] had his passport stamped with the new visa.

Between its introduction and July 15, 2015, there were reported to be 1,679 SIV applications, 90%Chinese, "mainly looking at NSW and Victoria".[62] As the majority of applicants become residents in Sydney and Melbourne, they become human locations in the traffic of the global city, secured nodal points freely in circulation, encouraged to relax and enjoy the events and lifestyles on offer, with this future guaranteed for their children, in an era when the atmospheres of Beijing and Shanghai are dangerous to breathe, or in case things suddenly turn nasty back home. The SIV is about bringing the HNWI and their offshore capital onshore into the global city, *with the promise of protection* from *sylon* (section 3.3, 6.6) – including by Border Force, whose staff will wave them through. Through the SIV, the Commonwealth is effectively granting asylum to the very rich, in exchange for money. This complicates any condemnation of people smuggling on moral grounds.

On July 1, 2015, on the same day that the Liberal Party announced a 'new era in border protection' with the inception of Border Force, the Premium Investor Visa (PIV) was added. The PIV is an invitation-only visa class targeted at

61 Since its introduction the mandated investment in bonds has been lifted and applicants are now less restricted in what and where they can invest. See: Bleby, Michael, 'Australia's First 888 Visa Investor Gets Passport Stamp', *Australian Financial Review*, May 16, 2013. www.afr.com/it-pro/australias-first-888-visa-investor-gets-passport-stamp-20130515-jyi0p

62 Reynolds, Emma, 'Will Rich Entrepreneurs Pay $15m to Get Australian citizenship?' *news.com.au*, July 14, 2015. www.news.com.au/finance/business/other-industries/will-rich-entrepreneurs-pay-15m-to-get-australian-citizenship/news-story/83c7e1e75eba0601ff9060dfe8ec90ba

'talented innovators and entrepreneurs', curated by Austrade as the sole nominator. Upon receipt of an invitation, prospective applicants are asked to invest 15 million (AUD) in exchange for permanent residency in one year, with a simplified application process. In its initial phase, Austrade are addressing invitations to American entrepreneurs in biotech, ICT and venture capital. What then is Australia, what is the value of its citizenship? Who and what are its global cities for? And what happens when Border Force enters it?

5.7 "Absolute, perfect, legitimate sense": the *Operation Fortitude* media release

At around 10am on Friday, August 28, 2015, 180 years after Melbourne's founding and precisely fourteen years after the tensest day of the Tampa Affair, a junior media officer working for Border Force posted the following media release on newsroom.border.gov.au:

5.7a ABF joining inter-agency outfit to target crime in Melbourne CBD

> This weekend Australian Border Force (ABF) officers will for the first time join forces with a diverse team of transport and enforcement agencies to target crime in the Melbourne Central Business District (CBD) as part of Operation Fortitude.
>
> Tonight and tomorrow evening (Friday 28 and Saturday 29 August 2015) Metro Trains, Yarra Trams, the Sheriff's Office, Taxi Services Commission and the ABF will join Victoria Police as part of the inter-agency operation.
>
> With a particular focus on people travelling to, from and around the CBD, the group of agencies will work together to support the best interests of Melbournians, targeting everything from anti-social behaviour to outstanding warrants.
>
> ABF Regional Commander Victoria and Tasmania, Don Smith, is proud the ABF will be participating in the operation.
>
> "While the ABF regularly conducts a range of compliance field-work, this is the first time we've been involved in an inter-agency operation of this nature and we're very proud be able to support each of our organisations to achieve our common mission of promoting a secure and cohesive society here in Melbourne."
>
> "ABF officers will be positioned at various locations around the CBD speaking with any individual we cross paths with," Mr Smith said.
>
> "You need to be aware of the conditions of your visa; if you commit visa fraud you should know it's only a matter of time before you're caught out."
>
> The inter-agency outfit will continue to work together on an ongoing basis to target crime in and around the Melbourne CBD to make the city a safer place for everyone.

5.7b Media opportunity

Operation Fortitude will be launched by representatives from each participating agency at 2pm today (Friday 28 August 2015) on the steps of Flinders Street Railway Station.

5.7c Media enquiries

Immigration and Border Protection Media (02) 6264 2244

By 11.30am, Twitter and Facebook were humming with protest posts, with a number of memes creatively expressing outrage, derision and scorn.[63] By around midday, news media and protest groups began to organise, while emails and instant messages percolated through the screened interfaces of the nation.

By 1.30pm, hundreds of protesters, dozens of police and clumps of news crews were assembled on Flinders St Steps, where a demonstration had just begun. By 2.30pm, officials from all the participating agencies were trapped in the police box just behind the ticket gates at Flinders St Station – the box they were supposed to emerge from to launch the Operation. At around 3pm – five or so hours after the media release had been posted, and two hours before it had been due to begin – *Operation Fortitude* was cancelled.

By 6pm, TV news coverage were framing the aborted Operation for evening free-to-air viewers as an 'embarrassing blackflip' caused by 'public backlash'. Even Socialist Alliance received neutral to favourable coverage. In some reports demonstrators were framed as heroic defenders of democracy, with only minor mention of the typical Murdoch framings 'disrupted traffic' and 'turned violent'. By the following morning across most news media, the hangover interpretation was that *Operation Fortitude* was most probably an untimely April Fools caused by some combination of stupidity, ineptitude and poor judgment that time and careful scrutiny would surely reveal.[64]

63 Schetzer, Alana, 'Border Force: Melburnians fight visa checks with memes', *The Age*, August 28, 2015. www.theage.com.au/victoria/border-force-melburnians-fight-visa-checks-with-memes-20150828-gja2b0.html and Groom, Nelson, 'Social Media Lights Up After the ABF Announces Plan to Carry Out Random Visa Checks on Melbourne Streets – Only to Cancel Operation Fortitude in the Wake of the Backlash', *Daily Mail Australia*. www.dailymail.co.uk/news/article-3213958/Social-media-lights-ADF-plans-carry-random-visa-checks.html

64 Mackenzie-Murray, Martin, 'Inside Border Force's Power', *The Saturday Paper*, September 5, 2015. www.thesaturdaypaper.com.au/news/immigration/2015/09/05/inside-border-forces-power/, Price, Jenna, 'Border Force's Operation Fortitude Was Beyond the Pale', *The Sydney Morning Herald*, August 31, 2015. www.smh.com.au/comment/border-forces-operation-fortitude-was-beyond-the-pale-20150831-gjbekz.html and Finnane, Mark, 'The Border Is Everywhere: The Policy Overreach Behind Operation Fortitude', *The Conversation*, August 31, 2015. http://theconversation.com/the-border-is-everywhere-the-policy-overreach-behind-operation-fortitude-46860

Yet how could this be known when no one appeared to confess, concede or take responsibility? ABF Regional Commander Don Smith, earlier quoted in the media release as 'proud to be participating in the operation', was seemingly not available for comment, based on his notable absence in the aftermath's widely sought clarifications and speculative justifications. Perhaps he was among those trapped inside the police box inside Flinders St Station? Echoing the norm established by Mr Morrison's weekly *Operation Sovereign Borders* briefings, spokesperson for the Minister for Immigration and Border Protection said only that Mr Peter Dutton "did not direct operational matters". *Operation Fortitude*'s many parents looked proudly forward to its arrival – then promptly orphaned it, the moment it proved an embarrassing failure (section 4.5).

The only spokesperson who appeared to explain the release was ABF's very broad shouldered Commissioner, Roman Quaedvleig, whose lunchtime doorstop – from 660km away in Canberra on the Friday of the Operation's launch – was the closest thing to an explanation offered by a senior Border Force official:

> Taken into context, it makes absolute, perfect, legitimate sense. But read through the layperson's eyes – which I absolutely openly acknowledge – it's clumsily worded and it's been misconstrued and it shouldn't have been worded that way.[65]

How should the media release be construed? Let's develop Mr Quaedvleig's comment by attending to the distinction he draws between contexts and the shifting position of the observer. On the one hand, there is a context in which the release makes absolute, perfect, legitimate sense. On the other hand, there is a context – which Quaedvleig describes via the layperson's reading eyes – in which the media release 'should have been worded differently'. The evaluation Quaedvleig's offers in his comment indicates that he knows both contexts well, and he's expert enough to read and judge that the media release makes perfect sense when read in one of them, as he's able to do. Let's call 'perfect sense' Quaedvleig refers to 'the expert context', making the assumption that it's an intra-operational perspective, which explains why Mr Dutton will not comment on it.

Quaedvleig concedes that, from the lay observer's position, the media release's expert-visible perfect sense is "clumsily worded", which he offers is why it has "been misconstrued": an awkwardness of expression generated problems of interpretation, and now the mechanics and semantics are off. Yet if you were aware of the context – like him – *you would know* the perfect sense it made, in the same way that contemporary Australians know of a viable context, existing on both sides of Bass Strait, in which the duck-billed platypus is a credible monotreme, and

65 'Statement by ABF Commissioner Roman Quaedvlieg on the ABF's Role in Operation Fortitude', *Border Force Newsroom*. http://newsroom.border.gov.au/releases/statement-by-abf-commissioner-roman-quaedvlieg-on-the-abf-s-role-in-operation-fortitude?mode=print

not the elaborate hoax it appeared when its seeming smile and poisonous spurs confronted Dr George Shaw in 1799.

Some journalists quickly read the media release as a surreal stuff up, and some publics responded with Internet memes and hashtagged barbs.[66] Other publics who assembled to protest in person carried placards reading 'Border Farce' and 'we experience racism every day', representing *Operation Fortitude* as a racist assault on liberal democracy in multicultural Australia. Some among these hundreds of protesters carried placards with crossed out swastikas referring to the Gestapo, perhaps gesturing toward the tendency of authoritarian regimes who govern using physical violence and racism to pick out and pick on vulnerable minorities, especially by a prominent 'show of force', especially on the streets of the city. The interpretation among these critical responses was also clear and consistent in its identification of racial profiling as the key street level tactic. In varying yet definite ways, the responses intuited that in a compact, crowded urban area through which 850,000 or so daily residents circulate, *Operation Fortitude* would have to be *about* racial profiling.

Information recovered from the observability of the expert context that Quaedvleig knows can be read as implying that the protesters were misguided: '*Fortitude* isn't racist, it's been misunderstood, and if the release had been worded differently, broader publics would have been able to know this'. But in the absence of a re-published, well-worded version of the release, this is something publics can only know if they read the artefact *Fortitude* left behind from the expert context in which it made this perfect sense – and this context is not readable "through the layperson's eyes". Just as Morrison's spokesperson announced that the minister had nothing to announce about this off-water operational matter, Quaedvleig was saying that there is an expert context within a media release – a piece of communication *intended for public dissemination* – that the public *cannot* read (section 2.2–2.3). With this in mind and what we've already explored by way of on-water operational matters, Quaedvleig's comment nonetheless offers us something indicative about border security's severances and world (section I.2): something that we've already encountered, but that shifted valence once more as it was re-positioned at the central public transport terminus of global city Melbourne.

'The people' *cannot* observe operational matters; 'the public' *cannot* see border security; the Minister *cannot* 'comment on operational matters'. With these observations we return to a central paradox encountered repeatedly in *Border Security*: border security's key (anti)political move is to keep placing operations beyond the shores of politics (section I.3). This is as operationally necessary when Border Force enters the city as when it interdicts in the Indian Ocean. But the global city is not the open ocean. In a densely populated, privileged site of intense public display, deliberation and resistance – which, moreover,

66 'Melbourne vs #Borderfarce', www.counteract.org. http://counteract.org.au/melbourne-vs-borderfarce/

the *Operation* sought to appropriate and leverage as a proud display of its new powers – *Operation Fortitude*'s political nature was immediately recognisable by large numbers of laypeople as a slightly grotesque and surreal thing. When the generated effects of the ordinary meanings read from the media release rendered the political nature of border security undeniable within a matter of hours – 'you are proudly announcing that your agents are intending to enter our city and racially profile the travelling public en masse?' – the *Operation* had to be cancelled. The audacity of *Operation Fortitude* was that it involved making the entirety of the CBD racially observable for border security purposes; the stupidity of *Operation Fortitude* was that its organisers didn't see the conspicuousness of this as obvious.

5.8 Concluding corollaries: criminals without justice and law, the 'violators' servicing circulation and the unravelling of *Operation Sovereign Borders*

The media release imbues *Operation Fortitude* with deep meaning by reference to high normative ideals. These are communicated as being *about* an empowered group, a group agent on a 'crime fighting mission'. Given that criminal law conventionally attributes criminal responsibility to individuals for acts they knowingly committed (or negligently omitted), on an operational and imaginary level this means:

- (good) groups collaborating to unify and face off against
- (bad) individuals.

Crucially, the collaborating groups are granted powers by the Commonwealth that many of the (bad) individuals cannot contest in the moment, nor contend with politically without facing deportation, nor protest legally, having been deported or detained offshore. Seen in this way, *Fortitude* empowered a group agent from Border Force's world to observe the city in the name of the nation, in order to:

- dominate individuals as categories of person;
- in ways that linked their presence in the city to crime; and
- empowered agents to work together to identify, check and detain them,
- in the name of the community and its safety.

Interestingly, this implies the attribution of criminal-like meaning to individuals, not actions; its routine and normal use would then bring forth the possibility of criminal beings prosecuted in the absence of the modern constraints of criminal law and political justice. *Operation Fortitude* opens onto a dystopian horizon at whose limit we can see a society capable of observing crime without law or justice.

In the media release, *Fortitude* is represented as contributing toward the realisation of a vision that involves 'working together to support the best interests of Melburnians' in order to promote "a secure and cohesive society". The consonance of this assertion can be read in relation to the theorisation of securing circulation developed in the introduction (section I.11) and pursued throughout *Border Security*. Since July 2015 the Border Force Act has given Customs new powers, equipment, uniforms and a broader, 'higher' purpose. But even in its new guise, ABF's broadened mission is not to 'target crime', but rather "[t]o protect Australia's border and manage the movement of people and goods *across* it".[67] The disjuncture between the high norms of its avowed societal mission, the workaday 'sniffer dog' banality of old-fashioned Customs work, and the dissonant effect that the media release itself secretes help us say more clearly what was conjuncturally specific *and* culturally peculiar about *Fortitude*.

Like receiving an invitation from Austrade to apply for a Premium Investor Visa, *Operation Fortitude* is something was only legally possible *from* July 1, 2015. But the style of declarative brazenness and self-sabotaging stupidity it was criticised for by protesting publics *seem* less likely since the (as of writing) current Prime Minister assumed office, on September 15, 2015, only a couple of weeks after the operation. I mention this not to praise Mr Turnbull, but to emphasise the time-sensitive specificity of the operation. In between *Fortitude* and the overthrow of the self-described 'stop the boats' Prime Minister, Tony Abbott, the photograph of a small, drowned boy on a beach, Aylan Kurdi, appeared, on September 2, 2015. A week after this photograph resonated throughout the mass mediated world, Australia committed to accepting twelve thousand Syrian refugees above the annual humanitarian intake – *and* expanded its aerial bombardment of Syria.[68] None of these events are factors that indicate that *Operation Fortitude* wouldn't have happened in some way at some point. Simultaneously, that it did *as it did* – through a media release whose authorising authors were unable to hear the bum notes that drew such an acute public wince – are highly characteristic of a surreal cultural moment of Australia in 2015 under the Abbott government.[69] In a very precise way, there were only seventy-six days in which *Operation Fortitude* was very likely to have happened exactly as it did. In this sense, *Fortitude* remains located where it was: fourteen years to the day after the

67 'Protecting Our Borders', *Australian Border Force*. www.border.gov.au/australian-border-force-abf/protecting

68 Henderson, Anna and Borello, Eliza, 'Australia Confirms Air Strikes in Syria, Announces Additional 12,000 Refugee Places', *www.abc.net.au*, September 9, 2015. www.abc.net.au/news/2015-09-09/australia-to-accept-additional-12,000-syrian-refugees/6760386

69 'Tony Abbott Eats a Raw Onion', *The Guardian*, March 13, 2015. www.theguardian.com/australia-news/2015/mar/13/tony-abbott-eats-raw-onion; www.news.com.au/entertainment/tv/john-olivers-hilarious-reaction-to-tony-abbott-eating-a-raw-unpeeled-onion/news-story/14f6fdbabb59ce1ac21232193a37cb9f and Williams, Evan, *Australian Leader Eats Raw Onion Whole: Headlines From the Government That Broke Satire*, Black Inc, Melbourne, 2015.

peak of the Tampa Affair; the intended apotheosis and the tragicomic unravelling of the *Operation Sovereign Borders* moment and its border security booster government.[70]

"You should know it's only a matter of time before you're caught out" is also connected to the political economy of any and all global cities whose growth and prosperity, like Melbourne's, have become structurally dependent on the provision of educational services and investment real estate to noncitizen residents. Working in the shadows of the CBD skyscrapers whose upper floors looked down on Flinders St that afternoon were hundreds of thousands of people, working: off the books, below minimum wage, in exploitative conditions. This is something new and disquieting in the city where the eight-hour working day was first won, in 1856, as well as the longstanding traditions of high minimum wages and no tipping. Many among the precarious populations of global city Melbourne are in violation of their visas *because* they work off the books, which they do because the conditions of their visas prohibit or limit authorised employment. But, in Australia as anywhere, this is integral work in the global city, just like banking, finance, real estate, education services and hedonism. The 'violators' prepare food and provide sexual services for local business people; they wait the tables of citizen students and wash the dishes of wealthy tourists; they clean the offices leased by multinational corporations where 'skilled temporaries' work alongside people with PR, and citizens.

That such street, basement, laneway and shadow economies – working quietly below the gleam of cleaned offices – is done off the books by noncitizens greatly increases the likelihood of illegal pay and exploitative conditions: basic matters of justice in a society where justice as fairness, the fair go, is still a widely held norm. *Fortitude* not only declared an intention to police individuals forced to work within these systemically exploitative constraints, it loaded petty compliance work with strong value judgments and stern criticism – as a way of making this work more meaningful to its targeting agents *and* more frightening to its target objects. The junior media officer who wrote the release may have had a tin ear, and their supervisor might have merely glanced at the email on their smartphone before replying with something like 'yep, that looks okay, send it out', but *Operation Fortitude* couldn't *not* have been designed to be addressed in some way to these many vulnerable locations within the global city. That the Operation was to 'target individuals' also draws focus away from whole industries working all over the city that are structurally reliant on exploitative conditions for profitability within their business models, which everyday life in the global city is now factoring in and accommodating itself to as the new normal, whether via 'disruptive' transport technologies like Uber and Deliveroo, or the suburban ubiquity of

70 Levy, Megan and Cox, Lisa, 'Prince Philip Awarded Knight of the Order of Australia by Prime Minister Tony Abbott', *The Sydney Morning Herald*, January 26, 2015. www.smh.com.au/federal-politics/political-news/prince-philip-awarded-knight-of-the-order-of-australia-by-prime-minister-tony-abbott-20150125–12xzk8.html

shady Thai 'massage' parlours. Two days after the Operation, a journalistic investigation revealed that 'dodgy bookkeeping, blackmail and mass underpayment' were systemic conditions faced by Melbourne employees of 7 Eleven.[71]

For many people working for these shadow economies and shady employers who became aware of its communicated intent, *Fortitude* must have seemed something imposed upon Melbourne from Canberra with no understanding of the actual conditions confronting the many classes of noncitizens, the several hundred thousand denizens who service circulation in the global city. As a strange effect of what was on its own terms a way of re-naturalising the city for the nation, *Operation Fortitude*'s aborted entry into the global city showed Border Force up as something alien and hostile, an out of touch otherness that landed in Melbourne. Border Force is a foreign country; they do things differently there.

71 Ferguson, Adele and Toft, Klaus, '7-Eleven: The Price of Convenience', *ABC 4 Corners*, September 30, 2015. www.abc.net.au/4corners/stories/2015/08/30/4301164.htm

Conclusion

Resistance against border security's world, horizons of justice beyond it

6.1 Summary of argument

In *Border Security* I examined how an improbable set of measures surfaced in society, emanating from Australia, creating border security's world, which is now an export policy model selectively migrating back to Europe and North America. Over the course of the book's chapters, I've explored how, via the continual co-presence of the threat environment, the arrival of threats from global space and the background ideal of secured circulation, border security emerged as a unilateral projection of national sovereignty in global space.

1 **as sovereignty:** border security relies on seeing vulnerable people seeking protection aboard boats as threats to the landed life of the nation. This has produced the operational necessity of observing human threat objects *who cannot be* eliminated *and must be* cared for, eventually filling vast maritime spaces with Australia's national sovereignty, in jurisdictions where it is and is not.
2 **as communication:** border security emerged in society as the message of border security as the sovereign right of the nation's spokespersons to decide who can arrive and now, and the communicated cultural ideal of deterrence and control: no way. Through the process of societal integration, onshore contestation about border security has reached the point where, by *Operation Sovereign Borders*, on-water operational matters *cannot* be discussed in public, placing border security's actions beyond the shores of politics, burying operations as unobservable critical national infrastructure: beneath contention, beyond critical regard.
3 **as offshore:** border security relies on the use of offshore's paradoxical form for the production of offshoring effects, circumventions within circulation that impose domination – on regional neighbours and asylum seekers. US Caribbean innovations revealed that maritime interdiction and offshore detention arose after a shift toward deterrence, which co-produced figures of rightfully harsh treatment, such as the 'illegal', and categories of warehouse-able person, such as the 'Cuban-Haitian entrant' and 'offshore entry person'. Offshore detention is the negation of asylum, and processing sites such

as Guantánamo, Christmas Island, Manus Island and Nauru are colonies of border security's world, *statifications* whose careful designs, like the irony of the phrase 'safe haven', reveal dystopian negatives, places beyond *sylon* – the 'haven' is a common utopia of global justice in the political present.

4 **as logistics:** border security is aligned with the *global* normative order of logistics, which as the technical art and science of getting things exactly where and when they need to be, *sans frontiers*, appears to be the opposite of a *national* political project of screening, impedance, stoppage, interdiction, nonarrival. Through Border Force's normative alignment with the goals and ideals of global logistics, undertaken reflexively by its human leaders during an integration process that has seen the promotion of customs over immigration and the paramilitarisation of Border Force, border security's third decade of Australian operations has been set up to serve the systemic necessity of maintaining seamlessly smooth circulation. This means that border security's projection of sovereignty, its message and its offshoring practices are no longer about living humans or legal persons, in turn revealing a future vision very partial to revenue but operationally unable to observe ecological catastrophe as crossing or risk, within the border continuum.

5 **as a matter of citizenship:** the message of border security is also addressed to key publics residing onshore in Australia's global cities. Global cities are the privileged addresses and addressees where the goods of global logistics are to be delivered, its successful residents are the greatest beneficiaries of secured circulation, and its CBDs are the spaces and places enjoying the highest value within the evaluative hierarchies underpinning Border Force's global logistical alignment. And yet, by glossing the demographic history of Melbourne's populations, their transformation from imperial subjects into national citizens and residents, and the extraordinary diversity, dependencies and unruliness this has produced in Melbourne's four-decade re-emergence as a global city, the entry of border security's world into the city, via *Operation Fortitude*, revealed Border Force as a foreign entity whose unwelcome advances had no rightful place among most of the peoples of the *polis*.

6.2 Sovereignty: authority over security objects, responsibility for vulnerable people

On December 15, 2010, a vessel observed by Border Protection Command[1] as SIEV 221 crashed into the rocks at Rocky Point, CI. In the language of the internal report, SIEV 221 was an 'unalerted and unattributed' vessel,[2] a total failure

1 Maritime Border Command was Border Protection Command (BPC) from 2006 until 2013.

2 On SIEV 221, see: 'Christmas Island Sinking of SIEV221 Class Action', *Supreme Court of New South Wales*. www.supremecourt.justice.nsw.gov.au/Pages/sco2_classaction/christmas_island.aspx Hope, Alistair, 'Christmas Island Findings', *Coroner's Court of Western Australia*, 2012. www.coronerscourt.wa.gov.au/_files/christmas_island_findings.pdf

of surveillance, interdiction and deterrence and the breakdown of the sovereign vision of border security later projected in the 'No Way' campaign (section 2.2). Operative paradoxes of offshore excised places notwithstanding (section 3.2), in a tragic sense, SIEV 221 actually arrived 'in' Australia in a way that few 'arrivals' do – because they are prevented from doing so. SIEV 221 struck the territory of Australia that border security works hard to deny asylum seekers, with Christmas Islanders and government employees watching, some trying to assist, as people drowned in front of them. SIEV 221 was in this sense a sovereign shipwreck, insofar as it involved the direct impact of Indonesian hull and Iraqi bodies on the rocks of the territory of Australia, eventuating in the drowning of fifty asylum seekers in Australian waters. The Christmas Island Shipwreck was Australia's worst peacetime maritime disaster in over a century.

On June 17, 2014, eight plaintiffs, relatives of SIEV 221 victims living in Australia, lodged a class action on the matter, suing the Commonwealth government for negligence. The pleadings and particulars allege that the Commonwealth "is liable in negligence and/or breach of statutory duty for:

a failure to have any, or alternatively, adequate search and rescue capabilities or capacity, including adequate systems, personnel and/or equipment to assess, detect, detain or rescue maritime arrivals at Christmas Island, as required;
b failure to have adequate systems, including chain of command, personnel and/or equipment to avert the disaster or effect a rescue of persons on SIEV 221 in a timely manner; and/or
c failure in its duty(s) as owner of the vessel, SIEV 221, arising by way of automatic ownership of the vessel upon entry into Australian territorial waters.[3]

In light of what has been developed throughout *Border Security*, and especially in Chapter 1's consideration of national sovereignty, the class action raises anew the side of the boundary left unmarked by security operations,[4] re-exposing the vulnerability of humans in the water and the Commonwealth's need to take

Chambers, Peter, 'Shipwreck With Spectator: Snapshots of Border Security in Australia', *Global Change, Peace and Security*, 26: 1, pp. 97–112, Marr, David, 'Sifting Through the Wreckage', *The Sydney Morning Herald*, December 3, 2011. www.smh.com.au/national/sifting-through-the-wreckage-20111202-1obnx.html and 'SIEV 221 Internal Review', *Australian Customs and Border Protection Service*, 2010. www.border.gov.au/ReportsandPublications/Documents/reviews-and-inquiries/110124CustomsInternalReview.pdf

3 'Statement of Claim, Christmas Island Sinking', *Supreme Court of New South Wales*. www.supremecourt.justice.nsw.gov.au/Documents/Class%20Actions/Christmas%20Island%20Sinking%20-%20Ibrahimi/christmas_island_statementofclaim_161213.pdf

4 "All negation accordingly potentialises what it explicitly negates, and preserves it, hence reestablishing the unmarked space into which every operation, including the negating operation, etches itself through a distinction", Luhmann, Niklas, *Theory of Society, Volume 1*, Stanford University Press, Stanford, 2012, p. 21.

responsibility for the lives of those it exercises authority over (sections 1.11–1.12). As the statement of claim details:

> At all material times the Defendant had the care, custody and responsibility for administering the *Migration Act 1958 (Cth)* in the area, being the land mass known as Australia as well as its external islands and/or territories, and which included:
>
> (i) between the baseline of its territorial sea as defined in the Seas and Submerged Lands Act 1973 and:
>
> (a) The contiguous zone; or
> (b) alternatively, the territorial waters; and
>
> (ii) any waters on the land side of the baseline of its territorial sea as defined in the *Seas and Submerged Lands Act 1973.* (hereinafter referred to as "Australian territory").

The action – which was denounced by Mr Scott Morrison in 2014 as "shameful and offensive", and proof of refugee ingratitude and impertinence[5] – was adjourned on September 27, 2016, and as of writing a new hearing date has not been set. As a possible horizon of justice within border security, future readers may wish to scrutinise the case.

6.3 Returning the message of border security: the fumigation of the Deutsche Bank's hull and the refoulement and possible torture of its occupants

On April 17, 2013, eight days after the Deutsche Bank sailed into Geraldton Harbour, with the Sri Lankans being held by immigration, pest controllers were hard at work fumigating the hull. The contractors, Allpest, had been called by the Department of Agriculture and Fisheries on Monday April 15. As the following news report notes,

> The company spent several hours yesterday wrapping the timber and fibreglass hull of the boat in white tarpaulins before it was fumigated. Customs and Border Protection officers and personnel from DAFF's Australian Quarantine and Inspection Service also attended the secured site.
>
> Meanwhile, seven of the sixty-six Sri Lankans who were on the boat remained in Perth yesterday – deemed 'unfit' to fly to Christmas Island for processing.

5 Owens, Jared and Taylor, Paige, 'Scott Morrison Condemns Lawsuit Launched Over Christmas Island SIEV 221 Disaster', *The Australian*, June 17, 2014. www.theaustralian.com.au/national-affairs/scott-morrison-condemns-lawsuit-launched-over-christmas-island-siev-221-disaster/news-story/d8ae0d9f371479ead807a287001cd92e

> The Department of Immigration would not comment on the condition of the seven or be drawn on the future of all the asylum seekers and whether or not they would be sent home.
>
> Customs said the boat would remain the property of the Commonwealth until DAFF's procedures had concluded.[6]

The moment encapsulates the conflation – simultaneously institutional and discursive – of quarantine and immigration, via border security.[7] The fumigation says what it does: 'the pests carried aboard the Deutsche Bank must be removed, and so they were.'

The next day, Thursday April 18, ABC News reported that thirty-eight of the sixty-six aboard were "being flown home to Sri Lanka after earlier being transferred to Christmas Island . . . heading to the Sri Lankan capital Colombo on an Australian Air Force plane".[8] The fate of all of those aboard the Deutsche Bank returned to Sri Lanka was as unreported as its arrival in Geraldton was hyped. As with Howard's concern about a diffuse coastline anxiety among ordinary Australians (section 2.8), what's striking is not just the confected hysteria the Deutsche Bank's arrival elicited, but – side by side with this – how little follow up there was on its occupants' fates. This is surely one of the ugliest aspects of op-ed writers captured by border security's world and partisan political commitments to the Coalition, such as Piers Akerman[9]: they are willing to screech panic when describing infinitesimal risks (assertions they are in any case never held accountable for justifying), simply because they may affect the nation and its sovereign borders. But they say little about people who are exposed to drowning, torture and violent death as the policy effects of the harsher measures they reliably advocate – because they are inflicted on non-white noncitizens. The spectre of the Haitian Program and the judgment in King haunts interdiction in Australia's maritime jurisdictions. For as in Haiti, the detention, beating and torture of returned Sri Lankan asylum seekers is routine (section 3.5): I do not know if this occurred with the sixty-six aboard the Deutsche Bank; it was not reported on. This is one precise point we might observe the lived effects of the asymmetries of infliction (sections 3.3–3.5).

On Friday April 19, 2013, then Immigration Minister Brendan O'Connor framed the forcible return of these thirty-eight people as a commanding instance of 'sending the message of border security':

> Returning this group to Sri Lanka sends the powerful message that people who pay smugglers are throwing their money away and risking their lives in

6 Davis, Tom, 'Geraldton Asylum Boat Fumigated', *The West Australian*, April 17, 2013. https://au.news.yahoo.com/thewest/wa/a/16766277/geraldton-asylum-boat-fumigated/#page1

7 On immigration detention and quarantine, see section 5.5, note 57.

8 'Sri Lanka Asylum Seekers Flown Home', *ABC News*. www.abc.net.au/news/2013-04-18/sri-lanka-asylum-seekers-flown-home/4637862

9 Akerman, Piers, 'Illegal Boat's Mainland Arrival Should Alarm All', *The Sunday Telegraph*, April 14, 2013. www.dailytelegraph.com.au/news/opinion/illegal-boats-mainland-arrival-should-alarm-all/story-e6frezz0-1226619898855

> the process. . . . There is no fast track. . . . If they do not engage Australia's protection obligations, they will be returned home.[10]

In a further direct echo of US authorities' treatment of Cuban-Haitian entrants in the post-Mariel Reagan era, in turn an echo of the systematic and racist denial of asylum claims in Haitian Program of the 1970s (section 3.8), Sri Lankans forcibly returned during this time were subjected to 'enhanced screening', which in practice meant conducting cursory on-water interviews, as the US Coast Guard had in the 80s (section 3.9–3.10). There as here, and paralleling the tragic irony of 'safe haven', enhanced screening was not set up to enhance the asylum prospects of the screened[11] – and this also indicates that, under a deterrence policy, screening means expulsion. Between August 13, 2012 and April 18, 2013, the Commonwealth returned 1004 Sri Lankans who attempted to arrive in Australia to seek asylum: 795 of these returns – roughly 80% – were reported as involuntary.[12] Forcible returns, and therefore probable detention and torture.

The lives of asylum seekers, harmed, spoiled and destroyed in ways beyond care or grievability[13] (section 3.8), comprise an invisible condition of seeing the ring of steel (section 2.12), believing in its shining necessity and greatness, investing ever further in its severances and the ever harsher inflictions they tend to call for. To the extent that agents of border security continue to interdict vulnerable people as security threats, the national sovereignty of Australia is predicated on the negation, expulsion and abandonment of noncitizens seeking protection – in ways that then tend to preclude public and critical discussions of what the contingent entrance of this passage of authority into society means for us, now that it is accepted as normal, necessary, infrastructural.

6.4 The shores of Australia: the legality of offshore, unconstitutional detention observed in PNG, and the hostage situation of 'take the package'

Excision and offshore processing remain durably legal in Australian law to the time of writing. The legality of offshore detention was most recently upheld by a decision of the High Court of Australia (HCA) that ruled that offshore detention

10 Hall, Bianca, '38 Geraldton Boat Arrivals Sent Back to Sri Lanka', *The Sydney Morning Herald*, April 19, 2013. www.smh.com.au/federal-politics/political-news/38-geraldton-boat-arrivals-sent-back-to-sri-lanka-20130418–2i31q.html

11 Evershed, Nick, Farrell, Paul and Laughland, Oliver, "In' or 'out': What We Know About 'Enhanced Screening' of Asylum Seekers', *The Guardian*, July 3, 2014. www.theguardian.com/world/2014/jul/03/asylum-seekers-may-be-subject-to-speedy-on-water-screenings

12 Crook, Andrew, 'Screened-Out Asylum Seekers Sent Straight Home Without Info, Review', *Crikey*, April 24, 2013. www.crikey.com.au/2013/04/24/screened-out-asylum-seekers-sent-straight-home-without-info-review/

13 Butler, Judith, *Frames of War: When Is Life Grievable?* Verso, London, 2009.

was lawful.[14] Onshore remonstrations emerged: how could something morally wrong be upheld as legal? This shows a lack of understanding: both of the jurisdiction and purpose of the High Court (of course legal, not moral), and the particularly logocentric, black letter culture of the current High Court. Reading section 198AHA (a section inserted by the Abbott government under duress, by making the lives of children its stake[15]), the High Court upheld that it is lawful to:

> take, or cause to be taken, any action in relation to the arrangement or the regional processing functions of the country . . . make payments, or cause payments to be made, in relation to the arrangement or the regional processing functions of the country . . . do anything else that is incidental or conducive to the taking of such action or the making of such payments. . . . Nothing in this section limits the executive power of the Commonwealth.[16]

Black letter legality and grey wigged white male judges aside, the societal momentum of border security recursively ensures its own onshore Australian support, while the expedient necessity of continuing to publicly uphold the defensible legality *and moral necessity* of offshore processing's deterrence effects provide a by now very durable, almost black boxed party-political impetus for continuing bipartisan support for border security. Since its election on its *Operation Sovereign Borders'* platform in 2013, the Coalition has continued to pursue a situational definition of border security that aligns legality, electoral supremacy and popular support with political and ethical rightness, then uses this alignment to beat down opponents and critics (sections 2.11–2.12). This framing was made explicit by Prime Minister Turnbull in response to the High Court's decision on the lawfulness of offshore processing: "the line has to be drawn somewhere and it is drawn at our border". For Turnbull, the High Court's decision underlined the legitimacy of border security's severences, while Labor's 'experiments with softer border protection', in contrast, 'led to 50,000 unauthorised boat arrivals and 'hundreds drowned at sea'.[17]

14 Hasham, Nicole, 'High Court Finds Offshore Detention Lawful', *The Sydney Morning Herald*, February 3, 2016. www.smh.com.au/federal-politics/political-news/high-court-finds-offshore-detention-lawful-20160202-gmk5q6.html

McKenzie-Murray, Martin, 'The Lawful Truth of the High Court's Offshore Detention Decision', *The Saturday Paper*, February 6, 2016. www.thesaturdaypaper.com.au/news/immigration/2016/02/06/the-lawful-truth-the-high-courts-offshore-detention-decision

15 The Abbott government pushed parliamentarians to accept the legislation so it could get children off Nauru, the implication being that: 'if you do not accept this legislation, I will not get children off Nauru (and their subsequent being there will then be your fault).

16 'Migration Act 1958, Section 198AHA', *www.austlii.edu.au*. www.austlii.edu.au/au/legis/cth/consol_act/ma1958118/s198aha.html

17 Hasham, Nicole, 'High Court Finds Offshore Detention Lawful', *The Sydney Morning Herald*, February 3, 2016. www.smh.com.au/federal-politics/political-news/high-court-finds-offshore-detention-lawful-20160202-gmk5q6.html

Support for excision and offshore processing, again lead by the Coalition and used as its 2013 electoral cudgel (sections 2.10–2.11) – but still retaining bipartisan support – is read as if it had always been put in place as an expression of moral opposition to children drowning, a position that, in turn, enables critics of detention to be read as supporters of the 'moral catastrophes' of people smuggling and drowning. Theses pretexts continue to recur, expand and shift, to the point where by early 2016 support for excision and offshore processing became the condition for Australia's *acceptance of Syrian refugees*. The Prime Minister,

> *If we wish to stop people drowning at sea*, if we want to keep our borders safe, if we want to maintain support for our whole immigration policy, if we want the capacity to bring in refugees from Syria, 12,000 additional refugees from persecuted minorities, *then we need a strong border protection regime* and this government will stand steadfast in protecting the border.[18]

Through the twists and turns of this trope we can read a consistent negation of justice as fairness and responsibility on whatever pretext expedience and compliance with the dictated terms the executive demands.

Yet as explored from the crab bridge onward (section I.11) all such rhetorical positions involve 'paying inattention' to historical conditions of possibility and the careful constructions observable through design intent – declared so often, in detail, and with a high degree of reflexivity and strategic vision (section 4.6). Most notably in *Border Security*: that offshore detention remains the deterrence policy it was clearly conceived and carefully executed as, in some measure based on the lessons Australian policy makers learned from the US' pioneering efforts to negate Haitian and Cuban asylum seeking. As in the US Caribbean of the 80s and 90s (section 3.10), so in contemporary Australia: offshore detention is devastatingly effective in achieving deterrence and control, *because* it exposes people to conditions so harsh that it breaks them, and people hear tell of that – Morrison's "very clear message" that those who will never see the shores of Australia "should warn others not to follow them" (section 3.5). Whether in the US Caribbean or contemporary Australia, offshoring is a consistent policy put in place for its known and foreseeable deterrence and control effects that propagates the proposition it accepts: 'if the price of sovereignty is cruelty, then seek sovereignty. If the price of international responsibilities is sovereignty, then seek sovereignty'.

On Tuesday April 26, 2016, Papua New Guinea's (PNG's) Supreme Court ruled that the detention centre on Manus Island was unlawful and unconstitutional, and that offshore processing conducted there breached international human rights norms by treating asylum seekers as if they were prisoners by

18 McKenzie-Murray, Martin, 'The Lawful Truth of the High Court's Offshore Detention Decision', *The Saturday Paper*, February 6, 2016, italics mine. www.thesaturdaypaper.com.au/news/immigration/2016/02/06/the-lawful-truth-the-high-courts-offshore-detention-decision

depriving them of liberty.[19] Where Australia's interdiction and consequential provisions gave authorised officers 'powers to move people' (section 3.12) – to interdict, move, detain and transfer people to offshore excised places and third countries the Commonwealth had entered into agreements with – the PNG Supreme Court decision meant that those held on Manus had been illegally detained from day one, while it also emphasised the extent to which the PNG government had been lent on by its Australian counterparts. Re-describing the nasty regional geopolitics of Australian bullying[20] in unambiguous legal language, the colonised spoke back to a past and present coloniser in a discursive instrument carrying an undeniable legitimacy (sections 1.2–1.3). On the same day as the Supreme Court delivered its decision, Dutton publicly conceded that Manus would have to close.

For detainees on Nauru as of writing (2,238km east of Manus, 4,287km north by northeast of Canberra), the current situation has likewise been imposed as a hostage situation whose phrasing is a dark coda of 'sending the message'. 2016 detainees on Nauru have been strongly encouraged to consider 'taking the package' – a phrasing used by government spokespeople – by acceding to the offer of permanent third country resettlement, in Cambodia and Papua New Guinea. For parents and young adults in detention on Nauru in 2016, the future is a bleak choice: take the package, or keep receiving the message of border security. In a sense, this hostage situation[21] and the stakes presented in its ultimatum again shows that the government knows very well: the message of border security is punishment.

6.5 The logistics of cruelty: the release of the Nauru Files and the value and status of children in offshore detention

On August 10, 2016, The Guardian leaked the Nauru Files,[22] the largest tranche of documents ever released from Commonwealth sources. The files report incidents reported in offshore detention over a period of two and a half years, from May 2013 to October 2015. The Files feature 2,000 incident reports – over 8,000 pages, 1,086 incidents – with more than half referring to children. The

19 Tlozek, Eric and Anderson, Stephanie, 'PNG's Supreme Court Rules Detention of Asylum Seekers on Manus Island is Illegal' *ABC News*, April 27, 2016. www.abc.net.au/news/2016-04-26/png-court-rules-asylum-seeker-detention-manus-island-illegal/7360078

20 See also section 2.2, note 69.

21 We can draw an interesting link from this instance back to Baudrillard's 'untimely realist' analysis of the Gulf War and hysterical mediation. See: Baudrillard, Jean, *The Gulf War Did Not Take Place*, Indiana University Press, Bloomington, 1995, pp. 24–27.

22 Evershed, Nick, Liu, Ri, Farrell, Paul and Davidson, Helen, 'The Nauru Files: The Lives of Asylum Seekers in Detention Detailed in a Unique Database', *The Guardian*, August 10, 2016. www.theguardian.com/australia-news/ng-interactive/2016/aug/10/the-nauru-files-the-lives-of-asylum-seekers-in-detention-detailed-in-a-unique-database-interactive

figures are staggering when considered against the average adult and child population in the centre over the reporting period: 783 adults, 144 children.

In these reports, incidents involving physical and sexual abuse are common, reports of infliction and experience of serious harm and inadequate care are frequent, while reports of children attempting self-harm are the most frequent of all. Here we are somewhere between the crab bridge and the electrocution of the robber crabs (section I.11), between extremely careful reflexive design working to secure circulation, and the failure to take into consideration the foreseeably harmful effects of designed choices.

Had the Commonwealth carefully designed a system to destroy the lives of a thousand children, it might have conceived of Nauru. In most criminal jurisdictions, conditions that are systemic on Nauru are legible as cruelty and child abuse, situations of acute harm and grave danger from which children are removed. In international humanitarian law, alongside this, the best interests of the child should be the primary consideration, and detention should only be used as a last resort.[23] On the day of the release, Border Force's newsroom spun the discursive wall of abuse incidents in the release as evidence of its agents' good work, "the rigorous reporting procedures that are in place in the regional processing centre – procedures under which *any* alleged incident must be recorded, reported and where necessary investigated".[24] The same media release also sought to minimise the kinds of claims appearing in the thousands of Nauru Files, over and over, as "unconfirmed allegations" "uncorroborated statements and claims" 'individual matters historical in nature',[25] without releasing a detailed point for point rejoinder giving some qualitative or quantitative assessment of these counterclaims. But of course this is a further tragic irony of on-water operational matters: as the childrens' lives are destroyed offshore, this is a security matter, and this also means that the Commonwealth is unable to refute the evidence when it leaks.

On October 15, 2016, the Guardian followed up the release of the Nauru Files by reporting that of the nineteen referrals made to Nauruan police during the period of time covered, there were eight allegations of "violence and sexual assault – including eight against children". In spite of this, there were 'no prosecutions or convictions'.[26] The Australian-imposed relations of domination, and their wilful obfuscation of Australian responsibility via *de jure* respect for state sovereignty, are stated in perfect governance PR syntax in the following passage

23 'Information About Children in Detention', *Australian Human Rights Commission*, updated January 6, 2016. www.humanrights.gov.au/information-about-children-immigration-detention

24 'The "Nauru Files"', *Border Force Newsroom*, August 10, 2016, underline in original. http://newsroom.border.gov.au/channels/NEWS/releases/the-nauru-files

25 Op.cit.

26 Doherty, Ben, 'Nauru Files: Review Confirms 19 Police Referrals Over Abuse Claims, Yet No Prosecutions', *The Guardian*, October 15, 2016. www.theguardian.com/australia-news/2016/oct/15/nauru-files-review-confirms-19-police-referrals-over-abuse-claims-yet-no-prosecutions

detailing procedures relating to child protection on Nauru, released on the same day in the Department of Immigration and Border Protection's Child Safeguarding Framework[27]:

> Nauru is a sovereign nation and child protection on Nauru is a matter for the Government of Nauru. Australia supports Nauru in their regional processing undertaking and as part of that support signs up to the Nauru Child Safeguarding Protocol for operation in the RPC. All child protection protocols within the RPC are agreed by all contracted service providers and led by the Government of Nauru Operations Managers with support from the Department.[28]

When the minister wishes to take 'any action' with regard to offshore processing, he may do so lawfully[29]; yet when allegations of the most serious nature are raised, the Commonwealth plays the sovereign trump card that has served the US so well with GITMO. In any argument between the agents of powerful states and populations fleeing war, poverty and violence, sovereignty tends to trump vulnerability. In relations of unequal authority or domination, this horizon of justice leaves us with an impasse. Those with authority are free to dominate and abuse; those with responsibility are left with people to care for. The beating hand is free, the caring hand is burdened.

6.6 The drowned and the saved; islands as havens from *sylon*, and groups who cannot see the shores and horizons of border security's world

Small groups of committed Australians have waged effective onshore campaigns against the cruelty of offshore detention, and its disproportionate impact on children and on women.[30] This has been strongly highlighted in scholarly and critical reporting for some time, has been used to significant critical effect. No doubt this is because (to paraphrase several variants on the thought), the way a culture treats the most vulnerable in its care – women, children, the elderly, the poor and homeless, animals, reefs – is the truest and rawest expression of its real values. Yet of all these groups of committed protesters, many if not all remain within the imposed boundaries of border security's world, insofar as they pursue or tacitly

27 'Child Safeguarding', *Department of Immigration and Border Protection*. www.border.gov.au/about/reports-publications/reports/corporate/child-safeguarding

28 'Child Safeguarding Framework Safeguarding Children in Our Care – A Shared Responsibility', *Department of Immigration and Border Protection*. www.border.gov.au/ReportsandPublications/Documents/child-safeguarding-framework.pdf, p. 65.

29 'Migration Act 1958, Section 198AHA', *www.austlii.edu.au*. www.austlii.edu.au/au/legis/cth/consol_act/ma1958118/s198aha.html

30 See section 3.12, notes 180–182.

accept border security's premises and necessity, insofar as they continue to be differential beneficiaries of secured circulation living in quiet safety and uncritical comfort within the climate controlled lounges of the border continuum.

Two unlikely groups of opponents bear final comment as people unable to see the meaning of the border continuum or understand themselves as living within it, subjected to its sovereignty: seafarers, and radical Christians.

On May 6, 2015, Admiral Donato Marzano responded directly to Tony Abbott's comments that "[t]he only way you can stop the deaths is to stop the people-smuggling trade. The only way you can stop the deaths is in fact to stop the boats",[31] made in a context where Mr Abbott was touring Europe, in part to promote the importation of the Australian policy model and trumpet its success. Admiral Marzano offered the following response to Mr Abbott's reasoning:

> There are several countries that apply a policy of expulsion, even by force of arms, others apply the international right to rescue. . . . I am a sailor who has spent 20 years on boats. If I find a boat adrift, I'm sorry, but I don't turn away . . . I intervene to help people at sea. I don't know if this reflects my Italian culture but I do know it is international law. . . . A vessel in difficulty, whether it is a boat full of migrants or a merchant ship, has to be assisted".[32]

We can see a recent condensation point of the disjuncture staged between Mr Abbott and Admiral Marzano that helps us consider border security as a part consequence of our failure to observe the simple ethical lesson brought to us through seafarers' encounter with the human-existential truth of the ocean – by returning attention to the Tampa Affair one last time.

After responding to the demand of the master's absolute obligation to rescue those aboard *Palapa* – a vessel in distress that Surveillance Australia directed him to – nothing in international humanitarian law could resolve authoritatively where and how they could be disembarked. But this *fait accompli* did nothing to diminish what Captain Rinnan could only observe as an immediate ethical imperative: an unhesitating responsibility to rescue, feed, house and shelter 'his' rescuees. The more complicated the international relations became in those final days of August 2001, the more strident Australia's unilateral claims to the decisionist prerogative (section 2.9), the more Captain Rinnan simply remained on duty, responding to a maritime imperative, the seafarer's world that sees nothing of border security's world. Rinnan's actions consistently supported the lives of the people who were actually at risk in the situation they were involved in, and this has remained something uncomplicated to Captain Rinnan. To the master,

31 A comment that by implication equates boats with death: perhaps electoral, perhaps national-sovereign.

32 'Italian Navy Chief Sceptical of Australian Asylum Seeker Solution to Mediterranean Migrant Ccrisis', *ABC News*, May 6, 2015. www.abc.net.au/news/2015-05-06/italy-navy-chief-sceptical-australian-solution-to-migrant-issue/6447708

the tricky complications of Border Force can only elicit a slightly exasperated shrug.[33]

Maritime law offers us one horizon of justice that border security and its projection of sovereignty cannot sink, internalise, re-enter into the threat environment (section 1.10–1.12), or expediently override like the international humanitarian commitments to which the Commonwealth is a signatory and lapsed believer. Indeed, border security's distinctions can only operate by failing to observe what was and is immediately obvious and existentially undeniable to Captain Rinnan as his primary obligation, which Border Force does by maintaining a security overlay over safety responsibilities (section 1.12). A horizon of justice was clearly visible to Arne Rinnan throughout the Tampa Affair, one tied in to his identity as a seafarer and the existential reality of what the drowning vastness of the ocean means to us as living humans.[34]

Side by side with maritime law, border security and all that it orders – onshore and offshore – are unobservable within universal saving power of God's love, as expressed by radical Christian groups protesting offshore detention. During a 2014 sit in protest of the #lovemakesaway campaign, protesters read the following passage from Leviticus:

> When an alien resides with you in your land, you shall not oppress the alien. The alien who resides with you shall be to you as the citizen among you; you shall love the alien as yourself, for you were aliens in the land of Egypt: I am the LORD your God.[35]

The campaign, "[a] movement of prayer & nonviolent direct action seeking to end Australia's cruel refugee policies", says directly that "we want to WELCOME, not abandon, people seeking safety".[36]

The earnest sincerity and directness of such avowals of love and vulnerability are totally at odds with the reward structure and self regard that has promoted and rewarded the careerists of Canberra and those of Australia's onshore living on the securing side of capital in its global cities. It is also, perhaps, embarrassing to hear words like love, welcome and cruelty so directly expressed, because it rips away the emotional distanciation necessary both for maintaining the remorseless pursuit of economic interest as something good, proper or rightful, and for continuing to function with acronyms like SUNC, SIEV and SIV. Love and care show up the supreme values propagated by neoliberalising globalisation as vulgar

33 See Rinnan's retrospective account in *Leaky Boat* (documentary). www.abc.net.au/tv/programs/leakyboat.htm

34 For one politico-ethical trajectory of exploration from this, see: Arendt, Hannah, *The Human Condition*, University of Chicago Press, Chicago, 1998.

35 Sherlock, Peter, 'Asylum Seekers: Praying for Change', *The Conversation*, May 20, 2014. http://theconversation.com/asylum-seekers-praying-for-change-26953

36 Op.cit.

and bereft of transcendence or greater meaning.[37] Like the co-presence of harsh treatment during the proud display of 'vibrant, brilliant' multicultural Australia during the Sydney Olympics (section 2.6) the simple loving act of 'welcoming vulnerable people' unconditionally exposes 'ordinary Australians' as mean, greedy, selfish, punitive and racist.[38]

My radicals are conservatives:[39]they believe what they believe, but they actually believe it, and they live it in a direct and full way. In the political present, this has become radical. Through its embrace and integration of border security, contemporary Australia has come to be shored up by dirty secrets, on-water operational matters: ungrievable ruined children, buried in its colonial backyard.[40] 'Cruise Ship Australia', the global enclave that Australia is becoming by denying people 'the shores of Australia' based on their inability to access a mode of transport, involves the profligate use of resources in defiance of the evidence of its effects on all of us, ultimately to defend the serene nullity of a deadening consumption lifestyle.[41] I remain amazed by the bracingly demanding openness of the ocean that nearly killed me as a child, when my mother saved me from drowning, at Clareville Beach, summer 1986: the way the unknown ocean was audaciously sailed into, in the age of discovery, by sailors who could not swim. It remains possible to life in this way,[42] a way that does not disavow that 'we are embarked'.[43] Likewise, it remains possible to live together in the enveloping communion of a living relation to country, to dance with strangers,[44] to pass one another on the street or landing with effusive warmth or relaxed indifference, and to be alive to one another and the living world that, in spite of everything, still provides us with a common future, if we are capable of sharing it.

37 See: Judt, Tony, 'Ill Fares the Land', *New York Review of Books*, April 29, 2010. www.nybooks.com/articles/2010/04/29/ill-fares-the-land/

38 For the co-presence of punitive urges, xenophobic nativist chauvinism and white Australian nostalgia among Hanson's One Nation supporters, see: Marr, David, 'The White Queen: One Nation and the Politics of Race', *Quarterly Essay*, 66, March 2017.

39 On the distinction between conservatives and reactionaries and an interesting exploration of the latter (except for the shallow exploration of Badiou and Schmitt), see: Lilla, Mark, *The Shipwrecked Mind: On Political Reaction*, New York Review of Books, New York, 2016.

40 See the discussion of Ursula LeGuin's 'Omelas' in: Sparrow, Jeff, 'What's the End Game for Australia's Border Policy – A World of Walled City-States? *The Guardian*, May 6, 2016. www.theguardian.com/commentisfree/2016/may/06/whats-the-end-game-for-australias-border-policy-a-world-of-walled-city-states

41 Delaney, Brigid, 'A Disco Cruise to the South Pacific Turns Downbeat', *The Saturday Paper*, February 13, 2016. www.thesaturdaypaper.com.au/2016/02/13/disco-cruise-the-south-pacific-turns-downbeat/ and Wallace, David Foster, 'Shipping Out: On the (nearly lethal) Comforts of a Luxury Cruise', *Harpers Magazine*, 1996. https://harpers.org/wp-content/uploads/2008/09/HarpersMagazine-1996-01-0007859.pdf

42 Taussig, Michael, 'The Beach (a Fantasy)', *Critical Inquiry*, 26: 2, 2000, pp. 248–278.

43 Pascal, quoted in: Blumenberg, Hans, *Shipwreck with Spectator: Paradigm of a Metaphor for Existence*, MIT Press, Cambridge, 1997, pp. 18–19.

44 Clendinnen, Inga, *Dancing With Strangers: Europeans and Australians at First Contact*, Cambridge University Press, Cambridge, 2005.

Book and journal bibliography

Adorno, Theodor, *Critical Models: Interventions and Catchwords*, Chicago University Press, Chicago, 2005.

Agamben, Giorgio, *Homo Sacer: Sovereign Power and Bare Life*, Stanford University Press, Stanford, 1998.

Agamben, Giorgio, *State of Exception*, University of Chicago Press, Chicago, 2005.

Albert, Matthias, Jacobson, David and Lapid, Yosef (eds.), *Identities, Borders, Orders*, University of Minnesota Press, Minneapolis, 2001.

Althusser, Louis, *On the Reproduction of Capitalism: Ideology and Ideological State Apparatuses*, Verso, London, 2014.

Arato, Andrew and Gebhardt, Eike, *The Essential Frankfurt School Reader*, Continuum, New York, 1982.

Arditi, Benjamin, 'On the Political: Schmitt contra Schmitt', *Telos*, 142, 2008.

Arendt, Hannah, *The Human Condition*, University of Chicago Press, Chicago, 1998.

Balibar, Étienne, *Politics and the Other Scene*, Verso, London, 1998.

Balibar, Étienne, *We, the People of Europe? Reflections on Transnational Citizenship*, Princeton University Press, Princeton, 2004.

Barry, Andrew, *Political Machines: Governing a Technological Society*, Athlone, London, 2001.

Bashford, Alison, 'Quarantine and the Imagining of the Australian Nation', *Health: An Interdisciplinary Journal for the Social Study of Health, Illness and Medicine*, 2: 4, 1998, 387–402.

Bashford, Alison and Strange, Carolyn, 'Asylum – Seekers and National Histories of Detention', *Australian Journal of Politics and History*, 48: 4, 2002.

Bauman, Zygmunt, *Wasted Lives: Modernity and Its Outcasts*, Polity Press, Cambridge, 2004.

Benton, Lauren, *A Search for Sovereignty: Law and Geography in European Empires, 1400–1900*, New York University, New York, 2010.

Bigo, Didier, 'Security and Immigration: Toward a Critique of the Governmentality of Unease', *Alternatives*, 27, 2002, 63–92.

Bissell, David and Fuller, Gillian, *Stillness in a Mobile World*, Routledge, Abingdon, 2011.

Black, Edwin, *War Against the Weak: Eugenics and America's Campaign to Create a Master Race, Expanded Edition*, Dialog Press, Washington, 2012.

Blumenberg, Hans, *Shipwreck With Spectator: Paradigm of a Metaphor for Existence*, MIT Press, Cambridge, 1997.

Blumenberg, Hans, *Work on Myth*, MIT Press, Cambridge, 1986.

Borch, Christian, 'Foam Architecture: Managing Co-Isolated Associations', *Economy and Society*, 37: 4, 2008, 548–571.

Borch, Christian, *Niklas Luhmann*, Routledge, Abingdon, 2011.

Bosworth, Mary, 'Border Control and the Limits of the Sovereign State', *Social and Legal Studies*, 17: 2, 2008, 119–215.

Bosworth, Mary and Kaufman, Emma, 'Foreigners in a Carceral Age: Immigration and Imprisonment in the United States', *Stanford Law and Policy Review*, 22: 2, 2011, 429–454.

Boyce, James, *1835: The Founding of Melbourne and the Conquest of Australia*, Black Inc, Melbourne, 2012.

Boyce, James, *Van Diemen's Land*, Black Inc, Melbourne, 2008.

Boyle, T.C., *The Tortilla Curtain*, Viking, New York, 1995.

Brenner, Neil, 'Global Cities, Glocal States: Global City Formation and State Territorial Restructuring in Contemporary Europe', *Review of International Political Economy*, 5, 1998, 1–37.

Brenner, Neil and Jessop, Bob, Jones, Martin and Macleod, *Gordon, State/Space: A Reader*, Blackwell, New Jersey, 2003.

Brittain-Catlin, William, *Offshore: The Dark Side of the Global Economy*, Farrar, Strauss and Giroux, New York, 2006.

Brown, Wendy, *Undoing the Demos: Neoliberalism's Stealth Revolution*, Zone Books, New York, 2015.

Brown, Wendy, *Walled States, Waning Sovereignty*, Zone Books, New York, 2010.

Burchell, Graham, Gordon, Colin and Miller, Peter (eds.), *The Foucault Effect: Studies in Governmentality*, Chicago University Press, Chicago, 1991.

Burke, Anthony, *Beyond Security, Ethics and Violence: War Against the Other*, Routledge, Abingdon, 2005.

Burke, Anthony, *Fear of Security: Australia's Invasion Anxiety*, Cambridge University Press, Cambridge, 1998.

Butler, Judith, *Frames of War: When Is Life Grievable?* Verso, London, 2009.

Butler, Judith, 'Human Shields', *London Review of International Law*, 3: 2, 2015, 223–243.

Butler, Judith, *Precarious Life: The Powers of Mourning and Violence*, Verso, London, 2004.

Butler, Judith and Spivak, Gayatri, *Who Sings the Nation-State? Language, Politics, Belonging*, University of Chicago Press, Chicago, 2007.

Buzan, Barry, 'Rethinking Security After the Cold War', *Co-operation and Conflict*, 32: 1, 1997, 5–28.

Chambers, Peter, 'The Embrace of Border Security: Maritime Jurisdiction, National Sovereignty, and the Geopolitics of Operation Sovereign Borders', *Geopolitics*, 20, 2015, 1–34.

Chambers, Peter, 'The Passage of Authority: Imagining the Political Transformation of Australia's Christmas Island, from Sovereignty to Governance', *Shima: The International Journal of Research into Island Cultures*, 6: 2, 2012, 116–137.

Chambers, Peter, 'Shipwreck With Spectator: Snapshots of Border Security in Australia', *Global Change, Peace and Security*', 26: 1, 2013, 97–112.

Chambers, Peter, 'Society Has Been Defended: Following the Shifting Shape of State through Australia's Christmas Island', *International Political Sociology*, 5, 2011, 18–34.

Clarke, Bruce and Hansen, Mark B., *Emergence and Embodiment: New Essays on Second-Order Systems Theory*, Duke University Press, Durham, 2009.

Clendinnen, Inga, *Dancing With Strangers: Europeans and Australians at First Contact*, Cambridge University Press, Cambridge, 2005.

Colangelo, Anthony J., 'What Is Extraterritorial Jurisdiction?' *Cornell Law Review*, 99: 6, September 2014, 1303–1352.

Connolly, William E., 'The Evangelical-Capitalist Resonance Machine', *Political Theory*, 33: 6, 2005, 869–886.

Connolly, William E., *The Fragility of Things: Self-Organizing Processes, Neoliberal Fantasies, and Democratic Activism*, Duke University Press, Durham 2013.

Coulter, Ann, *Adios, America: The Left's Plan to Turn Our Country into a Third World Hellhole*, Regnery Publishing, Washington, 2015.

Cowen, Deborah, *The Deadly Life of Logistics: Mapping Violence in Global Trade*, University of Minnesota Press, Minneapolis, 2014.

Crock, Mary, 'In the Wake of Tampa: Conflicting Visions of International Refugee Law in the Management of Refugee Flows', *Pacific Rim Law and Policy Journal*, 12: 1, 2003, 49–95.

Dahl, Erik J., 'Naval Innovation: From Coal to Oil', *Joint Force Quarterly*, Winter 2000–2001, 50–56.

Davison, Graeme, *The Rise and Fall of Marvellous Melbourne*, Melbourne University Press, Melbourne, 2004.

de Goede, Marieke, *Speculative Security: The Politics of Pursuing Terrorist Monies*, University of Minnesota Press, Minneapolis, 2012.

Deleuze, Gilles, 'Postscript on the Societies of Control', *October*, 59, 1992, 3–7.

Deneault, Alain, *Offshore: Tax Havens and the Rule of Global Crime*, The New Press, New York, 2011.

Derrida, Jacques, *The Beast and the Sovereign, Volume 1*, University of Chicago Press, Chicago, 2009.

Diken, Bülent and Laustsen, Carsten Bagge, *The Culture of Exception: Sociology Facing the Camp*, Routledge, Abingdon, 2005.

Donne, John, *Devotions Upon Emergent Occasions and Death's Duel*, Vintage, London, 1999.

Dorsett, Shaunagh and McVeigh, Shaun, *Jurisdiction*, Routledge, Abingdon, 2012.

Dorsett, Shaunagh and McVeigh, Shaun, 'Just So: The Law Which Governs Australia Is Australian Law', *Law and Critique*, 13, 2002.

Douglas, Mary, *Purity and Danger: An Analysis of Concepts of Pollution and Taboo*, Routledge, Abingdon, 2005.

Dreyfus, Hubert and Rabinow, Paul, *Michel Foucault: Beyond Structuralism and Hermeneutics*, University of Chicago Press, Chicago, 1982.

Elbe, Stefan, Roemer-Mahler, Anne and Long, Christopher, 'Securing Circulation Pharmaceutically: Antiviral Stockpiling and Pandemic Preparedness in the European Union', *Security Dialogue*, 45: 5, 2014, 440–457.

Elden, Stuart, *The Birth of Territory*, University of Chicago Press, Chicago, 2013.

Engstrom, David Wells, *Presidential Decision Making Adrift: the Carter Administration and the Mariel Boatlift*, Rowman & Littlefield, Lanham,1997.

Feldman, Allen, *Formations of Violence: The Narrative of the Body and Political Terror in Northern Ireland*, University of Chicago Press, Chicago, 1991.

Feldman, Allen, 'Philoctetes Revisited: White Public Space and the Political Geography of Public Safety', *Social Text*, 19: 3, Fall 2001, 57–89.

Feldman, Allen, 'Strange Fruit: The South African Truth Commission and the Demonic Economies of Violence', *Social Analysis*, 46: 3, 2002.

Finnane, Mark, *Police and Government: Histories of Policing in Australia*, Oxford University Press, Oxford, 1994.

Fischer, Gerhard, *Enemy Aliens: Internment and the Homefront Experience in Australia, 1914–1920*, University of Queensland Press, Brisbane, 1989.

Flinders, Matthew and Flannery, Tim, *Terra Australis: Matthew Flinders' Great Adventures in the Circumnavigation of Australia*, Text, Melbourne, 2012.

Ford, Lisa, 'Indigenous Policy and Its Historical Occlusions: The North American and Global Contexts of Australian Settlement', *Australian Indigenous Law Review*, 12: 1, 2008, 69–80.

Foucault, Michel, *The Birth of Biopolitics: Lectures at the Collège de France*, Palgrave Macmillan, London, 2008.

Foucault, Michel, *The Government of the Living: Lectures at the Collège de France*, Palgrave Macmillan, London, 2014.

Foucault, Michael, *The History of Sexuality, Volume One*, Penguin, London, 2008.

Foucault, Michel, 'Kant on Enlightenment and Revolution', *Economy and Society*, 15: 1, 1986, 88–96.

Foucault, Michel, 'Omnes et Singulatim: Towards a Criticism of 'Political Reason'', In *The Tanner Lectures on Human Values*, Stanford University, October 10 and 16, 1979.

Foucault, Michel, *Security, Territory, Population: Lectures at the Collège de France*, Palgrave Macmillan, London, 2007.

Foucault, Michel, *Society Must Be Defended: Lectures at the Collège de France, 1975–1976*, Picador, London, 2003.

Foucault, Michel, *Technologies of the Self: a Seminar With Michel Foucault*, Tavistock, London, 1998.

Galli, Carlo, *Political Spaces and Global War*, University of Minnesota Press, Minneapolis, 2010.

Galli, Carlo, 'The Rise and Fall of Modern Political Space', *Philosophy Kitchen*, 2: 2, 2015, 6–16.

Garland, David, *The Culture of Control: Crime and Social Order in Contemporary Society*, Oxford University Press, Oxford, 2001.

Garland, David, 'The Limits of the Sovereign State: Strategies of Crime Control in Contemporary Society', *The British Journal of Criminology*, 36: 4, 1996, 445–471.

Giddens, Anthony, *The Nation-State and Violence: Volume Two of a Contemporary Critique of Historical Materialism*, Polity Press, Cambridge, 1985.

Goldsworthy, David, *Losing the Blanket: Australia and the End of Britain's Empire*, Melbourne University Press, Melbourne, 2002.

Gregson, Nicky, 'Logistics at Work: Trucks, Containers and the Friction of Circulation in the UK', *Mobilities*, 2015. http://dx.doi.org/10.1080/17450101.2015.1087680

Gutekunst, Claire P., 'Interdiction of Haitian Migrants on the High Seas: A Legal and Policy Analysis', *Yale Journal of International Law*, 10: 151, 1984–1985, 151–184.

Habermas, Jürgen, *Legitimation Crisis*, Beacon Press, Boston, 1975.

Habermas, Jürgen, *Theory of Communicative Action Vol. 1: Reason and the Rationalization of Society*, Beacon Press, Boston, 1992.

Habermas, Jürgen, *The Theory of Communicative Action Vol. 2: Lifeworld and System: A Critique of Functional Reason*, Beacon Press, Boston, 1992.

Hannerz, Ulf, 'Notes on the Global Ecumene', *Public Culture*, 1: 2, 1989, 66–75.

Hansen, Jonathan M., *Guantánamo: An American History*, Hill and Wang, New York, 2011.

Harcourt, Bernard E., 'Reflecting on the Subject: A Critique of the Social Influence Conception of Deterrence, the Broken Windows Theory, and Order-Maintenance Policing New York Style', *Michigan Law Review*, 97: 2, 1998, 291–389.

Harvey, David, *A Companion to Marx's Capital, Volume 1*, Verso, London, 2010.

Heidegger, Martin, *The Question Concerning Technology and Other Essays*, Garland, New York, 1977.

Hobbes, Thomas, *Leviathan*, Penguin, London, 1982.

Hobsbawm, Eric, *The Age of Capital: 1848–1975*, Abacus, London, 1975.

Hobsbawm, Eric, *The Age of Empire: 1875–1914*, Abacus, London, 1989.

Horn, Eva, 'Logics of Political Secrecy', *Theory, Culture and Society*, 28: 7–8, 2011, 103–122.

Howard, John, *Lazarus Rising: A Personal and Political Biography*, Allen and Unwin, Melbourne, 2011.

Hugo, Graeme, 'From Compassion to Compliance? Trends in Refugee and Humanitarian Migration in Australia', *Geojournal*, 55, 2001, 27–37.

Huntley, Rebecca, *Still Lucky*, Penguin, Melbourne, 2017.

Iveson, Kurt and Scalmer, Sean, 'Contesting the "Inevitable": Notes on S11', *Overland*, 161, Summer 2000, 4–13.

Jacobs, Joren and Van Assche, Kristof, 'Understanding Empirical Boundaries: A Systems-Theoretical Avenue in Border Studies', *Geopolitics*, 19: 1, 2014, 182–205.

Jasanoff, Sheila and Kim, Sang Hyun, *Dreamscapes of Modernity: Sociotechnical Imaginaries and the Fabrication of Power*, University of Chicago Press, Chicago, 2015.

Jeffries, Stuart, *Hotel Grand Abyss: the Lives of the Frankfurt School*, Verso, London 2016.

Johnson, Chalmers, *The Sorrows of Empire: Militarism, Secrecy, and the End of the Republic*, Metropolitan Books, New York, 2005.

Juarrero, Alicia, *Dynamics in Action: Intentional Behaviour as a Complex System*, MIT Press, Cambridge, 2002.

Kanngeiser, Anja, 'Tracking and Tracing: Geographies of Logistical Governance and Labouring Bodies', *Environment and Planning: D*, 31: 4, 2013, 594–610.

Kapferer, Bruce and Morris, Barry, 'The Australian Society of the State: Egalitarian Ideologies and New Directions in Exclusionary Practice', *Social Analysis: The International Journal of Social and Cultural Practice*, 47: 3, 2003, 80–107.

Kaplan, Amy, 'Where is Guantánamo?' *American Quarterly*, 57: 3, 2005, 831–858.

Koselleck, Reinhard, *The Practice of Conceptual History: Timing History, Spacing Concepts*, Stanford University Press, Stanford, 2002.

LaCour, Anders and Philippopoulos-Mihalopoulos, Andreas (eds.), *Luhmann Observed: Radical Theoretical Encounters*, Palgrave Macmiilan, London, 2013.

Lemke, Thomas, *Biopolitics: An Advanced Introduction*, New York University Press, New York, 2011.

Licoppe, Christian, '"The Crisis of the Summons": A Transformation in the Pragmatics of "Notifications", From Phone Rings to Instant Messaging', *The Information Society: An International Journal*, 26: 4, 2010, 288–302.

Lilla, Mark, *The Shipwrecked Mind: On Political Reaction*, New York Review of Books, New York, 2016.

Lipman, Jana K., '"The Fish Trusts the Water, and It Is in the Water That It Is Cooked" The Caribbean Origins of the Krome Detention Center"', *Radical History Review*, 115, 2013, 115–141.

Lipman, Jana K., *Guantánamo: A Working-Class History between Empire and Revolution*, University of California Press, Berkeley, 2008.

Lowe, David, *Menzies and the Great World Struggle: Australia's Cold War 1948–1954*, UNSW Press, Sydney, 1999.

Loyd, Jenna, 'Carceral Citizenship in an Age of Global Apartheid', *Occasion*, 8, 2015, 1–15.

Luhmann, Niklas, 'Globalization or World Society: How to Conceive of Modern Society', *International Review of Sociology*, 7: 1, 1997. 67–79.

Luhmann, Niklas, 'The Paradoxy of Observing Systems', *Cultural Critique*, 31, 1995, 37–55.

Luhmann, Niklas, *Risk: A Sociological Theory*, Transaction Publishers, New Jersey, 2008.

Luhmann, Niklas, 'Speaking and Silence', *New German Critique*, 61, 1994, 25–37.

Luhmann, Niklas, *Theory of Society, Volume 1*, Stanford University Press, Stanford, 2012.

Luhmann, Niklas, *Theory of Society, Volume 2*, Stanford University Press, Stanford, 2013.

Luhmann, Niklas, 'What Is Communication?' *Communication Theory*, 2: 3, 1992, 251–259.

MacKenzie, Donald, 'Opening the Black Boxes of Global Finance', *Review of International Political Economy*, 12: 4, 2005, 555–576.

Marr, David, 'The White Queen: One Nation and the Politics of Race', *Quarterly Essay*, 66, March 2017.

Marx, Karl, *Capital, Volume 1: a Critique of Political Economy*, Penguin, London, 1992.

Maurer, Noel and Yu, Carlos, *The Big Ditch: How America Took, Built, Ran, and Ultimately Gave Away the Panama Canal*, Princeton University Press, London, 2010.

McCulloch, Jude, *Blue Army: Paramilitary Policing in Australia*, Melbourne University Press, Melbourne, 1997.

McCulloch, Jude, 'Paramilitary Surveillance: S11, Globalisation, Terrorists and Counter-Terrorists', *Current Issues in Criminal Justice*, 13: 1, 2001, 23–35.

McWilliams, Carey, *Southern California: An Island on the Land*, Peregrine Smith, Utah, 1980.

Mezzadra, Sandro and Neilson, Brett, *Border as Method, or, the Multiplication of Labor*, Duke University Press, Durham, 2013.

Mezzadra, Sandro and Neilson, Brett, 'Extraction, Logistics, Finance: Global Crisis and the Politics of Operations', *Radical Philosophy*, 178, March/April 2013, 8–18.

Mitchell, Timothy, 'Fixing the Economy', *Cultural Studies*, 12: 1, 1998, 82–101.

Mitchell, Timothy, *Rule of Experts: Egypt, Techno-Politics, Modernity*, University of California Press, Berkeley, 2002.

Moran, Dominique, Gill, Nick and Conlon, Dierdre (eds.), *Carceral Spaces: Mobility and Agency in Imprisonment and Migrant Detention*, Routledge, Abingdon, 2013.

More, Thomas, *Utopia*, Penguin, London, 2012.
Morin, Karen, '"Security Here Is Not Safe": Violence, Punishment, and Space in the Contemporary US Penitentiary', *Environment and Planning: D*, 31, 2013, 381–399.
Mountz, Alison, 'Specters at the Port of Entry: Understanding State Mobilities Through an Ontology of Exclusion', *Mobilities*, 6: 3, 2011, 317–334.
Mountz, Alison and Loyd, Jenna, 'Transnational Productions of Remoteness: Building Onshore and Offshore Carceral Regimes Across Borders', *Geographica Helvetica*, 69, 2014, 389–398.
Mussawir, Ed, *Jurisdiction in Deleuze: The Expression and Representation of Law*, Routledge, Abingdon, 2011.
Neilson, Brett, 'Bodies of Protest: Performing citizenship at the 2000 Olympic Games', *Continuum*, 16: 1, 2002, 13–25.
Nethery, Amy and Silverman, Stephanie J. (eds.), *Immigration Detention: The migration of a policy and its human impact*, Routledge, Abingdon, 2015.
Neuman, Klaus, *Across the Seas: Australia's Responses to Refugees*, Black Inc, Melbourne, 2015.
Nevins, Joseph, *Operation Gatekeeper and Beyond*, Routledge, Abingdon, 2010.
Nevins, Joseph, 'Remote Places at the Heart of Empire', *Political Geography*, 30, 2011, 351–354.
O'Grady, Nathaniel, 'Securing Circulation Through Mobility: Milieu and Emergency Response in the British Fire and Rescue Service', *Mobilities*, 9, 2014, 512–527.
Ong, Aihwa, *Neoliberalism as Exception: Mutations in Citizenship and Sovereignty*, Duke University Press, Durham, 2006.
Paik, A. Naomi, 'Carceral Quarantine at Guantánamo Legacies of US Imprisonment of Haitian Refugees', 1991–1994', *Radical History Review*, 115, 2013, 142–168.
Palan, Ronen, 'International Financial Centers: The British-Empire, City-States and Commercially Oriented Politics', *Theoretical Inquiries in Law*, 11: 1, 2010, 149–176.
Palan, Ronen, *The Offshore World: Sovereign Markets, Virtual Places, and Nomad Millionaires*, Cornell University Press, Ithaca, 2003.
Palmer, David, 'The Values Shaping Australian Asylum Policy: The Views of Policy Insiders', *Australian Journal of Public Administration*, 67: 3, 2008, 307–320.
Paton, Diana, 'An Injurious Population: Caribbean-Australian Penal Transportation and Imperial Racial Politics', *Cultural and Social History: The Journal of the Social History Society*, 5: 4, 2008, 449–464.
Perera, Suvendrini, *Australia and the Insular Imagination: Beaches, Borders, Boats, and Bodies*, Palgrave Macmillan, Basingstoke, 2009.
Philippopoulos-Mihalopoulos, Andreas, 'On Absence: Society's Return to Barbarians', *Soziale Systeme*, 14, 2008, Heft 1, S. 142–156.
Pias, Claus (ed.), *The Macy Conferences 1946–1953: the Complete Transactions*, University of Chicago Press, Chicago, 2016.
Pettit, Philip, 'Responsibility Incorporated', *Ethics*, 117: 2, 2007, 171–201.
Pickering, Sharon, 'Common Sense and Original Deviancy: News Discourses and Asylum Seekers in Australia', *Journal of Refugee Studies*, 14: 2, 2001, 169–186.
Pickering, Sharon, 'Floating Carceral Spaces: Border Enforcement and Gender on the High Seas', *Punishment and Society*, 16: 2, 2014, 187–205.
Plato, *The Republic*, Penguin, London, 2007.

Poerkson, Bernard, 'At Each and Every Moment, I Can Decide Who I am. Heinz von Foerster on the Observer, Dialogic Life, and a Constructivist Philosophy of Distinctions', *Cybernetics & Human Knowing*, 10: 3–4, 2003, 9–26.

Report of The House of Representatives Standing Committee on Legal and Constitutional Affairs, *Islands in the Sun: The Legal Regimes of Australia's External Territories and the Jervis Bay Territory*. Commonwealth of Australia, Canberra, 1991.

Ryan, Lyndall, 'The Black Line in Van Diemen's Land: Success or Failure?' *Journal of Australian Studies*, 37: 1, 2013.

Salter, Mark, 'Theory of the/: The Suture and Critical Border Studies', *Geopolitics*, 17: 4, 2012, 734–755.

Sassen, Saskia, *Expulsions: Brutality and Complexity in the Global Economy*, Belknap Press, Cambridge, 2014.

Sassen, Saskia, *The Global City*, Princeton University Press, Princeton, 1992.

Sassen, Saskia, *Global Networks, Linked Cities*, Routledge, Abingdon, 2002.

Sassen, Saskia, *Territory, Authority, Rights: from Medieval to Global Assemblages*, Princeton University Press, Princeton, 2008.

Saxton, Alison, 'I Certainly Don't Want People Like That Here': The Discursive Construction of "Asylum Seekers" ', *Media International Australia*, 109: 1, 2003, 109–120.

Shaxson, Nicholas, *Treasure Islands: Tax Havens and the Men who Stole the World*, Vintage, London, 2012.

Schmitt, Carl, *The Nomos of the Earth in the International Law of the Jus Publicum Europaeum*, Telos Press, New York, 2006.

Simon, Jonathan, 'Refugees in a Carceral Age: The Rebirth of Immigration Prisons in the United States', *Public Culture*, 10: 3, 1998, 577–607.

Sloterdijk, Peter, 'Foam City', *Distinktion: Journal of Social Theory*, 16, 2008, 47–59.

Sloterdijk, Peter, *Terror from the Air*, MIT Press, Cambridge, 2009.

Sloterdijk, Peter, *In the World Interior of Capital*, Polity Press, Cambridge, 2013.

Solomon, David (ed.), *Howard's Race: Winning the Unwinnable Election*, Harper Collins, Sydney, 2002.

Spencer-Brown, George, *Laws of Form*, The Julian Press, New York, 1969.

Steinberg, Philip E., *The Social Construction of the Ocean*, Cambridge University Press, Cambridge, 2001.

Stepick, Alex, 'Haitian Boat People: A Study in the Conflicting Forces Shaping U.S. Immigration Policy', *Law and Contemporary Problems*, 45:2, 1982, 163–196.

Stiegler, Bernard, *Technics and Time, 1: The Fault of Epimetheus*, Stanford University Press, Stanford, 1998.

Stumpf, Juliet P., 'The Crimmigration Crisis: Immigrants, Crime, and Sovereign Power', *American University Law Review*, 56, 2006, 368–418.

Swift, Jonathan, *Gulliver's Travels*, Penguin, London, 2003.

Taussig, Michael, 'The Beach (a Fantasy)', *Critical Inquiry*, 26: 2, 2000, 248–278.

Taussig, Michael, 'Culture of Terror – Space of Death: Roger Casement's Putomayo Report and the Explanation of Torture', *Comparative Studies in Society and History*, 26: 3, 1984, 467–497.

Teubner, Gunther, *Constitutional Fragments: Societal Constitutionalism and Globalization*, Oxford University Press, Oxford, 2012.

Toohey, Paul, 'That Sinking Feeling', *Quarterly Essay*, 53, March 2014.

Urry, John, *Offshoring*, Polity Press, Cambridge, 2014.

Vaughan-Williams, Nick, *Border Politics: The Limits of Sovereign Power*, Edinburgh University Press, Ediburgh, 2009.

Virilio, Paul, *Politics of the Very Worst*, Semiotext(e), New York,1999.

Vogl, Anthea, 'Over the Borderline: A Critical Inquiry into the Geography of Territorial Excision and the Securitisation of the Australian Border', *UNSW Law Journal*, 38: 1, 2015, 114–145.

Von Foerster, Heinz, *The Beginning of Heaven and Earth has No Name: Seven Days with Second-Order Cybernetics*, Fordham University Press, New York, 2013.

Von Foerster, Heinz, *Understanding Understanding: Essays on Cybernetics and Cognition*, Springer, Berlin, 2002.

Walsh, James P., 'Border Theatre and Security Spectacles: Surveillance, Mobility and Reality-Based Television', *Crime, Media, Culture: An International Journal*, 11: 2, 2015, 201–221.

Weizman, Eyal, 'Walking Through Walls: Soldiers as Architects in the Israeli-Palestinian Conflict', *Radical Philosophy*, 136, March/April 2006, 8–22.

Williams, Evan, *Australian Leader Eats Raw Onion Whole: Headlines From the Government That Broke Satire*, Black Inc, Melbourne, 2015.

Williams, Maslyn and Macdonald, Barrie, *The Phosphateers: A History of the British Phosphate Commissioners and the Christmas Island Phosphate Commission*, Melbourne University Press, Melbourne, 1985.

Ziegler, Garrett, 'The City of London, Real and Unreal', *Victorian Studies*, 49: 3, 2007, 431–455.

Zureik, Elia and Salter, Mark B. (eds.), *Global Surveillance and Policing Borders, Security, Identity*, Willan, Cullompton and Portland, 2005.

Newspapers, websites and online sources bibliography

'16 Ways to Benefit from Logistics', *UPS*. http://thenewlogistics.ups.com/guide/UPS-16Ways-Guide-PDF-US.pdf

'1788 The First Fleet, Botany Bay and the British Penal Colony', Migration Heritage Centre. www2.sl.nsw.gov.au/archive/discover_collections/history_nation/terra_australis/firstfleet.html

'40 Years of Change: 1975 to Today', *McCrindle*. http://mccrindle.com.au/the-mccrindle-blog/40-years-of-change-1975-to-today

Abbott, Tony, 'Abbott: I Was Right on National Security', *Quadrant Online*, March 26, 2016. https://quadrant.org.au/opinion/qed/2016/03/abbott-right-national-security/

'About Victoria Police', Victoria Police. www.police.vic.gov.au/content.asp?Document_ID=3

'Aboriginal and Torres Strait Islander Population, Year Book Australia, 2008', Australian Bureau of Statistics. www.abs.gov.au/ausstats/abs@.nsf/0/68AE74ED632E17A6CA2573D200110075?opendocument

'Aboriginal Customary Laws and Anglo-Australian Law After 1788 Australian Law as Applied to Aborigines', Australian Law Reform Commission. www.alrc.gov.au/publications/4.%20Aboriginal%20Customary%20Laws%20and%20Anglo-Australian%20Law%20After%201788/australian-law-applied

'Afghanistan Official Advice: Do Not Travel', *smartraveller.gov.au*. http://smartraveller.gov.au/Countries/asia/south/pages/afghanistan.aspx

Agamben, Giorgio, 'On Security and Terror', *www.libcom.org*, September 24, 2006. https://libcom.org/library/on-security-and-terror-giorgio-agamben

Akerman, Piers, 'Rudd's Red Carpet to Asylum Seekers', *The Daily Telegraph*, November 14, 2009. http://blogs.news.com.au/dailytelegraph/piersakerman/index.php/dailytelegraph/comments/rudds_red_carpet_to_asylum_seekers/

Akerman, Piers, 'Illegal Boat's Mainland Arrival Sshould Alarm All', *The Sunday Telegraph*, April 14, 2013. www.dailytelegraph.com.au/news/opinion/illegal-boats-mainland-arrival-should-alarm-all/story-e6frezz0-1226619898855

Allen, Frederick E., "Super Rich Hide $21 Trillion Offshore, Study Says", *www.forbes.com*, July 23, 2012. www.forbes.com/sites/frederickallen/2012/07/23/super-rich-hide-21-trillion-offshore-study-says/#73c8623873d3

Anderson, Stephanie, 'Immigration Department Secretary Michael Pezzullo Denies 5yo Asylum Seeker Raped on Nauru', *abc.net.au*, February 26, 2016. www.abc.net.au/news/2016-02-08/5yo-asylum-seekers-not-raped-on-nauru-immigration-official-says/7147492

'Apple Now Most Profitable Corporation in History of World', *People's Pundit Daily*, January 28, 2015. www.peoplespunditdaily.com/news/economy/2015/01/28/apple-now-most-profitable-corporation-in-history-of-world/

Australia: Island of Despair: Australia's 'Processing' of Refugees on Nauru', Amnesty International, October 17, 2016. www.amnesty.org/en/documents/asa12/4934/2016/en/

'Australian Border Force Act', 2015. www.austlii.edu.au/au/legis/cth/consol_act/abfa2015225/

'Average Weekly Earnings', September Quarter 1975, Australian Bureau of Statistics. www.ausstats.abs.gov.au/ausstats/free.nsf/0/5BACEEAF1C7DF296CA25750C00194241/$File/63020_SEP1975.pdf

Balogh, Stefanie, "Europe 'Needs an Asylum Solution': Jim Molan", *The Australian*, April 21, 2015. www.theaustralian.com.au/national-affairs/immigration/europe-needs-an-asylum-solution-jim-molan/story-fn9hml gu-1227312738365

Barlow, Karen, 'Parliament Excises Mainland From Migration Zone', *Radio Australia*, May 17, 2013. www.radioaustralia.net.au/international/2013-05-16/parliament-excises-mainland-from-migration-zone/1131736-0

Begley, Patrick, 'Gillian Triggs Refuses to Resign in Face of "Personal Attacks" From Abbott Government', *Sydney Morning Herald*, June 12, 2015. www.smh.com.au/federal-politics/political-news/gillian-triggs-refuses-to-resign-in-face-of-personal-attacks-from-abbott-government-20150611-ghm56b.htm

Bleby, Michael, 'Australia's First 888 Visa Investor Gets Passport Stamp', *Australian Financial Review*, May 16, 2013. www.afr.com/it-pro/australias-first-888-visa-investor-gets-passport-stamp-20130515-jyi0p

Boochani, Behrouz, 'Australia, Exceptional in Its Brutality', *Overland*, April 25, 2016. https://overland.org.au/2016/04/australia-exceptional-in-its-brutality/

'Beware the Supermarket Shopping Asylum Seekers', *Crikey*, March 29, 2010. www.crikey.com.au/2010/03/29/theyre-heeeeeeeere/

'Bilal Skaf: 15 Facts About the Crimes that Shook Sydney to Its Core 15 Years Ago', *The Daily Telegraph*, September 2, 2015. www.dailytelegraph.com.au/news/nsw/bilal-skaf-15-facts-about-the-crimes-that-shook-sydney-to-its-core-15-years-ago/news-story/d8a6f6c53b88e05328cfbe2909d7224f

'Boat Carrying Asylum Seekers Pulls into Geraldton', abc.net.au, updated April 10, 2013. www.abc.net.au/news/2013-04-09/boat-carrying-asylum-seekers-pulls-into-geraldton/4618844

'Border Protection (Validation and Enforcement Powers) Act 2001', *Federal Register of Legislation*. www.legislation.gov.au/Details/C2004A00886

Brough, Jodie and Millett, Michael, 'The Axeman Cometh', *Sydney Morning Herald*, November 1, 1997. http://australianpolitics.com/1997/11/01/the-axemen-cometh.html

Brown, Wendy, 'Desiring Walls', *LSE Public Lectures*, November 12, 2008. www.lse.ac.uk/publicEvents/events/2008/20080821t1104z001.aspx

Butterworth, Myra, 'So What's the REAL Price of Property in the UK? Average Is £2,216 per square metre But It's as High as £11,321 in London', *www.dailymail.co.uk*, May 20, 2016. www.dailymail.co.uk/property/article-3599013/Average-price-UK-property-2-216-square-metre-11-321-Kensington.html

'Canberra Preview – Wednesday', *RN Breakfast, ABC Radio National*, August 29, 2001. www.abc.net.au/radionational/programs/breakfast/canberra-preview–wednesday/3492086

Carter, Jimmy, '1980 Presidential Election Remarks With Reporters on the Results of the Election', November 5, 1980. *The American Presidency Project*, www.presidency.ucsb.edu/ws/?pid=45463

'A Certain Maritime Incident', Commonwealth of Australia, October 23, 2002. www.aph.gov.au/Parliamentary_Business/Committees/Senate/Former_Committees/maritimeincident/report/index

Chapman, Penny (producer), *Leaky Boat* (documentary), Matchbox Pictures, 2011. www.abc.net.au/tv/programs/leakyboat.htm

'The Coalition's Operation Sovereign Borders Policy', *Liberal Party of Australia*, 2013. sievx.com/articles/OSB/201307xxTheCoalitionsOSBPolicy.pdf

'The Day the Nauru Centre Was Closed', *sbs.com.au*, August 26, 2013. www.sbs.com.au/news/article/2013/02/08/day-nauru-centre-was-closed

The Future of Border Protection', The Lowy Institute, May 9, 2014. www.lowyinstitute.org/events/border-protection-scott-morrison (link dead), audio https://soundcloud.com/lowyinstitute/scott-morrison-future-border-protection

Chertoff, Michael, 'Managing Risk: A Global Imperative', *LSE Public Lecture*, Friday December 12, 2008. www.lse.ac.uk/publicEvents/events/2008/20081211t1517.aspx

'Child Safeguarding', *Department of Immigration and Border Protection*. www.border.gov.au/about/reports-publications/reports/corporate/child-safeguarding

'Child Safeguarding Framework Safeguarding Children in Our Care – A Shared Responsibility', *Department of Immigration and Border Protection*. www.border.gov.au/ReportsandPublications/Documents/child-safeguarding-framework.pdf

'Children in Immigration Detention: Statements by the United Nations', *Australian Human Rights Commission*, 2015. www.humanrights.gov.au/our-work/asylum-seekers-and-refugees/publications/children-immigration-detention-statements-united

'Christmas Island Sinking of SIEV221 Class Action', *Supreme Court of New South Wales*. www.supremecourt.justice.nsw.gov.au/Pages/sco2_classaction/christmas_island.aspx

Clifton, Tony, 'Fields of Dreams: The Battle for the Timor Sea, Home of Oil, Gas, Hot Air and Hope, *The Monthly*, July 2005. www.themonthly.com.au/monthly-essays-tony-clifton-fields-dreams-battle-timor-sea-home-oil-gas-hot-air-and-hope-63

'Coal "Good for Humanity", Prime Minister Tony Abbott says at $3.9b Queensland mine opening', *abc.net.au*, Updated October 13, 2014. www.abc.net.au/news/2014-10-13/coal-is-good-for-humanity-pm-tony-abbott-says/5810244

'Cook's Journal: Daily Entries', National Library of Australia, June 11, 1770. http://southseas.nla.gov.au/journals/cook/17700611.html

Colgan, Paul, 'Malcolm Turnbull Talks Up Australia's Border Protection as 'the Best in the World' Ahead of UN Talks', *Business Insider Australia*, September 18, 2016. www.businessinsider.com.au/malcolm-turnbull-talks-up-australias-border-protection-as-the-best-in-the-world-ahead-of-un-talks-2016–9

'Commonwealth of Australia Constitution Act, Section 127', *austlii.edu.au*. www.austlii.edu.au/au/legis/cth/consol_act/coaca430/s126.html

Conifer, Dan and Anderson, Stephanie, 'Refugee, Asylum Seeker Lifetime Visa Ban 'Extreme', 'Evil', 'Sick', Labor MPs Say', *abc.net.au*, updated October 31, 2016. www.abc.net.au/news/2016-10-31/asylum-seeker-refugee-lifetime-ban-extreme-evil-sick:-labor/7980686

'Convicts and the British Colonies in Australia', *australia.gov.au*. www.australia.gov.au/about-australia/australian-story/convicts-and-the-british-colonies

Corben, Billy (producer), *Cocaine Cowboys: Reloaded* (documentary), Magnolia Pictures, 2014.

Dailey, Peter, 'Haiti: The Fall of the House of Aristide', *The New York Review of Books*, March 13, 2003. www.nybooks.com/articles/2003/03/13/haiti-the-fall-of-the-house-of-aristide/

Dastyari, Azadeh, 'Explainer: The Legal Implications of 'Tow-Backs', *The Conversation*, January 20, 2014. http://theconversation.com/explainer-the-legal-implications-of-tow-backs-22151

Davies, Sara and Reilly, Alex, 'FactCheck: Have More Than 1000 Asylum Seekers Died at Sea Under Labor?' *The Conversation*, July 23, 2013. http://theconversation.com/factcheck-have-more-than-1000-asylum-seekers-died-at-sea-under-labor-16221

Davis, Tom, 'Geraldton Asylum Bboat Fumigated', *The West Australian*, April 17, 2013. https://au.news.yahoo.com/thewest/wa/a/16766277/geraldton-asylum-boat-fumigated/#page1

Delaney, Brigid, 'A Disco Cruise to the South Pacific Turns Downbeat', *The Saturday Paper*, February 13, 2016. www.thesaturdaypaper.com.au/2016/02/13/disco-cruise-the-south-pacific-turns-downbeat/

'Detention Centres Are Factories for Mental Illness', *The Drum*, November 17, 2011. www.abc.net.au/news/2011-11-18/tatz-ryan-detention-centres/3677942

Devine, Miranda, 'Racist Rapes: Finally the Truth Comes Out', *The Sydney Morning Herald*, July 14, 2002. www.smh.com.au/articles/2002/07/13/1026185124700.htm

'Detainees Have "No Right to Escape"', *The Sydney Morning Herald*, August 6, 2004. www.smh.com.au/articles/2004/08/06/1091732062324.html

Dodson, Louise, Mann, Simon and Taylor, Kerry, 'Refugees Stranded at Sea – Boat People Get Refuge in Containers, PM Sends a Message to the World', *The Age*, August 28, 2001.

Doherty, Ben, 'Nauru Files: Review Confirms 19 Police Referrals Over Abuse Claims, Yet No Prosecutions', *The Guardian*, October 15, 2016. www.theguardian.com/australia-news/2016/oct/15/nauru-files-review-confirms-19-police-referrals-over-abuse-claims-yet-no-prosecutions

Duff, Eamonn, 'Indonesia Prepares to Welcome Millionth Aussie Tourist for the Year', *Sydney Morning Herald*, November 9, 2014. www.smh.com.au/national/indonesia-prepares-to-welcome-millionth-aussie-tourist-for-the-year-20141108-11iuv4.html

Dusevic, Tom, 'Tampa Refugees Resurface as Kiwis', *The Australian*, August 20, 2011. www.theaustralian.com.au/national-affairs/tampa-refugees-resurface-as-kiwis/story-fn59niix-1226117936857

Dyett, Greg, 'The Day the Nauru Centre Was Closed', *sbs.com.au*, August 26, 2013. www.sbs.com.au/news/article/2013/02/08/day-nauru-centre-was-closed

'Economic Contribution of the Great Barrier Reef March 2013', Department of the Environment and Energy, Commonwealth of Australia. www.environment.gov.au/sustainability/publications/economic-contribution-great-barrier-reef-march-2013

Evershed, Nick, Liu, Ri, Farrell, Paul and Davidson, Helen, 'The Nauru Files: The Lives of Asylum Seekers in Detention Detailed in a Unique Database', *The Guardian*, August 10, 2016. www.theguardian.com/australia-news/ng-interactive/2016/

aug/10/the-nauru-files-the-lives-of-asylum-seekers-in-detention-detailed-in-a-unique-database-interactive

Evershed, Nick, Farrell, Paul and Laughland, Oliver, '"In" or "Out": What We Know About "Enhanced Screening" of Asylum Seekers', *The Guardian*, July 3, 2014. www.theguardian.com/world/2014/jul/03/asylum-seekers-may-be-subject-to-speedy-on-water-screenings

'Executive Order 12324 – Interdiction of Illegal Aliens', *The American Presidency Project*, September 29, 1981. www.presidency.ucsb.edu/ws/?pid=44317

'Fact Sheet – Abolition of the 'White Australia' Policy', *Department of Immigration and Border Protection*. www.border.gov.au/about/corporate/information/fact-sheets/08abolition

'Fees and Charges for Visas', *Department of Immigration and Border Protection*. www.border.gov.au/Trav/Visa/Fees

Ferguson, Adele and Toft, Klaus, '7-Eleven: The Price of Convenience', *ABC 4 Corners*, September 30, 2015. www.abc.net.au/4corners/stories/2015/08/30/4301164.htm

Finnane, Mark, 'The Border Is Everywhere: The Policy Overreach Behind Operation Fortitude', *The Conversation*, August 31, 2015. http://theconversation.com/the-border-is-everywhere-the-policy-overreach-behind-operation-fortitude-46860

'The First Fleet', *State Library of New South Wales*. www2.sl.nsw.gov.au/archive/discover_collections/history_nation/terra_australis/firstfleet.html

'The Future of Border Management: Maintaining Security; Facilitating Prosperity', *www.pwc.com*, 2015. www.pwc.com/gx/en/psrc/pdf/the-future-of-border-management.pdf

Frazer, Simon, 'Banks Place Many Interest-Only Home Loan Customers 'at Risk': ASIC Report', *www.abc.net.au*, August 20, 2015. www.abc.net.au/news/2015-08-20/many-interest-only-home-loan-customers-at-risk/6711784

Frum, David, 'America's Immigration Challenge', *The Atlantic*, December 11, 2015. www.theatlantic.com/politics/archive/2015/12/refugees/419976/

Frum, David, 'Closing Europe's Harbors: The Urgent Case for Stopping the Flow of Illegal Migrants Across the Mediterranean', *The Atlantic*, July/August 2015. www.theatlantic.com/magazine/archive/2015/07/closing-european-harbors/395321/

'The Future of Border Protection', *Australian Border Force*, 2014. www.ibrarian.net/navon/paper/The_future_of_border_protection.pdf?paperid=23143312

Gambaro, Teresa, 'Skilled Migrants Need to be Taught About Hygiene, Says Liberal Teresa Gambaro', *www.news.com.au*, January 10, 2012. www.news.com.au/finance/migrants-dont-know-how-to-wear-deodorant-or-queue-up-say-liberal-teresa-gambaro/story-e6frfm1i-1226240418996

Gerstein, Daniel M., Edwards, Karen, Woods, Delani, Newell, Julie and Moroney, Jennifer D.P., *Assessment of the Consolidation of the Australian Customs and Border Protection Service (ACBPS) with the Department of Immigration and Border Protection (DIBP)*, Commonwealth of Australia, 2016. www.rand.org/pubs/research_reports/RR1713.html

Gibney, Alex (director), *Taxi to the Dark Side* (documentary). www.imdb.com/title/tt0854678/

Gordon, Josh, 'Rudd Flips on 'Big Australia'', *abc.net.au*, April 4, 2010. www.smh.com.au/national/rudd-flips-on-big-australia-20100403-rkvo.html

Gordon, Michael, 'Revealed: The Cost of Stopping the Boats Put at $9.6 Billion', *The Sydney Morning Herald*, September 13, 2016. www.smh.com.au/federal-politics/political-news/revealed-the-cost-of-stopping-the-boats-put-at-96-billion-20160912-grea35.html

'Governor Bourke's Proclamation 1835 (UK)', Museum of Australian Democracy. www.foundingdocs.gov.au/resources/transcripts/nsw7_doc_1835.pdf

'Governor Bourke's 1835 Proclamation of Terra Nullius', *Migration Heritage Centre*. www.migrationheritage.nsw.gov.au/exhibition/objectsthroughtime/bourketerra/

Grattan, Michelle, 'Liberal Secrecy a Flawed Strategy', *The Conversation*, October 21, 2013. http://theconversation.com/liberal-secrecy-a-flawed-strategy-19406

Grattan, Michelle, 'Morrison Reacts to Heat Over Politicising the Military', *The Conversation*, November 13, 2013. http://theconversation.com/morrison-reacts-to-heat-over-politicising-the-military-20325

'Great Barrier Reef', *www.unesco.org*. http://whc.unesco.org/en/list/154

Grech, Alana and McCook, Laurence, 'Shipping in the Great Barrier Reef: The Miners' Highway', *The Conversation*, May 25, 2015. http://theconversation.com/shipping-in-the-great-barrier-reef-the-miners-highway-39251

'Grounding of the *Shen Neng 1* on Douglas Shoal, April 2010: Impact Assessment Report', *Great Barrier Reef Marine Park Authority*, June 2011. www.gbrmpa.gov.au/__data/assets/pdf_file/0019/17164/ShenNengGroundingImpactAssessmentReport.pdf

'Guide to Australian Maritime Security Arrangements (GAMSA)', 2013, *Commonwealth of Australia*. www.border.gov.au/AustralianBorderForce/Documents/GAMSA%202013.pdf

'Guugu Yimithir Country', *National Museum of Australia*. www.nma.gov.au/kspace/teachers/endeavour/learning/country

'Haitian Refugee Ctr. v. Civiletti, 503 F. Supp. 442 (S.D. Fla. 1980)', *Justitia US Law*. http://law.justia.com/cases/federal/district-courts/FSupp/503/442/1467096/

Hall, Bianca, '38 Geraldton Boat Arrivals Sent Back to Sri Lanka', *The Sydney Morning Herald*, April 19, 2013. www.smh.com.au/federal-politics/political-news/38-geraldton-boat-arrivals-sent-back-to-sri-lanka-20130418–2i31q.html

Hanson, Pauline, 'Pauline Hanson's Maiden Speech in the House of Representatives', September 10, 1996. http://australianpolitics.com/1996/09/10/pauline-hanson-maiden-speech.html

Harding, Jeremy, 'The Uninvited', *London Review of Books*, 22: 30, 2000. www.lrb.co.uk/v22/n03/jeremy-harding/the-uninvited

Hasham, Nicole, 'High Court Finds Offshore Detention Lawful', *The Sydney Morning Herald*, February 3, 2016. www.smh.com.au/federal-politics/political-news/high-court-finds-offshore-detention-lawful-20160202-gmk5q6.html

Henderson, Anna and Borello, Eliza, 'Australia Confirms Air Strikes in Syria, Announces Additional 12,000 Refugee Places', *www.abc.net.au*, September 9, 2015. www.abc.net.au/news/2015-09-09/australia-to-accept-additional-12,000-syrian-refugees/6760386

'A History of the Department of Immigration – Managing Migration to Australia', *Commonwealth of Australia*. www.border.gov.au/CorporateInformation/Documents/immigration-history.pdf

Hope, Alistair, 'Christmas Island Findings', *Coroner's Court of Western Australia*, 2012. www.coronerscourt.wa.gov.au/_files/christmas_island_findings.pdf

Hopkins, Katie, 'Rescue Boats? I'd Use Gunships to Stop Migrants: You May as Well Set Up a Libya to Italy P&O ferry', *The Sun*, April 17, 2015. www.thesun.co.uk/news/1541491/rescue-boats-id-use-gunships-to-stop-migrants/

Howard, John, 'Delivered at Sydney, NSW, October 28th, 2001', Museum of Australian Democracy. http://electionspeeches.moadoph.gov.au/speeches/2001-john-howard

Hunt, John, 'Revolt on Christmas Island', *Sydney Morning Herald*, March 14, 2012. www.smh.com.au/entertainment/revolt-on-christmas-island-20120313-1uy5q.html

'Immigration Restriction Act (1901)', Museum of Australian Democracy. www.foundingdocs.gov.au/resources/transcripts/cth4ii_doc_1901a.pdf

'Independent Investigation into the Grounding of the Chinese Registered Bulk Carrier Shen Neng 1 on Douglas Shoal, Queensland 3 April 2010', *Australian Transport Safety Bureau*. www.atsb.gov.au/media/2478832/mo2010003.pdf#page=0

'Indigenous Australia Timeline 1901–1969', Australian Museum. http://australianmuseum.net.au/indigenous-australia-timeline-1901-to-1969

'Information About Children in Detention', *Australian Human Rights Commission*, updated January 6, 2016. www.humanrights.gov.au/information-about-children-immigration-detention

'Inquest into the Death of Mohammed Hassan Ayubi, Muzafar Ali Sefarali, Mohammed Amen Zamen, Awar Nadar, Baquer Husani', (SIEV 36 Inquest), *Darwin Coroner's Court*, 2010. www.defence.gov.au/siev36/pdf/findings%20-%20SIEV%2036%20inquest.pdf

Ireland, Judith, 'Tony Abbott Blasts National Broadcaster: ABC Takes 'Everyone's Side But Australia's'', *Sydney Morning Herald*, January 29, 2014. www.smh.com.au/federal-politics/political-news/tony-abbott-blasts-national-broadcaster-abc-takes-everyones-side-but-australias-20140129–31lt8.html

Isaacs, David, 'Nauru and Manus Island Are Australia's Guantanamo Bay', *The Sydney Morning Herald*, February 29, 2016. www.smh.com.au/comment/nauru-and-manus-island-are-australias-guantanamo-gay-20160228-gn5qtg.html

'Is Australia Responsible for Asylum Seekers Detained on Manus Island?' *ABC Fact Check*, updated February 28, 2014. www.abc.net.au/news/2014-02-27/who-is-responsible-for-asylum-seekers-detained-on-manus/5275598

'Is It Illegal to Turn Back Boats in International Waters to Indonesia?' *ABC Fact Check*, updated November 17, 2014. www.abc.net.au/news/2013-09-26/government-turn-back-boat-policy/4979898

'Italian Navy Chief Sceptical of Australian Asylum Seeker Solution to Mediterranean Migrant Crisis', *ABC News*, May 6, 2015. www.abc.net.au/news/2015-05-06/italy-navy-chief-sceptical-australian-solution-to-migrant-issue/6447708

Ives, Mike, 'New Zealand Property Boom Attracts Overseas Buyers', *New York Times*, May 7, 2015. www.nytimes.com/2015/05/08/greathomesanddestinations/new-zealand-property-boom-attracts-overseas-buyers.html?_r=0

Johanson, Simon, 'Apartment Correction to Cause Australia-Wide Recession: Report Warns', *The Sydney Morning Herald*, September 2, 2016. www.smh.com.au/business/property/apartment-correction-to-cause-australiawide-recession-report-warns-20160902-gr7bce.html

Judt, Tony, 'Ill Fares the Land', *New York Review of Books*, April 29, 2010. www.nybooks.com/articles/2010/04/29/ill-fares-the-land/

Kelly, Joe, 'Gillian Triggs Debases Her Position: Peter Dutton', *The Australian*, June 7, 2015. www.theaustralian.com.au/in-depth/terror/australian-born-jihadis-to-lose-citizenship-says-peter-dutton/news-story/0474b153fead5fd3ba82b1678659c3b3

Kelly, Sean, 'Things Peter Dutton Has Said Since May: The Words of the Nation's Minister for Immigration Tell Their Own Sad Story', *The Monthly*, August 18, 2016. www.themonthly.com.au/today/sean-kelly/2016/18/2016/1471504197/things-peter-dutton-has-said-may

Klapdor, Michael, Coombs, Moira and Bohm, Catherine, 'Australian Citizenship: A Chronology of Major Developments in Policy and Law', *Parliament of Australia*, September 11, 2009. www.aph.gov.au/About_Parliament/Parliamentary_Departments/Parliamentary_Library/pubs/BN/0910/AustCitizenship

Knott, Matthew, 'Gough Whitlam's Free University Education Reforms Led to Legacy of No Upfront Fees', *The Sydney Morning Herald*, October 21, 2014. www.smh.com.au/federal-politics/political-news/gough-whitlams-free-university-education-reforms-led-to-legacy-of-no-upfront-fees-20141021–119bws.html

'The Labour Force, February 1975', *Australian Bureau of Statistics*. www.ausstats.abs.gov.au/ausstats/free.nsf/0/BF171A1080225CA2CA2576CC00197D60/$File/62030_02_1975.pdf

Lane, Sabra, 'Greens Push for Legal Guarantees for Geraldton Boat Arrivals', *The World Today, ABC Radio National*, April 11, 2013. www.abc.net.au/worldtoday/content/2013/s3734670.htm

Laughland, Oliver, 'Angus Campbell Warns Asylum Seekers Not to Travel to Australia by Boat', *guardian.com.au*, April 11, 2014. www.theguardian.com/world/2014/apr/11/angus-campbell-stars-in-videos-warning-asylum-seekers-not-to-travel-by-boat

Laughland, Oliver, Bennett, Christian and Code, Bill, 'Scott Morrison Visit Sent Manus Tension Soaring, Says G4S Whistleblower', *www.theguardian.com*, Monday 28 April, 2014. www.theguardian.com/world/2014/apr/28/scott-morrison-visit-sent-manus-tension-soaring-says-g4s-whistleblower

Levy, Megan and Cox, Lisa, 'Prince Philip Awarded Knight of the Order of Australia by Prime Minister Tony Abbott', *The Sydney Morning Herald*, January 26, 2015. www.smh.com.au/federal-politics/political-news/prince-philip-awarded-knight-of-the-order-of-australia-by-prime-minister-tony-abbott-20150125–12xzk8.htm

Leys, Nick, 'No Expense Spared for High Rollers' New Home at Crown Casino', *The Herald Sun*, September 10, 2010. www.heraldsun.com.au/news/no-expense-spared-for-high-rollers-new-home-at-crown-casino/story-e6frf7jo-1225916687016

Manne, Robert, 'The History Wars', *The Monthly*, November 2009. www.themonthly.com.au/issue/2009/november/1270703045/robert-manne/comment

'Maritime Interception and Screening of Asylum Seekers at Sea', *Kaldor Centre for International Refugee Law*, July 1, 2015. www.kaldorcentre.unsw.edu.au/publication/maritime-interception-and-screening-asylum-seekers-sea

Marr, David, 'Sifting Through the Wreckage', *The Sydney Morning Herald*, December 3, 2011. www.smh.com.au/national/sifting-through-the-wreckage-20111202-1obnx.html

Marszalek, Jessica, Scarr, Lanai and Tin, Jason, 'Scrapping Carbon Tax "My First Act" Says Opposition Leader Tony Abbott', *news.com.au*, August 5, 2013. www.news.com.au/national/federal-election/scrapping-carbon-tax-8216my-first-act8217-says-opposition-leader-tony-abbott/story-fnho52ip-1226691201649

'Martin Luther King Jr's "Letter From Birmingham Jail"', *The Atlantic*, April 16, 2013. www.theatlantic.com/politics/archive/2013/04/martin-luther-kings-letter-from-birmingham-jail/274668/

Martin, Peter, 'The Extraordinary Cost of Keeping Asylum Seekers in Detention: Over $500,000 Each', *The Sydney Morning Herald*, September 14, 2016. www.smh.com.au/comment/the-extraordinary-cost-of-keeping-asylum-seekers-in-detention-over-500000-each-20160914-grftcj.html

McCluskey, Ian, 'Boat Arrivals on the Mainland: What Difference Does It Make?' *Parliament of Australia*, posted April 12, 2013. www.aph.gov.au/About_Parliament/Parliamentary_Departments/Parliamentary_Library/FlagPost/2013/April/Boat_arrivals_on_the_mainland_what_difference_does_it_make

McGrath, Kim, 'Oil, Gas and Spy Games in the Timor Sea', *The Monthly*, April 2014. www.themonthly.com.au/issue/2014/april/1396270800/kim-mcgrath/oil-gas-and-spy-games-timor-sea

McIlroy, Tom, 'Government-Dominated Committee Finds Lifetime Visa Ban Pointless and Cruel', *The Sydney Morning Herald*, November 22, 2016. www.smh.com.au/federal-politics/political-news/lifetime-visa-ban-pointless-and-cruel-parliamentary-committee-20161122-gsv78j.html

McKenzie-Murray, Martin, 'The Lawful Truth of the High Court's Offshore Detention Decision', *The Saturday Paper*, February 6, 2016. www.thesaturdaypaper.com.au/news/immigration/2016/02/06/the-lawful-truth-the-high-courts-offshore-detention-decision

McKenzie-Murray, Martin, 'Nauru Rapes: "There Is a War on Women"', *The Saturday Paper*, August 22, 2015. www.thesaturdaypaper.com.au/news/immigration/2015/08/22/nauru-rapes-there-war-women/

Meers, Daniel and Benson, Simon, 'Ring of Steel to Protect Our Borders', *The Daily Telegraph*, September 24, 2016. www.dailytelegraph.com.au/news/nsw/sea-and-air-patrols-are-securing-australian-borders-like-never-before/news-story/135aea6297f4eb50744867245c980763

'Mental Trauma on Nauru Worse Than War Zones: Neistat', *ABC RN Breakfast*, October 18, 2016. www.abc.net.au/radionational/programs/breakfast/refugee-mental-trauma-worse-than-war-zones/7941392

Middleton, Karen, 'Department of Immigration and Border Protection's Lack of Preparedness on Organised Crime', *The Saturday Paper*, September 24, 2016. www.thesaturdaypaper.com.au/news/immigration/2016/09/24/department-immigration-and-border-protections-lack-preparedness

'Migration Act (1958)', *austlii.edu.au*. www.austlii.edu.au/au/legis/cth/consol_act/ma1958118/

'Migration Amendment (Excision from Migration Zone) (Consequential Provisions) Act 2001', Commonwealth of Australia. www.legislation.gov.au/Details/C2004A00888

Millar, Lisa, 'Australia's Asylum Seeker Policies Heavily Criticised at UN Human Rights Council Review', *abc.net.au*, November 10, 2015. www.abc.net.au/news/2015-11-10/australias-asylum-policies-heavily-criticised-at-united-nations/6926032

'Ministerial Statements, Illegal Immigration: MV Tampa', *Parliament of Australia*, Wednesday, August 29, 2001. http://parlinfo.aph.gov.au/parlInfo/search/dis

play/display.w3p;query=Id%3A%22chamber%2Fhansardr%2F2001-08-29%2F0067%22

'Minister for Immigration and Border Protection – Address to the Australian Strategic Policy Institute', *Liberal Party of Australia*, September 20, 2016. www.liberal.org.au/latest-news/2016/09/20/minister-immigration-and-border-protection-address-australian-strategic

Moore, Tony, 'Costs to Remove Toxic Paint From Great Barrier Reef 'Triples' to $141 Million', *Brisbane Times*, May 7, 2016. www.brisbanetimes.com.au/queensland/costs-to-remove-toxic-paint-from-great-barrier-reef-triples-to-141-million-20160506-gooe84.html

Mondale, Walter and Mondale, Walter, 'Speech to the U.N. Conference on Indochinese Refugees at the Palais de Nations', July 21, 1979. http://nakbaeducation.com/wp-content/uploads/UNSpeech19MONDALE.pdf

'Montevideo Convention on the Rights and Duties of States', Council on Foreign Relations. www.cfr.org/sovereignty/montevideo-convention-rights-duties-states/p15897

'National Parks', *australia.gov.au*. www.australia.gov.au/about-australia/australian-story/national-parks

'National Service, 1965–72 – Fact sheet 164', National Archives of Australia. www.naa.gov.au/collection/fact-sheets/fs164.aspx

Neighbour, Sally, 'The Christmas Party', *4 Corners*, July 1, 2002. www.abc.net.au/4corners/archives/2002b_Monday1July2002.htm

Neuman, Klaus, 'Boat People and Gunships in the Mediterranean', *Inside Story*, May 12, 2015. http://insidestory.org.au/boat-people-and-gunships-in-the-mediterranean

Neuman, Klaus, '"Queue Jumpers" and the Perils of Crossing Sydney Harbour on a Manly Fery', *Inside Story*, October 1, 2014. http://insidestory.org.au/queue-jumpers-and-the-perils-of-crossing-sydney-harbour-on-a-manly-ferry

'New Thinking About Borders: ACBPS CEO Michael Pezzullo', *Border Force News Room*, August 30, 2013. http://newsroom.border.gov.au/channels/Speeches/releases/ceo-speech-to-university-of-canberra-national-security-lecture-series

Norman, Jane, 'Pauline Hanson Calls for Muslim Immigration Ban in Maiden Speech to Senate', *abc.net.au*, updated September 14, 2016. www.abc.net.au/news/2016-09-14/one-nation-senator-pauline-hanson-makes-first-speech-to-senate/7845150

'Norway Pressures Australia Over Refugee Ship', *bbc.co.uk*, August 27, 2001. http://news.bbc.co.uk/2/hi/asia-pacific/1511202.stm

Ockenden, Will, 'Apple Pays $193m Tax in Australia on $27b Revenue as Federal Government Vows to Capture Lost Taxes', *abc.net.au*, March 7, 2014. www.abc.net.au/news/2014-03-06/tax-expert-explains-how-apple-pays-193m-tax-on-27b-revenue/5303426

'Office of Fossil Energy', *energy.gov*. http://energy.gov/fe/about-us/our-history

'Our Operating Environment', *Australian Border Force*. www.border.gov.au/australian-border-force-abf/protecting#Our%20operating%20environment

Owens, Jared and Taylor, Paige, 'Scott Morrison Condemns Lawsuit Launched Over Christmas Island SIEV 221 Disaster', *The Australian*, June 17, 2014. www.theaustralian.com.au/national-affairs/scott-morrison-condemns-lawsuit-launched-over-christmas-island-siev-221-disaster/news-story/d8ae0d9f371479ead807a287001cd92e

Paddenburg, Trevor and Mullany, Ashlee, 'War of Words Over Geraldton Arrivals as Cyclone Victoria Stops Flights', *The Australian*, April 10, 2013. www.theaustralian.com.au/news/asylum-boat-carrying-72-sri-lankan-passengers-sails-into-geraldton/story-e6frg6n6–1226617279185

'The Panama Papers: Politicians, Criminals and the Rogue Industry that Hides Their Cash', *The International Consortium of Investigative Journalists*, https://panamapapers.icij.org/

Parr, Nick, 'Who Goes to University? The Changing Profile of Our Students', *The Conversation*, May 25, 2015. http://theconversation.com/who-goes-to-university-the-changing-profile-of-our-students-40373

Perpitch, Nicolas, 'Yongah Hill Detainees Face Transfer to Christmas Island After Failed Escape Attempt', *ABC News*, June 3, 2015. www.abc.net.au/news/2015-06-03/yongah-hill-detainees-fail-in-escape-attempt/6517866

Pezzullo, Mike, 'CEO Speech to University of Canberra National Security Lecture Series: New Thinking About Borders', *newsroom.border.gov.au*, August 30, 2013. http://newsroom.border.gov.au/channels/Speeches/releases/ceo-speech-to-university-of-canberra-national-security-lecture-series

Pezzullo, Mike, 'Keynote Address at Mobility Symposium 2016', *Crawford School of Public Policy*, March 21, 2016. www.border.gov.au/about/news-media/speeches-presentations/keynote-mobility-symposium-2016

Pezzullo, Mike, 'Pezzullo: Immigration Department Won't Be Trapped by History', *The Mandarin*, June 2, 2016. www.themandarin.com.au/65969-michael-pezzullo-immigration-department-wont-be-trapped-by-history/

Phillips, Janet, 'The 'Pacific Solution' Revisited: A Statistical Guide to the Asylum Seeker Caseloads on Nauru and Manus Island', Parliamentary Library of Australia. http://parlinfo.aph.gov.au/parlInfo/download/library/prspub/1893669/upload_binary/1893669.pdf

Phillips, Janet and Spinks, Harriet, 'Boat Arrivals in Australia Since 1976', *Parliament of Australia*. www.aph.gov.au/About_Parliament/Parliamentary_Departments/Parliamentary_Library/pubs/rp/rp1314/BoatArrivals

Phillips, Janet and Spinks, Harriet, 'Immigration Detention in Australia', *Parliament of Australia*. www.aph.gov.au/About_Parliament/Parliamentary_Departments/Parliamentary_Library/pubs/BN/2012-2013/Detention

Phillips, Melissa and Boese, Martina, 'From White Australia to Stopping the Boats: Attitudes to Asylum Seekers', *The Conversation*, June 21, 2013. http://theconversation.com/from-white-australia-to-stopping-the-boats-attitudes-to-asylum-seekers-15244

'The President's News Conference, June 14, 1984', *The American Presidency Project*, www.presidency.ucsb.edu/ws/?pid=40049

'Protecting Our Borders', Australian Border Force. www.border.gov.au/australian-border-force-Border Force/protecting

'Questions Without Notice, Illegal Immigration: MV Tampa' (Hansard), *Parliament of Australia*, Monday August 27, 2001. http://parlinfo.aph.gov.au/parlInfo/search/display/display.w3p;query=Id%3A%22chamber%2Fhansardr%2F2001-08-27%2F0051%22

Raschella, Adrian, 'Former SAS Commander Breaks Silence on Tampa', *abc.net.au*, updated July 8, 2013. www.abc.net.au/news/2011-07-07/former-sas-commander-breaks-silence-on-tampa/2785164

'Record Number of Students in Higher Education in 2015', Department of Education and Training. https://ministers.education.gov.au/birmingham/record-number-students-higher-education-2015

'Remarks at the Signing of the Immigration Bill, Liberty Island, New York', October 3, 1965, LBJ Presidential Library. www.lbjlib.utexas.edu/johnson/archives.hom/speeches.hom/651003.asp

Renshaw, Catherine, 'The Problems With Recognising Sri Lankan Boat Arrivals as Refugees', *The Conversation*, May 3, 2013. http://theconversation.com/the-problems-with-recognising-sri-lankan-boat-arrivals-as-refugees-13895

Reynolds, Emma, 'Will Rich Entrepreneurs Pay $15m to Get Australian Citizenship?' *news.com.au*, July 14, 2015. www.news.com.au/finance/business/other-industries/will-rich-entrepreneurs-pay-15m-to-get-australian-citizenship/news-story/83c7e1e75eba0601ff9060dfe8ec90ba

Richardson, David, 'Asian Financial Crisis', *Parliament of Australia*, June 29, 1998. www.aph.gov.au/About_Parliament/Parliamentary_Departments/Parliamentary_Library/Publications_Archive/CIB/CIB9798/98cib23#July

Rosenblum, Marc R., 'Border Security: Immigration Enforcement Between Ports of Entry', *Congressional Research Service*, 2012. fpc.state.gov/documents/organization/180681.pdf

'RSL Alarm at New Migrant Plan', *The Sydney Morning Herald*, July 24, 1947. http://trove.nla.gov.au/newspaper/article/18036458

'Rudd Welcomes "Big Australia" ', *abc.net.au*, updated October 23, 2009. www.abc.net.au/news/2009-10-23/rudd-welcomes-big-australia/1113752

Rundle, Guy, 'Rundle Mythbusts Abbott's Victory, *crikey.com.au*, September 10, 2013. www.crikey.com.au/2013/09/10/rundle-mythbusts-abbotts-victory/

'Secret Instructions to Captain Cook, 30 June 1768', Museum of Australian Democracy. www.foundingdocs.gov.au/resources/transcripts/nsw1_doc_1768.pdf

Sewell, Dan, 'Haitians Escape Guantanamo, Not HIV Shadow: Miami: Immigrants Infected With Virus That Causes AIDS Fight to Build New Lives in United States, a Country That Has Made Them Feel Unwanted, Deeply Suspicious', *LA Times*, December 12, 1993. http://articles.latimes.com/1993-12-12/news/mn-1026_1_united-states

Schetzer, Alana, 'Border Force: Melburnians Fight Visa Checks With Memes', *The Age*, August 28, 2015. www.theage.com.au/victoria/border-force-melburnians-fight-visa-checks-with-memes-20150828-gja2b0.html

'Ships, 1940–1970', Museum Victoria. https://museumvictoria.com.au/discoverycentre/websites-mini/journeys-australia/1940s60s/ships-1940s70s/

'SIEV 221 Internal Review', *Australian Customs and Border Protection Service*, 2010. www.border.gov.au/ReportsandPublications/Documents/reviews-and-inquiries/110124CustomsInternalReview.pdf

'A Snapshot of Australia, 1901', Australian Bureau of Statistics, www.abs.gov.au/websitedbs/D3110124.NSF/24e5997b9bf2ef35ca2567fb00299c59/c4abd1fac53e3df5ca256bd8001883ec!OpenDocument

Sparrow, Jeff, 'The Real Problem Is Not the Lamb ad But the Militarisation of Australian Nationalism', *theguardian.com.au*. www.theguardian.com/commentisfree/2016/jan/12/the-real-problem-is-not-the-lamb-ad-but-the-militarisation-of-australian-nationalism

Sparrow, Jeff, 'What's the End Game for Australia's Border Policy – A World of Walled City-States? *The Guardian*, May 6, 2016. www.theguardian.com/commentisfree/2016/may/06/whats-the-end-game-for-australias-border-policy-a-world-of-walled-city-states

Spinks, Harriet, 'Breaking the Deadlock? The Report of the Expert Panel on Asylum Seekers', *Parliament of Australia*, August 13, 2012. www.aph.gov.au/About_Parliament/Parliamentary_Departments/Parliamentary_Library/FlagPost/2012/August/Breaking_the_deadlock_The_Report_of_the_Expert_Panel_on_Asylum_Seekers

Spinks, Harriet, 'Tampa: Ten Years On', *Parliament of Australia*. www.aph.gov.au/About_Parliament/Parliamentary_Departments/Parliamentary_Library/FlagPost/2011/August/Tampa_ten_years_on

'The Squattocracy', State Library of Victoria. http://ergo.slv.vic.gov.au/explore-history/land-exploration/pastoral-practices/squattocracy

'Sri Lanka Asylum Seekers Flown Home', *abc.net.au*, April 18, 2013. www.abc.net.au/news/2013-04-18/sri-lanka-asylum-seekers-flown-home/4637862

'Standards Catalogue: 55.180.10: General Purpose Containers', *www.iso.org*. www.iso.org/iso/iso_catalogue/catalogue_ics/catalogue_ics_browse.htm?ICS1=55&ICS2=180&ICS3=10

'The State of the World's Refugees', *www.unhcr.org*. www.unhcr.org/3ebf9bad0.pdf

Statement by ABF Commissioner Roman Quaedvlieg on the ABF's Role in Operation Fortitude', *Border Force Newsroom*. http://newsroom.border.gov.au/releases/statement-by-abf-commissioner

Steketee, Mike, 'Refugees: Asians May Be "Twisting Our Tails"', *Sydney Morning Herald*, November 26, 1977.

'Stolen Generations History', *National Sorry Day Committee*. www.nsdc.org.au/stolen-generations-history

Taylor, Savitri, 'Sri Lankan Boat Arrivals: Enhanced Screening, Diminished Protection', *The Conversation*, November 1, 2013. http://theconversation.com/sri-lankan-boat-arrivals-enhanced-screening-diminished-protection-19601

Thomas, Jo, 'Castro Turns the Tables', *New York Times*, April 25, 1980. http://query.nytimes.com/gst/abstract.html?res=9803EEDD153BE732A25756C2A9629C94619FD6CF&legacy=true

'Three Nations Cast Refugees Adrift', *Sydney Morning Herald*, August 28, 2001.

Ting, Inga and Walters, Conrad, 'Asylum Seekers' time in detention soars', *The Sydney Morning Herald*, May 2, 2014. www.smh.com.au/federal-politics/asylum-seekers-time-in-detention-soars-20140503-zr3eg.html

Tlozek, Eric and Anderson, Stephanie, 'PNG's Supreme Court Rules Detention of Asylum Seekers on Manus Island is Illegal', *ABC News*, April 27, 2016. www.abc.net.au/news/2016-04-26/png-court-rules-asylum-seeker-detention-manus-island-illegal/7360078

'Tony Abbott Eats a Raw Onion', *The Guardian*, March 13, 2015. www.theguardian.com/australia-news/2015/mar/13/tony-abbott-eats-raw-onion; www.news.com.au/entertainment/tv/john-olivers-hilarious-reaction-to-tony-abbott-eating-a-raw-unpeeled-onion/news-story/14f6fdbabb59ce1ac21232193a37cb9f

'Torture Claims Emerge From Sri Lanka', *ABC 7.30 Report*, April 24, 2013. www.abc.net.au/7.30/content/2013/s3749532.htm

Towell, Noel, 'Border Force Accused of Wearing Fake Uniforms to Campaign Against Turnbull', *Canberra Times*, May 17, 2016.

Transcript: Tony Abbott's Controversial Speech at the Margaret Thatcher Lecture', *The Sydney Morning Herald*, October 28, 2015. www.smh.com.au/federal-politics/political-news/transcript-tony-abbotts-controversial-speech-at-the-margaret-thatcher-lecture-20151028-gkkg6p.html

'Transcript: Press Conference – Operation Sovereign Borders', September 23, 2013. http://sievx.com/articles/OSB/20130923OSBPresser.html

Transcript: Press Conference – Operation Sovereign Borders', Friday November 1, 2013. http://sievx.com/articles/OSB/20131101OSBPresser7.html

'Trauma on Nauru and Manus', *RN Late Light Live*, July 4, 2016. www.abc.net.au/radionational/programs/latenightlive/paul-stevenson/7557752

'Trøstesløs situasjon om bord i "Tampa"', *Dagbladet*, August 27, 2001. www.dagbladet.no/nyheter/2001/08/27/277706.html

Tsavdaridis, Noula, 'TURNED AWAY 'We Have a Lot of Sick People on Board: These People Are in Really Bad Shape', *The Daily Telegraph*, August 28, 2001.

Turnbull, Malcolm, 'Beneath the Boulevards: Malcolm Turnbull on James Boyce's 1835: The Founding of Melbourne & the Conquest of Australia', *The Monthly*, July 2011. www.themonthly.com.au/issue/2011/june/1309412782/malcolm-turnbull/beneath-boulevards

'Under the Radar: Dog-Whistle Politics in Australia', The Australia Institute. www.tai.org.au/node/1290

'United Nations Convention on the Law of the Sea (UNCLOS)', *www.un.org*. www.un.org/depts/los/convention_agreements/texts/unclos/unclos_e.pdf

'Victoria's Future Industries International Education Discussion Paper', *State Government Victoria*, July 2015. http://yoursay.business.vic.gov.au/futureindustries/application/files/5114/3676/6619/DEDJTR_InternationalEducation_Discussion_Paper.pdf

Victoria's Historic Population Growth: Annual Population Growth, Victoria, European Settlement to Present, 1836–2011', *Department of Environment, Land, Water and Planning*. www.dtpli.vic.gov.au/data-and-research/population/presentations-and-bulletins/victorias-historic-population-growth

Wadham, Ben, 'Operation Sovereign Borders: Dignified Silence or Diminishing Democracy?' *The Conversation*, January 8, 2014. http://theconversation.com/operation-sovereign-borders-dignified-silence-or-diminishing-democracy-21294

Wallace, David Foster, 'Shipping Out: On the (Nearly Lethal) Comforts of a Luxury Cruise', *Harpers Magazine*, 1996. https://harpers.org/wp-content/uploads/2008/09/HarpersMagazine-1996-01-0007859.pdf

'Where Do We Work', *Australian Border Force*. www.border.gov.au/AustralianBorderForce/PublishingImages/australian-border-force-abf/protecting/where-do-we-work/Border%20continuum.png

Whitmont, Debbie, 'To Deter and Deny: The Inside Story of Operation Relex – The Defence Forces' Mission to Stop Asylum-Seekers Reaching Australian Shores', *4 Corners*, April 15, 2002. www.abc.net.au/4corners/archives/2002a_Monday15April2002.htm

Wright, Tony and Narushima, Yuko, 'Casino for Asylum Housing', *The Sydney Morning Herald*, July 1, 2009. www.smh.com.au/national/casino-for-asylum-housing-20090630-d43h.html

'Why Did Sun Delete Katie Hopkins' 'Gunships to Stop Migrants' Tweet?' *The Guardian*, September 4, 2015. www.theguardian.com/media/mediamonkeyblog/2015/sep/03/why-did-sun-delete-katie-hopkins-gunships-to-stop-migrants-tweet

Whyte, Sarah, 'Doctors and Teachers Gagged Under New Immigration Laws', *Sydney Morning Herald*, June 4, 2015. www.smh.com.au/federal-politics/political-news/doctors-and-teachers-gagged-under-new-immigration-laws-20150603-ghft05.html

Wilkie, Andrew (MP), 'Manus Island More Illegal Than Ever', *www.andrewilkie.org*. http://andrewwilkie.org/manus-island-more-illegal-than-ever/

Wilkinson, Marian, 'Ruddock Discussed Piracy During Boat People Crisis', *Sydney Morning Herald*, March 8, 2003. www.smh.com.au/articles/2003/03/07/1046826532276.html

Wroe, David, 'Angus Campbell to Become Australia's Next Chief of Army', *The Sydney Morning Herald*, February 24, 2015. www.smh.com.au/federal-politics/political-news/angus-campbell-to-become-australias-next-chief-of-army-20150224–13nng7.html

Wroe, David and Snow, Deborah, 'Minister Takes General Out of the Political Fray', *The Sydney Morning Herald*, November 16, 2013. www.smh.com.au/federal-politics/political-news/minister-takes-general-out-of-the-political-fray-20131115-2xmmu.html

York, Barry, 'Australia and Refugees, 1901–2002: An Annotated Chronology Based on Official Sources', *Parliament of Australia*. www.aph.gov.au/About_Parliament/Parliamentary_Departments/Parliamentary_Library/Publications_Archive/online/Refugeess3

Index

Note: Italic indicates a figure on the corresponding page.

For Product Safety Concerns and Information please contact our EU
representative GPSR@taylorandfrancis.com
Taylor & Francis Verlag GmbH, Kaufingerstraße 24, 80331 München, Germany

www.ingramcontent.com/pod-product-compliance
Ingram Content Group UK Ltd.
Pitfield, Milton Keynes, MK11 3LW, UK
UKHW022012180926
475701UK00003B/328